Kuroda Institute
Studies in East Asian Buddhisn

GW00995131

Traditions of Meditation in Chinese Buddhism

Edited by
Peter N. Gregory

UNIVERSITY OF HAWAII PRESS
HONOLULU

KURODA INSTITUTE
Studies in East Asian Buddhism

STUDIES IN CH'AN AND HUA-YEN
Robert M. Gimello and Peter N. Gregory

DŌGEN STUDIES
William R. LaFleur

THE NORTHERN SCHOOL AND THE FORMATION
OF EARLY CH'AN BUDDHISM
John R. McRae

The Kuroda Institute for the Study of Buddhism and Human Values is a
non-profit, educational corporation, founded in 1976. One of its primary
objectives is to promote scholarship on Buddhism in its historical, philosophical, and cultural ramifications. The Institute thus attempts to serve the
scholarly community by providing a forum in which scholars can gather at
conferences and colloquia. To date the Institute has sponsored six conferences in the area of Buddhist Studies. The present volume is the outgrowth
of the fourth such conference, held at the Institute in May, 1983. Volumes
resulting from other and future conferences, as well as individual studies,
are planned for publication in the present series. The Institute also publishes
a series with the University of Hawaii Press devoted to the translation of
East Asian Buddhist classics.

© 1986 KURODA INSTITUTE
ALL RIGHTS RESERVED
MANUFACTURED IN THE UNITED STATES OF AMERICA
90 92 93 94 95 96   6 5 4 3 2

Library of Congress Cataloging-in-Publication Data
Traditions of meditation in Chinese Buddhism.

(Studies in East Asian Buddhism ; 4)
Based on papers presented at a conference sponsored
by the Kuroda Institute for the Study of Buddhism and
Human Values in 1983.
Includes index.
1. Meditation (Buddhism)   2.   Buddhism—China.
I.   Gregory, Peter N., 1945–   . II.   Kuroda
Institute.   III.   Series: Studies in East Asian
Buddhism ; no. 4.
BQ628.T72   1986   294.3'443   86–19243
ISBN 0–8248–1088–0

Contents

Preface

The papers collected in this volume grew out of a conference I organized in the spring of 1983 through the Kuroda Institute for the Study of Buddhism and Human Values, the fourth such conference on Buddhist Studies sponsored by the Kuroda Institute. All the original conference papers have been revised to varying degrees in light of the discussion that ensued and in response to the other papers. In this regard I would like to acknowledge the contributions of Professors Donald S. Lopez, Jr. (Middlebury College), John R. McRae (Fairbank Center for East Asian Research at Harvard University), and William F. Powell (University of California at Santa Barbara), all of whom took part in the conference as discussants. Their perceptive comments and enthusiastic participation did much to enhance the quality of the resulting volume. In preparing the papers for publication, I have made every effort to make them work together synergistically to present a coherent overview of the traditions of Chinese Buddhist meditation.

I would like to take this opportunity to gratefully acknowledge our *dānapati,* Dr. Steven Rockefeller. His generous contribution to the Kuroda Institute made the conference possible, and his continued support of the Kuroda Institute's series, Studies in East Asian Buddhism, has helped make possible the publication of this volume. I would also like to thank Stephan Bodian, the production editor for the series, and Stuart Kiang and the staff at the University of Hawaii Press for their diligent and careful attention to detail in the preparation of this volume. Finally, I would like to thank Robert Burger for compiling the index.

PETER N. GREGORY

Introduction

Peter N. Gregory

During the past two decades there has been a steady profileration of books in the West on Buddhist meditation. This trend reflects a growing interest in Buddhism both as a viable religious alternative and as an academic field of study. But this broader interest in Buddhism is also very much an outgrowth of our fascination with Buddhist meditation. For it is on the theory and practice of meditation that Buddhism may have the most to offer us, whether we are interested in it for personal reasons (as a vehicle for our own spiritual growth) or for more academic ones (for gaining a broader understanding of the nature of religion). In the course of its long and varied development, Buddhism has produced a veritable treasury of reflection on meditation, one whose extensiveness and subtlety cannot be matched by any of the other great religions. Whether it is practiced or not, meditation remains central to the tradition as a whole, and without appreciating its importance one simply cannot begin to understand Buddhism.

The wealth of English language books on Buddhist meditation ranges from translations of classical texts, academic studies, and personal accounts by Westerners to expositions by modern masters. Many are excellent, and some have even achieved the status of classics in their own right, contributing not just to our deeper understanding of Buddhism but also, in many instances, to our personal insight as well. Most, however, deal with either the Theravāda or Tibetan Buddhist tradition, whether in classical or contemporary guise. Very few deal with the kinds of meditation typical of the East Asian Buddhist traditions. The outstanding exception, of course, is Zen; most bookstores that trade in Buddhism even have a separate section reserved exclusively for Zen. Yet the majority of books written about Zen meditation tend to treat it in isolation from the larger Buddhist historical and cultural context of which it is a part. Zen meditation, zazen, is often discussed or recommended as a spiritual technique free of the usual cultural and doctrinal impediments that discourage all but the most dogged or those specially drawn to the exotic. Such a representation is, undoubtedly, the result of a number of factors: the increasingly pyschological orientation of educated Americans; an American penchant for the practical and experiential accompanied by an impatience with the theoretical; the apologetic and missionary character of some publications; the lack of familiarity with Zen's Buddhist legacy on the part of many Western enthusiasts, and so forth. But it is also very much a reflection of Zen's own professed stance, its disdain for traditional Buddhist doctrine and its insistence on cutting through to the ultimate with a single thrust of the sword.

But such a stance is itself the result of a long and complex historical evolution, one in which Zen came to define itself as the Sudden Teaching in contrast to the other more textually oriented traditions within Chinese Buddhism—a teaching, that is, that dispensed with the usual compromises suited to the less spiritually adept in order to grasp the ultimate directly. Zen claims to represent a special mind-to-mind transmission outside of the textual tradition, a transmission that ultimately traces back to the enlightenment experience of the historical Buddha. Zen's stance is thus related to its emergence as a distinct tradition within the sectarian arena of Chinese Buddhism. As the chapters by Bernard Faure and Carl Bielefeldt well demonstrate, Zen's public attitude toward meditation is deeply colored by its own sectarian claims and the kind of rhetorical posture they entailed.

While clear presentations of the techniques and psychology of Zen meditation are valuable, Western familiarity with Zen has now reached a point where an understanding of the larger historical context within which Zen articulated itself is also necessary. Such an understanding is important not only for a more balanced academic view, but also for a more serious appraisal of the meaning of Zen practice for contemporary American life. The radical character of Zen emerged as part of a complex dialectic within Buddhism, and we cannot understand Zen until we understand what it is critiquing. If we take its statements out of their Buddhist context and interpret them instead within our own cultural context, they are apt to mean something quite different, particularly in the realm of ethics. Zen's iconoclasm had a different meaning within a cultural context where Buddhist moral teachings were widely affirmed than it does today to contemporary Americans who lack any such background and who are probably already suffering from an excess of moral relativism.

Philip Kapleau records the shock that he and a fellow seeker experienced when they first witnessed the unabashed religiosity of a modern Japanese rōshi bowing before an enshrined image of his temple founder. Recalling the stories of the great T'ang Dynasty Chinese Ch'an masters

(masters who did not hesitate to use a carved image of the Buddha as firewood to keep warm), Kapleau's friend could barely hold back his disdain. When the rōshi asked them if they would also like to offer incense, the friend asked the rōshi why he didn't spit on the statue instead. To this, the rōshi replied: "If you want to spit you spit; I prefer to bow."[1] Like Kapleau's friend, it is easy for us to be misled by Zen rhetoric. We would do well to pay attention to the overall context within which Zen's radicalism evolved: the highly regimented monastic lifestyle of disciplined training and prescribed ritual that structures the details of the monk's daily life and defines the larger rhythms of his year.

Like Zen's radical pronouncements, meditation—itself originally a structured activity within an institutionalized lifestyle intended to exemplify the Buddhist ideal—is also related to the ethical realm. In the *Platform Sūtra* the Sixth Patriarch does not abrogate seated meditation when he criticizes the Northern School's practice of "sitting without moving" by alluding to Vimalakīrti's upbraiding of Śāriputra for his mistaking "meditation" for its ritualized posture.[2] Like Vimalakīrti, he redefines a prescribed practice in completely internalized and formless terms, terms that lack convenient handles onto which one might grasp. This move, of course, is only another aspect the *Platform Sūtra's* emphasis on non-abiding *(wu-chu)*. When he defines seated meditation (*tso-ch'an,* zazen), the Sixth Patriarch does so in a way that makes no reference to any physical activity: sitting *(tso)* means not activating thoughts in regard to external objects, and meditation *(ch'an)* means seeing one's original nature and not being confused.[3] While this may be a more profound way to talk about meditation, it also leaves open the question of what one actually *does* when one meditates. How, for instance, might one go about realizing a state in which one does not activate thoughts in regard to external objects? What must one do to see one's original nature?

Hu Shih is surely wrong when he says, playing on the meaning of *ch'an* as dhyāna (here loosely meaning meditation), that the Southern Ch'an denunciation of Northern Ch'an meditation practices was "a revolutionary pronouncement of a new Ch'an which renounces *ch'an* itself and is therefore no *ch'an* at all."[4] The Sixth Patriarch's criticism of the formal practice of meditation in the *Platform Sūtra* only makes sense within the context of the daily regimen of the Ch'an or Zen monk, where seated meditation was an integral part of his practice, if not the major focus of his life. But it is important to note how easily Zen rhetoric allows Hu Shih to come to this conclusion. And Hu was not alone; many Buddhists also came to this same conclusion, as David Chappell makes clear in his chapter on Pure Land criticism of Ch'an. It even seems that some of the schools of Ch'an that developed in the eighth century took Zen rhetoric quite literally, if Tsung-mi's account of the Pao-t'ang School in Szechwan can be given any credence.[5] The problematic of the radical character of Zen rhetoric about meditation versus the actual practice of meditation within the Zen School is sensitively explored by Carl Bielefeldt in his chapter on the first Ch'an meditation manual, Tsungtse's *Tso-ch'an i.*

But this book is not about Zen per se, although Zen (or, more properly speaking, Ch'an) is the central focus of three of its chapters. Rather, it deals with the matrix of Chinese Buddhist practices and concepts of which Zen was a part, and should thus help to fill out our understanding of the historical and doctrinal context from which Zen emerged. By treating the larger context of Chinese Buddhist meditation theory and practice, it should also fill a significant gap in our knowledge and understanding of Buddhist meditation: the lack of any readily available and trustworthy discussion of those forms of Buddhist meditation developed and practiced in East Asia. It thereby seeks to balance our acquaintance with Zen meditation—which, because it is the only East Asian practice with which many Westerners are familiar, is often held up as the archetypal form of East Asian Buddhist meditation—by placing it alongside other, equally representative and important forms of meditation: the invocation of the Buddha's name *(nien-fo)* in Pure Land; visualization (as exemplified by Hsüan-tsang's visualization of Maitreya); and Chih-i's monumental T'ien-t'ai synthesis of Buddhist ritual, cultic, and meditation practices. By exploring the characteristic forms of East Asian Buddhist meditation, the present volume should also contribute further to delineating the distinctive features of East Asian Buddhism.

Alan Sponberg, in the opening chapter on "Meditation in Fa-hsiang Buddhism," raises the hermeneutical problem of how we, as contemporary Westerners doubly distanced from the East Asian Buddhist meditation traditions, should properly interpret them. Not only are they the products of a different time and culture, they are also based on a world view that is fundamentally different from ours in its structure and orientation. He points out, for example, that, although we use a word like "meditation" without a second thought in our discussions of Buddhism, our word does not correspond to any specific term or general concept within Buddhism. Sponberg's discussion of the range of traditional Buddhist terms encompassed by our word "meditation" provides a useful basis for approaching the various kinds of meditation discussed throughout this book and at the same time helps us clarify our own assumptions about the use of meditation as a general category in the study of religion. His more general point is also one we would do well to heed: we must become aware of the presuppositions behind the categories with which we interpret Buddhist meditation as a first step toward gaining some understanding of it.

The hermeneutical issue, of course, not only confronts us as contemporary Westerners—it also confronted medieval Chinese Buddhists.

If our language frequently seems ill equipped to deal with the subtle psychological and epistemological distinctions found in the great Indian Buddhist meditation manuals, classical Chinese was even less well suited to the task. One could argue that the Chinese were culturally even further distanced from the world view embodied in the Buddhism they received from India than are we (who share, at least, a language with the same Indo-European roots and who also have more sophisticated hermeneutical tools at our disposal). One can outline the chronological development of Chinese Buddhism in terms of an increasingly sophisticated series of hermeneutical frameworks devised to understand a religion as alien conceptually as it was geographically.

The hermeneutical issue of the Chinese understanding of Buddhism raises the whole question of "sinification"—how the Chinese adapted Buddhism within their own conceptual framework and how Buddhism, in turn, irrevocably transformed that framework. Our awareness of the hermeneutical problems that framed the context in which the Chinese appropriated Buddhism should remind us, as the modern interpreters, that, while we must be sensitive to how our own assumptions affect our understanding of Buddhism, we must be open to how our understanding of Buddhism may also transform those assumptions. Understanding is a process of hermeneutical engagement. And here again, Buddhist meditation—as a systematic methodology for uncovering and transforming the basis of our understanding of the world—can be seen as an essentially hermeneutical enterprise and may have yet something further to offer us. Although these more general hermeneutical issues are not the focus of this book, they are inevitably raised by our consideration of Buddhist meditation within its cultural and historical context. It is hoped that, with the further understanding toward which studies such as those collected here will contribute, such issues will become not only more sharply focused but the subject of more detailed exploration in their own right.

The question of sinification, in addition to its hermeneutical ramifications, is also important for clarifying those general features that distinguish East Asian Buddhist meditation from that of South or Southeast Asian Buddhism, as well as from that of Tibet. The major traditions discussed in the chapters that follow (T'ien-t'ai, Ch'an/Zen, and Pure Land) are all products of what Yūki Reimon has characterized as the New Buddhism of the Sui/T'ang Period. In other words, they are examples of thoroughly assimilated forms of Chinese Buddhist thought and practice, forms that are at once genuinely Buddhist and uniquely Chinese. They thus offer a convenient base of comparison with the meditation traditions characteristic of other, more widely known forms of Buddhist practice.

The only tradition of Buddhism discussed in this book that does not neatly fit into Yūki's rubric is that of Fa-hsiang. Though it had its incep-

tion in the early years of the T'ang Dynasty, this Chinese form of Yogācāra in many ways represents a far less "sinified" form of Buddhism, one
that self-consciously rejected, in favor of a more purely Indian model,
those new forms of Chinese Buddhism that were taking shape during the
sixth and seventh centuries. Fa-hsiang thus can be seen as offering a
bridge between more Indian forms of Buddhist practice and those more
typically Chinese forms discussed in the other chapters of this book. At
the same time, K'uei-chi's five-level discernment of *vijñaptimātratā* (discussed in Alan Sponberg's chapter on Fa-hsiang meditation), can also be
seen as a deliberate response to those new forms of Chinese Buddhist
thought. If, as Sponberg suggests, K'uei-chi's five-level discernment can
be seen as an attempt "to co-opt or preempt . . . some of the distinctive
analytical structures of the new Chinese Buddhism of the sixth century,
seeking thereby to appropriate the vitality of these new developments
while remaining true to his own, more conservative tradition," it also represents a distinctly Chinese twist to the more Indian teachings of Hsüan-
tsang.

We cannot easily detach the practice of meditation from its doctrinal
context. The various Buddhist meditation techniques are deeply embedded in a larger world view. Buddhist meditation puts into practice the
Buddhist understanding of the world. It involves a sophisticated epistemology based on an analysis of the psychological process by which we
"construct" our experience of the world, and it has a definite soteriological orientation. The distinction between theory and practice, like that
between form and content, breaks down when applied to meditation.
Although it may seem obvious, this point is well worth stressing within
the context of East Asian Buddhism, where the Zen practice of zazen is
often taken as the reigning model. Even those forms of Buddhist meditation that involve nondiscursive modes of awareness are set within the
larger soteriological context of the Buddhist understanding of the world.
Buddhist meditation practice is inextricably linked with Buddhist meditation theory. The practice exemplifies the theory; the theory is informed
by the practice.

Nowhere is this more apparent than in the traditional Buddhist practice of vipaśyanā (P. *vipassanā*), discernment or insight into the true
nature of existence. As Winston King remarks in his recent study of
Theravāda meditation, "Vipassanā is the methodological embodiment of
the Buddhist (Theravāda) world view."[6] Vipaśyanā entails the experiential internalization of Buddhist categories—a practice in which the adept
systematically applies Buddhist categories to his own experience so that
his own experience becomes the living exemplification of the reality of
those categories. In the case of Theravāda Buddhism, "vipassanā is the
total, supersaturated, existentializing of the Theravāda world view that
all existence in personal and individual modes of being, intrinsically and

ineradicably embodies impermanence [*anicca*], pain [*dukkha*], and impersonality [*anattā*]."⁷ In the case of the the Chinese Fa-hsiang tradition of Buddhism, K'uei-chi's five-level discernment of *vijñaptimātratā* embodies the systematic and progressive understanding of the central Yogācāra teaching that our notion of self and external objects "are nothing but cognitive constructions." In Chih-i's comprehensive systematization of T'ien-t'ai meditative practice (as it is laid out in detail in the chapter by Daniel Stevenson), discernment ultimately involves insight into the emptiness of all forms.

While these various examples of vipaśyanā all illustrate how this central Buddhist practice relates to the Buddhist understanding of the world, they also suggest how that understanding of the world differs according to different traditions of Buddhism. Given the intimate interrelationship in Buddhism between the theory and practice of meditation, this last point further suggests that the kind of *experience* that one might have as a result of practicing different kinds of meditation would vary not just according to the kind of technique involved, but also according to the doctrinal setting in terms of which that technique is framed.

By way of illustration, we might well consider the modern form of Theravāda vipassanā, or "insight meditation," that has become popular in both Southeast Asia and the United States. Often referred to as the practice of "bare awareness," this form of vipassanā is based on the traditional practice of mindfulness (P. *sati*) as taught in the *Mahāsatipaṭṭhāna-sutta*. As elaborated by such modern advocates as Nyanaponika Thera in *The Heart of Buddhist Meditation,* the mindful attention it cultivates often seems barely distinguishable from the T'ien-t'ai practice of *sui-tzu-i* ("cultivating samādhi wherever mind is directed") or the Ch'an practice of one-practice samādhi *(i-hsing san-mei).* All involve concentrating one's total attention on whatever one happens to be experiencing in the moment. The immediate content of one's consciousness itself becomes the "object" of the meditation. From the bare descriptions of the techniques involved, one would be hard pressed to determine how the practices differ, and we might well suppose that the experience of practicing the modern Theravāda form of insight meditation would be similar to the experience of practicing T'ien-t'ai *sui-tzu-i* samādhi or Ch'an one-practice samādhi.

It is because the techniques seem so strikingly similar that we must pay particular attention to their doctrinal contexts. In the Theravāda practice, vipassanā is a method for realizing the true nature of all existents as being impermanent *(anicca),* entailing suffering *(dukkha),* and lacking any abiding self *(anattā).* Vipassanā thus involves insight into the so-called three marks of existence, which came to express the core of the Theravāda world view. To these was often added a fourth term, impurity *(asubha).* The opposite of these four—permanence *(nicca),* bliss *(sukha),* selfhood *(attā),* and purity *(subha)*—constituted the four upside-down views. These upside-down views were considered the constituents of ignorance *(avijjā),* which, in turn, was the basis for our continual suffering in an endless round of births. As such they also served as a doctrinal litmus test for determining the truth of any teaching: any teaching that held that the true nature of existence could be characterized as permanent, blissful, having a self, or pure was to be rejected as false.

The corresponding Chinese practices were based on an entirely different understanding of the ultimate nature of all existents, a Mahāyāna view that saw all forms of existence not only as ultimately empty of any defilement, but also as manifestations of an intrinsically pure nature. Such a perspective offered a vision in which the phenomenal world of everyday experience could be revalidated in light of an understanding of emptiness *(śūnyatā; k'ung),* especially as that understanding was qualified by the *tathāgatagarbha* doctrine. The Chinese inherited this doctrine from Indian Mahāyāna, but developed it further in texts such as the *Awakening of Faith,* and it assumed a centrality for the tradition as a whole that it never had in India and never was to enjoy in Tibet. The doctrine was important for Chinese Buddhists because it explained how Principle *(li)* interpenetrated with phenomena *(shih)* without obstruction, thus providing an ontological ground for an affirmation of the realm of phenomenal activity.[8]

The understanding of emptiness within the *tathāgatagarbha* tradition differs from that found within Mādhyamika: ultimate reality is empty of all defilement but also full (literally, "not empty"; *aśūnya*) of infinite Buddha-dharmas. This understanding enabled Chinese Buddhists to interpret Buddhism in more ontological terms, terms that could be used to make positive ascriptions about the ultimate nature of reality —that is, to say what it *was* as well as what it was *not.* In such representative texts as the *Nirvāṇa Sūtra, Śrīmālā Sūtra, Ratnagotravibhāga,* and *Awakening of Faith,* the four upside-down views were turned upside-down and were thereby made the marks of true discernment into the ultimate nature of absolute reality. Whereas the ignorant ordinary person mistakes what is impermanent for what is permanent, what causes suffering for what is blissful, what lacks self for what has self, and what is impure for what is pure, the Hīnayāna disciples were correct in realizing the impermanent to be impermanent, and so forth. Their understanding was limited and partial, however, for they did not yet realize what was truly permanent, what was truly blissful, what was truly endowed with self, and what was truly pure. Such Buddha-knowledge was only available to advanced bodhisattvas. The *tathāgatagarbha* was thus said to represent the perfection of permanence, bliss, self, and purity.[9]

The chapters that follow underline the importance that the *tathāgatagarbha* doctrine had for Ch'an. Bernard Faure discusses the important role in seventh- and eighth-century Ch'an of the *Awakening of Faith* and its ontological interpretation of one-practice samādhi. Carl Bielefeldt notes that the theory of how wisdom is related to the practice of seated meditation in Tsung-tse's *ch'an* manual is based on "the model of the pure, enlightened mind covered by discursive thinking." As both these chapters point out, the *tathāgatagarbha* doctrine was especially prominent in the teaching of Tao-hsin and Hung-jen, the fourth and fifth Ch'an patriarchs. Although the more radical teaching of Hui-neng and Shen-hui, which came to define the orthodox Southern Ch'an position, moved away from such explicit identification with the *tathāgatagarbha* doctrine, it did not reject it altogether, as evidenced by the characteristically Southern Ch'an emphasis on "seeing the Nature" (Ch. *chien-hsing;* J. *kenshō*). The crucial role of this doctrine in providing an ontological undergirding for Ch'an practice was reemphasized by the great Ch'an theoretician and historian of the early ninth century Tsung-mi, who adapted Hua-yen metaphysics as a buttress against the more radical interpretations of the Southern position that he witnessed in the burgeoning Ch'an movements of his day. Tsung-mi's theory of the ontological basis of Ch'an practice later became the cornerstone around which Chinul laid the foundation for Korean Ch'an (Sŏn) in his masterful synthesis of Chinese Buddhist theory and practice, as Robert Buswell amply documents in his closing chapter. Buswell's discussion of the practice of "tracing back the radiance of the mind" is particularly interesting for showing how the *tathāgatagarbha* doctrine was applied to Ch'an practice.

Indeed, the *tathāgatagarbha* doctrine was central to all of the schools of the New Buddhism of the Sui/T'ang Period because it provided the basis on which they affirmed the universal accessibility of Buddhahood. Although it was especially pronounced in Hua-yen and Ch'an, it also figured in Pure Land and T'ien-t'ai. The doctrine occupied a prominent position in the thought of Hui-ssu, but played a more qualified role in that of Hui-ssu's disciple Chih-i. Chih-i was careful to dissociate his use of the doctrine from the more ontological interpretations of the Ti-lun and She-lun traditions. Nevertheless, he frequently referred to it, and the understanding of the nature of consciousness that underlay his systematization of Buddhist practice was based on a *tathāgatagarbha* model. Chan-jan, the great eighth-century reviver of the T'ien-t'ai tradition, reemphasized the importance of the *tathāgatagarbha* within T'ien-t'ai doctrine. His incorporation of the *Awakening of Faith's* analysis of mind can be seen as an attempt to accommodate the metaphysics of his major scholastic rival, Hua-yen, as well as a reflection of his close relationship to the Northern School of Ch'an. This version of T'ien-t'ai became the basis for the so-called *hongaku shisō* ("theory of intrinsic enlightenment") that was the hallmark of medieval Japanese Tendai and served as the watershed from which emerged the great medieval reform movements of Pure Land, Zen, and Nichiren.

Although all of the new schools of Buddhism drew upon the *tathā-gatagarbha's* teaching of an intrinsically pure, enlightened mind, this doctrine was notably absent from the Fa-hsiang tradition. For this reason Hua-yen thinkers such as Chih-yen and Fa-tsang classified Fa-hsiang as only a quasi-Mahāyāna teaching within their hierarchy of Buddhist teachings. As the chapters in this volume make clear, this doctrine underlay much of the typically Chinese theory of meditation practice and was a characteristic feature of the sinified forms of Buddhism that emerged during the Sui and T'ang dynasties. Thus it must be considered in any attempt to assess the major features that distinguish Chinese Buddhism, and more broadly East Asian Buddhism, from that of other areas of Asia.

Not only can we not detach the practice of meditation from its theory (or doctrinal setting), we also cannot separate meditation from various ritual, cultic, and devotional practices, as Daniel Stevenson so well illustrates in his chapter on "The Four Kinds of Samādhi in Early T'ien-t'ai Buddhism." In Chih-i's systematic synthesis of Chinese Buddhist meditative practices, careful prescriptions for purification, the preparation of offerings, the enshrinement of holy images, the solicitation of auspicious dreams, prostrations, circumambulation, repentance, prayer, the making of vows, the recitation of sacred texts, the incantation of dhāraṇīs, the invocation of the Buddha's name, and the performance of intricate visualizations are all harmoniously integrated within a thoroughgoing discernment of the emptiness of all phenomenal forms. The means by which these various practices are balanced with one another and incorporated within a larger and more penetrating understanding of the nature of the mind and the noetic act itself can be found in Chih-i's understanding of *upāya,* the "skillfull means" by which the Buddha devised a panoply of practices and teachings suited to the varying capacities and diverse levels of experience of different beings. Chih-i draws upon a crucial distinction within Chinese Buddhism in his treatment of *upāya:* that of *li* (Principle) and *shih* (phenomenal activities). The various phenomenal means *(shih)* encompassed within the four kinds of samādhi are all necessary as *upāya* and, as they become suffused with the discernment of Principle *(li-kuan),* lead to the realization of the ultimate emptiness of all phenomenal forms.

As Stevenson points out, Chih-i's system thus contains two distinct approaches to meditation: a radical one (based on *li*) that takes ultimate reality itself as its "object" and an expedient one (based on *shih*) that relies on the mediation of various phenomenal forms. These two approaches, exemplified by Chih-i's treatment of one-practice samādhi, were already apparent in the *Wen-shu shuo ching* passage he cites for scriptural authority for that practice. The importance of this passage for the Chinese traditions discussed in this book reverberates throughout four of the chapters. While Chih-i held these two approaches together in a creative tension in his comprehensive framework, they became separately embodied in the Ch'an and Pure Land interpretations of the practice, as Bernard Faure argues. While Ch'an emphasizes the direct apprehension of ultimate reality (the Dharmadhātu), Pure Land stresses the importance of visualizing the ideal form of a particular Buddha or calling upon his name *(nien-fo)*. Faure goes on to show how these approaches, based on their different emphases on *li* and *shih,* relate to other sets of polarities within the discourse of T'ang Buddhism, one of the most important being that of sudden *(tun)* and gradual *(chien)*. Chih-i's disciple Kuan-ting, in his preface to the *Mo-ho chih-kuan,* had defined the "perfect sudden" *(yüan-tun)* practice as that which directly took ultimate reality as its "object". In its rejection of all forms and expedients, Ch'an could thus at once proclaim itself as the Sudden Teaching and put down other teachings (such as Pure Land) as inferior forms of gradualistic practice because they relied on expedient approaches. The *li/shih* polarity, insofar as it was conceptually related to the Chinese Buddhist understanding of *upāya,* thus became inextricably bound up with the "sudden/gradual" discourse as well.

In the section of his chapter discussing *sui-tzu-i* samādhi, Stevenson notes a tension inherent in Chih-i's treatment of the discernment of Principle. Since the ultimate success of all the various forms of meditation Chih-i discusses under the rubric "four kinds of samādhi" depend on the discernment of Principle, the question naturally arises, why can't they simply be dispensed with altogether in favor of the practice of *sui-tzu-i,* which does not depend on any phenomenal form but constitutes the very discernment of Principle that is the essence of the other practices? Chih-i, of course, draws back from such a radical conclusion and is careful to hedge in *sui-tzu-i* with a series of accessory practices and cautions. In championing itself as the Sudden Teaching, however, the Southern School of Ch'an took the step against which Chih-i warned. This move led to a tension within the tradition regarding such mundane but all-important matters as the actual technique of meditation. Given its ideological identification as the Sudden Teaching, the tradition could say nothing at all about the very practice from which it took its name. The resulting paradox is perceptively explored in the chapter by Carl Bielefeldt.

In his chapter on the Pure Land response to Ch'an, David Chappell discusses the two different approaches to practice found in one-practice samādhi in terms of the Perfection of Wisdom dialectic so important for both Pure Land and Ch'an. He notes how in the eighth century Fei-hsi sought to reconcile the split that had taken place between these two

12 Peter N. Gregory

forms of Chinese Buddhist practice by resorting to the *li/shih* paradigm. This paradigm thus provided the conceptual basis for the dual cultivation of Pure Land and Ch'an characteristic of later Chinese Buddhism. Such a resolution was possible, as Chappell indicates, because *li* and *shih* offerred Chinese Buddhists a convenient framework in which to interpret the Indian Buddhist doctrine of the two truths.

Indeed, the theme of *li* and *shih* runs as a *leitmotif* throughout this volume. It can even be found in K'uei-chi's five-level discernment of *vijñaptimātratā*. These terms, drawn from the indigenous Chinese philosophical vocabulary, provided Chinese Buddhists with one of their most convenient tools for adapting Buddhism to forms that were both more comprehensible and more compatible with their own religious and philosophical preoccupations. The terms are thus also a part of the unique conceptual framework that distinguishes the Buddhism of China in particular and East Asia in general from that of other areas of Asia.

As a conclusion to this volume, the chapter by Robert Buswell on the great Korean Buddhist figure Chinul is both appropriate and welcome. It is appropriate because Chinul can be seen as operating within the same doctrinal problematic as the Chinese Ch'an and Hua-yen traditions he inherited. His thought is thus a fitting extension of Chinese Buddhist thought. It is welcome because it shows how the Chinese Buddhist tradition carried over into other East Asian countries to become the matrix for East Asian Buddhism as a whole. Buswell's chapter also illustrates how, in forging a new synthesis of Chinese Buddhist theory and meditation practice, Chinul helped to define a distinctively Korean form of Buddhism. Indeed, Chinul's achievement can in many ways be compared to Chih-i's. Not only did both figures succeed in creating an impressive synthesis of a broad range of practices within a comprehensive vision of the path, but both also occupied similar positions in the development of unique forms of Buddhism that served as watersheds for all that followed.

Notes

1. *The Three Pillars of Zen* (Boston: Beacon Press, 1967), pp. 211–212.
2. See Philip Yampolsky, *The Platform Sutra of the Sixth Patriarch* (New York: Columbia University Press, 1967), p. 137.
3. *Ibid.,* p. 140.
4. "Ch'an (Zen) Buddhism in China: Its History and Method," *Philosophy East and West,* vol. 3 (1953), p. 7.
5. See *Yüan-chüeh ching ta-shu ch'ao,* ZZ1/14/3.278c–d; see also Yanagida Seizan, "The *Li-tai fa-pao chi* and the Ch'an Doctrine of Sudden Awakening," translated by Carl Bielefeldt, in Whalen Lai and Lewis R. Lancaster, eds., *Early Ch'an in China and Tibet* (Berkeley: Asian Humanities Press, 1983), pp. 31–32.

6. *Theravāda Meditation: The Buddhist Transformation of Yoga* (University Park: Pennsylvania State University Press, 1980), p. 16.
7. *Ibid.,* p. 94.
8. These points are discussed more fully in my article "Chinese Buddhist Hermeneutics: The Case of Hua-yen," *Journal of the American Academy of Religion,* vol. 51 (1983), pp. 231–249.
9. See, for example, *Sheng-man shih-tzu-hou i-sheng ta-fang-pien fang-kuang ching,* T12.222a18–25; translation by Alex and Hideko Wayman, *The Lion's Roar of Queen Śrīmālā* (New York: Columbia University Press, 1974), pp. 101–102. Cf. *Ta-sheng ch'i-hsin lun,* T32.579a14–20; translation by Yoshito S. Hakeda, *The Awakening of Faith* (New York: Columbia University Press, 1967), p. 65.

Meditation in Fa-hsiang Buddhism

Alan Sponberg

I. Some Introductory Reflections

Buddhism and meditation have become virtually synonymous in the Western mind, so much so that contemporary efforts to discuss Buddhism in contrast to other world religions usually include some reference to the centrality of meditative practice along with the older characterization of Buddhism as "the world's only atheistic religion." Although such generalizations probably tell us more about Western religious conceptions and presuppositions than about Buddhism, there is no question that meditation does hold a central place in the history of Buddhist practice. But to what specific activities within the range of Buddhist religious practice are we referring when we use this term "meditation"?

In asking that question we raise an underlying problem that runs throughout this chapter, and indeed throughout all the chapters of this volume. My assignment was to provide a discussion of the meditation traditions of the Fa-hsiang school of early T'ang Buddhism—an exercise that would seem at first glance to be fairly straightforward. In practice, however, it turns out to be rather more complicated. I might begin by asking the most obvious questions: What were the meditational practices of the Chinese Yogācāra masters, and how did their meditation differ from that of the other schools of Chinese Buddhism? Yet the very clarity of these questions obscures the fact that they already presuppose a common concept of meditation, an understanding of meditation as a category of religious experience that would have to be shared not only among us, the Western interpreters, but also by the sixth-century Buddhists of China, a tradition from which we are doubly distanced, both temporally and culturally. But is such an assumption warranted in this case? Do we have, among ourselves, a reasonably clear consensus regarding the meaning of "meditation," that is, regarding what activities are "meditative" and what activities are not? And can our understanding of meditation be mapped directly onto the range of practices we find in early China? Can it accommodate and illuminate the distinctiveness of what those Buddhist practitioners considered meditation, and what they did not? I am not so sure. Before I attempt to present some material that will, I think, tell us something of great interest about meditative practice among the Fa-hsiang monks of the seventh century, let us pause a moment to consider the precariousness of such an assumption.

First, we should reflect on what we, as contemporary Westerners, are likely to include under the rubric "meditation" or "meditative practice"—and, perhaps of even more significance, on what we are likely *not* to include, consciously or otherwise. Meditation, as a Western category of religious practice, suffers from a twofold confusion: it is at once too vague and too specific. It is too vague in the sense of being extremely open-ended, and too specific in the sense of being too narrowly represented or instantiated in the minds of those who use it. We all feel quite comfortable using the term loosely, assuming some commonly understood but never clearly defined referent. Yet, at the same time, even in our apparent agreement, each of us is likely to be taking some overly narrow and specific instance or example of meditation as normative for the category as a whole. Indeed, I suspect that our conception of meditation is thus often framed in overly narrow terms because of its very lack of more explicit definition as a category of religious experience.

In fact, in the history of religions, meditation has been a notoriously vague and multivalent concept—a circumstance that stems, no doubt, from its relative lack of elaboration and systematization in the Western religious traditions, especially in their post-Enlightenment forms. That the concept lacks any clearly defined and generally accepted referent in our own general cultural experience does not restrict its attractiveness— indeed, it actually enhances it. Meditation is a very useful category precisely because it can be understood in so many ways.

Consider how much our various personal conceptions are likely to vary. For some of us, meditation is exemplified by the contemplative exercises of St. Ignatius, or perhaps by the seven mansions of St. Teresa of Ávila. For others, meditation may suggest some more contemporary practice, a new biofeedback technique for "total relaxation and lower blood pressure," or perhaps the Transcendental Meditation® taught by Maharishi Mahesh Yogi. Or again, in the case of Westerners interested in Buddhism, meditation may refer to the formal seated meditation (zazen) of the Ch'an and Zen lineages, or perhaps to the modern insight meditation of Southeast Asian Theravāda.

Certainly these various examples bear a family resemblance to one another; they are clearly instances of meditation understood in a very broad sense. My point here is not to argue that we need some normative definition of meditation to carry on our scholarship, if not our lives. The problem I do wish to address is that a conception of meditation shaped exclusively by any one of these instances would be inappropriately restrictive. We must be sure that we are understanding the term in a suitably comprehensive sense before we begin looking for meditation in another culture. We must recognize the extent to which our respective individual conceptions of meditation do in fact vary; and I am not at all convinced that what meditation means to each of us is as clear as it might seem. As scholars attempting a phenomenological study of "meditation" in Buddhism, we must not allow our particular conception of the term to constrict our view of the alien tradition we are seeking to interpret and understand. Meditation *is* unquestionably a useful and necessary category to bring to our study of Buddhism, *but only* if we are careful to determine how it is understood *within* Buddhism. We must consider what range of practices are included under that category, and we must try to reveal how those practices are understood to be interrelated within the tradition itself.

Consider for a moment what technical term in the traditional Buddhist vocabulary corresponds to this concept. If the Western technical vocabulary for psychophysical spiritual cultivation is clumsy because it is too vague and too limited, the corresponding South Asian vocabulary tends to be intractable for just the opposite reason: it is characterized by a historical proliferation of refinements and differentiations that has led to a surprising range and variety of terms, a wealth of distinctions that are highly standardized in some traditions and more free-floating in others. Several scholars of Indian Buddhism have already pointed out that the Sanskrit technical vocabulary is far richer in terms that describe techniques and aspects of psychophysical conditioning or cultivation than the corresponding vocabulary in European languages.[1] Let me draw attention to just a few of the problems that are relevant to the present discussion.

Even the most limited group of Sanskrit terms encountered in technical discussions of Buddhist meditation practice would include *dhyāna, samādhi, śamatha, vipaśyanā, samāpatti, anusmṛti, yoga,* and *bhāvanā.* Although some of these terms are occasionally used synonymously in Sanskrit, they are usually carefully distinguished in the technical literature, each having its own specific referent. The problem with introducing our own concept of meditation is that we may tend to use it interchangeably for all of these, usually without recognizing that "meditation" does not adequately express any of them in their technical specificity. When more of an effort is made to retain the distinctions of this technical vocabulary, "meditation" is usually used to render one (or more) of the three most common terms: dhyāna, samādhi, and bhāvanā. Since each of these has been proposed at some point as the best and most appropriate equivalent for "meditation," it will be helpful for our purposes to review the meaning of each in turn and to consider why we should be careful about too readily assigning any one of them to the concept "meditation."

The Sanskrit term that most often comes to mind when one speaks of Buddhist meditation is "dhyāna," the term transcribed by the early Chinese as *ch'an(-na)* and by the Japanese as *zen*. In his major study of the Buddhist meditation literature, Mahāthera Paravahera Vajirañāṇa, the eminent Sri Lankan monk and Pāli scholar, has argued that this is the Buddhist term that should be rendered as "meditation." He says we must understand "dhyāna" in its broadest etymological sense (Pāli: *jhāna,* from the verb *jhāyati:* "to think closely [upon an object]"), pointing out that this sense comes closest to the literal meaning of the English term.[2] Etymologically this is appropriate, though on looking more closely we find that "dhyāna" seems to be used in two ways within the tradition: in the broader sense Paravahera emphasizes, but also in a more restricted sense, which is thoroughly documented as well.

In its narrower sense "dhyāna" is frequently used to refer specifically to the various states or levels that make up an early system of successive stages of mental absorption or trance, each level having a corresponding plane in Buddhist cosmology.[3] As the tradition develops, the term comes to be used more frequently in its broader sense, referring to psychophysical practices in general. In this broader sense, dhyāna is said to consist of both śamatha and vipaśyanā, of both psychophysiological calming or centering and insight into or discernment of the nature of existence. This insistence on the importance of the latter component, discernment or insight, distinguished the early Buddhists from other, parallel South Asian traditions that recognized the same system of successive levels of dhyānic absorption—states that for the Buddhists still fell within the cultivation of centering (śamatha) rather than that of discernment (vipaśyanā). Thus, used in its older, pre-Buddhist sense, "dhyāna" may refer to certain specific states or levels of attainment *(samāpatti);* used in a broader or more inclusive sense, it could also refer to mental cultivation that included the distinctive Buddhist notion of vipaśyanā as well. This broader sense appears to be the one most often implied when we encounter "dhyāna" in its Chinese transcription, though certainly the more specific system of the four, eight, or nine dhyānic attainments was also well known.

Another term that occurs quite often in the technical literature is "samādhi," which is found in the Eightfold Path taught in Gautama's first sermon. Samādhi is a more general concept than dhyāna in its narrower sense, which has led some to favor "samādhi" as the proper equivalent for "meditation." If we look more closely at how the term "samādhi" is actually employed, however, we will quickly see that it is still too restricted to correspond to our usual notion of meditation. With the etymological sense of "bringing or putting together," this term most often refers to a state of mental concentration, usually the result of some particular technique or practice. A verbal noun, it tends more often to be used for the resultant state than for the activity itself, for the one-pointed concentration of mind *(cittasya ekāgratā)* that results from meditative practice rather than for meditative practice in general. At times, "samā-dhi" is also used in place of "śamatha" in contrast to "vipaśyanā," thus representing only one of the dual aspects of meditative practice in Buddhism. The closest parallel in the Buddhist tradition to our notion of meditation thus does appear to be dhyāna, as long as we are careful to take it in its generic sense, in which it comprises both śamatha and vipaś-yanā.

There is, however, still another term that we must note. Of all the terms mentioned thus far, certainly the broadest in its semantic range is "bhāvanā." Here we have another verbal noun, derived from the root *bhū,* "to be, become; to cultivate, develop, increase; to produce; to prac-tice." In Buddhism "bhāvanā" can refer to any form of spiritual cultiva-tion or practice, "dhyānic" or not, and it is by far the most inclusive of all the terms mentioned thus far. Recently Walpola Rahula has argued that "Buddhist meditation" must be understood in the broader sense of bhāvanā rather than dhyāna, so that Western audiences will realize that there is more to mental cultivation in Buddhism than "sitting quietly like a statue, with legs crossed and eyes cast down."[4] But to assert "bhāvanā," by virtue of its inclusiveness, as a more suitable analog for "meditation" still does not resolve our problem. Were we to insist on "bhāvanā" as the proper Sanskrit equivalent for "meditation," we would simply have a new problem: a term that is *more* inclusive than what we usually under-stand by "meditation" and also one that I think answers rather different questions as a categorizing tool.

Even so, Rahula's point is an important one. In Buddhist practice, there is a crucial connection between the concepts of dhyāna and bhāvanā. The sense in which dhyāna, the exercise of meditation, is con-sidered to be bhāvanā, a soteriologically productive practice, can tell us a great deal about how meditation is understood in Buddhism. To apply our notion of meditation to Buddhism in the most effective way then, we must look to the notion of dhyāna, being particularly careful to under-stand dhyāna in the still broader context of bhāvanā, even though many aspects of bhāvanā might fall outside of our notion of meditation. To focus, in our examination of Buddhist meditation, on only those aspects of bhāvanā that fit neatly into our concept of meditation would obscure much of what is unique about the Buddhist understanding of religious practice. What is most distinctive about bhāvanā as a category is its lack of any restrictive specificity: virtually any activity can be considered bhāvanā, as long as it is conducive to enlightenment and liberation in the Buddhist sense. What makes a given activity bhāvanā is not the presence of any particular quality—whether it is individual or corporate, devotional or "meditative," mental or physical, active or passive, etc. The focus of bhāvanā as a category is not on distinguishing a particular type of activity in that way, but rather on indicating the "productive" nature of various activities undertaken in the distinctive context of Buddhist soteriology. Any activity done in such a way as to be productive of nirvāṇa is deemed bhāvanā; the important point is how a given practice is integrated into a comprehensive soteriology, not whether it has certain predetermined definitive qualities. Thus a given activity might well be bhāvanā for one person but not for another; similarly, a given practice might be appropriate as bhāvanā at one point in time but not at another.

Although Rahula raises a valid concern, we must be careful not to reduce bhāvanā to our more specific notion of meditation. A whole dimension of bhāvanā would be lost if we were to understand it as meditation in any narrow or reductive sense. That bhāvanā was not by definition more rigidly restricted to a limited range of specific techniques is one of the circumstances that has contributed to a high degree of toleration within the tradition and, in turn, to Buddhism's unique ability to adapt itself historically and culturally. Through a process of creative assimilation and revalorization, indigenous forms of religious practice in many Asian cultures have been brought within the realm of orthopraxis, a process whereby a given practice is reoriented to become "productive" within a Buddhist framework. We must not lose sight of this distinctive feature of the Buddhist concept of bhāvanā.

It should be clear by now that determining which of these Buddhist concepts corresponds to our notion of meditation is no simple task—and for good reason: to attempt such a correlation is wrongheaded in a fundamental way. To ask which Buddhist technical term should be rendered by the word "meditation" is to map Buddhist data onto our own conception of meditation. A more fruitful approach would start in the opposite direction: rather than trying to determine which Buddhist term best fits our concept of meditation, we should consider what modification our concept requires in light of Buddhist experience. As interpreters of an alien culture, we cannot be content simply to assign aspects of Buddhist experience to the best available category from our own culture. Rather, we need to expand and elaborate our categories to better encompass what we find in the alien culture: in this case, we must modify our understanding of meditation as a category of human religious experience in whatever ways are required to make sense of the Buddhist experience as it emerges from our study. In doing this, we must look for "Buddhist meditation" in its broadest sense—that is, in the sense of dhyāna understood as bhāvanā—and we must take into consideration the full range of activities designated by these two Sanskrit terms, seeking to discover how and why the Buddhist tradition sees as interrelated a variety of practical techniques. To do this with sensitivity and respect, and in a way that broadens our own understanding, we must be careful to adapt *our own* conception of meditation to accommodate the range of Buddhist dhyāna, and not vice versa.

In my conclusion, I shall return to these hermeneutical reflections on the theme of cross-cultural interpretation. First, however, we should proceed with the task at hand. So far I have argued that we must recognize the interpretative concept or category of meditation as a product of our own contemporary culture. I have attempted to illuminate some of the ways in which that concept is understood in our culture. And I have briefly reviewed the technical vocabulary of traditional Buddhist praxis, pointing out that any discussion of Buddhist meditation must take into account the full range of practices indicated by the terms "dhyāna" and "bhāvanā." With this framework in mind, we can turn now to a consideration of meditation understood as dhyāna-bhāvanā among the Fa-hsiang monks of sixth-century China.

II. Two Examples of Fa-hsiang Praxis

To assay the range of meditative practice in Fa-hsiang Buddhism, I will discuss two different and quite distinctive exercises, both of which were designated by the same Chinese term, *kuan:* "to view" or "to contemplate". The first involves a technique of eidetic visualization whereby one enters into a different level of existence. In contrast to that highly specific technique, the second practice involves a set of "discernments" or "contemplations" presenting the successive steps by which one gains insight into the nature of existence as understood by the Yogācārins. Although each of these exercises warrants a more extended discussion in its own right, here I hope only to show how each represents a different aspect of Buddhist practice in this particular school. To do this we must examine the context, the content, and the respective objectives of each technique.

Of course, other meditative practices were current among the early Fa-hsiang monks. I will limit the present discussion to these two, however, because they appear particularly representative, both being relatively well-documented in contemporary works pertaining to important Fa-hsiang figures, and because they demonstrate how different in content and technique meditative practices can be. The activities we will consider here are quite different from zazen-type techniques, not just in detail, but in conception as well. These are not just different ways of doing zazen; they are fundamentally different types of praxis. Even so, they must be included in any discussion of meditation in its broadest sense, and they certainly fall within the Buddhist category of dhyāna as bhāvana.

1. MAITREYA VISUALIZATION

The first type of practice is one of a class of visualization exercises in which the practitioner mentally constructs an eidetic image of some specific object or scene, in this case Maitreya Bodhisattva as he resides in Tuṣita Heaven or, more specifically, an image of the meditator himself in the presence of Maitreya in Tuṣita.[5] Various types of visualization practice appear relatively early in Buddhist texts, both Mahāyāna and Hīnayāna, and one finds visualization employed in a number of different ways to achieve a variety of ends. Sometimes visualization serves simply as an aid to establishing one-pointed concentration *(ekāgratā)*. At other times, it is part of a more elaborate praxis directed toward identification and appropriation. Within this range of visualization practices, we can find numerous instances in which the technique involves a devotional attitude directed toward some specific cult figure, though again, even within this particular subset of visualization techniques, the specific objective or goal of the exercises appears to have varied significantly from case to case.

In China there is substantial evidence of a prominent tradition of cult visualization involving devotional reverence, a tradition documented from as early as the first half of the fifth century.[6] A number of different cult figures served as the object of visualization in this tradition: the earliest Chinese texts talk of visualizing the Buddhas of the Ten Directions, and in later works we find Maitreya, Baiṣajyarāja, Mañjuśrī, and eventually Amitābha coming to the fore. At the end of the sixth century, just prior to the ascendance of Pure Land devotionalism, Maitreya appears to have become to be quite prominent as a focus of much of Chinese Buddhist cult activity, especially in association with praxis that involved visualization techniques. Given these antecedents and the special place of Maitreya in the Yogācāra tradition, it is hardly surprising to find that the Maitreya cult and Maitreya visualization had a special place in the religious life of the early Fa-hsiang masters.

The place of the Maitreya cult in Fa-hsiang circles is not difficult to establish. An analysis of references to cult figures in Hsüan-tsang's travelog and in his principal biography[7] shows that the central objects of devotion in his religious life were Śākyamuni Buddha and the three bodhisattvas Maitreya, Avalokiteśvara, and Mañjuśrī.[8] Although Hsüan-tsang regarded all four of these figures with great veneration, Maitreya was especially important, it seems, both because of the bodhisattva's association with the Yogācāra literature and because of Hsüan-tsang's fervent desire to be reborn in Tuṣita Heaven. We can see this in the record of his pilgrimage, for example, where he reports at several points going out of his way to visit Maitreya statues in Central Asia and

India.[9] Later, his contemporary and biographer, Hui-li, reports that after Hsüan-tsang returned to China, he compiled a record of the religious activities performed during his lifetime, a catalog of good works that prominently included, in addition to his translation activities, the production of one thousand images of both Śākyamuni and Maitreya.[10] At the end of his life, moreover, we are told that Hsüan-tsang dedicated the merit of all his efforts to ensuring that all present at his death bed would be born among the inner circle around Maitreya in Tuṣita Heaven. He went on to express the further aspiration that when Maitreya is reborn as the next Buddha, they should all descend with him to continue doing Dharma works until finally attaining supreme perfect enlightenment *(anuttarasamyaksaṃbodhi)*. His final words came a few moments later in response to a disciple's question. Asked whether it was certain that he would be reborn in Tuṣita Heaven, he replied: "Quite certain!"[11]

These references should suffice to establish the general importance of Maitreya in Hsüan-tsang's religious life. For our purposes here, another incident from Hsüan-tsang's travels is especially informative. The details are reported in the biography cited earlier as part of an account of the master's encounter with river pirates on the Ganges River, an incident that very nearly cost him his life. In this passage we find some of the best evidence in Fa-hsiang materials for a specific visualization technique with Maitreya and his heaven as its object. The story has already been briefly summarized by Demiéville, Lamotte, and others.[12] Still, it warrants further analysis here, along with a full translation, because I would like to draw attention to the fact that it presents us with something more than an instance of simple Maitreya devotionalism.

According to his biographer, the incident occurred not long after Hsüan-tsang had first reached the Ganges River Valley; he had already spent some time in both Gandhāra and Kashmir but had not yet reached Nālandā. Most recently, he had come from the thriving Buddhist community of Ayodhyā, a city visited by Gautama and also the site of one of Aśoka's stūpas. While in the vicinity of Ayodhyā, Hsüan-tsang had stayed at the nearby monastery where Asaṅga had resided, the site where, according to legend, the great Yogācāra master had ascended by night to Tuṣita Heaven to learn the Yogācāra treatises and then returned by day to teach. Hui-li provides us with the following account:

> Having worshipped the holy places in Ayodhyā, the master sailed eastwards down the Ganges in a boat along with more than eighty other people intending to go to the country of Hayamukha. They had sailed for some thirty-five miles, reaching a place where the forest of *aśoka* trees on both banks was unusually dense. All at once, out of the trees on each bank came more than ten boats of pirates flailing their oars as they entered the current. There was panic and confusion on the boat, and several people threw themselves into

the river. The pirates forced the boat to the shore and ordered all the passengers to take off their clothes so that they could be searched for valuables.

Now these pirates were by custom devotees of the goddess Durgā, and
every fall they would search for a man of fine character and handsome features whose flesh and blood they could sacrifice to the goddess in prayer for
her blessings. They saw that the master's physical form suited their needs,
his deportment being quite impressive. They looked at each other, saying
happily, "The time for our sacrifice to the goddess is almost past, and we
haven't yet been able to find anyone. Now this monk is pure and handsome
in appearance. Wouldn't it be auspicious to use him for our sacrifice
to her?"

In response the master said, "Truly I could not begrudge it if this
despicable body of mine would serve for your sacrifice. However, my purpose in coming from afar was to worship the Bodhi Tree and Buddhist
images, to visit Vulture Peak, and to inquire about the Dharma of the Buddhist scriptures. Since I have not yet fulfilled my intention, I fear it might
not be so auspicious if you, generous sirs, were to sacrifice me to your goddess."

The other people from the boat all pleaded for him, and some even
wanted to take his place, but the pirates would not allow it. The leader of
the pirates sent some men for water to build an altar of smoothed mud on a
spot they cleared in the vegetation. He then ordered two men with drawn
swords to lead the master to the altar. As they were about to wield their
swords, the Master's face showed no fear, and the pirates were quite
astonished. Knowing that he would not be spared, the master said to the
pirates, "I wish only that you would grant me a little time without disrup-
tion so that I might die with a quiet mind *(an-hsin)*."

The master then concentrated his mind *(chuan hsin)* on the palace in
Tuṣita Heaven and reflected *(nien)* on Maitreya, vowing to be reborn there
where he could pay homage to the bodhisattva and learn from him the
Yogācārabhūmi while listening to the fine Dharma. After having gained
complete wisdom, he would then be reborn to this world again where he
would teach these same men, bringing them to practice good deeds and to
abandon all evil acts and where he would propagate the Dharma widely for
the benefit of all beings.

Next the master paid homage to the Buddhas of the Ten Directions, and
then he sat mindfully *(cheng-nien erh tso)*, fixing his thoughts on Maitreya,
free of any other [mental] object *(wu fu i yüan)*. It seemed that in his mind
(yü hsin-hsiang chung) he ascended Mount Sumeru, passed through the
first, second, and third heavens, and then saw the palace in Tuṣita Heaven
with Maitreya Bodhisattva sitting on a dais made of marvelous gems and
surrounded by heavenly beings. With that he became so enraptured, both
mentally and physically, that he was no longer aware of being on the sacrifi-
cial altar and had forgotten all about the pirates.[13]

In his discussion of this same incident, Demiéville has quite aptly
stressed its significance, pointing to it as one example illustrating the
importance of the role of Maitreya *l'inspirateur*.[14] In the present context,

however, there is more to be said about Hsüan-tsang's actions, more to be gleaned from this intriguing bit of text. In addition to Demiéville's observations, we should note that the incident reported here also reveals an elaborate and structured visualization procedure, a soteric technique that was apparently of crucial importance to Hsüan-tsang. A close reading of the translation will reveal how structured this procedure was.

Note carefully the sequence of events. Once Hsüan-tsang determines that the pirates are not to be dissuaded and that his death is at hand, he requests that the pirates delay the sacrifice long enough for him to undertake his preparations for death. What he wishes to do is not simply to have Maitreya in mind at the moment of death. There is more to be done, and for that he needs an uninterrupted period of time before the knife falls. With his request granted, Hsüan-tsang first fixes his thoughts *(chuan-hsin)* on Tuṣita Heaven and calls Maitreya to mind *(nien Tz'u-shih P'u-sa)*. In doing this he also reaffirms his vow to be reborn in the bodhisattva's paradise. Once that is done, Hsüan-tsang appears to have completed his preparations and is ready to proceed with the visualization.

Next, we read, he offers obeisance to the Buddhas of the Ten Directions, proceeding, we can imagine, to perform prostrations to each of the respective cardinal points in turn.[15] Then, seating himself meditatively in a state of proper mindfulness *(cheng-nien > samyaksmṛti)*, he turns his mind once again to Maitreya, making an effort to remove any other mental object (*[so]-yüan > ālambana*).[16] Next, having begun the visualization proper, he imagines or visualizes a progress in which he proceeds first to Mt. Sumeru, highest point of the terrestrial world and *axis mundi* of this world system. He then continues ascending through the first, the second, and third heavens of this realm of desire, the *kāmadhātu*. Finally he sees *(chien)* his ultimate goal, the Tuṣita Heaven of Maitreya. Note the introduction of eidetic detail at this point. In the preliminary preparations for this exercise, Hsüan-tsang had already called Maitreya to mind; now he "sees" or visualizes Tuṣita in all of its overwhelming splendor. Consistent with other texts describing Maitreya visualization,[17] the exercise described here enables Hsüan-tsang to envision the scene in the most minute detail, from the gems covering Maitreya's dais to the heavenly beings arrayed in attendance. Finally, we are told, he becomes so enraptured with the splendor of the vision that he is no longer aware of what is happening back on the river bank, not aware even of the imminence of his own death.

As one might expect, this edifying tale reaches a dramatic climax and concludes on a highly inspirational note. With Hsüan-tsang still in the midst of his rapture, a fierce storm suddenly blows up, tearing down trees and overturning all the boats. The pirates, thinking at this point that perhaps they have made a mistake, inquire among the other passengers about this peculiar foreign monk. Learning of the master's fame, they become convinced that the gods are angered with their sacrifice and quickly reconsider. Meanwhile, oblivious to what has been going on, Hsüan-tsang returns to awareness, asking if his time has come. The pirates, by then quite contrite, plead to be forgiven, vow to give up their evil ways, throw their weapons in the river, and receive the five precepts from Hsüan-tsang. All present are greatly impressed with the master's virtue, so amply revealed by this display of supernatural power, and he is free once again to continue on his journey.

Under close examination the activities reported in this passage present us with an instance of Maitreya visualization having clear parallels to the visualization exercises discussed in the other Chinese visualization *(kuan)* texts. Several further observations remain to be made about the nature of this Maitreya visualization as a meditation technique. In this exercise we find Hsüan-tsang progressing through successively higher levels of existence according to generally accepted notions of Buddhist cosmography. This procedure recalls the well-established tradition associating these various levels of existence with the attainment of specific meditative states, the dhyānas or *samāpattis*.[18] There is, however, a significant difference between that older tradition and what we see here. In this exercise Hsüan-tsang never attempts to go beyond the fourth of the six heavens still within the desire realm *(kāmadhātu),* lowest of the three realms of this world system. No effort is made to reach the Nirmāṇarati or Paranirmitavaśavartī heavens, or to attain the still higher abodes of the form realm *(rūpadhātu)* and the formless realm *(arūpadhātu)*.

The older traditions of Buddhist meditation, by contrast, considered it soteriologically beneficial to cultivate the ability to enter these higher realms by means of meditative absorption or trance. Hsüan-tsang certainly had knowledge of those traditions of meditation and, indeed, as a Yogācārin might be expected to have had some competence in their techniques. Nonetheless, his objective in this exercise had nothing to do with any pursuit of the more traditional attainments of meditative practice. In fact, what he accomplishes by this exercise would have to be considered quite negligible in terms of traditional Buddhist meditation. To gain the Tuṣita Heaven does not involve going beyond the desire realm; one is still left well short of even the first dhyāna, the lowest of the eight or nine traditional attainments. The goal here has nothing to do with cultivating meditative states *per se*. Clearly Hsüan-tsang's aspiration is to gain a vision of Maitreya now, the best guarantee of being reborn later with him in Tuṣita after one's death.

Nevertheless, this visualization technique does share with the older dhyāna tradition a characteristic that distinguishes it sharply from the prevailing Ch'an understanding of dhyāna meditation. In the narrative we are told that Hsüan-tsang becomes so enraptured with his vision of

Maitreya in Tuṣita Heaven that he loses all awareness of what is going on around him. He forgets about the sacrifice and the pirates, and then later, when the pirates arouse him after the storm, he is quite unaware of what happened, asking if they are ready to proceed with the slaughter. In other words, the type of visualization meditation depicted here does involve an absorptive trance state requiring sensory withdrawal from any awareness of one's immediate environment.[19] Sensory withdrawal is, of course, a common feature of many South Asian meditation techniques, including the older dhyāna tradition in early Buddhism. On the other hand, the single most distinctive feature of the techniques that came to dominate East Asian Ch'an practice was, of course, the emphatic *rejection* of any trance-like sensory withdrawal in favor of total mindfulness of one's surroundings. The contrast is intriguing; but we must still look more closely at the use of sensory withdrawal in this case.

Even though an affinity in this respect might help relate Hsüan-tsang's visualization technique more closely to South Asian meditation traditions, we must be careful to remember that sensory withdrawal can be employed in a variety of ways. Although this visualization technique and the older dhyāna tradition both require a significant degree of sensory withdrawal, the latter seeks ultimately to eliminate sensation altogether. Hsüan-tsang's visualization technique, in contrast, seeks to block external stimulation only to enhance the meditator's involvement in the eidetic imagery of an alternative sensorium, one meant to be fully experienced in all of its sensual and affective detail. With regard to sensory withdrawal, it thus becomes very useful to distinguish an *enstatic* form of introversion from a more *ecstatic* form. The older dhyāna traditions can be thought of as enstatic in that they seek a state of stasis, the complete cessation of sensory processing. The visualization technique we find here, however, is clearly ecstatic: the practitioner seeks a state of enhanced sensation by throwing himself into an alternative reality rich in aesthetic and emotional detail.[20] Indeed, the apparent distinction between "visualizing" and actually "seeing" Maitreya probably becomes meaningless as one's skill in the technique is perfected.

The older dhyāna tradition did, of course, employ some visualization of mental objects. The mental re-creation of meditational objects *(kasiṇa)* was used for preliminary training in concentration, as an exercise for cultivating "one-pointed" attentiveness *(ekāgratā)*. In the case of Hsüan-tsang's visualization, however, the creation of an eidetic image was not a preparatory exercise; it was the consummation of the exercise.[21] And that, in turn, brings us back to the important question of what Hsüan-tsang sought to achieve by this practice. What exactly, in Buddhist terms, did one accomplish by perfecting this visualization practice? We have already seen that Maitreya played a central role in the religious life of the Fa-hsiang master. The same sources also show that he took his aspiration to be reborn in Tuṣita Heaven very seriously. Now we can also see, from this incident with the pirates, that the master felt that this visualization technique was very important to achieving that goal of rebirth in Tuṣita Heaven. The trouble that he went to in gaining the consent of the pirates to undertake the visualization exercise suggests that the Maitreya visualization had a specific objective. Hsüan-tsang practiced this technique not just to achieve inspiration from the future Buddha and not just to see Maitreya while still in this life. More than anything else he sought thereby to assure his own rebirth in the bodhisattva's heaven.

Was rebirth in Tuṣita seen as an end in itself? Or was it understood more as an intermediate goal, the next step to some more ultimate objective? With regard to that question, we can glean a bit more from this passage and also from the passage referred to earlier that recounts the scene at Hsüan-tsang's death bed.[22] In both cases Hsüan-tsang makes it clear that rebirth in Tuṣita Heaven was an intermediate goal that would allow one the opportunity to study Yogācāra Buddhism with Maitreya before returning to be reborn in this world to continue working for the salvation of all beings while achieving perfect enlightenment under the guidance of the future Buddha. Like all Buddhist practice, this particular exercise contributed ultimately to the realization of enlightenment, but it also had the more immediate objective of ensuring rebirth in Tuṣita, the place where one can most beneficially pass the time until Maitreya's advent.

We can thus reasonably conclude that this passage presents a specific and distinctive meditation technique involving a visualization exercise organized as a sequential progression by which one moves from the familiar levels of this world to the more sublime realm of Maitreya's abode. While showing some features in common with more traditional dhyāna meditation, this visualization practice differed significantly in that it did not seek to attain a state of non-perception, but sought rather an ecstatic participation in an elaborate and highly detailed realization of Maitreya's presence in Tuṣita Heaven. Proficiency in this technique apparently assured the practitioner of subsequent rebirth in Maitreya's realm, where one could best bide one's time until the advent of the new era to be presided over by the future Buddha. Because of its functional specificity and the intermediate nature of its purpose, Hsüan-tsang probably considered this exercise to be only one among a variety of practices. At the same time, this technique would have been of crucial importance with regard to one particular aspect of Buddhist religious life: one's confrontation with the inevitable end of this life and the necessary preparation for one's next rebirth. This was not the only realm of practical concern, but, as Hsüan-tsang's biography indicates, it was certainly an important concern for a Buddhist of his time. Although this technique was thus associated with only one aspect of Hsüan-tsang's religious life, he undoubtedly devoted a significant portion of his energies to it. Such a visualization exercise would almost certainly have required some extended practice to perfect, and especially to perfect to the degree that it could be performed even under the duress of imminent decapitation. The opportunity, moreover, to be reborn in Maitreya's heaven—and an effective technique for securing such a rebirth—would no doubt have been very attractive to anyone (and especially to a Yogācārin) who had lived through the apocalyptic times of the pre-T'ang period in China.

One further question needs to be addressed before we move on to look at the second type of Fa-hsiang meditation. We must ask whether the Maitreya visualization technique we find here was peculiar to Hsüan-tsang or whether it was, in fact, a practice important in the religious life of other monks associated with the Fa-hsiang School.[23] Although the question is difficult to answer conclusively, it seems likely that such a powerful visualization technique would have been part of the practice of Hsüan-tsang's followers as well. As we have seen, textual evidence indicates that some form of Maitreya visualization was popular in various Chinese Buddhist circles prior to Hsüan-tsang's journey. I have not yet found other biographical sources that report Maitreya visualization in such detail, but there is ample evidence to verify the importance of Maitreya cult practice in the religious life of other Fa-hsiang masters.

The best additional evidence for the place of Maitreya cult practice in Fa-hsiang circles can be drawn from biographical sources for Hsüan-tsang's collaborator and successor, K'uei-chi (632–682), the scholar-monk later designated the first patriarch of the Fa-hsiang School. K'uei-chi's funerary inscription informs us, for example, that as part of his practice the monk made a Maitreya statue every month.[24] His official (though less reliable) biography, written later by Tsan-ning during the Sung, adds that his daily recitation of the Bodhisattva Vows was performed in front of a Maitreya statue.[25] K'uei-chi himself writes of Maitreya visualization in his commentary on the Maitreya sūtras, where he tells us that Maitreya visualization was practiced by the great Yogācāra masters of India, mentioning Asaṅga and Vasubandhu by name.[26] We should note also that in this same work he extols at some length the advantages of seeking rebirth in Maitreya's Tuṣita Heaven rather than in Amitābha's Pure Land, a fact that again suggests the functional specificity of this particular meditative exercise.[27]

In sum, then, we can safely conclude that Fa-hsiang practice placed special emphasis on the Maitreya cult and, further, that one of the specific exercises employed was a technique of eidetic visualization of the sort described in the story of Hsüan-tsang's encounter with the pirates. Given the weight of Hsüan-tsang's example within the school, it seems reasonable to assume the presence of this specific technique in the practice of his colleagues, especially because of its functionally specific objective. We can find some further confirmation of this in the fact that there are indeed references to Maitreya visualization in various exegetical works associated with the school. Though not exclusive to Fa-hsiang circles, this practice was probably given a special place in the school, both because of the school's affiliation with Maitreya generally and because of the practice's obvious importance in Hsüan-tsang's religious life on his return from India.

2. THE FIVE-LEVEL DISCERNMENT OF *VIJÑAPTIMĀTRATĀ*

The first example of meditative practice, Maitreya visualization, was prominent in, but not limited to, the Fa-hsiang School. The second example, in contrast, appears to have been a distinctly Yogācāra doctrine, one first discussed in the commentaries and essays of K'uei-chi (632–682). Though both examples are referred to as *kuan,* this second example reveals a rather different type of activity. We have seen that *kuan* is best rendered as "visualization" in the first case, perhaps ultimately going back to the Sanskrit *anusmṛti,* "meditative mindfulness." Now we will take up a doctrine in which the same term *kuan* is used in way much closer to its more standard meaning of vipaśyanā, "discernment" or "insight" into the nature of existence.[28] In this case we will be dealing with the cultivation of a cognitive realization of specific philosophical principles, an activity that is not limited to a certain occasion of practice and does not seem to have been directly associated with any specific or structured technique comparable to the visualization procedure we considered earlier. In spite of these differences between the two cases, the second still presents us with a soteriologically oriented activity—that is, with a practice of religious transformation. And it is certainly one that we would want to include in any discussion of meditation understood in the broadest sense.

The doctrine I have in mind as my second example is the five-level discernment of *vijñaptimātratā (wu-ch'ung wei-shih kuan),* a theme K'uei-chi discusses in his *Commentary on the Heart Sūtra (Po-jo po-lo-mi-to hsin ching yu-tsan)* and also in his *Essay on Vijñaptimātra (Wei-shih chang).*[29] This teaching became one of the best-known Fa-hsiang doctrines in the subsequent history of the school and was central to K'uei-chi's exposition of the Yogācāra path. Although it has important associations with a number of Fa-hsiang views, I will focus here on the way in which the five-level discernment presents a systematic and progressive understanding of the central doctrine of *vijñaptimātratā,* the teaching that there is "nothing but cognitive construction."[30]

The derivation and origins of this five-level discernment are somewhat unclear. No specific mention of **evijñaptimātratā-vipaśyanā* or **evijñaptimātratā-abhisamāya* is to be found, to the best of my knowl-

edge, in any of the surviving Sanskrit or Tibetan sources for the early Yogācāra tradition. The Chinese expression *"wei-shih-kuan"* does occur in the early Chinese translations of the *Mahāyāna-saṃgraha* done by both Paramārtha and Dharmagupta, though the *kuan* appears to be more of an interpolation than a translation of a Sanskrit term.[31] Some of the language K'uei-chi employs in his discussion of the five levels can be traced to the *Ch'eng-wei-shih-lun,* but the five-level discernment as such is not mentioned in that work either, which leads me to assume that it was an innovation of K'uei-chi's or perhaps of his teacher, Hsüan-tsang. A doctrinal antecedent for the distinctive five-fold structure of the discernment and for the designation of the five divisions as "gates" *(men >
mukhāni)* can be seen in the doctrine of the five contemplations for stilling the mind, the *wu-t'ing-hsin-kuan,* an early Buddhist doctrine found in a number of Chinese sources and one that had become an established part of the new Chinese Buddhism of K'uei-chi's period with its inclusion in the systematic works of both Chih-i and Chih-yen.[32] K'uei-chi would, of course, have been quite familiar also with the Indian origins of this latter doctrine, particularly since it is found in the *Yogācārabhūmi* and the *Abhidharmakośa.*[33]

Although structural antecedents for K'uei-chi's five-level discernment can be found in the *wu-t'ing-hsin-kuan* doctrine, these two teachings differ significantly. The five entrances of the older doctrine represent alternative practices, each appropriate as a corrective to specific psychological problems. That doctrine represents a typological paradigm of a sort frequently encountered in early Buddhist meditation manuals, which present therapeutically specific techniques to be employed as antidotes for specific forms of delusion. What we find in K'uei-chi's five-level discernment, however, are not five *alternative* points of entry to the path, but rather five *interconnected* gateways through which one passes progressively in the cultivation of insight into the principle or truth of *vijñaptimātratā.* In this doctrine the five are still spoken of as "gates" or "entrances" *(men),* but they are meant to mark the stages by which one can penetrate progressively deeper into the basic soteric truth of Yogācāra Buddhism: the view that the world, as we experience it, is nothing but cognitive construction *(vijñapti).*

This aspect of K'uei-chi's doctrine suggests another model for his notion of a structured, sequential discernment of reality, one that helps to show why the doctrine played such an important role in Fa-hsiang thought. A similar sequence of progressive steps is found in Tu-shun's threefold discernment of Dharmadhātu, a key Hua-yen doctrinal theme elucidated in the influential *Hua-yen fa-chieh kuan-men.*[34] K'uei-chi's more immediate model was most probably this indigenous Chinese doctrine—a possibility suggested even more strongly by his incorporation of some of Tu-shun's technical vocabulary, most notably the categories of

Principle *(li)* and phenomena *(shih)*. In fact, in K'uei-chi's five-level discernment can, I think, be best understood as his attempt to summarize in
distinctly Chinese terms the core *vijñaptimātratā* doctrine of scholastic
Indian Yogācāra. It was an attempt, moreover, in which he sought quite
intentionally to use—indeed to co-opt or preempt—some of the distinctive analytical structures of the new Chinese Buddhism of the sixth century, seeking thereby to appropriate the vitality of these new developments while remaining true to his own, more conservative tradition.[35] In
his attempt to revalorize preemptively the hermeneutical innovations of
his Hua-yen and T'ien-t'ai critics, K'uei-chi uses his five-level discernment to reinterpret some of their key concepts in terms of more "orthodox" Yogācāra doctrines, particularly the *trisvabhāva* theory explicating
the three aspects of phenomenal existence.[36] According to the view presented in K'uei-chi's five-level discernment, one is to penetrate the true
nature of reality by understanding the three aspects of existence in five
successive steps or stages.

The first level K'uei-chi calls "dismissing the false—preserving the
real" *(ch'ien-hsü ts'un-shih)*. At this level one must realize that what one
ordinarily clings to as existing or real is, in actuality, purely imaginary
(parikalpita). In the normal state of human delusion these misconstrued
objects of attachment appear to have an abiding reality, but ultimately,
we are told, they must be seen as having neither substance *(t'i)* nor function *(yung)*. Emotionally *(ch'ing)*, we are by nature inclined to cling to
these imaginary delusions, taking them to be truly existent. In fact *(li)*,
however, they should be seen as nonexistent. At the same time, the meditator must make an effort to preserve as real the remaining two aspects
of existence, the dependent *(paratantra)* and the consummate *(pariṇispanna)*, for they are in fact *(li)* real, even though emotionally *(ch'ing)* one
is inclined to overlook or even to deny their reality in order to continue
clinging to imaginary delusions. At this first level K'uei-chi introduces
the basic structure of reality in terms of the interrelation among its three
aspects. This structure provides a common ground for the remaining
four levels, which, according to K'uei-chi, culminate in a full realization
of what is presented in essence in the first level.[37]

At the second level or next gate, entitled "relinquishing the diffuse
—retaining the pure" *(she-lan liu-ch'un)*, K'uei-chi initiates a phenomenological reduction of the cognitive process by which our experience
of the world is constructed. The point at this level is to shift one's attention from what are naively assumed to be predeterminate objects in the
external world and to focus instead on the fact that every perception,
every consciousness of something in the world, comprises an "inner"
subjective awareness and also an "inner" intentional object. Projecting
these intentional objects out onto what is taken to be a separate "external" world—allowing them to "overflow" or diffuse—one clings to them
as intrinsically real, predeterminate objects, thus failing to recognize

their interdependent nature as cognitive constructs. At this stage we are enjoined to let loose of—to bracket—these "diffused" or projected objects, so that we might begin to recognize the more basic or "pure" interaction of intentional object and perceiving awareness.

The third level is called "gathering in the extensions—returning to the source" *(she-mo kuei-pen)*. Having recognized the interdependent, correlative *noema-noesis* relationship between the intentional object and the perceiving awareness, between constituted object and constituting subject, one must, we are then told, go yet deeper. At this level K'uei-chi brings in a notion dating from the scholastic period of Yogācāra thought, the doctrine of the *svasaṃvittibhāga* or self-verifying component of perception. The idea is that meditative discipline gives an experience of an underlying, unbifurcated mode of cognition that verifies the distinctive correlative relationship of what we take to be a separate subject and object in ordinary experience. The objective at the third gate is to return to the source of that subject-object division, to gain direct awareness of unbifurcated cognition by means of the *svasaṃvittibhāga.*

Next comes "suppressing the subordinate—manifesting the superior" *(yin-lüeh hsien-sheng)*. At this point K'uei-chi takes up the relationship between *citta* and *caittāh,* between "thought" in its most basic sense and the various subordinate mental states or attitudes that it assumes—or, in K'uei-chi's metaphor, that it governs. Thought is not only bifurcated into subject and object, *noesis* and *noema;* it is also differentiated into a variety of dispositional attitudes, the apparently discrete components *(caittāh)* making up the process of thought *(citta).* These mental coefficients had been the subject of extensive phenomenological analysis in Buddhist psychology, giving rise to various speculations regarding their experiential and ontological status. The scholastic Yogācāra doctrine advocated by K'uei-chi sought to salvage the phenomenological analysis of the old Abhidharma tradition, but in so doing it had to avoid the same mistake that precipitated the Mādhyamika critique of the Hīnayāna Abhidharma masters. The Yogācāra Abhdharmikas could remain true to their notion of the emptiness doctrine, they felt, as long as they avoided reifying the product of any phenomenological analysis. This would have to be true in the case of *all* elements of our experience, of course, the "external" dharmas we take to be objects *as well as* the "internal" states that apparently characterize our subjective individuality. K'uei-chi's point here at the fourth level is that we must recognize that the most immediate and subjective mental states are not to be perceived as discrete or independent. We must not cling to them, for they, too, are simply functions or constructs of the unbifurcated process of thought. As such, we must see them as subordinate or derivative in order to realize the true nature of "thought," the dynamic activity of reality construction that cannot be reduced to either its apparently "objective" or "subjective" components.

Finally we come to the fifth entrance, the gateway entitled "dismissing the phenomenal aspects—realizing the true nature" *(ch'ien-hsiang cheng-hsing),* which marks the culmination of the phenomenological reduction that has brought the meditator to an understanding of his "own" mind, understood now as the process of unbifurcated thought. At this last stage K'uei-chi would have us turn outward once again to realize the basic nature of all phenomenal existence, what in Yogācāra terms is called its "thusness" or "suchness" *(tathatā).* He would have us find within the phenomenality of existence the underlying universal Principle *(li)* or nature that all things share: the condition of being simply as they are, all interdependently related in one constructive process. To effect this realization the meditator must turn from the differentiated, phenomenal appearance of existence in order to realize the true nature of that phenomenality. He must turn from "things" in their apparent independent objectivity before he can recognize the underlying interdependence and relatedness that characterizes those "things." Only then can that same phenomenality, which does make up reality, be perceived free of delusion.

In terms of the threefold nature of existence, one must realize the consummate *(pariṇispanna)* before one can see the dependent *(paratantra)* as it truly is, free of the imaginary *(parikalpita).* To see the *dependent* free of the *imaginary* is, in fact, to see it as the *consummate;* for in delusion the dependent aspect of existence is inseparable from the imaginary, but with the realization of "thusness" it is inseparable from the consummate.[38]
We must understand K'uei-chi's five discernments as progressive levels of "seeing" or "viewing" *(kuan)* the world, as ways of seeing and understanding the nature of our experience of existence. Each of these successive views is undertaken or put into practice as one progresses on the path to enlightenment, yet it would be inappropriate to think of these five levels or "gateways" as meditations, in the narrow sense—that is, as specific procedures for which the practitioner might set aside a certain time each day. The cultivation of this fivefold discernment was meant to be an ongoing process, unlike the Maitreya visualization which was a single, discrete activity with a distinct, functionally specific objective.

3. VISUALIZATION AND DISCERNMENT

Now we can see more clearly just how much the two types of meditation presented here do indeed differ. The Chinese term *"kuan,"* used to refer to both, seems to have a rather different meaning in each case. In the exercise performed by Hsüan-tsang, *"kuan"* refers to the visualization of a particular scene, to an activity undertaken at a particular time to achieve a particular intermediate goal. In K'uei-chi's five-level discernment, by contrast, *"kuan"* does not refer to a specific exercise or technical procedure, something one would sit down to do on a certain occasion. Rather it refers to a longer-term activity, to the overall manner in which one views the world. In this doctrine K'uei-chi presents a paradigm of the gradual transformation of the practitioner's normal, deluded experience of existence, a paradigm of the successive development of insight into the ultimate emptiness of "self" and "things" conceived as predeterminate entities—insight, that is, into the impossibility of ontologically grounding the apparent dualism that characterizes ordinary awareness. K'uei-chi's concern is unquestionably practical, in that he is attempting to chart the direction in which the practitioner must move. Yet his concern is not with the specific, tactical exercises appropriate for a particular person at a particular time. The five-level discernment or "viewing" of existence is a more generalized model of Buddhist practice, a strategic overview of what everyone is to do, each employing the tactics most appropriate to his or her personality and circumstances. While we can think of the formulation of such a strategic overview as falling within the category of "praxis" in the sense of vipaśyanā-bhāvanā, we do not have here a specific "practice" undertaken to attain some particular meditative state or level of dhyāna. Nor do we find any single structured procedure or technique as we do with the visualization exercise and with certain samādhi practices.

The picture that emerges, then, from this brief exploration of Fa-hsiang praxis reveals a range of activities as well as a distinction in levels of practical concern. We see evidence of a complex and disparate group of different "meditative techniques," as well as a more abstract discussion of the development of insight into the nature of existence that should come with proper practice. This picture suggests a rich and complex religious life encompassing a variety of practices, a repertoire of meditative techniques and procedures variously applied at different times in the composite practice of a given individual and directed toward specific, and often distinct, intermediate goals. At the same time, all of this practice was directed, in a more ultimate sense, toward the realization of a distinctively Buddhist view of the world, toward a particular insight into the nature of existence. It is the Fa-hsiang formulation of that Buddhist insight into existence, along with an analysis of the successive stages of its realization, that we find expressed in K'uei-chi's five-level discernment of *vijñaptimātratā,* whereas the Maitreya visualization technique represents one of a number of different exercises that could be employed to progress along the path. The particular technique employed at any given time would depend on the temperament and situation of the practitioner, certain exercises being more appropriate for certain circumstances. In the context of concern over one's future rebirth, for example, the practice of Maitreya visualization would undoubtedly take on special significance and utility.

The range of different techniques employed by various Buddhists in different cultural and historical settings is strikingly diverse. Certainly many of those functionally specific practices had non-Buddhist analogs and origins—hence, no doubt, the necessity felt by the more reflective Buddhist thinkers to articulate what made these various activities "Buddhist." We can, I think, best understand K'uei-chi's formulation of the five-level discernment as an attempt to connect the more abstract principles of Buddhist philosophy with the immediate and real concerns of religious practice. The strategic paradigm presented in the five-level discernment is meant to provide, in other words, a practical link between principle and practice, a guide to indicate how the latter must be oriented to realize successfully the former.

III. Some Further Reflections on Meditation as a Concept

We are all familiar with the danger of assuming that a category of experience fundamental to our own culture must be, by virtue of its apparently "universal" stature, present in all other cultures, or at least in any other comparably developed culture. And we have become, as a consequence, more careful in our efforts to interpret an alien culture not to assume (or to require), for example, some concept of an anthropomorphic, creator god or some progressive, teleological conception of history. Indeed, the naïveté of such assumptions in earlier scholarship often strike us now as surprisingly blatant. There is, however, another, perhaps more insidious form of mismapping to which we are all still quite prone. Even if, in our interpretive mapping, we avoid the pitfall of "finding" the necessary and expected analog to every concept taken as essential and universal in our own cultural framework, we run the risk of not recognizing that any effort of interpretation, of mapping in this sense, must be a two-way street. Where we do succeed in establishing some appropriate conceptual link between two cultures, where our mapping activity has yielded some understanding, we must still recognize that both sides of the equation are involved in the understanding. If the analog in the alien culture is mapped onto our own experience in a way that yields true understanding, then both are being transformed, in a sense. The alien concept is being interpreted or translated, certainly, and at the same time our own concept must also undergo a transformation, must be both expanded and refined. Otherwise, the product is not understanding but simply reduction in the most negative sense—a reduction that actually restricts our access to the alien culture. Specifically, we must be careful in our interpretive mapping not to allow the semantic restrictions of our own concept to limit our view of the data we are assigning to that concept.

What does this mean in the context of the present examination of

Chinese Buddhist meditation practice? Given some success in recognizing the priority of "meditation" in the Buddhist perspective of religious practice, we must be all the more careful to ensure that we are not working with an inappropriately restricted conception of what "meditation" involves and includes. We can acknowledge the interpretive value of employing our category of meditation in the study of Buddhist praxis, but we must do so in a way that allows that concept to be informed and transformed by the subject of our interpretation. We can, indeed, learn something about another culture, even one so doubly distanced in time and culture, but that understanding comes only to the extent that we are open to an expansion of our own framework—something perhaps not so difficult to see in principle, but more difficult to put into practice than we often realize. In seeking to understand better the Chinese Buddhist perspective on religious practice, we are exploring what elements of that Buddhist experience might best be mapped onto our concept of meditation. In doing so we hope to discover what that interpretation will reveal about Buddhist culture and what it might teach us about our own. The material I have presented in this chapter provides us with two instances in which this dual objective might be seriously undermined if we are not attentive to the problems raised in the opening section. With an overly narrow, unexamined conception of meditation, we might be tempted to exclude from our consideration of "Chinese meditation traditions" both of the examples I have outlined earlier.

With too narrow a notion of the range of meditative practice within Buddhism, we might take Hsüan-tsang's Maitreya visualization to be simply a case of "devotional cult practice," rather than "meditation" proper—perhaps without even stopping to consider the validity of the dichotomy asserted in such a distinction. Indeed, scholars of East Asian Buddhism might be especially prone to this pitfall. Working with a conception of meditation informed by later sectarian debates between Japanese Pure Land and Zen, the Buddhist scholar might begin with an overly narrow conception of Buddhist meditation and then look back on the earlier history of East Asian Buddhism for *only* those forms of practice that resemble zazen, a highly specific technique of meditation that would have analogs in only a few of the practices available to Hsüan-tsang and his contemporaries. Of course, the historical development of zazen practice is an important line to trace back historically; but this should not be done in a way that overlooks the diversity of other practices characteristic of medieval Chinese Buddhism. Certainly we must be aware of the differences between zazen and Hsüan-tsang's Maitreya visualization. At the same time, we must also note what, in terms of the Buddhist conception of dhyāna as bhāvanā, they have in common. We must recognize the sense in which the tradition considered both Maitreya visualization and zazen to be instances of meditative practice. Any conception of meditation that cannot readily accommodate *both* of these techniques, no matter how apparent and how important their differences, would be likely to distort, rather than inform, our understanding of religious practice in Buddhism, simply because what relates these two activities in the minds of many Buddhists is still more significant than what distinguishes them. Therefore, I would argue, we must include forms of "devotional cult practice" in our discussion of meditation traditions.

But what of K'uei-chi's fivefold discernment of *vijñaptimātratā*, which appears not even to be a "practice" in the strictest sense? Must we expand our conception of meditation to include this as well? Certainly there is value in noting the significant differences between the two aspects of Buddhist praxis I have presented here. And one might well argue that the term "meditation" should be employed in the narrowest possible sense, that its semantic range should be limited to the various practical *procedures* Buddhists employ to attain enlightenment, in contrast to the more abstract and theoretical paradigms employed to speculate about the nature of enlightenment. That would still allow us to include a wide range of practices, devotional activities, and visualization techniques as well as the more traditional dhyāna cultivation. However, it would require another category or level of discourse for the type of enlightenment paradigm we find in K'uei-chi's five-level discernment. Pursuing that line of argument for the moment, one could point out that the second type of activity is, in fact, the *product* of the first: that practices like dhyāna cultivation, visualization, and the various samādhis, etc., are what we should call "meditation," whereas the resulting insight is better understood as the *fruit* of that practice, the enlightenment toward which the practice is directed. That would allow us a neat conceptual distinction between the two senses of *kuan* found in the material we have examined here, *kuan* as "visualization" and *kuan* as "discerning" or gaining insight into reality. A useful distinction, perhaps, but again one that is likely to distort our understanding of the Buddhist notion of praxis.

To force a distinction between meditative practices and their "resulting insight" would be to overlook a fundamental Buddhist insight into the nature of religious practice. It is crucial to any understanding of Buddhist soteriology, certainly in a Mahāyāna context, to recognize that no meaningful distinction can be drawn between practice and result. We are familiar with this theme in later Ch'an and Zen, but actually it expresses a tension that runs throughout the history of Buddhist thought, one that can be seen already in the earliest Buddhist speculation on the necessary relationship between śamatha and vipaśyanā, the psychophysical exercises of "calming" or centering and the transformative vision or "insight" characteristic of the liberated or enlightened individual. Certainly this theme was an issue in K'uei-chi's mind—one reason, no doubt, why he formulated his paradigm of enlightenment under the rubric of *"kuan,"* the term used to render "vipaśyanā" and, perhaps even more significantly, a verb indicating an ongoing, transitive activity, rather than the apparently static state implied, for example, by the Chinese term *"chih"* ("wisdom"), which was often employed for enlightenment in the sense of understanding. In this light, the five-level discernment should not be seen simply as a result, it should be seen as itself praxis, as dhyāna in the sense of vipaśyanā-bhāvana, because for K'uei-chi enlightenment can only be a dynamic activity, not a passive, quiescent state. Enlightenment is something one does, an active way of viewing the world that matures over a period of time, gradually perfected by the whole range of practices that make up the Buddhist religious life.

In sum, then, I feel that it is appropriate to begin our examination of Chinese Buddhist meditation traditions with these two examples from Fa-hsiang circles and also with a caveat regarding our understanding of "meditation." I think we must employ "meditation" in the broadest possible sense—in the same sense that we find Buddhists using the term "dhyāna" to include both śamatha-bhāvanā and vipaśyanā-bhāvanā. There are two reasons for doing this—both important, and both inextricably interrelated. First, we must recognize that such an inclusive conception of meditation is necessary if we are not to obscure what is most distinctive and characteristic about the Buddhist perspective on religious practice. Second, only by coming to terms with what is distinctive and characteristic in Buddhist culture can we gain a better understanding of ourselves. Our goal is not just to gain the ability to make sense of (and to manipulate) what is separated by both time and culture. The understanding we seek should not only inform our perception of the alien culture; it should also transform our own experience, the understanding of our own culture. The true value of any cross-cultural exploration, after all, lies not in how successful we are in reducing the alien culture to the terms of our own experience. True understanding, rather, is born only when we must expand our own perspective to accommodate what initially appears to be alien.

Notes

1.   The best modern study of the canonical tradition of Buddhist meditation is the Mahāthera Paravahera Vajirañāṇa's *Buddhist Meditation, In Theory and Practice* (Colombo: Gunasena, 1962), a careful survey of material from the Nikāyas and the Theravāda Abhidhamma along with some reference to the Sanskrit Abhidharma as well. See also Friedrich Heiler's study *Die Buddhistische Versenkung* (Munich: E. Reinhardt, 1918), Edward Conze's *Buddhist Meditation* (London: Allen & Unwin, 1956), and the articles by Stephen Beyer cited below in note 20. For a valuable discussion of the relationship between Buddhist meditation and the general category of mysticism see Robert M. Gimello's excellent article "Mysticism and Meditation"

40   *Alan Sponberg*

in Steven T. Katz, ed., *Mysticism and Philosophical Analysis* (New York: Oxford University Press, 1978), pp. 170–199.

2. Vajirañāṇa, *Budddhist Meditation,* pp. 23–25 and 35. There is a tradition that derives *jhāna* also from the homonymic *jhāyati,* "to burn," in the causative sense of burning away opposition and obstruction. Although probably more an exegetical device than a historical etymology, this derivation does underscore further the close relationship between Buddhist meditation and the *tapas*-oriented ascetic traditions of South Asia.

3. Vajirañāṇa discusses this narrower sense of dhyāna also; see *Buddhist Meditation,* pp. 37–43.

4. Walpola Rahula, "Psychology of Buddhist Meditation," in *Indianisme et Bouddhisme: Mélanges offerts à Mgr Étienne Lamotte* (Louvain: Université Catholique de Louvain, Institut Orientaliste, 1980). Rahula, a prominent figure among the reform-minded, Western-educated Theravāda intelligentsia, makes this point in order to argue the view that attainment of the traditional *rūpa-* and *arūpa-jhānas* is "not a *sine qua non,* not a *must* for the realization of *Nirvāṇa,"* a position that has some scriptural foundation but must be seen also in the historical and social context of the contemporary movement to emphasize *vipassanā* over *samatha* in certain Theravāda circles.

5. For further research on this topic drawing on other sixth-century Chinese sources, see my article "Wŏnhyo on Visualization: Maitreya Cult Practice in Early China and Korea" in Alan Sponberg and Helen Hardacre, eds., *Maitreya, the Future Buddha* (Cambridge University Press, forthcoming).

6. Alexander Soper and others have made very convincing attempts to trace this tradition back to the frontier regions of Indian culture, especially Kashmir and Gandhāra. See his *Literary Evidence for Early Buddhist Art in China* (Ascona, Switzerland: Artibus Asiae, 1959), pp. 144, 184, 215, and 222.

7. Hsüan-tsang's own account of his travels is found in his *Ta-t'ang hsi-yü chi* (*T*#2087), available in the rather dated translation of Samuel Beal, *Si-yu-ki, Buddhist Records of the Western World* (London, 1884; rpt. Delhi: Motilal Banarsidass, 1981). The most detailed biography is the *Ta-t'ang ta-tz'u-en-ssu san-tsang-fa-shih chuan* (*T*#2053), written by his contemporary Hui-li and edited by Yen-tsung. Though still including frequent ellipses, the best and most complete translation of this biography is that of Li Yung-hsi, *The Life of Hsuan-tsang* (Peking: The Chinese Buddhist Association, 1959).

8. On Maitreya, Avalokiteśvara, and Mañjuśrī as a triad, note also the account of the three appearing together in a dream to Śīlabhadra, the great Yogācāra master of Nālandā in the seventh century, a story recorded by Hui-li in Hsüan-tsang's biography, *T*50.236c4–237a14.

9. See, for example, Hsüan-tsang's account of his visit to the colossal Maitreya statue at Darel recorded in the *Ta-t'ang hsi-yü chi, T*51.884b.

10. *Ta-t'ang ta-tz'u-en-ssu san-tsang-fa-shih chuan, T*50.276c2–277b10, especially 277a2–3. For Tao-hsüan's report of Hsüan-tsang's final words, see *T*50.458b3–4.

11. *T*50.277b4–6; for additional reports of Hsüan-tsang's aspiration to be reborn in Tuṣita, written by Tao-hsüan, K'uei-chi, and other eminent contemporaries, see *T*50.458a–b, *T*38.277c, *T*54.6c–7a, *T*50.219a and c, and *T*47.106c.

12. See, for example, Demiéville's "La *Yogācārabhūmi* de Saṅgharakṣa," *Bulletin de l'École Française d'Extrême-orient,* vol. 44, no. 2 (1954), p. 338.

13. *T*50.233c21–234a21; truncated versions of this story can be found in Samuel Beal, *The Life of Hsüan-tsang by Hwuy-Le* (London: Routledge & Kegan Paul, 1911), pp. 86–90, and in Li Yung-hsi, *The Life of Hsüan-tsang*, pp. 85–88.

14. See note 12 above.

15. It is useful to remember here that several early meditation texts in China took the Buddhas of the Ten Directions as their focus; see Soper, *Literary Evidence*, p. 143.

16. On the use of *ālambana/ārammaṇa* as a technical term in discussions of meditation in the early Indian literature, see Paravahera Vajirañāṇa's *Buddhist Meditation*, pp. 30–31.

17. Cf. K'uei-chi's commentary on the Maitreya sūtras (*T*#1772) as well as that of Wŏnhyo, which is quite detailed (*T*#1773; especially *T*38.299c1–24 and 300b12–22). The relevant portions of the latter work have been translated and discussed in the article cited in note 5.

18. Some accounts of Śākyamuni's biography relate his progression through the four *dhyānas* at the time of his enlightenment and again just prior to his death. For canonical references to the dhyānas and the *samāpattis*, see Paravahera Vajirañāṇa, *Buddhist Meditation,* especially chapters 4 and 34.

19. The sixth-century Korean exegete Wŏnhyo affirms this observation in an extended discussion of Maitreya visualization. He notes that the exercise produces samādhi, but a samādhi of a relatively low degree as it is without *praśrabdhi,* the functional integration of mind and body that is a prerequisite of the advanced dhyānic attainments. See Sponberg, "Wŏnhyo on Visualization."

20. Stephen Beyer (following Heinrich Zimmer) has explored this enstatic/ecstatic distinction as it characterizes two fundamentally opposed soteric orientations or postures present in Indian culture during the Upaniṣadic period. See Beyer's articles "The Background to Buddhism," "The Doctrine of Meditation in the Hīnayāna," and "The Doctrine of Meditation in the Mahāyāna," all found in Charles S. Prebish, ed., *Buddhism, a Modern Perspective* (University Park: Pennsylvania State University Press, 1975), pp. 3–9 and 137–158. To consider the history of Buddhist meditative practice as an attempt to mediate or reconcile the tension between an enstatic and an ecstatic ideal is a theme worthy of further exploration.

21. Antecedents for this type of visualization exercise are most likely to be found in *anusmṛti* rather than in *kasiṇa* techniques.

22. See note 11 above. Although Hui-li's account of Hsüan-tsang's death includes no elaborate description of any Maitreya visualization technique, it does say that Hsüan-tsang, after bidding his attendants farewell, entered *samyaksmṛti (cheng-nien).*

23. That question is, in turn, related to another, more difficult, and perhaps also more tantalizing question: Where did Hsüan-tsang learn these visualization techniques? Was he familiar with them already before leaving China? Or did he learn them during his travels? We have already seen that a visualization tradition was well established in China prior to Hsüan-tsang's departure. At the same time, however, it is probably no coincidence that the most detailed description of visualization in all of the Hsüan-tsang material comes at the point in his biography just shortly after his sojourn in Kashmir and immediately after he visited Asaṅga's old monastery with its stories of meditative transport Heaven.

24. *Ta-t'ang ta-tz'u-en-ssu fa-shih-chi-kung pei,* which can be found in a collection of K'uei-chi's biographical materials, "Jion daishi denki monjū," published in *Shōsō,* vol. 9 (1940), pp. 41–48; see 45a13.
25. For a study of the primary sources for K'uei-chi's biography, including an excellent critique of Tsan-ning's account, see Stanley Weinstein's "A Biographical Study of Tz'u-en," *Monumenta Nipponica,* vol. 15, nos. 1 and 2 (1953), pp. 119–149.
26. *T*38.277c24–278a3.
27. *Ibid.,* 277a–c.
28. In this context, *kuan* might also render *abhisamāya,* a frequently occuring Abhidharma term of great soteriological importance referring to the liberating comprehension produced by meditative practice, as *satya-abhisamāya,* the comprehension of the four noble truths. While *abhisamāya* would be quite plausible in this context, it is a term that Hsüan-tsang and K'uei-chi normally render more precisely with the expression *hsien-kuan.* Of course *vipaśyanā* and *abhisamāya* are not unrelated in meaning, and certainly most Chinese Buddhists, not knowing any Sanskrit, would have used *kuan* without distinguishing clearly between the various Sanskrit terms it rendered in Buddhist Chinese.
29. The *Po-jo po-lo-mi-to hsin ching yu-tsan, T#*1710, see specifically *T*33.526c16–527b10; and the *Wei-shih chang,* a long essay found as part of Kuei-chi's encyclopedic compendium the *Ta-sheng fa-yüan i-lin chang, T#* 1861, see specifically *T*45.258b21–259a27.
30. I plan to discuss this five-level discernment doctrine more fully in a monograph on early Fa-hsiang Buddhism. K'uei-chi's "Essay on Vijñaptimātratā" was translated in my Ph.D. dissertation, "The Vijñaptimātratā Philosophy of the Chinese Buddhist Monk K'uei-chi (A.D. 632–682)" (University of British Columbia, 1979). Some of the ideas in this chapter were presented as part of an unpublished paper read at the Association of Asian Studies annual meeting, 1979.
31. There is nothing to correspond to the *kuan* in the Tibetan versions of the Saṃgraha, and it was dropped in Hsüan-tsang's later and more literal translation. Cf. all four Chinese versions of the passage in Sasaki Gesshō's *Kanyaku shihon taishō Shōdaijōron* (Tokyo: Hōbunsha, 1938), p. 56b and c.
32. Chih-i discusses two different versions of the *wu t'ing-hsin kuan,* one in his *Ssu-chiao-i (T*46.732c) and the other in both the *Fa-hua-ching-hsüan-i (T*33.707c) and the *Mo-ho chih-kuan* (*T*46.92c–93a). Chih-yen's discussion is found in his *Hua-yen-ching k'ung-mu-chang* (*T*45.552b). For references to the five discernments in earlier Chinese works, those of Kumārajīva and Ching-ying Hui-yüan, see Sakurabe Hajime's brief but informative article "On the *wu-t'ing-hsin-kuan,*" in *Indianisme et bouddhisme,* pp. 307–312.
33. For references see Sakurabe, *op. cit.,* p. 307.
34. Included in Ch'en-kuan's *Hua-yen fa-chieh hsüan-ching, T#*1883. For an excellent study of this work and a very useful summary of current scholarship on the early history of Hua-yen Buddhism, see Robert M. Gimello's "Chih-yen and the Foundations of Buddhism" (Ph.D. dissertation, Columbia University, 1976).
35. The relationship of K'uei-chi's thought to that of the early Hua-yen masters is a fascinating and highly complex topic that I plan to examine more fully elsewhere.
36. For a fuller discussion of K'uei-chi's understanding of this key Yogācāra

notion, see my article, "The *Trisvabhāva* Doctrine in India and China," in the *Ryūkoku daigaku bukkyō bunka kenkyūjo kiyō,* vol. 21 (1982), pp. 97–119.

37. At the end of his discussion of the fifth level, K'uei-chi concludes with the observation: "At the stage that one realizes the contemplation of thusness *(chen-[ju] kuan),* conventional phenomena *(su-shih)* are made evident by understanding the ultimate universal Principle *(chen-li).* Once the universal Principle *(li)* and phenomenal existence *(shih)* have become evident, [the deluded notions of] 'self' and 'things' cease to exist. It is precisely this that is the substance, the essential structure *(t'i),* of what was contemplated at the first level" (*T*45.259a25–27).

38. Cf. *Mahāyānasaṃgraha,* II.2.4 and II.25; Étienne Lamotte, *La somme de la grade véhicule d'Asaṅga,* vol. 2 (Louvain: Université de Louvain, Institut Orientaliste, 1938), pp. 90–91 and 120.

The Four Kinds of Samādhi
in Early T'ien-t'ai Buddhism

Daniel B. Stevenson

I. The Institutional Context of the Four Kinds of Samādhi

In the *Kuo-ch'ing pai-lu* ("Record of One Hundred Items [Pertaining to] Kuo-ch'ing [Monastery]"), a text consisting of miscellaneous documents relating to the founding of the early T'ien-t'ai community, there is a short piece entitled *Li chih-fa* ("Establishing the Regulations").[1] Chih-i (538–597), the great systematizer of early T'ien-t'ai thought and practice and the author of this treatise, began his teaching career in the Ch'en capital of Chin-ling in 568. Desiring a more stable environment in which to train his disciples and pursue his own practice, he withdrew to Mt. T'ien-t'ai in Chekiang province in 575, remaining there for ten years until 585, when he left the mountain to embark upon a period of intensive preaching in central and south China. When Chih-i once again returned to Mt. T'ien-t'ai in 595, he discovered that the monastic community had grown considerably larger and, along with its growth, discipline and spiritual commitment had declined. To redress this problem, Chih-i composed the *Li chih-fa*.

The work is brief, consisting of a short introduction and a set of ten items that outline the basic routine of the monastery and prescribe rules and punishments for those areas of monastic life that Chih-i considered to be most essential. As is clear from the orientation and tone of the work, the primary concern is not to present a comprehensive code of temple organization and procedure, but simply to rectify and strengthen the spirit of a system that was already well established and quite familiar. The details are taken for granted, and, where the highlights of monastic life are mentioned, the emphasis is not so much on giving us a clear picture of procedure as it is on ensuring that it be pursued with the proper spirit. Nevertheless, as fragmentary as it is, the *Li chih-fa* presents the only firsthand account of the religious life as it was actually instituted by

Chih-i. It thus affords us a precious glimpse into the realities of early T'ien-t'ai self-cultivation.

In the first entry of the *Li chih-fa,* Chih-i describes two basic approaches to liberation. The first is to practice alone deep in the mountains or forests far removed from others. The second approach, the one with which the *Li chih-fa* is predominantly concerned, is to practice with the support of a monastic community.

Altogether Chih-i distinguishes three basic modes of religous life within the T'ien-t'ai community: (1) "practicing seated meditation by resorting to the [community] hall" *(i t'ang tso-ch'an);* (2) "attending to the practical affairs of the community of monks" *(chih seng shih);* and (3) "performing repentance in a sanctuary or place of practice set apart from others" *(pieh ch'ang ch'an-hui).*

The life of the main meditation hall appears to have been the focal point of the community at large. Individuals enrolled there submitted to a fixed regimen—comprised of communal meditation, worship, and attendance at lectures on Buddhist doctrine—that structured all aspects of their daily lives. This regimen was designed not only to provide an environment most conducive to realizing their own personal spiritual goals, but also to engender a momentum and sense of common commitment in the community that could, in turn, uplift everyone involved. Four periods of meditation, amounting to approximately eight hours, were scheduled over a given day and night.[2] In addition, community worship services were held at the six intervals of morning, noon, late afternoon, evening, midnight, and late night.[3] Communal meals were served twice daily, once in the morning and once at noon.

Tardiness, disruptiveness, lack of spirit, or any deviation from the established procedure was met with swift discipline. Yet these rules themselves, and the measures taken to deal with such offenses, were not conceived in purely legalistic terms. In the case of minor infractions, the monk was required to prostrate and repent before the assembly. For more serious offenses, he was removed from the main hall and assigned, as a *wei-na,* to attend to menial affairs of the monastery. If a monk proved to be incorrigible, he was expelled from the temple entirely. No doubt removing trouble makers from the hall helped to ensure that the highest standards were maintained there, but the overriding message in the institutions of the *Li chih-fa* (even in such radical measures as these) was not so much one of exclusion as one of education and cooperation. Chih-i tell us, "Through yielding [on the part of the individual] there is harmony; from mutual acknowledgment there is joining together [in cooperation]."[4] His aim is to urge the student toward a genuine appreciation of the seriousness of both his own religious commitment and that of the community as a whole. As long as the monk in question makes progress in this regard, he has a place in the monastery. But if he persists in being a problem for the community, there is no question what course of action will be taken. In the closing lines of the *Li chih-fa,* Chih-i sums up the principles guiding the regulations as follows:

> We establish the procedures on the basis of the sūtras, and, upon seeing the illness, we determine the medicine. If you disregard the procedures and spit out the medicine, what benefit could there possibly be? Even in the case of one whose repentance regarding the nine regulations has already been heard, even though he may repent again and again, if he shows no sense of remorse, then he is a person who spits out the medicine, and it is fitting to expel him from the community. If he is able to change, one may later reconsider his return. But if he flaunts all the regulations and, always defending himself, is not willing to repent, then he is one who has absolutely no regard for the rules. If he cannot accord with the collective procedure of the community, he should not remain within it.[5]

The second form of religious activity described in the *Li chih-fa,* managing the affairs of the monastery, was designed, as Chih-i notes, "to promote the benefit and ensure the stability of the community at large."[6] By dedicating their time and labor to handling the practical demands of the monastery, the managerial monks apparently enabled the community of monks in the main hall (or in solitary retreat) to devote themselves single-mindedly to worship and meditation. Unfortunately Chih-i does not give us any clear indication of how the ranks of managerial monks (or lay menials) were organized, what their various duties were, or what relation (if any) they had with the daily routines of the main hall. As we have already noted, the position of *wei-na,* which was a sort of managerial duty, was sometimes assigned as a form of penance for going against the regulations of the main hall. Elsewhere in the *Kuoch'ing pai-lu* we hear of a type of temple menial known as *ching-jen,* "pure person." By the context in which the title is used, we can surmise that the *ching-jen* were probably laymen or novices *(śramaṇa),* often of low class and little education, who were attached to the temple as laborers or servants. In one instance we hear of a young *ching-jen* named Shan-hsin, who was later given full bhikṣu precepts and admitted into the main assembly, indicating that a certain degree of mobility was available to the *ching-jen.* However, for the most part such persons seem to have been prohibited from participating in the community meditation, worship, and teachings.[7]

Such examples create the impression that the managerial ranks were filled with delinquent monks or persons not worthy or capable of meeting the high standards of monastic life. Yet we must be cautious in drawing such conclusions, for our information is limited. As in the Zen monasteries of later periods, managerial duties may well have been taken up also by senior monks who, by virtue of their advanced abilities, did not need to rely upon the meditation hall but could effectively continue their practice in the midst of any and all circumstances.[8]

From Chih-i's brief descriptions of these two main functional aspects of the T'ien-t'ai community—the collective life of worship and meditation and the services of the managerial monks that supported it— we can see that the main hall was the heart of the monastery, the place where its fundamentals of learning and training were both preserved and imparted. However, Chih-i describes yet a third mode of religious practice that takes precedence even over this: the "repentance in a separate sanctuary" *(pieh ch'ang ch'an-hui)* or "practice [in a hall] apart from others" *(pieh hsing)* spoken of earlier. Monks, or on occasion even laymen, who showed exceptional motivation and promise were encouraged to leave the community meditation hall periodically and isolate themselves in retreat for given periods of time. There they took up any one of a set group of highly intensive and effective forms of practice known collectively as the "four kinds of samādhi" *(ssu-chung san-mei).* As Chih-i comments in the *Li chih-fa:*

> [A monk] zealously applies himself to cultivating the four kinds of samādhi because [practice] in the context of the community is lax. This is the point of practicing apart from others. Merely making a pretense of entering the sanctuary [to practice] cannot be considered [to be in line with] its basic purpose.[9]

As used in the T'ien-t'ai expression "four kinds of samādhi," the term "samādhi" (Ch. *san-mei*) can have two basic meanings. On the one hand, it carries the more familiar sense of a general state of meditative absorption or ecstasy, which, in a strictly Buddhist context, may cover a variety of experiences. There are the nine grades of mundane dhyāna and various states of genuine liberative insight and cessation, such as the supramundane *nirodha samāpatti,* that are emphasized in the Hīnayāna tradition. Or there are the grand displays of omniscience characteristic of the samādhis of the Buddhas and bodhisattvas of the Mahāyāna where, as Étienne Lamotte has so appropriately stated, "L'accent est mis non plus sur la technique de la concentration, mais sur la force magique *(ṛddhibala)* qui en découle pour le plus grand bien des êtres."[10]

On the other hand, as it is used in T'ien-t'ai treatises, the term "samādhi" at times designates not only the fruits of meditative practice but also the various mental and physical disciplines designed to evoke them. Lotus samādhi *(fa-hua san-mei),* for example, can refer both to an experience of samādhi *cum* enlightenment and to the particular form of practice, derived from the *Lotus Sūtra,* that produces it.

The expression "four kinds of samādhi," which is unique to the T'ien-t'ai school, does not describe four states of samādhi, but four ways of cultivating samādhi. In his *Mo-ho chih-kuan* ("[Treatise on] the Great Calming and Discernment"), Chih-i gives what has become the classic definition of the four kinds of samādhi:

> Now if you wish to ascend to the stage of wondrous realization, you will not be able to reach it unless you practice. But if you become skilled at stirring and agitating [the raw milk], then the essence of ghee may be obtained. The *Lotus Sūtra* says, "I also see the sons of Buddha cultivating all manner of practices in order to seek the path to Buddhahood."[11] There are many methods of practice, but we may summarize them under four sorts: (1) constantly sitting, (2) constantly walking, (3) part walking part sitting, and (4) neither walking nor sitting. By refering to them collectively as "samādhis," we mean [that one thereby] attunes, rectifies, and stabilizes [the mind]. The *Ta-[chih-tu] lun* ("Great [Perfection of Wisdom] Treatise") says, "Skillfully to fix the mind on one spot and abide there without shifting—that is called samādhi."[12] The Dharmadhātu is a "single spot," and through true discernment you can abide there and never stray from it. These four types of activity constitute the supporting condition [for meditation]. By discerning the mind and resorting to the supporting condition [of the four activities], one attunes and rectifies [the mind]. For this reason we call them samādhis.[13]

The four categories of practice that Chih-i describes here are quite comprehensive in scope. As they are defined solely in terms of simple posture and physical activity, they could conceivably incorporate any form of spiritual discipline or technique of mental discernment. Undoubtedly this was in part the impression that Chih-i wished to convey when he remarked that virtually all forms of practice could be grouped under these four. However, in those instances throughout his works where Chih-i actually describes the contents of the four kinds of samādhi, the four categories of sitting, walking, part sitting part walking, and neither sitting nor walking are themselves identified with a very specific (and consistent) group of practices.[14]

The technique of cultivating samādhi through constant sitting *(ch'ang-tso san-mei)* is equated with a meditation known as one-practice samādhi *(i-hsing san-mei),* where the practitioner applies himself to sitting in meditation for a period of ninety days. Cultivating samādhi through constant walking *(ch'ang-hsing san-mei)* is identified with a practice known as *pratyutpanna* samādhi *(pan-chou san-mei),* in which the meditator, also over a period of ninety days, cultivates samādhi while slowly circumambulating an altar dedicated to the Buddha Amitābha. Cultivating samādhi through part walking and part sitting *(pan-hsing pan-tso san-mei)* is associated with two practices: the Lotus samādhi *(fa-hua san-mei)* and *fang-teng* repentance *(fang-teng ch'an-fa).* Both of these meditations are structured around repeated cycles of walking and seated meditation. Cultivating samādhi neither through walking nor through sitting *(fei-hsing fei-tso san-mei)* describes two types of practice. The first includes any form of structured meditation, worship, or spiritual discipline that does not fit neatly into the rubric of walking and/or sitting described by the previous three categories. As his primary example, Chih-i cites the *ch'ing Kuan-yin* repentance *(ch'ing Kuan-yin ch'an-fa)*. The second sort refers to a particular kind of free-form meditation that actively disavows adherence to any specific pattern or mode of activity. This he calls *"sui-tzu-i,"* which essentially means "doing as one will" or, in a more technical sense, "cultivating samādhi wherever one's mind happens to be directed at the moment."

The works of Chih-i's master, Hui-ssu (515–577), as well as various references that appear in the biographies of both Hui-ssu and his immediate disciples, reveal that the one-practice, *pratyutpanna,* Lotus, and *sui-tzu-i* samādhis and the *fang-teng* and *ch'ing Kuan-yin* repentances were also used in Hui-ssu's community.[15] More significantly, at that early date they appear to have already been established as a fixed set, with the same sort of importance that Chih-i outlined more fully some years later in such works as the *Li chih-fa* and *Mo-ho chih-kuan*. Hui-ssu's biography in the *Hsü kao-seng-chuan* ("Continued Biographies of Eminent Monks") records that, in his last address to his disciples just before his death, he remarked:

> If there were but ten of you who, without concern for body or life, would constantly apply yourselves to the practice of the Lotus, *pratyutpanna,* and mindfulness of Buddha *(nien-fo)* samādhis, as well as the *fang-teng* repentance, and [moreover would dedicate yourselves to] constant sitting in meditation and [the practice of] ascetic disciplines, then I personally would supply you with whatever you need. It would without question be to our mutual benefit.[16]

In the biography of Hui-ch'eng, one of Hui-ssu's foremost disciples, we find an indication of the way in which these practices were actually applied by Hui-ssu. In many respects it anticipates the role that Chih-i defines for the four kinds of samādhi in his *Li chih-fa*. The biography states:

> At the time [when Hui-ch'eng joined the assembly], there were several tens of persons applying themselves to the practice of dhyāna, all of whom had already experienced attainments. As Ch'eng was a latecomer, he feared that he would not be able to fit in with them. So from dusk until dawn he would sit in meditation with his eyes open. Altogether he passed fifteen years doing this. [Hui-]ssu [also] had him repeatedly enter the sanctuaries for the practice of the *fang-teng* and *Kuan-yin* [repentances] and the Lotus and *pratyutpanna* [samādhis] in order to dissolve his obstructions. For three years he resorted to these practices. Finally his demonic disturbances, the demons

that plague dhyāna practice, and the subtle causes of biased [attachment] having been dispersed, [Hui-ssu] revealed the True Dharma for him.[17]

Chih-i himself experienced his first taste of enlightenment while practicing the Lotus samādhi under Hui-ssu's tutelage on Mt. Ta-su.[18] When he left Hui-ssu in 568 to begin his own career as a dhyāna master, he employed these six practices as effective methods for training his own disciples. During the earliest phase of his career—the years between 568 and 575, when he first taught in Chin-ling—Chih-i composed manuals for the *fang-teng* repentance and the Lotus samādhi at the very least.[19] All six practices (one-practice samādhi, *pratyutpanna* samādhi, and so forth) are mentioned in his *Shih ch'an po-lo-mi tz'u-ti fa-men* ("Elucidation of the Successive Dharma Gates of Perfection of Dhyāna"), which also dates from this period.[20] Dating from the years beginning with Chih-i's withdrawal to Mt. T'ien-t'ai in 575, we find manuals for *sui-tzu-i (chüeh-i san-mei), fang-teng* repentance, *ch'ing Kuan-yin* repentance, and *pratyutpanna* samādhi. Additional references throughout Chih-i's works, as well as his biographies and those of his major disciples, corroborate that these six samādhi and repentance techniques continued to hold a major place in his scheme of practice. Consequently, even though the one-practice, *pratyutpanna,* Lotus, and *sui-tzu-i* samādhis and the *fang-teng* and *ch'ing Kuan-yin* repentances were never explicitly systematized into an identifiable set prior to their being incorporated into the form of the four kinds of samādhi, they nevertheless had long functioned as a mainstay of meditation practice in the communities of both Hui-ssu and Chih-i and, as a group, received no noticeable additions or subtractions from their original number.

The term *"ssu chung san-mei"* ("four kinds of samādhi") itself is not found in any of Hui-ssu's extant works, nor is it used in any of the materials dating from the earlier phases of Chih-i's career (i.e., his first period of residence in Chin-ling and his ten year sojourn on Mt. T'ien-t'ai).[21] It appears for the first time in Chih-i's *Fa-hua hsüan-i* ("Abstruse Meaning of the *Lotus Sūtra*"), which was compiled from lectures he delivered in Ching-chou in 593, only five years before his death. From this point on it is used regularly throughout most of his works, such as the *Mo-ho chih-kuan, San-kuan i* ("The Meaning of the Three Discernments"), *Ssu-chiao i* ("The Meaning of the Four Teachings"), and the short *Kuan-hsin lun* ("Treatise on Discerning the Mind"), his last composition.

In terms of the volume of material that survives from these last years of Chih-i's life—from the time he departed Mt. T'ien-t'ai in 585 until his death in 597—this period seems to have been the most prolific of his career. Perhaps most significant, however, is the fact that in these last works we witness the maturation of those concepts and formulations that came to be revered by subsequent tradition as the orthodox statement of T'ien-t'ai thought and practice. In the area of meditation we see the emergence of such schemes as the three [approaches to] calming and discerning *(san chih-kuan),* the ten spheres of discernment *(shih kuanching),* and the famous ten modes of discernment *(shih ch'eng kuanfa).*[22] Through such concepts as these, Chih-i sought to provide the general practitioner with fundamental principles of meditation practice that he could systematically apply to any one of the great variety of meditative techniques—Indian and Central Asian as well as native Chinese—that were circulating in China during his time. The scheme of four kinds of samādhi, which strives to classify and group different forms of meditation on the basis of their dominant mode of physical activity, may be numbered among these formulae.

Yet, when we actually examine the references to the four kinds of samādhi in Chih-i's works, we find that the four categories are not only closely tailored to the ritual descriptions of the one-practice, *pratyutpanna,* Lotus, and *sui-tzu-i* samādhis and the *fang-teng* and *ch'ing Kuanyin* repentances, but on numerous occasions are explicitly identified with them. This suggests, first of all, that Chih-i devised this scheme of the four kinds of samādhi specifically to accommodate this group of practices and, second, that, despite his intentions to extend this scheme to include any and all forms of meditation, he had essentially these six samādhi and repentance practices in mind when he used the expression "four kinds of samādhi." Therefore, when we begin to consider what forms of spiritual discipline were really at the heart of the early T'ien-t'ai school, or in what way Chih-i's more abstract models of meditation were put into concrete practice, this group of meditations, otherwise known as the four kinds of samādhi, emerges as one of the true pillars of T'ien-t'ai practice. Perhaps there is no better illustration of the importance with which Chih-i regarded them than his final admonition to his disciples while on his deathbed—an admonition that is strikingly similar to the one made by his master, Hui-ssu. When asked, "Whom can we regard as our teacher when you are gone?" Chih-i replied, "Haven't you ever heard [the Buddha's parting words]? The *prātimokṣa* is your master. Or, as I have always told you, take the four kinds of samādhi as your guide."[23]

The aim of this chapter is to describe in detail the individual practices of the four kinds of samādhi and to identify some of the features they have in common. The four kinds of samādhi were themselves one of the wellsprings from which T'ien-t'ai thought and practice originally flowed, and, over succeeding generations, they continued to function as one of the primary means by which T'ien-t'ai teachings and religious aspirations were put into practice. Furthermore, in their choice of practices—what they deemed most suitable and most effective—the T'ien-t'ai founders in many ways reflect some of the preferences in meditation and self-cultivation that later came to characterize East Asian Buddhism as a whole. The most notable example along these lines is the practice of mindfulness of the Buddha *(nien-fo)*, which became the basis of the Pure Land traditions in China and Japan. The more formless approach of one-practice samādhi, as well as such techniques as *sui-tzu-i* and the advanced approach to the Lotus samādhi known as *an-lo hsing*, suggest certain parallels with the Ch'an tradition. The invocation of specific Buddhas and bodhisattvas through the use of dhāraṇī and visualization, as found in such quasi-esoteric practices as the *fang-teng* and *ch'ing Kuan-yin* repentances, anticipates the interest in esoteric Buddhism of the T'ang period and the emergence of the great traditions of Shingon and Tendai esotericism in Japan. Finally, such activities as performing offerings, doing repentance, prostrating before the Buddhas, and reciting sūtras represent an important facet of spirituality that touched the lives of all Buddhists throughout East Asia irrespective of sectarian distinctions.

It is hoped, therefore, that this undertaking will not only contribute significantly to our appreciation of the realities of religious practice in the early T'ien-t'ai tradition, but also further our understanding of some of the underlying religious sensibilities that helped shape the character of East Asian Buddhism as a whole.

II. The Contents of the Four Kinds of Samādhi

Descriptions of the different practices that were incorporated into the scheme of the four kinds of samādhi can be obtained from a number of early T'ien-t'ai sources. As has already been mentioned, Hui-ssu and Chih-i both composed treatises dealing with these meditations.

Preserved in the *Taishō Daizōkyō* edition of the Buddhist canon are *Fa-hua san-mei ch'an-i* ("The Procedure for [Performing] the Lotus Samādhi Repentance"), *Fang-teng san-mei hsing-fa* ("The Method for the Practice of *Fang-teng* Samādhi"), and *Chüeh-i san-mei hsing-fa* ("The Method for Practicing the Samādhi of Maintaining Awareness of Mind [Wherever Mind is Directed]")—manuals for the practice of Lotus samādhi, *Fang-teng* repentance, and *sui-tzu-i* samādhi (cultivating samādhi wherever mind is directed), respectively. All three works date from early in Chih-i's career.[24]

Kuo-ch'ing pai-lu, the compendium of T'ien-t'ai-related documents mentioned previously, contains three more brief manuals of this sort, all by Chih-i: *Ch'ing Kuan-yin ch'an-fa* ("The Method for [Performing] the *Ch'ing Kuan-yin* Repentance"), a second *Fang-teng ch'an-fa* ("The Method for [Performing] the *Fang-teng* Repentance"), and *Chin kuang-*

ming ch'an-fa ("The Method for [Performing] the *Chin kuang-ming* Repentance").[25]

The *Ta-t'ang nei-tien lu,* a catalog of Buddhist texts in the T'ang imperial collection that was compiled by the monk Tao-hsüan (596–667) about fifty years after Chih-i's death, includes among Chih-i's works a *Pan-chou cheng-hsiang hsing-fa* ("The Method for the Practice and [Verification of] Signs of Successful Realization of *Pratyutpanna* Samādhi") and a *Ch'ing Kuan-yin hsing-fa* ("The Method for the Practice of *Ch'ing Kuan-yin* Repentance"). The former was a manual for the *pratyutpanna* samādhi. The latter is thought to have been another, longer, guide to the *ch'ing Kuan-yin* repentance.[26] Unfortunately both works have been lost.

Looking back to Chih-i's master, Hui-ssu, we find that he composed a *Sui-tzu-i san-mei* ("[Method for] Cultivating Samādhi Wherever Mind is Directed"), which is preserved in the *Zoku Zōkyō* edition of the canon, and a work expounding the practice of the Lotus samādhi known as *Fa-hua ching an-lo hsing i* ("The Essential Meaning of the Course of Ease and Bliss [Set Forth] in the *Lotus Sūtra*"), which appears in the *Taishō Daizōkyō.*[27]

Apart from the individual manuals themselves, the best overall account of the contents of these practices is found in the *Mo-ho chih-kuan,* where Chih-i treats them together under a single lengthy discussion of the four kinds of samādhi.[28] The descriptions in the *Mo-ho chih-kuan,* however, are too brief and too lacking in the necessary details of procedure to function as guides to practice, and clearly were not intended to do so. In the case of the Lotus samādhi, *fang-teng* and *ch'ing Kuan-yin* repentances, and *sui-tzu-i* samādhi, where seperate manuals exist, our descriptive analysis of the four kinds of samādhi will rely on both sources, taking care to draw attention to any major discrepancies between the different accounts. For the one-practice and *pratyutpanna* samādhis we have no choice but to resort exclusively to the *Mo-ho chih-kuan.*

i. Cultivating Samādhi Through Constant Sitting

Chih-i identifies the first of the four kinds of samādhi with the practice known as *i-hsing san-mei.* The term *"i-hsing san-mei,"* rendered here as "one-practice samādhi," is the Chinese translation of the Sanskrit *eka-vyūha-samādhi,* which originally meant "samādhi of a single array." The *Ta-p'in ching* (*Pañcaviṃśatisāhasrikā-prajñāpāramitā-sūtra,* "The Sūtra of the Perfection of Wisdom in Twenty-five Thousand Lines") and its large commentary, the *Ta-chih-tu-lun* (both of which had a major impact on the thought of Hui-ssu and Chih-i), give this samādhi as the eighty-first member in a list of one hundred and eight great samādhis of the Mahāyāna. The latter text says:

This samādhi constantly avails itself of a single practice [wherein the practitioner] is in touch with ultimate emptiness. In this samādhi there is no cultivation by successive stages of practice of the sort that [we find in the four stations of mindfulness], where from the cultivation of [the insight of] impermanence there next develops the practice of [mindfulness] of pain, and from [mindfulness of pain] it progresses to the [mindfulness] of no-self. Furthermore, [when coursing in this samādhi, the practitioner] does not see this shore [of birth and death] nor any other shore [of nirvāṇa].[29]

Although Chih-i and Hui-ssu were certainly aware of this reference, they chose to rely, as a scriptural basis for the practice, on the more substantial account of *i-hsing san-mei* that appears in the *Wen-shu-shih-li so-shuo po-jo po-lo-mi ching (Saptaśatikā-prajñāpāramitā-sūtra;* "Sūtra on the Perfection of Wisdom Spoken by Mañjuśrī"—hereafter *Wen-shu shuo ching),* supplementing it with material from the *Wen-shu-shih-li wen ching (Mañjuśrī-paripṛcchā-sūtra;* "Sūtra [Spoken at] the Behest of Mañjuśrī").[30]

As Chih-i describes it in the *Mo-ho chih-kuan,* one-practice samādhi is to be performed in a quiet room or a secluded and untrammeled spot. The essential requisite is that the immediate environs be free of any disturbance, human or otherwise. Only a single rope bed for meditation is to be placed in the hall; no other seats or daises should be added. The practice itself lasts for a fixed period of ninety days and may be performed alone or in a small group. Over the entire duration of this three month period the meditator applies himself zealously to the practice of sitting motionless in the traditional "lotus" meditation posture. With the exception of brief stretches of walking meditation *(ching-hsing)* and attending to such necessities as eating and relieving himself, he vows never to sleep, lie down, stand, wander aimlessly about, or lean against any object for support. For this reason the practice is referred to as "constant sitting."

In accordance with the *Wen-shu shuo ching,* Chih-i distinguishes two basic approaches to meditative practice in the one-practice samādhi: the radical approach of directly contemplating the reality of the Dharmadhātu (or the Dharma-body of the Buddha) and the more expedient approach of concentrating the mind on the name, idealized image, and merits (body of form) of a particular Buddha.

Providing that the meditator posesses the requisite meditative skill, the ideal approach is to "renounce all fallacious theories, cast aside all confused thinking, refrain from any random pondering, avoid seizing upon any characteristics, and simply absorb oneself completely in the direct experiencing of all objects as [identical to] the Dharmadhātu and in contemplating one's own [subjective] mind as [also] being uniform with the Dharmadhātu."[31] Chih-i goes on to explain:

[To think of trying to] realize the Dharmadhātu by means of the
Dharmadhātu is absurd. There is no realization, nor is there any attaining
of anything. One discerns that the characteristics [peculiar to] sentient
beings are the same as the characteristics of a Buddha and that the extent of
the realm of sentient beings is just the same as the extent of the domain of
the Buddha. The extent of the domain of the Buddhas is inconceivable,
and, likewise, the extent of the realm of sentient beings is also inconceivable. Dwelling in the realm of sentient beings is [ultimately] like dwelling in
empty space. Through this teaching of non-abiding and this teaching of no-
characteristics, one comes to dwell in prajñā. Not seeing any profane qualities, what is there to cast off? Not finding any sagely qualities, what is there
to appropriate? The same is true for nirvāṇa and cyclic existence, purity and
defilement. Neither rejecting nor grasping, one abides directly in ultimate
reality.[32]

If the meditator becomes exhausted, or illness and other forms of
obstruction begin to overwhelm his powers of contemplation, or if he is a
novice who has not yet developed the powers of meditative insight necessary to take up this first type of discernment effectively, then he turns to
the second more tangible approach. Selecting a Buddha of his own
choosing, he faces in the direction of that particular Buddha's realm and
single-mindedly "invokes that Buddha's name *(ch'eng i fo ming-tzu),*
generates a deep sense of shame [over his own inability to practice as he
should], repents, and entrusts his fate to him."[33]

Viewed purely from a psychological perspective, these more tangible
techniques function therapeutically as valuable aids to meditation. The
figure of a particular Buddha and the repeated recitation of his name
provide a solid support for concentration, enabling the meditator quickly
to focus and calm his mind when it is disturbed or to ward off drowsiness
when he is exhausted. Prayer, self-reflection, and repentance can help to
release emotional pressures that oppress the practitioner's spirit and hinder the equilibrium and ease necessary for deeper meditation.

However, the benefit of these techniques need not be limited solely
to the psychological. In theory the simple act of reciting the name,
repenting, and professing faith in even a single Buddha is itself capable
of generating great religious power, for such a deed, Chih-i tells us, "is
fully equivalent in merit to invoking the names of all the Buddhas of the
Ten Directions."[34] If the practitioner can apply himself to this kind of
practice with wholehearted faith and sincerity, not only can it help to
bring his mind under control, but he can move the Buddhas to communi-
cate their power and blessings to him, thereby removing his obstructions
directly. Chih-i explains:

When a person is joyous or depressed, if he raises his voice to sing or cry
out, then his sorrow or humor will be released. It is similar for the practi-

tioner. The wind [of emotion] touches the seven spots and initiates a physical response, and, when the voice comes forth from the lips, it becomes the act of speech. These two deeds [of body and speech] are able to assist the mind in forming a stimulus that moves the Buddha to send down [his blessings].[35]

Apparently, such expedients as fixing one's mind on the Buddha, repenting, and chanting his name were intended to function in close conjunction with the meditation on the Dharmadhātu. Unfortunately, Chih-i does not give us a full explanation of how this meditation on the Buddha is to be performed and how it is ultimately to be reconciled with the meditation on the Dharmadhātu.

The account of one-practice samādhi in Kuan-ting's *Kuan-hsin lun shu* ("Commentary to the Treatise on Discerning the Mind") suggests that visualization of the Buddha's form and mindfulness of his merits may have been practiced concurrently with the invocation of his name. The treatise says: "When the practitioner takes up mindfulness of a particular Buddha *(nien i fo)*, he must [grasp the fact that] the merits [of this Buddha] are fully equivalent to the merits of [all] the Buddhas of the Ten Directions. He should also [accompany this] with invoking [that] Buddha's name out loud *(ch'eng-ch'ang fo-ming)*."[36]

Furthermore, embedded in the *Mo-ho chih-kuan's* description of the meditation upon the Dharmadhātu, we find a discussion of the expressions "discerning or visualizing the Tathāgata" *(kuan ju-lai)* and "seeing the marks of a Buddha" *(chien fo hsiang hao)*. The main thrust of this particular section is to assert that any image or characterization of a Buddha is ultimately equivalent to "no mark" and that the discernment of such features is fundamentally an empty enterprise, akin to "seeing the reflection of one's own image on the surface of water."[37] Significantly, much of the discussion here revolves around a passage from the *Wen-shu wen ching*, which reads:

> By resorting to [invocation of the Buddha's] name, mindfulness is strengthened. [Once one] perceives the minor and major marks of the Buddha [through visualization], samādhi proper is complete. Once samādhi proper is complete, one perceives all the Buddhas. These Buddhas are perceived in the same manner as one sees one's own image reflected on the surface of water. This is known as the initial [experience of] samādhi.[38]

Chih-i's interest in this passage may well indicate that he used such expedients as reciting the Buddha's name and visualizing the Buddha's form in a manner similar to the one described in the passage. If so, his critique of these expedients from the standpoint of emptiness and the dialectics of prajñā was perhaps a necessary step for ultimately linking them with the meditation on the Dharmadhātu. We shall say no more about such a procedure here, for the account of *pratyutpanna* samādhi in the section that follows deals with this phenomenon in considerable detail and may itself serve as a suitable explanation.

The essential point to bear in mind for now is that the radical approach of complete "non-abiding" and immediate identification with the Dharmadhātu and the expedient approach of fixing the mind on the Buddha's form and reciting his name were intended to function in close support of one another. If thoroughly pursued enough, either can convey the meditator to the same end, whereby, as Chih-i describes it, he "enters one-practice samādhi, perceives all the Buddhas face to face, and ascends to the stage of assurance of full bodhisattvahood *(ju p'u-sa wei)*."[39]

2. Cultivating Samādhi Through Constant Walking

Constantly walking samādhi is identified with the practice known as *pratyutpanna* samādhi. The term *"pan-chou san-mei,"* which for the sake of convenience we render as *"pratyutpanna* samādhi," is a Chinese transliteration of the lengthy Sanskrit compound *pratyutpanna-buddha-saṃmukhāvasthita-samādhi,* "the samādhi wherein one finds oneself standing face to face with all the Buddhas of the present age." This particular samādhi appears to have been one of the better known Mahāyāna samādhis, for mention of it can be found throughout any number of early Mahāyāna sūtras and commentaries.[40] Chih-i derives his views concerning this samādhi and its practice from two main scriptural sources. The first is the *Pan-chou san-mei ching (Pratyutpannasamādhi-sūtra).* The earliest Chinese translation of this scripture (the one on which Chih-i relies) is said to have been done by the Central Asian monk Lokakṣema during the last years of the second century.[41] The second is the *Shih-chu pi-p'o-sha lun (Daśabhūmika[sūtra]vibhāśa),* a lengthy work consisting of a detailed exegesis of the first two of the ten bodhisattva stages of the *Daśabhūmika-sūtra.* This text is attributed to Nāgārjuna and was translated into Chinese by Kumārajīva during the first decade of the fifth century.[42] In addition to the *Shih-chu pi-p'o-sha lun,* we find that *pratyutpanna* samādhi also figures prominently in the *Ta-chih-tu-lun.*[43] Both works cite the *Pan-chou san-mei ching* as the *locus classicus* for this samādhi. Therefore, it would be quite natural for Hui-ssu and Chih-i to use Lokakṣema's ancient translation of this sūtra (the only one available at the time) together with the *Shih-chu pi-p'o-sha lun* as their two primary sources for this practice.

Like the one-practice samādhi, the *pratyutpanna* samādhi is to be performed in isolation. The meditator selects and adorns a hall for practice, prepares all the necessary accoutrements of offering, and lays out various delicacies, fruit, incense, and flowers. Having washed himself thoroughly, he changes into a new set of robes, which is to be worn at all times in the inner sanctuary where the practice is performed. Whenever he leaves this chamber to tend to necessities, he changes once again into an older set. The practice itself lasts for a fixed period of ninety days, over the duration of which the meditator must contiuously circumambulate an altar to the Buddha Amitābha. He vows never to entertain worldly thoughts or desires, never to lie down or leave the hall, and, aside from the times when he eats his meals, never arbitrarily to sit down or stop to rest until the three months are completed.[44]

Given the strenuous nature of the practice, its success depends heavily on the support and close interaction of three other individuals aside from the practitioner himself. They are the instructor, the outer attendant, and the companion in the practice. The instructor must be well versed in the practice and skilled in recognizing and alleviating obstructions. The practitioner, in turn, must have absolute faith in his guidance. The outer attendant takes care of all the meditator's practical needs and watches over him day and night, "as a mother protects her child." The exact nature of the third party, the "companion in the practice" *(t'ung-hsing),* is ambiguous. There are certain indications that the term referred to additional meditators, which would mean that *pratyutpanna* samādhi (like the one-practice samādhi and the *fang-teng* and *ch'ing Kuan-yin* repentances) was not necessarily practiced alone, but could be undertaken collectively. Yet another possibility is that the companion in the practice was a monitor whose duty it was constantly to encourage the meditator and ensure that he kept his vows. In either case, Chih-i tells us that this individual must be "stern in appearance and strict [in character]" and otherwise fully capable of inspiring the meditator to persevere.[45]

The meditative discernment itself centers around the visualization of the thirty-two major marks and eighty minor excellent qualities of the Buddha Amitābha. This practice is performed repeatedly, "in reverse order from the thousand-spoked wheels on the soles of his feet to the indiscernable *uṣṇīṣa* on the crown of his head, and then in the normal order from the crown of the head back to the thousand-spoked wheel." The visualization is carried out concurrently with the invocation of the Buddha's name and slow circumambulation of the hall so that, "step after step, recitation after recitation, recollection after recollection, [the practitioner's] mindfulness is wholly upon the Buddha Amitābha."[46]

The devotional element in this practice, just as in the one-practice samādhi, undoubtedly plays a key role; however, as the practitioner becomes more skilled at constructing the mental image of the Buddha, the orientation of the visualization begins to shift radically. Eventually the eidetic image of Amitābha loses its devotional character altogether and instead becomes the basis for a simple dialectical investigation into the nature of mind and the noetic act itself.[47] Citing a passage from the *Pan-chou san-mei ching,* Chih-i describes the technique as follows:

Where does the Buddha that I am contemplating come from? [He does not come from somewhere else, and] I do not go off to reach him. Whatever [feature] I turn my attention to thereupon appears. This Buddha is simply mind perceiving mind. Mind is the [visualized] Buddha [that is the object, and likewise] mind is the [subjective] "I" [that sees the Buddha]. When it perceives the Buddha, mind is not itself aware of mind, nor does it itself perceive mind. When the mind gives rise to thoughts, then there is delusion. When it is free of thoughts, it is nirvāṇa.[48]

On the basis of the *Shih-chu pi-p'o-sha lun,* Chih-i distinguishes three levels to the practice of "mindfulness of Buddha" *(nien-fo).* The first involves the mindfulness or contemplation of a Buddha through the visualization of the major marks and minor excellent qualities of his idealized physical form. The second is the contemplation of the more abstract qualities that mark a Buddha's spiritual omniscience, such as the forty qualities unique to a Buddha *(āveṇikabuddhadharmāh).* The third and final stage involves the contemplation or mindfulness of Buddha as he is in his essence—the essential nature or true character of all phenomena *(sarvadharmabhūtatā).*[49] At this stage all vestiges of discrimination and dualistic thinking, together with any sense of Buddha being a real entity or an object of devotion, completely vanish, and reality stands directly revealed. Citing the *Shih-chu pi-p'o-sha lun,* Chih-i explains:

He does not cling to the [Buddha's] body of form, nor does he adhere to the [Buddha's essence] body of Dharma, but thoroughly realizes that all phenomena are eternally quiescent just like empty space.[50]

The manner in which *pratyutpanna* samādhi integrates various devotional elements and expedient supports for meditative discernment with the more abstract and intangible discernments of the Dharma-body or the Dharmadhātu suggests close parallels with one-practice samādhi. Both meditations recognize the effectiveness of resorting to the image and grace of the Buddhas as a powerful medium for practice, yet place final emphasis on mind (and a critique of the mind's fundamental role in the generation of all forms of deluded existence) as the ultimate ground of discernment and realization. The *Pan-chou san-mei ching* designates three main factors from which *pratyutpanna* samādhi draws its strength and by virtue of which it is able to produce enlightenment quickly. The first is the sustaining power or grace *(adhiṣṭhāna)* of the Buddha. The second is the power of samādhi of the practitioner himself. And the third is the power that derives from the stock of merit that the practitioner has accumulated over his past (and present) lives.[51]

This rationale may just as easily be applied to one-practice samādhi or any other form of meditation involving the two elements of reliance on the supportive grace of Buddhas and bodhisattvas and the powers of one's own meditative discernment. In the particular case of *pratyutpanna* samādhi, the source of supportive grace is the Buddha Amitābha. Naturally this feature calls to mind the practice of seeking rebirth in the Pure Land of *Sukhāvati* through meditation upon the Buddha Amitābha. Chih-i openly states that rebirth there is one of the benefits to be derived from *pratyutpanna* samādhi but is not its principal aim. "Invoking Amitābha's [name] is equivalent to invoking [the names of] all the Buddhas," Chih-i tells us, "so in this case we simply focus on Amitābha as the essential gate of access to Dharma."[52] Through his grace and the practitioner's own powers of meditation and merit, the practitioner does not simply perceive Amitābha and his Pure Land but is able to achieve the climactic vision of *pratyutpanna-buddha-saṃmukhāvasthita-samādhi* itself:

> On entering samādhi, he is able to perceive all the Buddhas of the present age in all the Ten Directions standing directly before him. As many stars as a person with keen eyesight can see on a clear night—that is how many Buddhas he sees![53]

3. CULTIVATING SAMĀDHI THROUGH PART WALKING AND PART SITTING

Partly sitting and partly walking samādhi is identified with two different practices: the *fang-teng* repentance and the Lotus samādhi.

A. The Fang-teng *Repentance*

The *fang-teng* repentance is based on the *Fang-teng t'o-lo-ni ching* ("*Fang-teng* or Vaipulya Dhāraṇī Sūtra"), a quasi-esoteric Buddhist scripture translated into Chinese by the monk Fa-chung during the Northern Liang dynasty.[54] Like the previous two samādhi practices, this repentance is to be performed in a secluded hall that has been carefully purified and arranged for this purpose. As the *fang-teng* repentance places great emphasis on ritual purity and strict adherence to ritual procedure, instructions concerning the preparations and performance of the ceremony are far more detailed than in either the one-practice or *pratyutpanna* samādhis.[55]

The *Fang-teng san-mei hsing-fa,* Chih-i's earliest and lengthiest manual for the practice, specifies that there be four separate rooms consisting of a central sanctuary, a bath house, and two antechambers. During the course of the retreat, the meditator must perform ritual ablutions three times a day. Whenever he passes in or out of the inner sanctum, whether he be on his way to or on his way from the performance of his ablutions or any other necessity, he must change robes and undergo vari-

ous rituals of purification in the two antechambers. These are designed
to protect the sanctuary from defilement.

In the event that the meditator finds himself unable to make such
elaborate preparations, he is permitted to reduce the number of rooms to
three, two, or even one. However, if he uses a single chamber he must rit-
ually demarcate (and carefully maintain) specific areas for performing
the required purifications and changes of garb.

In the initial preparation of the repentance chambers, the inner
sanctuary is first rubbed with perfumed mud or paste, then sprinkled
with purified water and dried with fire. A circular altar is constructed, on
which the practitioner places twenty-four raised thrones; on these
thrones he then enshrines images of the twenty-four patron deities of the
practice.[56] Finally a mirror is added to protect the hall from evil influ-
ences, and a five-colored cloth canopy is suspended over the altar. To
complete the preparation of the site, a low dais (presumably for the practitioner himself) is arranged facing the images on the altar, and numerous
multicolored paintings and banners are draped around the walls to give
the hall "the semblance of a Pure Land." The repentance ceremony
proper must commence on either the eighth or the fifteenth day of the
lunar month. A period of seven days is stipulated as the minimum length
of the retreat; however, this may be extended, at the practitioner's discre-
tion, to a period of several months or even years.[57] As many as ten persons may take part. Prior to beginning the practice itself, all prospective
participants must undergo a week of purification and preparation. During this time they maintain constant vigilance over themselves, repent
past sins, and offer prayers in an effort to seek an auspicious dream from
one of the twelve dream kings *(meng-wang)* who protect the *Fang-teng
t'o-lo-ni ching* and its practices. If a dream occurs, it signifies that permission has been granted for that individual to perform the repentance.
Once this condition has been fulfilled, the participants then master the
essential dhāraṇī and ritual procedures to be used in the practice and are
administered twenty-four special precepts that they must adhere to over
the course of the retreat. By the time the repentance itself is ready to
begin, "their minds must be set solely upon [the goal of] the most
supreme and perfect enlightenment."[58]

The daily regimen of the *fang-teng* repentance consists of repeated
cycles of the following pattern of activities:[59]

1. Making offerings, followed by prostrations, repentance, vows,
   and ritual ablutions
2. Circumambulation of the hall, accompanied by recitation of the
   dhāraṇī
3. Prostrations, repentance, and vows
4. Sitting in meditation

5. Circumambulation of the hall, accompanied by recitation of the dhāraṇī
6. Sitting in meditation

On the morning of the first day, extended invocations are performed, and the altar is adorned with elaborate offerings of flowers, rare incenses, lamps, and various fragrant broths and delicacies. Over the remainder of the retreat, however, this phase of the ritual cycle is reduced to a bare minumum and greater emphasis is placed on the two main activities of walking (while concurrently reciting the dhāraṇī) and seated meditation. It is for this reason that Chih-i classifies the *fang-teng* repentance as a partly walking partly sitting samādhi.

All three sources for the *fang-teng* repentance give rather rigid specifications for the number of circumambulations and recitations to be performed by the meditator during each ritual cycle. In the *Fang-teng san-mei hsing-fa,* however, Chih-i indicates that the length and frequency of the periods of seated meditation and walking meditation have some degree of flexibility and can be adjusted to suit the practitioner's particular needs or inclinations of the moment. Walking, for example, can be used to counteract drowsiness, and sitting can be applied to ease exhaustion and collect the scattered mind, or to provide warmth (if the practice is being performed in a cold climate). "The practitioner," Chih-i explains in the chapter on "Adjusting [the Practice of] Circumambulation" in the *Fang-teng san-mei hsing-fa,* "must be well acquainted with [the principles of applying different procedures to] counteract [problematic states of mind] and should employ these [techniques] to his benefit."[60]

Regarding the dhāraṇī, or "spell," that lies at the heart of the *fang-teng* repentance, Chih-i says:

> [The practitioner] contemplates *(ssu-wei)* the *Mo-ho t'an ch'ih t'o-lo-ni.* In translation this means, "The Great Secret Essence That Checks Evil and Secures the Good." The "secret essence" is none other than the genuine emptiness of the Middle Way, [which is itself] the true character [of all phenomena].[61]

The Sanskrit term "dhāraṇī," derived from the root *dhā,* "to hold" or "to retain," carries the general meaning of something that enables one to retain, recollect, secure, hold, and so forth. Chih-i's description of dhāraṇī as "securing the good" and "checking evil" renders this basic idea and, in fact, itself seems to derive directly from a definition of the term given in the *Ta-chih-tu-lun,* which states:

> "Dhāraṇī" is a word from the western regions. In this region it translates as "able to secure" or else "able to check." As for being able to secure, it

gathers and secures various wholesome qualities and is able to hold and
secure them and prevent them from being scattered or lost. . . . As for
being able to abolish, when evil or unwholesome propensities arise, it is able
to check them and prevent them from manifesting.[62]

The term "dhāraṇī," however, also took on the more commonly
known meaning of a spell or incantation that secures a particular power
or spiritual essence. This meaning is probably the basis for Chih-i's additional rendering of "dhāraṇī" as "secret essence" *(mi-yao)*. In the case of
the dhāraṇī employed in the *fang-teng* repentance, the power or essence
with which it is identified is the liberating insight of the Middle Way
itself. Significantly, we find the same sort of association made for the
dhāraṇī of the *ch'ing Kuan-yin* repentance as well. Chih-i's disciple
Kuan-ting remarks in his commentary to the sūtra on which the *ch'ing
Kuan-yin* repentance is based:

> The essential substance [of this dhāraṇī] is none other than the essential sub-
> stance of the true discernment of the reality [of all phenomena]. It is neither
> empty nor existent. It checks the evil activities (karma) [that arise on the
> basis] of the two extremes [of dualistic thinking] and secures the genuine
> good of the Middle Way.[63]

Consequently, the evil that these dhāraṇī remove is not simply evil or
unwholesome qualities as they are conventionally understood, but the
misconceptions and evil propensities that comprise the very root of cyclic
existence itself.

In his explanation of how the *fang-teng* repentance removes sins,
Chih-i distinguishes three fundamental layers or types of obstruction
(san-chang). The first, and most fundamental, is known as the obstruction of vexation *(fan-nao chang)*, which refers to the three basic poisons
of lust, anger, and delusion that form the root of birth and death.[64] The
second is the obstruction of reciprocity or endowment *(pao chang)*,
which refers to obstructions posed by defects of mental and physical
endowment such as illness, impairment of the mind and senses, and so
forth. The third is known as the obstruction of deed or karma *(yeh
chang)*, which refers to obstructions that arise in response to deeds—
deeds in this case referring to those that contravene the Buddhist teachings and codes of morality and consequently cause the individual to
become further and further removed from the Path.

The dhāraṇī used in the *fang-teng* repentance is in theory capable of
removing all three types of obstructions. But the actual accomplishment
of this end is not something automatically guaranteed by simple recitation of the dhāraṇī. The key to the dhāraṇī's efficacy (and that of the
repentance as a whole) lies in the extent to which the practitioner's own

mind is in touch with the "secret essence"—the true insight of the Middle Way—that the dhāraṇī embodies. Therefore, Chih-i emphasizes the necessity of incorporating meditative discernment into all phases of the practice. In the manual from the *Kuo-ch'ing pai-lu,* he describes meditation amidst the activities of recitation, circumambulation, and sitting as follows:

> When [the practitioner] discerns the sound of the voice while he is reciting the spell, he finds that the sound cannot be apprehended. It is without any self-substance, like an echo in an empty valley. When he discerns his feet while circumambulating, he finds that the feet cannot be apprehended. They are [insubstantial] like a cloud or a reflected image and neither come nor go. When he sits to practice meditation, he contemplates the mind of the instant and sees that it does not arise from the faculty of mind alone, does not arise solely on the basis of external objects, does not arise from any combination of the two, and does not arise totally independent of them. . . . Ultimately there is no instant of thought to be found, and he cannot determine where mind arises. There is only the name "arising." The name is not inside, outside, or in between; therefore this name is no-name. Having discerned mind in this fashion, he finds that the same also holds true for all phenomena produced from the mind. . . . What is sin? What is blessing? By virtue of his powers of insight, he suddenly realizes enlightenment. His insight into emptiness is bright and thorough. Only when [a person himself] drinks does he know that the water is cool; so similarly [this practitioner] alone is totally clear [about this] while others do not see it. The merits of wisdom and samādhi that he has acquired are completely inexpressible. Once you have experienced awakening like this, you will know for yourself that your obstructions have been eliminated, and you will not [need to] wait for further discrimination [regarding this fact].[65]

The general procedure that Chih-i prescribes for meditating amidst the different ritual activities of walking, reciting, sitting, and so forth, is quite close in character to the sort of dialectic we find applied to the discernment of the eidetic image of the Buddha in the one-practice and *pratyutpanna* samādhis. Attention is shifted away from the professed religious value or significance of the ritual acts themselves and directed instead toward a critique of the fundamental mental processes by which they (together with all other phenomena) are conceived. Through dialectical exposure of the assumptions that undergird this process, mind and phenomena are revealed as inherently empty and identical with the single and unchanging Dharmadhātu. In the *Fang-teng san-mei hsing fa,* Chih-i remarks:

> Even though [at this point the meditator does not experience any sense of] discerner or discerned, nevertheless [this is not a blank state of mind, for he is clearly aware that] in their essential nature [the multitude of] phenomena

are perfectly uniform and are neither defiled nor pure. This in itself [constitutes their] true nature. This true nature [of all phenomena] is not defiled by birth and death in the twenty-five states of [deluded] existence, nor is it purified by the myriad [Buddhist] practices. As such, defiled and pure are a single continuum . . . like empty space. This is known as "ultimate purity." It is also referred to as "the true suchness that is the very nature of mind [itself]," or "the Dharmadhātu that is the nature of mind [itself]." It is the fundamental wellspring of all the Buddhas, the ultimate reality of all sentient beings.[66]

On the basis of the practitioner's relative skills of meditative discernment, Chih-i distinguishes two general approaches to the *fang-teng* repentance. The first is known as repentance [based solely on] phenomenal activities *(shih ch'an-hui)* and the second, as repentance that accords with Principle *(li ch'an-hui).*[67] Repentance based on phenomenal activities is directed toward the unskilled or novice practitioner—the practitioner who is unable to discern the emptiness of mind and phenomenal features effectively and thus has no other recourse but to fix his mind as well as he can on the phenomenal features of the activity at hand. Repentance that accords with Principle is conceived in terms of the more advanced meditator who is able to maintain a steady awareness of the Principle *(li)* that mind and any activities or distinctions it initiates are themselves none other than the "true emptiness of the Middle Way" or the all pervading Dharmadhātu.

Together these two approaches to the *fang-teng* repentance mark the upper and lower limits of an entire continuum of possibilities for meditative discernment. In a manner quite similar to the one-practice and *pratyutpanna* samādhis, they allow the meditator freedom to adjust the practice to suit his particular level of ability. As circumstances require, he may resort wholly to phenomenal features, or he may apply dialectical discernment to those features in an effort to elicit insight into their emptiness. He may also dispense with such expedients altogether and contemplate the Dharmadhātu directly. His approach is by no means limited to the extremes of either phenomena or Principle alone.

Theoretically speaking, repentance (and invocation of the dhāraṇī) performed solely on the basis of phenomenal activities can at best remove the two obstructions of endowment and deed; it cannot remove the root obstruction of vexation. This means that it may eliminate sins that obstruct the path and help to reinstate a practitioner to the Buddhist teachings and precepts, or it may change the individual's karmic fortune, cure illness, remove impairment of the senses or the physique, and so forth. Since this approach is weak in meditative discernment, however, it alone cannot liberate one from birth and death. Only when the *fang-teng* repentance is performed in accord with Principle does it become capable of uprooting the obstruction of vexation together with all the forms of deluded existence that evolve from it. Drawing upon a passage from the *Ta fang-teng t'o-lo-ni ching,* Chih-i explains that, when the approach of Principle reaches its culmination and the obstruction of vexation is removed, "[the practitioner] comes to perceive all the Buddhas of the Ten Directions, hear them preach Dharma, and attain the stage of non-retrogression [on the bodhisattva path]."[68]

B. Lotus Samādhi

Fa-hua san-mei, or the Lotus samādhi, takes two basic forms. The first is a twenty-one day practice based upon the twenty-eighth chapter of the *Lotus Sūtra,* "The Chapter on the Exhortations of the Bodhisattva Samantabhadra" *(P'u-hsien p'u-sa ch'üan-fa p'in),* and on a short scripture known as the *Kuan p'u-hsien p'u-sa hsing-fa ching* ("The Sūtra on the Practice of Visualizing the Bodhisattva Samantabhadra").[69] This meditation centers around intensive worship and recitation of the *Lotus Sūtra* and the performance of a formalized confession ceremony known as repentance of the six senses *(liu-ken ch'an-hui).* For this reason the practice is often referred to by the alternate name of Lotus repentance *(Fa-hua ch'an-fa).*

The second form of Lotus samādhi is called *an-lo hsing* ("the practice or course of ease and bliss"), after the title of the fourteenth chapter of the *Lotus Sūtra (An-lo hsing p'in),* from which it was originally derived.[70] This approach dispenses with the format of the twenty-one day practice and concentrates wholly on the cultivation of deep samādhi without the hindrance of fixed time limits or the interruption of ritual proceedings.

Chih-i's master, Hui-ssu, refers to these two approaches to Lotus samādhi as practice possessing distinguishing characteristics *(yu-hsiang hsing)* and practice devoid of distinguishing characteristics *(wu-hsiang hsing).* Hui-ssu explains their differences as follows:

> Practice devoid of characteristics is none other than the course of ease and bliss *(an-lo hsing).* While in the very midst of all phenomena, [the practitioner discerns that] mental characteristics are quiescent and extinguished and ultimately do not arise. Therefore it is called practice devoid of characteristics. He is constantly immersed in all the profound and wonderful dhyāna absorptions because in all activities—walking, standing, sitting, lying down, eating, or speaking—his mind is always settled [in samādhi].
> . . . The profound and wonderful dhyāna absorptions that are experienced in the course of ease and bliss are not at all like [the nine successive grades of mundane dhyāna taught in the Abhidharma]. [The practitioner] does not resort to the desire realm, nor dwell in the form or formless realms. When he courses in this kind of [wonderful] dhyāna, it is the universally pervading

practice of the bodhisattva. Because there is no mental fluctuation whatsoever, it is called practice devoid of characteristics.

   Further, there is the practice possessing characteristics, which is the
practice of reciting the *Lotus Sūtra* and striving diligently with the ordinary
scattered mind as is taught in "The Chapter on the Exhortations of Samantabhadra" [of the *Lotus Sūtra*]. A person undertaking this [approach] neither cultivates dhyāna nor strives to enter samādhi. Whether sitting, standing, or walking, he concentrates his whole attention on the words of the
Lotus Sūtra and perseveres zealously without lying down [to rest], as though
he were trying to put out a fire blazing on his head. This is called the practice possessing characteristics [that relies upon] the written text.[71]

   According to Chih-i's manual for the Lotus samādhi, *Fa-hua san-
mei ch'an-i*,[72] the twenty-one day Lotus repentance is to be performed
alone in a hall consisting of a central sanctuary with an adjoining room
for seated meditation. A high throne is set up in the sanctuary, on which
a single copy of the *Lotus Sūtra* is enshrined. No other images, relics, or
scriptures of any kind may be added. A canopy is placed over the altar,
and banners are hung about the room. Two sets of robes are prepared—a
new one to be worn only in the inner sanctum and an older set to be worn
elsewhere. The practitioner must change robes whenever he passes in or
out of the sanctuary.

   Prior to beginning the actual repentance, the meditator undergoes a
week of purification during which he strives to prepare himself spiritually (through worship, reflection, and repentance) and perfect the recitations and ritual procedures that will be used in the practice.

   At dawn on the day he is to enter the hall, the practitioner cleans and
sweeps the floor of the sanctuary, sprinkles it with perfumed water, and
scours it with perfumed mud. On the altar he arranges oil lamps and
flowers and burns rare incense powders. The repentance commences with
elaborate invocations and offerings to the Three Jewels and a host of
Buddhas and bodhisattvas. However, just as in the *fang-teng* repentance,
this rite is performed only in an abbreviated form over the rest of the
retreat.

   During the twenty-one days of the practice the meditator performs
the following set of rituals at each of the six intervals of the day and
night:

1. Offering of the Three Deeds of body, speech, and mind
2. Praising of the Three Jewels of Buddha, Dharma, and Sangha
3. Prostrations and veneration of various Buddhas
4. Recitation of the formula for repentance of the [sins of the] six
   sense faculties
5. Closing praises of the Three Jewels and recitation of the formula
   of the Three Refuges

The repentance of the six senses, the longest and most intricate part of the ceremony, consists of five phases that have subsequently come to be known in T'ien-t'ai tradition as the five penances or the fivefold repentance *(wu-hui):* (1) actually confessing or repenting for one's sins *(ch'an-hui);* (2) imploring the Buddhas to remain in the world and turn the wheel of the teaching *(ch'üan-ch'ing);* (3) sympathetically rejoicing in the merits of others *(sui-hsi);* (4) dedicating one's merits toward the enlightenment of all beings *(hui-hsiang);* and (5) setting forth the vow to save all beings *(fa-yüan).* [73]

The name, "repentance of the six senses," derives from the fact that the first phase of this five-part penance—the confession of sins—involves the ritual recitation of six long formulae for confessing all the sins that one has accumulated over one's past lives due to the misuse of the six sense faculties. Throughout the entire procedure, the meditator visualizes the bodhisattva Samantabhadra seated atop a six-tusked white elephant and surrounded by a vast retinue of attendants. "As though [Samantabhadra] were situated right before your very eyes," Chih-i tells us, "single-mindedly and with all your heart perform this repentance on behalf of all sentient beings. Generate a deep sense of shame and confess all the evils that you together with all other sentient beings have committed over innumerable kalpas down to the present day. Cut off the mentality that [desires to] continue to indulge in these sins and [vow] never again to commit any such evil from the present until the end of time." [74]

Over the remainder of the day and night the meditator alternates between slowly circumambulating the altar reciting the *Lotus Sūtra* and sitting in meditation. Chih-i describes the method of recitation as follows:

> You should make the sentences distinct and enunciate the sound [of the words] clearly. [Your recitation] should be neither too lethargic nor too hurried. Fix your attention on the text of the sūtra and do not stray from the passage at hand. Mistakes are not permissible. Next you should quiet your mind and [strive to] comprehend the nature of the voice as being like an echo in an empty valley. Although the sound itself cannot be apprehended, yet the mind [is able] to illumine the meaning of every line, and the words [themselves] are spoken clearly. Visualize this sound of Dharma as spreading throughout the Dharmadhātu, [spontaneously] making offerings to the Three Jewels, giving donations to sentient beings everywhere, and causing them all to enter the realm of the single reality of the Great Vehicle. [75]

No specific length of time or number of circumambulations is prescribed for reciting the sūtra and performing walking meditation. Likewise, no limits are set on sitting in meditation. The two activities may be adjusted to suit the needs of the individual. A practitioner who is not skilled in meditative discernment may find it more beneficial (or easier) to recite for longer periods, sitting briefly in meditation only to rest.[76] By contrast, one who finds seated meditation to be the most effective approach may sit for longer periods and take up recitation as an expedient for concentrating or stimulating the mind when he becomes anxious or exhausted. In either case, however, the meditator is not permitted to dispense with either practice entirely.

Chih-i describes the method of meditative discernment for seated meditation as follows:

> [The practitioner] seeks for the mind in all the various causes and conditions [that present themselves in any given instant of thought], but ultimately finds that it cannot be apprehended. Mind is insubstantial, like a dream or an illusion of magic. Being quiescent, it is like empty space. It is without name, without distinguishing characteristics, and it defies discrimination. At this point the practitioner does not even see the mind of birth and death; how could he yet [expect to] find a mind of nirvāṇa? As he does not [apprehend] any object of discernment or retain any notion of [a subjective] discerner, he does not grasp hold of anything, does not abandon anything, does not depend on anything, and does not adhere to anything. No mental activity whatsoever arises. His mind is ever quiescent, yet he does not dwell in stillness. Beyond the reach of words and speech, it is indescribable.[77]

In identifying the twenty-one-day Lotus repentance as a practice "possessing characteristics," Hui-ssu defines it as an approach that resorts primarily to phenomenal activities of recitation and ritual. He does not give us any clear indication whether or not it involves meditative discernment as well. Hui-ssu describes the approach that is "devoid of characteristics," in contrast, as primarily meditative in character. Although we cannot be sure of the exact nature of Hui-ssu's version of the twenty-one-day practice, Chih-i, in his *Fa-hua san-mei ch'an-i,* explicitly incorporates the approach that is "devoid of characteristics" into the phenomenal activities of the twenty-one-day Lotus repentance. Therefore we find this practice endowed with the same two basic approaches of Principle *(li)* and phenomenal activities *(shih)* as the *fang-teng* repentance. In the practice that resorts to the support of phenomenal activities, the meditator simply focuses his attention on the phenomenal features of the activity at hand (such as prostrating, reciting, repenting, and so forth) and does his best to prevent his mind from drifting away from that particular object. In the practice that resorts to Principle, he continues to perform the same prescribed ritual activities but concurrently elicits the insight of the fundamental emptiness of mind and characteristics and, "turning back to discern the wellspring of mind, he maintains this [insight] from moment to moment, thereby completing the entire twenty-one days without apprehending any mental characteristics.[78]

Consequently, the distinction between the twenty-one-day Lotus repentance and the more formless course of ease and bliss *(an-lo hsing)* seems to become less absolute than originally suggested by Hui-ssu. Nevertheless, an important functional difference remains between the two practices that continues to reflect Hui-ssu's basic model.[79] As Chih-i explains at the end of his *Fa-hua san-mei ch'an-i:*

> It should be known that taking the twenty-one days as the fixed period of practice and cultivating according to the six intervals of the day as described above is for the purpose of training bodhisattvas who have just begun to practice. If [such a person] has not yet been able to enter deep samādhi, then to start with he uses phenomenal methods to subdue and harmonize his mind and eliminate heavy sins that obstruct the Path. Through this his body and mind are purified and he obtains a taste of Dharma joy. If he wishes single-mindedly to cultivate constant quiescence so that he may enter profound samādhi, he must dispense with his previous practice and rely directly on the course of ease and bliss. He constantly delights in sitting in meditation and discerning the emptiness of all phenomena. He does not give rise to any internal or external transgressions, and, feeling great compassion, he sympathizes with [the plight of] all sentient beings. When in his mind he can maintain this without a moment's interruption, then this is cultivating samādhi.[80]

The twenty-one-day Lotus repentance and the featureless course of ease and bliss may be seen as constituting different phases of a single course of training. In a manner similar to the one-practice and *pratyut-panna* samādhis, they are capable of accommodating persons of a wide range of abilities and levels of experience and, through the skillful blend of a variety of expedients, can convey them all to the deepest reaches of the bodhisattva path. If, in undertaking the twenty-one-day Lotus repentance, the meditator is truly able to penetrate the practice, then, just as the "Exhortations of Samantabhadra" chapter of the *Lotus Sūtra* and the *Kuan p'u-hsien p'u-sa hsing fa ching* profess, the bodhisattva Samantabhadra and the Buddhas will appear and remove his obstructions. Chih-i says:

> Through these causes and conditions [of the practice], he will come into responsive accord with samādhi. Through the power of samādhi he will see Samantabhadra and all the Buddhas of the ten directions [appear before him], massage the crown of his head, and preach Dharma for him. In a single instant of thought all [the different] accesses to Dharma will manifest in their entirety [and will be understood as being] neither identical nor different and as having no obstruction between them.[81]

In his *An-lo hsing i* ("The Meaning of the Course of Ease and Bliss"), Hui-ssu describes a similar experience for the successful realization of the course of ease and bliss:

[On perceiving and] hearing the preaching of all the Buddhas [of the Ten Directions], the bodhisattva's mind becomes filled with great rapture, and he acquires vast spiritual powers. Sitting in the midst of empty space he perceives all the Buddhas of the Ten Directions and becomes endowed with the wisdom of all the Buddhas. In an instant of thought he totally knows the minds of all the Buddhas of the Ten Directions and also knows the mental activities of every sentient being. . . . In order to deliver sentient beings, his physical form and his insight [respond and take form] differently in accordance with the [varying] capacities [of beings]. In an instant of thought he manifests all [types of] forms. In a single moment of expounding Dharma, with one sound he can create infinite voices. At one and the same moment countless beings thereby come to attain the Way.[82]

4. CULTIVATING SAMĀDHI THROUGH NEITHER WALKING NOR SITTING

As has already been mentioned, neither walking nor sitting samādhi can be divided into two sorts of practices. The first includes any ritualized or structured form of samādhi or repentance practice (derived from the Buddhist scriptures) that does not immediately fall into one of the three categories of constantly walking; constantly sitting; and partly walking and partly sitting. In the *Mo-ho chih-kuan,* Chih-i describes the *ch'ing Kuan-yin* repentance under this heading and mentions two other practices by name: the repentance of the seven Buddhas and eight bodhisattvas *(ch'i-fo pa-p'u-sa ch'an-fa)* and the practice of cleaning latrines for eight hundred days [as taught by] the bodhisattva Ākāśagarbha *(hsü-k'ung-tsang pa-pai-jih t'u ts'e).*[83] The practice known as the *chin kuang-ming* repentance *(chin kuang-ming ch'an-fa),* a brief manual of which appears in the *Kuo-ch'ing pai-lu,* might also be included here.[84] The second form of practice described as neither walking nor sitting is the freeform approach to meditation known as *sui-tzu-i* ("cultivating samādhi wherever the mind is directed at the moment").

A. The Ch'ing Kuan-yin *Repentance*

The *ch'ing Kuan-yin* repentance derives its content as well as its name from the *Ch'ing Kuan-shih-yin hsiao-fu tu hai t'o-lo-ni ching* ("The Sūtra of the Dhāraṇī That Invokes the [Bodhisattva] Avalokiteśvara to Dissipate Poison and Harm"), which was translated into Chinese by the Indian Nan-t'i during the last years of the Eastern Chin Dynasty.[85]

The practice is to be undertaken in an isolated hall. The meditator rubs the floor of the sanctuary with perfumed mud and adorns the room with banners, canopies, lamps, and the usual equipment of offering. Atop an altar situated on the western side of the chamber, he enshrines the trinity of Amitābha Buddha and his two attendant bodhisattvas,

Avalokiteśvara (Kuan-yin) and Mahāsthāmaprāpta (Ta-shih-chih).[86] Finally, a mat or a low dais (to be used by the meditators) is arranged facing the altar, and new sets of robes are prepared for use in the sanctuary. As in the *fang-teng* and Lotus repentances, the participants must change clothes and purify themselves whenever they enter or leave the inner sanctuary.

Up to ten persons may take part in the practice, which must commence on one of the six monthly *uposatha* days—i.e., the eighth, fourteenth, fifteenth, twenty-third, twenty-ninth, and thirtieth days of the lunar month. The *Mo-ho chih-kuan* does not prescribe any fixed length for this practice, but the manual contained in the *Kuo-ch'ing pai-lu* specifies a period of either twenty-one or forty-nine days. The basic ritual cycle for the *ch'ing Kuan-yin* repentance proceeds as follows:

1. Invocation of and obeisance to the Three Jewels, the seven Buddhas of antiquity, the Buddha Amitābha and the two bodhisattvas Avalokiteśvara and Mahāsthāmaprāpta, the assembly of sages, and the three dhāraṇī of the sūtra.[87]
2. Offering of incense and flowers.
3. Seated meditation, which begins with counting the breath, followed by mindfulness of the Buddhas of the Ten Directions and the seven Buddhas of antiquity, "whose bodies of form and wondrous bodies of Reality have the appearance of empty space." Furthermore, the meditator generates thoughts of compassion for all sentient beings.
4. Invocation of the Three Jewels, invocation *(ch'eng-ming)* of the bodhisattva Avalokiteśvara's name, and the offering of a sprig of willow and purified water to the bodhisattva.[88]
5. Recitation of verses and the three dhāraṇī from the sūtra (i.e., the dhāraṇī for dispersing poison, the dhāraṇī for eradicating [evil] karma, and the dhāraṇī of six-syllable phrases).
6. Confession of sins, repentance, and making of vows.[89]
7. Obeisance to the Three Jewels.
8. Three or seven rounds of circumambulation, after which one person from among the group of practitioners ascends a high seat and recites the *Ch'ing Kuan-shih-yin hsiao-fu tu hai t'o-lo-ni ching* in its entirety. The others listen attentively.[90]

This ritual cycle is to be performed, in its entirety, over two of the six intervals that normally make up a single day and night of worship—morning and early evening. The remaining four intervals—noon, afternoon, midnight, and late night—are taken up with extended periods of meditation and the usual procedure for making obeisance to the Buddhas at these junctures of the day and night.

The key to successful cultivation of the *ch'ing Kuan-yin* repentance is meditative discernment. As in the *fang-teng* and Lotus repentances described earlier, the practitioner strives to discern the fundamental emptiness of mind and phenomena throughout all phases and activities of the ritual. Chih-i explains:

> In every instant of mental activity he brings the discernment of emptiness to completion. He must practice this diligently in order to bring [the fundamental discernment of Reality and the phenomenal activities of the repentance] into mutual response. The foundation of meditative insight must not be neglected.[91]

Each of the three dhāraṇī recited during the repentance has a different efficacy, depending on the type of obstruction it is designed to remove. The dhāraṇī for dispersing poison eliminates karma pertaining to the obstruction of endowment. The dhāraṇī for destroying karma removes karma pertaining to the obstruction of [evil] deeds. The dhāraṇī of six-syllable phrases eliminates the root propensities of the obstruction of vexation.[92] The dhāraṇī of six-syllable phrases may therefore be considered the most potent of the three. Through meditating and invoking this dhāraṇī, the practitioner himself invokes and identifies with the compassion and omniscient powers of salvation of the bodhisattva Avalokiteśvara. In a single instant he is able to remove not only his own obstructions but those of sentient beings throughout all realms of birth and death as well. To illustrate the miraculous function of this dhāraṇī, Chih-i resorts to two ways of interpreting the significance of the number six in the expression "dhāraṇī of six-syllable phrases."[93]

According to the first scheme, the number six is identified with the six realms of birth and death. Through recitation of the dhāraṇī, the meditator invokes six forms of Avalokiteśvara, each of which manifests in and removes the obstructions peculiar to one of these six realms:

1. Avalokiteśvara of Great Compassion appears in the hells.
2. Avalokiteśvara of Greindness appears in the realm of the *pretas* (hungry ghosts).
3. Avalokiteśvara Who Has the Fearlessness of a Lion appears in the animal realms.
4. Avalokiteśvara Who Is a Virile Hero Among Gods and Men appears in the human realm.
5. Avalokiteśvara of Great Radiance appears in the realm of the *asuras* (titans).
6. Avalokiteśvara Who [Appears as] Great Brahma, Profound and August, manifests in the heavens of the *devas*.

In his second illustration, Chih-i subdivides the six realms of existence into a total of twenty-five modes or states of existence. Borrowing

a scheme from the *Nirvāṇa Sūtra,* where the twenty-five states of existence are matched with the twenty-five kingly samādhis *(erh-shih-wu
wang san-mei),* he explains that, through recitation of the dhāraṇī of six-
syllable phrases, the twenty-five states of existence are instantaneously
transformed into the twenty-five kingly samādhis, thereby effecting total
omniscience over all modes of existence.[94]

In theory the *ch'ing Kuan-yin* repentance is accessible to followers
of all three vehicles of Buddhism—śrāvaka, pratyekabuddha, or bodhisattva—and is not the exclusive property of the Mahāyāna. If successfully pursued, it can convey any practitioner to his particular religious
goal. A follower of the path of the śrāvaka will realize the fruit of arhat.
One who inclines towards the path of the pratyekabuddha will become a
pratyekabuddha. And, if the individual intent upon the Mahāyāna, the
path of the bodhisattva, out of great compassion seeks the liberation of
all sentient beings,

> His body will appear like glass, and in its finest hair pores he will perceive
> [the vast realms of] the Buddhas. He will acquire *śūraṅgamasamādhi* and
> come to dwell in the stage of non-retrogression.[95]

B. Sui-tzu-i: *Cultivating [Samādhi] Wherever Mind is Directed*

The last of the six meditations that Chih-i includes in the four kinds
of samādhi is *sui-tzu-i* ("cultivating samādhi wherever mind is directed"). *Sui-tzu-i* does not have the clearly stated basis in scripture of
the other five practices. The name itself, to the best of our knowledge,
appears for the first time in Hui-ssu's manual for this practice, the *Sui-
tzu-i san-mei,* and may well have been coined by him. In the opening
pages of that text, the *Śūraṅgamasamādhi-sūtra (Shou-leng-yen san-mei
ching)* is mentioned, suggesting that Hui-ssu may have regarded it a
source of inspiration for this practice. Moreover, the literary format of
the *Sui-tzu-i san-mei* and certain themes repeated throughout each of its
six chapters indicate that it was modeled on a specific section of this
sūtra. However, no technique having either the name or form of *sui-tzu-i*
(as ited by Hui-ssu and Chih-i) is to be found in the *Śūraṅgamasamādhi-
sūtra,* and its connection with this sūtra remains tenuous.[96]

Chih-i inherited the practice of *sui-tzu-i* from his teacher, Hui-ssu,
as a comparison of their respective works on the subject clearly corro-
borates. However, in addition to the original designation of *sui-tzu-i,*
Chih-i adopts two new names for the practice: *chüeh-i san-mei* ("the
samādhi of maintaining awareness of mind [wherever mind happens to
be directed]") and *fei-hsing fei-tso* ("neither walking nor sitting").

In Chih-i's writings we hear no further mention of any connection
with the *Śūraṅgamasamādhi-sūtra.* When he takes up the question of a
scriptural source for *sui-tzu-i,* he identifies the practice as *chüeh-i san-*

mei and points to Kumārajīva's twenty-seven fascicle translation of the *Pañcaviṃsatisāhasrikā-prajñāpāramitā-sūtra* ("The Sūtra of the Perfection of Wisdom in Twenty-Five Thousand Lines"), where *chüeh-i san-mei* appears as the seventy-second member in the list of one hundrd eight great samādhis of the Mahāyāna.[97]

The term *"chüeh-i"* is a Chinese translation of the Sanskrit term *"bodhyaṅga,"* which has the long-established technical meaning of "limb or factor of enlightenment" (as in the well-known formula of seven limbs of enlightenment). The *Ta-chih-tu lun,* in its exegesis of the passage in which the name *"chüeh-i san-mei"* appears, interprets its meaning in full conformity with the term's classical usage. "Dwelling in this samādhi," the treatise tells us, "one is able to render all samādhis devoid of outflows and bring them into response with the seven limbs of enlightenment, just as one *chin* of the mineral *shih-han* can transform one thousand *chin* of copper into gold."[98]

Chih-i is clearly aware of the technical meaning of the expression *"chüeh-i,"* as well as the definition of *chüeh-i san-mei* that is given in the *Ta-chih-tu lun.* However, he chooses to downplay its importance and instead takes the liberty of giving the term the peculiar Chinese reading of "maintaining awareness of mind [wherever mind is directed]." This interpretation, as will become evident shortly, is a capsule description of the practice of *sui-tzu-i,* much like the term *sui-tzu-i* itself. His decision to adopt the name *"chüeh-i san-mei,"* therefore, seems to be no more than a thinly veiled attempt to locate a more credible scriptural basis for the practice.

The third name, *"fei-hsing fei-tso"* ("neither walking nor sitting") is simply the title of the fourth category of the four kinds of samādhi. In the *Mo-ho chih-kuan,* Chih-i explains the relationship and significance of these three designations as follows:

> [In the other practices of the four kinds of samādhi described] above, sitting and/or walking are always used. Here it is different from these previous cases. The name "neither walking nor sitting" is adopted simply to complete [the set of] four phrases. In actuality this practice [of *sui-tzu-i*] runs through both sitting and walking, as well as [any and] all activities. For this reason, Nan-yüeh [Hui-ssu] styled it *"sui-tzu-i."* As mental activity [or intent] arises one cultivates samādhi right on the spot. The *Ta-p'in ching (Pañcaviṃsati)* calls it *chüeh-i san-mei* ("the samādhi of maintaining awareness of mind wherever mind is directed"). Wherever one's mind happens to be directed, one always [strives] to remain thoroughly aware of it. Although there are three different names for this practice, in actuality they are one and the same thing.[99]

Sui-tzu-i, as this passage indicates, focuses primarily on the mind. It takes as its object the mental processes that initiate and undergird action as a whole and tends to disregard the specific character or conventional value of the activity itself. "Whenever mental factors arise," Kuan-ting relates in the *Kuan-hsin lun shu,* "[the practitioner] turns back to illumine and discern [mind that initiates the action] and does not perceive any evolution of thought. He does not see a source [from which mind springs] or a culmination [to which mind and action proceed], or any place from which it comes or to which it goes."[100] From such a perspective as this, any type of activity or circumstance—religious as well as mundane—can serve as an equally effective ground for meditative discernment. Therefore, in the case of *sui-tzu-i,* the appellation "neither walking nor sitting" is not entirely suitable, for it does not adequately express the nature of the practice. If it is to be described in terms of the purely physical categories of the four kinds of samādhi, it would more properly be described as availing itself of any and all activities.

In order formally to indicate the comprehensiveness of *sui-tzu-i,* Chih-i (in the *Mo-ho chih-kuan*) distinguishes four broad categories of action to which *sui-tzu-i* may be applied: (1) any explicit form of structured meditation or religious discipline derived from the sūtras, (2) wholesome activities (in a general sense), (3) unwholesome activities, and (4) activities that do ot have any particular moral valence.[101] Together these four categories comprehend all possible modes of action—actions that have a religious motive and design as well as those that are purely mundane, those that are sacred as well as those that are profane.

The actual method for discerning mind while in the midst of activity centers around what Chih-i calls the four phases or marks of mental activation *(ssu yün hsin hsiang):* (1) not-yet-thinking *(wei-nien),* (2) being about-to-think *(yü-nien),* (3) actually thinking *(cheng-nien* or *tang-nien),* and (4) having thought *(nien-i).* There are a limitless variety of activities with which an individual may become involved, as well as a multitude of ways to distinguish the different psychological and physical circumstances that attend each moment of activity. However, at the heart of each instant of activity lies this pattern of four phases repeating itself over and over in endless succession. In the face of constantly changing circumstances, this pattern provides the consistency necessary for meditation. In the *Chüeh-i san-mei hsing-fa* Chih-i says:

Someone asked, "The [different] features of mental activity are quite numerous. Why do you only select these four phases or characteristics of activation?" [Chih-i] replied, "These four phases of mental activation embrace all states of mind. If one becomes occupied with an evil object, [there are the phases of] not yet thinking of that evil object, being about to think of that evil object, actually thinking of that evil object, and having thought of that evil object. If one becomes occupied with a wholesome object, [there are the phases of] not yet thinking of that wholesome object, being about to think of that wholesome object, actually thinking about it, and having thought about it. If one becomes involved with the six sense objects, or with any of the vexations such as the three poisons, or even with the performance of any form of [external] activity such as walking, standing still, sitting, lying down, speaking, or eating, in all cases the four mental phases described earlier are always present. Moreover, even if one becomes occupied with any supramundane object, these four mental phases are always there. For this reason we only concern ourselves with these four types of mental characteristics. Taking them as the basis for discernment, there is nothing that is not comprehended by them."[102]

As such, the four phases of mental activation provide the kind of consistent basis necessary for maintaining meditative discernment throughout all types of activity. The first task that confronts the practitioner in the cultivation of *sui-tzu-i* is to familiarize himself with these four phases and develop his meditative concentration to the point where he can clearly distinguish their presence in each moment of mental activity. When this basic field of discernment has been stabilized, he focuses his attention on the first two phases of not-yet-thinking and being about-to-think, which mark the actual arising of thought and action. Maintaining constant awareness of the point when mental interest takes shape, the meditator subjects the two phases of not-yet-thinking and about-to-think to a rigorous analysis in terms of the four possible alternatives of logical proposition *(ssu-chü; catuṣkoti)*. In an effort to understand the basis on which the intent to act first arises, he investigates the mental condition that lies prior to it—the phase of not-yet-thinking. When the second phase of being about-to-think arises, he inquires:

1. Does this first phase of not-yet-thinking perish?
2. Does this phase of not-yet-thinking not perish?
3. Does not-yet-thinking both perish and not perish?
4. Does not-yet-thinking neither perish nor not perish?

Next he turns his attention to the arising of mental intent proper—the emergence of the second phase of mind-about-to-think. He asks:

1. Does the phase of being about-to-think arise?
2. Does the phase of being about-to-think not arise?
3. Does being about-to-think both arise and not arise?
4. Does being about-to-think neither arise nor not arise?[103]

Having exposed and systematically refuted all possible stances regarding the inception of action in the mind, the practitioner comes to grasp the baselessness of all aspects of mind and activity. The emptiness of the remaining two phases of actually thinking and having thought follows as a matter of course, requiring no additional effort. As Chih-i describes it in his *Chüeh-i san-mei hsing-fa:*

> It is due solely to common misconception and delusion that [a person] distinguishes the existence of [any one of the four logical propositions] from arising-and-perishing to neither arising-and-perishing nor not arising-and-perishing in these two phases of not-yet-thinking and being about-to-think or in any phenomena [produced from them]. They are false, insubstantial, and in all cases cannot be apprehended. They exist only as designations. Furthermore, as designations themselves are not to be located internally, externally, or in between and ultimately have no [genuine] self-existence, then [what he takes to be a designation] is actually no designation. If [the practitioner] does not apprehend [the existence of] the designations of the four logical possibilities of arising-and-perishing and so forth, he will not come up with [the notion of] no-designation either. Because he does not apprehend any designation, he does not [dwell in] the provisional. Because he does not posit [the idea of] no-designation, he does not [adhere to] emptiness. . . . Discerning [the phases of] not-yet-thinking and being about-to-think in this manner, if the practitioner does not seize upon any dualistic extremes, he will not adhere to dualistic extremes. [Not being mired in dualistic extremes, he will not] go on to generate all the various sorts of karma. Once he is free of dualistic extremes, free of karma that induces bondage, and free of obscurations, then the mind of true discernment will [appear] lucid and pure, like empty space. As a result of this, the genuine insight of the Middle Way will brilliantly open forth, and [the meditator] will come to illumine both of the two truths [of emptiness and provisional reality] together at the same time. Thought after instant of thought, his mind will be quiescent and extinguished, and he will effortlessly flow into the ocean of the great nirvāṇa. If he discerns the [two phases of] not-yet-thinking and being about-to-think in this way, then the other [mental phases of] actually thinking and having thought, as well as any and all mental phenomena [that arise on the basis of them], can categorically be known.[104]

Viewed in light of the other practices of the four kinds of samādhi, *sui-tzu-i* can be seen to have an immediate affinity with the more advanced techniques for discerning mind that are advocated in the one-practice, *pratyutpanna,* and Lotus samādhis and in the *fang-teng* and *ch'ing Kuan-yin* repentances. Although each of these practices has its own particular devotional orientation and ritual format, they share a common ground in their tendency to uphold meditation upon the emptiness of mind and phenomena as the most essential element in the practice. Rather than the devotional and ritual gestures themselves, it is the practitioner's ability (at any given moment) to elicit the emptiness of these activities, together with the mind that conceives them, that ultimately determines the efficacy of the practice. This in itself may well be the reason why Chih-i insists that *sui-tzu-i* does not obviate the highly structured and ritualistic practices "based on the sūtras" but in fact is "common to [the samādhis] both of walking and of sitting, as well as to any and all activities." In other words, *sui-tzu-i* constitutes that very discernment of mind that is central to the other meditations of the four kinds of samādhi.

However, there remains a key difference between *sui-tzu-i* and the other practices of the four kinds of samādhi. While in theory such meditations as the one-practice samādhi, *pratyutpanna* samādhi, and so forth might be considered to lie within the domain of *sui-tzu-i,* the fact that they actively promote the importance of ritual and devotional forms (whereas *sui-tzu-i* disregards them) sets *sui-tzu-i* apart as an independent and unique form of practice in its own right. In a concluding discussion of the four kinds of samādhi, Chih-i describes the relationship between *sui-tzu-i* and the other practices as follows:

> In terms of the respective methods they use, the practices of the four kinds of samādhi are distinct from one another; but in [their common use of] the discernment of Principle *(li-kuan)* they are the same. Basically the methods found in the other three types of practice [e.g., constantly walking, constantly sitting, partly walking and partly sitting] make liberal use of techniques for assisting the path. They also tend to pose certain obstructions to the path. As *sui-tzu-i* makes little use of [these kinds of] methods [for assisting the path], it produces this kind of phenomenon to a lesser degree. If you merely understand [a practice] in terms of the assistance to the path that these methods [are designed to] afford, then you will never be able to penetrate beyond the phenomenal features [of the practice]. If you understand the discernment of Principle, there will be no phenomenal feature that you will not penetrate. On the other hand, if you do not grasp the basic import of the discernment of Principle, then even the assistance to the path [to be gained by relying on] these phenomenal features will not be achieved. However, once you have grasped the basic idea behind the discernment of Principle, you will be able to realize the samādhis associated with these phenomenal features at will. If you cultivate the path by resorting primarily to these phenomenal practices, then, when you enter the sanctuary [for isolated retreat], you will be able to apply yourself effectively; but when you come out, you will not be able to [continue to do so]. In the case of *sui-tzu-i,* however, there is no interruption. Phenomenal methods belong to three [of the four kinds of samādhi]. Discernment of Principle is common to all four.[105]

What Chih is referring to when he uses the expression "phenomenal features" or "methods that assist the path" are those features of ritual format and religious cult that give the different meditations of the four kinds of samādhi their distinct character—such elements as mindfulness of Buddha and the rigorous discipline of ninety days of sitting or walking of the one-practice and *pratyutpanna* samādhis; recitation of the *Lotus Sūtra,* repentance of the six senses, and visualization of Samantabhadra of the Lotus samādhi; and the elaborate rituals of offering, repentance, and recitation of daranī of the *fang-teng* and *ch'ing Kuan-yin* repentances. Each practice has its particular justification, its scriptural and devotional orientation, its prescriptions, and its claims to efficacy. As expedient approaches to Dharma, they can help the practitioner to remove his obstructions and enter the path. However, the objects they venerate, the religious emotions they evoke, and the images and goals they set up are not in themselves ultimate, but are mere conventions designed for expedient purposes. In this sense they pose the danger of seducing the practitioner deeper into delusion and attachment by encouraging him to cling to these features as though they were real and constituted a legitimate end in their own right. As such, on certain levels they actually obstruct the Way.

The decisive factor as to whether these practices bring liberation or further bondage ultimately lies in the practitioner's ability to utilize them in a way that enables him to penetrate beyond their stated value and meaning—to critique them in light of the emptiness of both mind and phenomena, ultimately reconciling them with the Dharmadhātu. In other words, the success of these techniques finally comes down to the essential discernment of mind (or Principle) that is identified with *sui-tzu-i*.

This, of course, creates a certain amount of tension and ambiguity between *sui-tzu-i* and the other practices of the four kinds of samādhi. If the religious claims and ritual specifications of the one-practice samādhi, *pratyutpanna* samādhi, and so forth are simply expedients—expedients that have no real inherent value other than serving the end of the discernment of Principle—then why bother to adhere to them? Why take such a roundabout approach and run the risk of being waylaid by them when one can turn to *sui-tzu-i* directly?

Chih-i was well aware of the seductive appeal of *sui-tzu-i* and its potential, when misconstrued, for eclipsing other forms of Buddhist faith and practice. For this reason he consciously refrains from extolling the virtues of this approach in the *Mo-ho chih-kuan*. He embarks, instead, on a lengthy discourse in which he cautions against its abuse, citing examples of dhyāna masters who ruined both themselves and their disciples by seizing upon this practice as supreme and teaching it indiscriminately to others. "The six defiling obscurations [that we consider to be] the antithesis of the Way are themselves the very path of liberation," Chih-i tells us. "But, when individuals whose [spiritual] capacities are dull and obscurations heavy hear these words, they are immediately swamped. If one were to go on to give them specific encouragement to practice this teaching, their misunderstanding of its actual meaning would become even more severe."[106]

Sui-tzu-i, as such, was not a practice to be taught to just anyone; nor was it ever intended to devalue or wholly replace other forms of Buddhist discipline. Although in theory it disavowed employing expedients or any subsidiary religious goals or beliefs, its use was subject to certain strict practical conditions. Primarily this approach was reserved for those individuals who could measure up to it—persons whose inherent spiritual endowments were especially keen or who, through previous training, had reached an advanced stage of practice where they could effectively dispense with the coarser forms of discipline. Chih-i makes this point forcefully in both his *Chüeh-i san-mei hsing-fa* and his *Mo-ho chih-kuan* by carefully circumscribing the discernment of *sui-tzu-i* proper with various preliminary conditions that the meditator must fulfill before he is ready to devote himself to this more formless approach.

The *Chüeh-i san-mei hsing-fa* describes the following preparatory disciplines leading up to the full practice of *sui-tzu-i:*

1. Setting forth the vow
2. Taming the mind with the Six Perfections
3. Eliciting the mental phases
4. General Discernment of mind (while seated)
5. Specific discernment amidst all activivies[107]

The vow to save all sentient beings and strive for the perfect enlightenment of a Buddha is a standard pledge that generally marks the initial step on the Mahāyāna path. That Chih-i would make it the foundation of *sui-tzu-i* is not at all unusual. However, as it is applied within the specific context of this practice, the initial vow has a more immediate function than a generalized profession of commitment to the Mahāyāna faith. Through its lack of emphasis on devotional fervor and ascetic discipline, *sui-tzu-i* seems, on the surface, to be rather passive and easygoing. It does not pose the sort of challenge or summon the kind zeal that we find in the other more stringent practices of the four kinds of samādhi. In order to avoid slipping into a false or complacent understanding of the practice (a problem that can develop quite easily when all that one is required to do is attend to the activity at hand), the mediator must maintain a keen sense of self-integrity and constantly remind himself of the fundamental premises and aims of *sui-tzu-i*. "At this point," Chih-i tells us in the *Chüeh-i san-mei hsing-fa*, "[the practitioner's] mind is like diamond. With absolute decisivenesss he holds the conviction that all phenomena are utterly empty and quiescent; yet he does not abandon any of the counless sentient beings. On [their] behalf he undertakes the myriad activities."[108]

With his determination firmly established, the practitioner turns his attention to subduing the coarse emotional reactions and negative states of mind that obscure more forms of meditative insight. Chih-i summarizes these negative qualities by a formula known as the six coverings or obscurations: (1) craving and attachment, (2) inability to conform to the prohibitions of the precepts, (3) anger and hatred, (4) laziness and habitual lassitude, (5) scattered and confused mind, and (6) lack of awareness and stupidity. Each of these faults is eliminated by cultivating its counterpart among the Six Perfections: (1) giving, (2) discipline, (3) patience or endurance, (4) zeal, (5) meditative concentration, and (6) insight.[109] As he begins to loosen the hold of his habitual entanglements and comes into closer and closer conformity with the positive qualities described by the Six Perfections, the practitioner's mind and feelings undergo a substantial change in quality. The view of intrinsic emptiness, purity, and quiescence that was originally just a matter of faith begins to become an actuality. "If the practitioner understands that mind and the myriad phenomena are all nonexistent, neither arise nor perish, and are [actually] quiescent and pure, and he is able to apply the expedients of the Six Perfections skillfully to subdue his own deluded and false mind," Chih-i explains, "then, once the deluded mind comes to rest, samādhi will appear of its own accord."[110]

In the *Chüeh-i san-mei hsing-fa,* Chih-i summarizes the role of the Six Perfections as follows:

> If the practitioner does not cultivate these six qualities of mental purity that function as approaches to the Way, then his mind will not be fit for cultivating deep samādhi. Therefore, if you wish to practice the samādhi of maintaining awareness of mind wherever it is directed at the moment *(chüeh-i san-mei),* you must thoroughly verse yourself in the practice of the Six Perfections as described above. These Six Perfections embrace all expedients. Once you are able to apply them skillfully to subdue the six obscured and coarse states of mind and can render the mind supple and tame, only then will you be able to investigate and discern with a subtle mind and finally enter the door of true discernment. These are known as the preliminary expedients for cultivating truly deep samādhi.[111]

The Six Perfections constitute the general expedients for the practice of *sui-tzu-i,* but they alone are not sufficient to prepare the practitioner for directly taking up the discernment of mind amidst all activities. Even though he may well have removed his coarser obstructions, he must still strive to develop the meditative skills necessary to penetrate the "wellspring of mind." At first this is accomplished primarily through the practice of seated meditation, the practice that Chih-i refers to as the "general discernment."[112] The meditator begins by developing a firm grasp of the meditative object—the four phases of mental activation—and training himself to apply the discernment of the four alternatives of logical proposition. After he has achieved an initial degree of insight into the emptiness of mind and phenomena, he may then begin to apply this awareness to other activities. At first he continues to bolster this practice with a regular regimen of seated meditation; but "once he knows that mind and all forms of mental consciousness do not exist and cannot be apprehended, he should [extend this] and carefully discern both the internal and external aspects of mind according to whatever activity he finds himself involved in."[113] As his powers of meditation develop, he may reduce his dependence on sitting, until finally his discernment of mind flows continuously without interruption.

If the practice is successful, the meditator will attain *śūraṅgamasamādhi.* Hui-ssu, in his text of *Sui-tzu-i san-mei,* gives the following vivid description:

> By discerning that the mind that is not-yet-thinking or about-to-think is pure in its essential self-nature and free of any change or transformation, the practitioner acquires the unshakable samādhi, manifests omniscient wisdom, and comes to comprehend the totality of Buddha Dharma. [He realizes that] from the stage of first truly putting forth the thought [of enlightenment] up to the final attainment of the full fruit of Buddhahood, [mind] has never once undergone any change. Nor does [its spiritual development] proceed from one stage to another [through a series of successive stages of development]. In an instant of thought he knows the affairs of the three periods of time in their entirety. The mental dispositions of both sages and ordinary beings, lands, and world realms over numbers of aeons both far and near, the afflictions of sentient beings as well as differences in their respective spiritual capacities—in a flash he knows them all exhaustively. This is the samādhi of universal awareness. It is also termed the samādhi of illumination. Through the supernatural powers of this samādhi, he is able to manifest physical forms throughout the realms of the Ten Directions, responding differently according to each respective stimulus. All the while he remains perfectly lucid and experiences no sense of transformation [on his own part]. It is the same for the voice. At this point it is known as the power of *śūraṅgamasamādhi,* [the practice of] cultivating samādhi wherever mind is directed having been perfected to the full.[114]

III. Conclusions

This chapter has sought to provide a glimpse of early T'ien-t'ai religious training not simply as it was expressed in theory, but also as it was actually instituted among the followers of Chih-i and Hui-ssu. Central to this picture is the set group of practices identified as the four kinds of samādhi—one-practice samādhi, *pratyutpanna* samādhi, Lotus samādhi, *Sui-tzu-i, fang-teng* repentance, and *ch'ing Kuan-yin* repentance. Having described their contents, as well as the principles governing their application, what general statements can we make about the nature of T'ien-t'ai meditation as a whole?

First, we find that, despite their apparent diversity, the four kinds of samādhi are structured according to a common set of principles. At their core stands the fundamental discernment of the emptiness of mind and phenomena, the discernment of Principle *(li-kuan)*. This practice is responsible for their ultimate success, and to this practice all other practices, consequently, must aspire. However, to effectuate this discernment, the practitioner must meet certain practical conditions. The fulfillment of these conditions is enhanced by the rich variety of "techniques for assisting the path" that carefully circumscribe the core discernment of mind. The view of practice that Chih-i presents is a holistic one. The various disciplines—ranging from basic precepts, worship, ritual, diet, sleep, and so forth to more subtle forms of mental discipline and meditative discernment—are fundamentally inseparable. Effective practice on the part of the individual depends on his understanding of the principles that govern the meditative path as well as on his ability to assess and apply the measures appropriate to his situation.

Second, in his tendency to reduce and unify different meditative practices in terms of underlying principles that govern meditation as a whole, Chih-i does not thereby obviate the multiplicity of religious disciplines taught in the Buddhist scriptures or handed down within the tradition. On the contrary, his attitude is highly eclectic. A diversity of available meditative practices ensures that the individual practitioner may deal more adequately with the vicissitudes of his own practice. It also makes the benefits of Buddhist teaching and practice as a whole available to a much wider audience, allowing persons of different abilities and spiritual inclinations to choose the approach best suited to them. Practically speaking, we see this attitude at work in the extraordinary diversity of disciplines made available through the four kinds of samādhi themselves. Along more theoretical lines, Chih-i's views may be summarized by the following exchange cited from his concluding discussion of the four kinds of samādhi in *Mo-ho chih-kuan:*

> Someone asked: "In [applying] the true discernment of the Middle Way, through the very act of unifying one's mind, [both] the practice and its function are complete. What need is there to make so many [distinctions] such as the four kinds of samādhi, the application of [discernment] to good and evil [circumstances], or [meditating] amidst the twelve [different forms of] activity? When the water is muddy, the pearl is concealed. When the wind blows heavily, waves beat on the surface. What use could [such concerns] have for realizing lucidity and calm?" Chih-i replied: "[Your attitude] is analogous to a poor person who, upon obtaining a little advantage, considers it sufficient and doesn't care to do even better. If you use only one form of mental discernment, what happens when you are confronted with all sorts of [different] mental states? In such a case you will be at a loss in your own practice. If you [consider] trying to use [this one method] to train others, the spiritual endowments of others are all different from one another. One person's afflictions are in themselves infinite, how much more so [the afflictions of] many people! [Let us say] there is a master of medi-

cines who gathers all varieties of medicines to remove all the different types of illness. Then a person [comes along] who suffers from one particular illness and needs one particular medicine to cure that illness and thinks it strange that the doctor should carry so many other [useless] medicines [apart from the particular one he requires]. Your question is like this."[115]

Notes

1. The *Kuo-ch'ing pai-lu* (*T*#1934) was begun by Chih-i's disciple Chih-chi and taken over and completed by Kuan-ting when Chih-chi passed away. The work consists of miscellaneous pieces of correspondence, short treatises, inscriptions, and so forth, totaling 104 entries in all. They range in date from relatively early in Chih-i's career (around the time that he first entered Mt. T'ien-t'ai) to approximately a decade after his death. Chih-i's main temple on Mt. T'ien-t'ai (actually located on Fo-lung Peak) was known as Hsiu-ch'an ssu. Permission and funds for building a larger complex at the foot of the mountain were received just before his death, and construction was finally completed in 601. The new name, Kuo-ch'ing ssu, was not attached to the monastery until 605. The *Li chih-fa* is the first entry in the *Kuo-ch'ing pai-lu* (*T*46.793b–794a). For a discussion of its contents and date, see Satō Tetsuei, *Tendai daishi no kenkyū* (Kyoto: Hyakkein, 1961), pp. 20, 62; Ikeda Rozan, *Kokusei Hyakuroku no kenkyū* (Tokyo: Daizō shuppan, 1982), pp. 135–142; and Shioiri Ryōdō, "Shoki Tendaizan no kyōdanteki seikaku," Nihon Bukkyō Gakkai, ed., *Bukkyō kyōdan no shomondai* (Kyoto: Heirakuji shoten, 1974), pp. 133–149.

2. It is not clear at exactly what time these periods of meditation were held and for how long they lasted. Ikeda Rozan suggests that they might have been similar to the four periods of meditation of early evening, late night, mid morning, and late afternoon stipulated in Southern Sung and later Japanese Ch'an/Zen monastic codes (*Kokusei Hyakuroku no kenkyū*, p. 139). Martin Colcutt notes that such periods of meditation (in Zen monasteries) were one hour in length (see *Five Mountains: The Rinzai Zen Monastic Institution in Medieval Japan* [Cambridge: Harvard University Press, 1981], p. 143). Chang Sheng-yen, in a recent conversation, has suggested that two periods of meditation may have been held over the two watches of the early night, and the other two periods over the two watches of the late night (a total of approximately eight hours). The two watches of time around midnight (comprising four hours) were used for rest, as this particular part of the night was considered unsuitable for meditation. At the end of Hui-ssu's biography in the *Hsü kao-seng-chuan* (hereafter *HKSC*), Tao-hsüan remarks that in Hui-ssu's community the monks meditated at night and occupied their days primarily with study (*T*50.564a2). Curiously, the "Perfection of Dhyāna" chapter of the *Ta-chih-tu-lun* (one that had a major impact on the system of meditation espoused by Hui-ssu and Chih-i) contains a passage stating that meditation is to be practiced during the two intervals of early night and late night (*T*25.185c28–9). This may well have been an established Indian or Central Asian model later adopted by Hui-ssu and Chih-i.

3. Manuals of recitation for the ceremonies of obeisance held at the six intervals are included as the second and third entries in the *Kuo-ch'ing pai-lu:*

Ching-li-fa (*T*46.794a–795a) and *P'u-li-fa* (*T*46.795a–b). The former draws its material primarily from the *i-hsing, ch'u-yeh,* and *fen-pieh kung-teh* chapters of the *Shih-chu pi-p'o-sha lun* (*T*26.40c–49b). The later draws mainly upon the *Avataṁsaka Sūtra.*

4. *Kuo-ch'ing pai-lu* (hereafter abbreviated *KCPL*), *T*46.794a5.
5. *KCPL, T*46.794a13–17.
6. *KCPL, T*46.793c21.
7. *KCPL,* entry 7, *Shun Chih-shih-jen, T*46.798c21–799a7. Also see Ikeda, *Kokusei Hyakuroku no kenkyū,* p. 208, n. 13.
8. Colcutt, *Five Mountains,* pp. 236–243.
9. *KCPL, T*46.793c18–20.
10. Étienne Lamotte, *La Concentration de la Marche Héroique (Śūraṅgamasa-mādhi Sūtra)* (Brussels: Institut Belges des Hautes Études Chinoises, 1975), p. 31.
11. *Miao-fa lien-hua ching, T*9.3a3–4.
12. *Ta-chih-tu-lun* (hereafter *TCTL*), *T*#1509, location unclear.
13. *Mo-ho chih-kuan* (herafter *MHCK*), *T*46.11a22–28. The simile of raw milk and ghee originally comes from the *Shih-tzu-hu p'u-sa* chapter of the *Nirvāṇa Sūtra* (*T*12.530b– 532a). Raw milk signifies the human potential for enlightenment. Heating and stirring the raw milk (through practice) ulti-mately produces the finest essence of ghee, which represents the most pro-found realization.
14. Such references may be found in Chih-i's *MHCK* (*T*46.11a– 21b), *Fa-hua hsüan-i* (*T*33.806c), and *Ssu chiao i* (*T*46.761c) as well as Kuan-ting's *Ssu nien-ch'u* (*T*46.574b–c) and *Kuan-hsin lun shu* (hereafter *KHLS*) (*T*46.600b–603c).
15. Hui-ssu composed manuals for two of these practices—*Sui-tzu-i san-mei* (*ZZ*2/3/4) for the practice of *sui-tzu-i* and *Fa-hua ching an-lo hsing i* (*T*# 1926) for the Lotus samādhi. The text of *Sui-tzu-i san-mei,* in its opening lines, mentions mindfulness of Buddha samādhi *(nien-fo san-mei), pratyut-panna* samādhi, Lotus samādhi, and *sui-tzu-i* as especially effective tech-niques that should be practiced if one wishes "speedily to enter the stage of [the conviction of full] bodhisattvahood and acquire the wisdom of a Bud-dha" (*ZZ*2/3/4.344a). Along with the practices just mentioned, *fang-teng* and *ch'ing Kuan-yin* repentances appear in biographies of several of Hui-ssu's more prominent disciples.
16. *HKSC, T*50.563c19–21. Sekiguchi Shindai suggests that the mindfulness of Buddha samādhi *(nien-fo san-mei)* that appears here is an alternate name for one-practice samādhi *(i-hsing san-mei),* because mindfulness of Buddha is a major aspect of this practice (see *Tendai shikan no kenkyū* [Tokyo: Iwanami shoten, 1969], p, 150). More substantial proof of this can be found in Chih-i's *Shih ch'an po-lo-mi tz'u-ti fa-men,* where *nien-fo san-mei* is identified with the *Wen-shu-shih-li suo shuo po-jo po-lo-mi ching,* which is the very sūtra from which one-practice samādhi itself derives (*T*46.538b21–22).
17. *HKSC, T*50.557a29–b2.
18. This event is recorded in *Sui t'ien-t'ai chih-che ta-shih pieh chuan* (*T*50.191c22–192a1), in Kuan-ting's preface to the *MHCK* (*T*46.1b14–15), and in the biography of Chih-i in *HKSC* (*T*50.564b15–20).
19. These are the *Fa-hua san-mei ch'an-i* (*T*46.949b) and *Fang-teng san-mei hsing-fa* (*T*46.943a). For a more detailed discussion of these and other man-uals by Chih-i, see below.

20. Chih-i, *Shih ch'an po-lo-mi tz'u-ti fa-men, T#*1916. See especially
    *T*46.479b3–7, 481a11–14, 481b26–c12, 485c–487a, 499a12–15, etc.
21. Chih-i's teaching career can be divided into roughly two major periods. The
    years 568–575, when he was in Chin-ling, and 575–585, when he was on
    T'ien-t'ai, generally represent his early period. The remaining years of his
    life, i.e., from 585 until his death in 597, represent his later period. In cer-
    tain respects, the decade on Mt. T'ien-t'ai (575–585) can be seen as a tranisi-
    tional period. This scheme of periodization is based primarily on the thesis
    that Chih-i's thought underwent an important transformation while he was
    on Mt. T'ien-t'ai, the results of which are to be seen in new forms of doctri-
    nal expression that became characteristic of his later works. For a resumé
    and assessment of various references in Chih-i's works that have a bearing
    on the formation of the scheme of four kinds of samādhi, see Satō Tetsuei,
    "Tendai daishi ni okeru shishu zammai no keisei katei," *IBK,* vol. 12, no. 2
    (1964), pp. 51–65; Shioiri Ryōdō, "Shishu zammai ni atsukawareta Chigi
    sanbō," *IBK,* vol. 8, no. 2 (1960), p. 269; and Sekiguchi Shindai, *Tendai shi-
    kan no kenkyū,* pp. 148–154.
22. The three approaches to calming and discernment are: (1) the gradual and
    successive calming and discernment, (2) the sudden and complete calming
    and discernment, and (3) the unspecified calming and discernment. To-
    gether they outline (in theory) three basic approaches to meditative practice.
    The ten objects or spheres of discernment present a digest of the different
    conditions, phenomena, or states of mind that may confront the practi-
    tioner in the course of his practice (and therefore constitute a range of possi-
    ble fields of discernment). The ten modes of discernment outline basic prin-
    ciples governing the internal dynamics of meditative discernment itself and
    supply a rationale by which the meditator can logically assess and take
    appropriate measures to deal with whatever phenomena or situation may
    confront him at the moment. Along with the formula mentioned above, we
    should include the well-known twenty-five preliminary expedients *(erh-shih-
    wu fang-pien),* which outline certain preliminary physical and mental condi-
    tions that the meditator must fulfill before he can begin to take up medita-
    tion effectively. However, this scheme already appears fully developed in
    Chih-i's earliest works and must be distinguished from those that were
    devised late in his career.
23. *Sui t'ien-t'ai chih-che ta-shih pieh chuan, T*50.196b15–17.
24. The *Fang-teng san-mei hsing-fa* (*T#*1940) is the oldest among these three
    works, dating from the first years of Chih-i's sojourn in Chin-ling (568–
    575). *Fa-hua san-mei ch'an-i* (*T#*1941) is thought to date from slightly later,
    possibly from the period when Chih-i moved to T'ien-t'ai. *Chüeh-i san-mei
    hsing-fa* (otherwise listed in *Taishō daizōkyō* as *Shih Mo-ho po-jo po-lo-mi
    ching chüeh-i san-mei, T#*1922), although it is probably later than the *Fa-
    hua san-mei ch'an-i,* also seems to have been written at about the same time.
    For further discussion of the dating of these works, see Satō, *Tendai daishi
    no kenkyū,* pp. 149, 188, 219.
25. *KCPL, T*46.795b–8c. This second manual for *fang-teng* repentance is
    clearly later than the *Fang-teng san-mei hsing-fa* but earlier than the
    description of the practice that appears in *MHCK* or *KHLS.* The *chin
    kuang-ming* repentance is not mentioned in any of Chih-i's other works, nor
    is it generally listed among the four kinds of samādhi. The practice itself is
    based upon and focuses on the recitation of the *Suvarnaprabhāsottama-
    sūtra (Chin kuang-ming ching).*

26. Tao-hsüan, *Ta-t'ang nei-tien lu,* T55.284b. The possibility that the two fasci-
    cle *Ch'ing Kuan-yin hsing-fa* mentioned in this catalog is another, older
    manual for the *ch'ing Kuan-yin* repentance is corroborated by a reference to
    an "earlier *(chiu)* manual for repentance previously devised on the basis of
    this sūtra" in Kuan-ting's *Ch'ing Kuan-yin ching shu* (T39.973a). For fur-
    ther discussion of this question, see Satō, *Tendai daishi no kenkyū,* pp. 504–
    509. Tao-hsüan's catalog also attributes a "Method for the Practice of *Chin
    Kuang-ming*" *(Chin Kuang-ming hsing-fa)* to Kuan-ting.
27. Hui-ssu, *Sui-tzu-i san-mei,* ZZ2/3/4; *Fa-hua ching an-lo hsing i,* T46.697c.
    Both works most likely date from the period of Hui-ssu's stay on Mt. Ta-su
    (ca. 555–568). As the *An-lo hsing i* cites the *Sui-tzu-i san-mei,* it is clear that
    Sui-tzu-i san-mei is the earlier work.
28. A second lengthy description of the four kinds of samādhi nearly identical
    to that of the *MHCK* in both form and content, appears in Kuan-ting's
    KHLS. Satō Tetsuei has suggested that this version in the *KHLS* may have
    been taken, almost verbatim, from an earlier edition of the *MHCK* known
    by the title *Yüan-tun chih-kuan.* Therefore, even though the commentary is
    by Kuan-ting, the description of the four kinds of samādhi itself may be
    closer to Chih-i's original lecture, before it was once again edited (and in
    some instances further supplemented) by Kuan-ting some years later. See
    Satō, *Tendai daishi no kenkyū,* pp. 382–400.
29. *TCTL,* T25.401b20–25. The Chinese name for this samādhi is commonly
    read *i-hsing san-mei,* but in light of the original Sanskrit term *vyūha,* the
    second character should perhaps be read as *hang,* meaning "arrangement"
    or "array." Despite the original Sanskrit meaning, Chinese monks, since the
    time of its translation, seem to have interpreted the character to mean *hsing,*
    or "practice, activity" and not *hang.* The T'ang period T'ien-t'ai master
    Chan-jan carries this particular interpretation to its extreme by specifically
    defining the "practice" of one-practice samādhi solely in terms of the activ-
    ity of constant sitting, rather than accepting its more abstract meaning of
    meditating on oneself as being contemporaneous with the "single" Dhar-
    madhātu (*Chih-kuan fu-hsing chuan-hung-chüeh,* T46.182b3–6.)
30. T#232. This scripture was translated by the monk Mandrasena during the
    Liang period. The particular passage on which Chih-i bases his twofold
    description of the practice (T8.731a26–b8) is translated in the chapter in this
    volume by David Chappell.
       The notion of constant sitting, the ninety-day period of practice, and
    the details of (1) the expedient practice of repentance, (2) generating a sense
    of shame, (3) invoking the Buddha's name, and (4) entrusting him with
    one's fate are all taken from the *Wen-shu-shih-li wen ching* (T14.506c–
    507b), which was translated by the monk Sanghapala in 518. The *KHLS* de-
    scription of one-practice samādhi cites the *Wen-shu shuo ching* as a source
    for this practice, but does not mention the *Wen-shu wen ching.* Instead, the
    practices of reciting the Buddha's name and repenting are said to be com-
    mon to any number of Buddhist sūtras, no source being named in particular.
    This has led Satō Tetsuei to the conclusion that the material from the *Wen-
    shu wen ching* may not have appeared in the earlier editions of the *MHCK,*
    but was added later by Kuan-ting (*Tendai daishi no kenkyū,* pp. 383–385).
    For a thorough study of the basic scriptural sources for the description of
    one-practice samādhi in the *MHCK,* see Ōno Eijin, "Shishu zammai no
    tenkyo to sono kōsatsu," *Zen kenkyūsho kiyō,* nos. 6 & 7 (1976), p. 271.
31. *MHCK,* T46.11b21–23.

32. *MHCK, T*46.11c15–21.
33. *MHCK, T*46.11b11–12.
34. *MHCK, T*46.11b12–13.
35. *MHCK, T*46.11b13–16. Chih-i's description of how the voice is formed appears to derive originally from fascicle six of the *TCTL* (*T*25.103a–b). Both this treatise and Chan-jan's commentary to *MHCK* give the seven spots as the crown, teeth, lips, gums, tongue, throat, and chest (*Chih-kuan fu-hsing ch'uan-hung-chüeh, T*46.183a).
36. Kuan-ting, *KHLS, T*46.600c3–4.
37. *MHCK, T*46.11c2–12.
38. *Wen-shu wen ching, T*14.506c–507a.
39. *MHCK, T*46.11b19–20.
40. For an excellent summary discussion of this samādhi and its significance in various Mahāyāna treatises (especially the *TCTL*), see Étienne Lamotte, *Le Traité de la Grande Vertue de Sagesse,* vol. 5 (Louvain: Université de Louvain, 1980), pp. 2263–2272.
41. Two versions of this sūtra are attributed to Lokakṣema, one in three fascicles (*T*#417) and one in one fascicle (*T*#418). It has been suggested that the longer version may have been translated by Dharmarakṣa, but this seems untenable, as the two texts are too similar in content to have been translated by different people. Chih-i appears to have relied on the three fascicle version. Tokiwa Daijō has shown that the translation was not done by Lokakṣema alone but in collaboration with Chu Shuo-fo. Various early catalogs give the date as A.D. 179. See Tokiwa Daijō, *Yakukyō sōroku* (repr. ed., Tokyo: Kokusho kankyōkai, 1973), pp. 492–498, 523–524.
42. *T*#1521. The *Pi-p'o-sha lun* is not a line by line exegesis of the *Daśabhūmika-sūtra* but consists of root verses, composed on the basis of the sūtra, and prose commentary on the verses. The work (or translation) itself is incomplete, covering only the first two of the ten *bhūmi.* Takemura Shōhō has suggested that the prose commentary of the text may have been based on the recitation and interpretation of Buddhayeshe, whom Kumārajīva sought out in order to gain a clearer understanding of the meaning of the system of ten *bhūmi* and to facilitate his translation of the *Daśabhūmika-sūtra* itself. See Takemura Shōhō, *Jūjūbibasharon no kenkyū* (Kyoto: Hyakkaen, 1979), pp. 15–16, 21–22. Discussion of the *Pratyutpannasamādhi-sūtra* and its practice takes up the greater part of six chapters of the *Shih-chu pi-p'o-sha lun* (*T*26.68c7–88c18).
43. Lamotte, *Le Traité de la Grande Vertue de Sagesse,* vol. 5, pp. 2266–2272.
44. These stipulations are based on the third chapter of three fascicle version of the *Pratyutpannasamādhi-sūtra* and are known as the "four affairs" *(ssu shih).* See *T*13.906a–b.
45. The *Fang-teng san-mei hsing-fa* (*T*46.944a) calls for the same arrangement of personnel for the *fang-teng* repentance as is described here. Furthermore, these three type of supportive personnel are defined in the discussion of the "spiritual friend" *(shan-chih-shih)* that appears as one of the entries in the *MHCK*'s treatment of the twenty-five preliminary expedients. Here the companion in the practice *(t'ung-hsing)* is stated to be a necessary feature of the *pratyutpanna* samādhi and the *fang-teng* repentance, but not of *sui-tzu-i* or *an-lo hsing.* Presumably such a companion was not needed in these latter two practices because of their less restrictive and physically demanding nature. No mention is made of the other practices of the four kinds of samādhi.

46. *T*46.12b23-29.
47. Chih-i refers to this aspect of the practice as "mindfulness in accordance with or on the basis of distinguishing characteristics" *(ju hsiang nien)*. Paraphrasing the *Pan-chou san-mei ching* (*T*13.905c), he makes the interesting point that this form of discernment is akin to "a jewel being reflected in glass when it is placed in close proximity to it, or like a bhikṣu visualizing *(kuan)* bones [in the white bone meditation on impurity], where the white bones give off radiant light. [In the case of the glass and the gem] there is no appropriating [of the image of the gem on the part of the glass], and [in the case of the bones] the bones do not really exist. They are mentally produced" (*T*46.12c15-18).
48. *T*46.12c20-24. This passage is abstracted almost verbatim from a discussion in the *Pan-chou san-mei ching* (*T*13.906a1-11). Due to its ambiguities, I have consulted *KHLS* and a Sui period translation of the sūtra (*Ta fang-teng ta-chi-ching hsien-hu fen*, *T*13.877b-c) as well as *TCTL* (*T*25.276b8-13) (where this passage appears) to help clarify its meaning.
49. These three levels of mindfulness of Buddha are based on chapters nineteen *(nien-fo p'in)* through twenty-five *(chu nien-fo san-mei p'in)* of the *Shih-chu pi-p'o-sha lun* (*T*26.68-88).
50. *MHCK, T*46.13a5-6; *Shih-chu pi-p'o-sha lun, T*26.86a.
51. *MHCK, T*46.12a21-22; *Pan-chou san-mei ching, T*13.905c16-17.
52. *MHCK, T*46.12b22-23.
53. *MHCK, T*46.12a24-25.
54. *T*#1339. Tokiwa Daijō notes that the four-fascicle version of this sūtra, translated by Fa-chung, is also listed in various early catalogs as having the alternate title *Ta fang-teng t'an-ch'ih* (or *t'an-t'eh*) *t'o-lo-ni ching*. An earlier translation of a *Ta fang-teng t'o-lo-ni ching* in one fascicle dating from between 291 and 299 is mentioned in certain early catalogs as well, but whether it represented an earlier recension of the work is unknown (see *Yakukyō Sōroku,* pp. 900 and 728).
55. The three manuals of the *fang-teng* repentance are in close agreement regarding the general procedure of the practice. However, we will rely primarily on the *Fang-teng san-mei hsing-fa* (*T*46.943a), which offers the most detailed account of the preliminary ritual preparations.
56. The exact identity of these thirty-four divinities is not clear. However, the *KCPL* manual of *Fang-teng ch'an-fa* (*T*46.797b) mentions ten Buddhas (of the Ten Directions), the *"vaipulya* mother and father of the *Mo-ho t'an-ch'ih t'o-lo-ni,"* the ten Dharma princes, and the twelve dream kings—totaling thirty-four deities. Subhuti and other Arhats are also worshipped in the ceremony, but it is possible that they were not enshrined.
57. All three manuals agree that seven days is a minimum length for the repentance. The *Fang-teng san-mei hsing-fa,* on the basis of the *Fang-teng t'o-lo-ni ching* itself, lists, in addition to a period of seven days, periods of eighty-seven, ninety-seven, forty-seven, and sixty-seven days, based, according to the sūtra, on whether the practitioner was a full bhikṣu, a full bhikṣunī, a śrāmana, a śrāmanerikā, or a holder of the bodhisattva precepts, respectively. Each type of practitioner was also to use a different dhāraṇī. The later manuals, however, do not mention such distinctions at all and simply state that the length of the practice may be extended as one desires.
58. *Fang-teng ch'an-fa, T*46.797a28-29.
59. This basic procedure is found in all three manuals of *fang-teng* repentance.
60. *Fang-teng san-mei hsing-fa, T*46.945c8-16.

61. This discussion of the nature of the dhāraṇī appears only in *MHCK* (*T*46.13b22–23) and *KHLS* (*T*46.602b24–25).
62. *TCTL T*25.95c10–16. This same passage is cited (and the *TCTL* acknowledged as the source) in Chih-i's *Fa-chieh tz'u-ti ch'u men, T*46.692a.
63. Kuan-ting, *Ch'ing Kuan-yin ching shu, T*39.974a2–5.
64. Although the obstruction [of root] vexation *(fan-nao chang)* is none other than the *kleśāvarana,* in this context it should not be understood in its better known Yogācāra sense as being distinct from *jñeyāvarana.* Chih-i is well aware of these two terms (as other works show), but in this case we might properly understand *fan-nao chang* to cover both meanings. This discussion of the three obstructions appears in *MHCK* (*T*46.13c), *KHLS* (*T*46.602c), and *KCPL, Fang-teng ch'an-fa* (*T*46. 798b).
65. The *Fang-teng san-mei hsing-fa* also includes explicit instructions for walking meditation (*T*46.945c8–16) and seated meditation (*T*46.945c17–946a6). In the latter, the practitioner first calms and collects his mind through meditating on the breath and then discerns "the true suchness that is the nature of mind, the Dharmadhātu that is itself the nature of mind."
66. *Fang-teng san-mei hsing-fa, T*46.945a1–6.
67. *MHCK, T*46.13c22–23; *KHLS, T*46.602c. This scheme does not appear in the *KCPL, Fang-teng ch'an-fa.*
68. *MHCK, T*46.13c25–26; *KHLS, T*46.602c. This illustration of s repentance of the obstruction of vexation is taken from the sūtra itself.
69. Chih-i relies on Kumārajīva's translation of the *Lotus Sūtra (Miao-fa lien-hua ching; Saddharmapundarīka Sūtra), T*#261. The term *fa-hua san-mei,* "Lotus samādhi," appears only three times in the *Miao-fa lien-hua ching,* and in each case is merely included in a list along with various other samādhis. No description or definition of its content is given. Its content seems to have been supplied entirely by Hui-ssu and Chih-i. The principal passage in the "Exhortations of Samantabhadra" chapter of the *Lotus Sūtra,* on which this twenty-one day repentance is based, reads:

    If in the latter age, in the last five hundred years, in the midst of a muddied and evil age, a bhikṣu or a bhikṣuṇī, an upāsaka or an upāsikā, who keeps, reads and recites, and copies, wishes to cultivate and practice this Scripture of the Dharma Blossom, then for three weeks he must single-mindedly persevere with vigor. When he has fulfilled three weeks, I (Samantabhadra), mounted on my white elephant with six tusks, will together with incalculable bodhisattvas personally circumambulate him, appearing before that person in a body beheld with joy by all living beings, preaching Dharma to him, demonstrating to him, teaching him, benefitting and delighting him. I will also give him this dhāraṇī charm. (Leon Hurvitz, trans., *Scripture of the Lotus Blossom of the Fine Dharma* [New York: Columbia University Press, 1976], pp. 333–334.)

The *Kuan p'u-hsien p'u-sa hsing-fa ching* (*T*#277) was translated by the Kashmiran monk Dharmamitra during the first half of the fifth century. Given the close connection between this sūtra and the "Exhortations of Samantabhadra" chapter of the *Lotus Sūtra,* these two sūtras, together with the *Wu-liang i ching,* came to be regarded as a single set and were often referred to as the Three Great Scriptures of the Lotus."

70. *Miao-fa lien-hua ching, T*9.37a–39c. Hui-ssu bases this practice of the course of ease and bliss *(an-lo hsing)* on *T*9.37a12–20, especially the lines that read:

If, further, he performs no act with respect to the dharmas, but views the dharmas in keeping with their true marks; if, also, he performs no act and commits no discrimmination, this is called "the place where the bodhisattva-mahāsattva acts" (Hurvitz, *Lotus*, p. 208).

71. Hui-ssu, *Fa-hua ching an-lo hsing i,* T46.700a19–29.
72. Both the *MHCK* and *KHLS* accounts of Lotus samādhi mention the existence of the manual *Fa-hua san-mei ch'an-i* and cite it as the primary guide for the practice. As this manual, even late in Chih-i's career, continued to be regarded as so important, and as it also offers a much more complete account of the practice than either of these two later sources, we will rely on it primarily in the course of the discussion that follows.
73. The same set of five penances is used in the *P'u ching li* (*KCPL,* T46.794c23–a12)—one of the main procedures used during the worship services conducted in the community meditation hall at the six intervals of the day. Curiously, however, the fifth element in the set described in the *Fa-hua san-mei ch'an-i*—the setting forth of vows—involves not the vow to save all living beings, but the vow "to be reborn in the [Pure Land] of ease and nourishment, be received by Amitābha face to face, meet the sagely retinue, and cultivate the ten stages [of the bodhisattva path]" (T46.953b23–24).
74. *Fa-hua san-mei ch'an-i,* T46.952b1–2. The passages to be recited for the confession of the sins of the six senses, and the instructions for the visualization that accompanies it, are drawn from the text of the *Kuan p'u-hsien p'u-sa hsing-fa ching* (T#277). The accounts of Lotus samādhi in the *MHCK* and *KHLS,* apart from giving an outline of the ten sections of the *Fa-hua san-mei ch'an-i,* say little about the actual procedure of the practice itself. At one point they go into an extended analysis of the meaning of the iconographical symbolism of Samantabhadra, but this would seem to have no active bearing on the meditation itself, apart from facilitating the practitioner's sensitivity to the spiritual significance of the imagery. Chan-jan, in his commentary to this section of the *MHCK,* suggests that Chih-i chose to expand there on the meaning of this visualization simply to augment and further explain the sparse description of it that appears in the *Fa-hua san-mei ch'an-i* (*Chih-kuan fu-hsing ch'uan hung-chüeh,* T46.192b).
75. *Fa-hua san-mei ch'an-i,* T46.954a3–8.
76. For those who prefer recitation, or who are unskilled in meditative discernment, recitation of the sūtra may be continued while sitting in meditation. However, at the very least the four normal watches of seated meditation (presumably those normally performed in the community hall) must be kept (see T46.953c22–25).
77. *Fa-hua san-mei ch'an-i,* T46.954a19–25.
78. *Fa-hua san-mei ch'an-i,* T46.950a2–15.
79. Satō Tetsuei regards Chih-i's version of Lotus samādhi, as described in *Fa-hua san-mei ch'an-i,* as considerably different from that of Hui-ssu. His primary criterion for this assertion is that Chih-i integrated the two approaches of "possessing characteristics" and "devoid of characteristics" into one and the same practice, whereas Hui-ssu kept them totally separate. This conclusion is suspect. Satō fails to notice that Chih-i quite clearly preserves Hui-ssu's distinction between the ritualistic twenty-one day repentance and the extended (and unstructured) course of ease and bliss. Therefore, the only real difference between Chih-i's version of Lotus samādhi and that of Hui-ssu is that Chih-i explicitly finds a place for the "featureless" approach (of

Principle) in the twenty-one day repentance (as well as *an-lo hsing*), whereas Hui-ssu describes the twenty-one day repentance solely as a "phenomenal" practice of concentrating on recitation of the text. Nevertheless, Hui-ssu's description of this twenty-one day practice is quite brief (and not the main focus of the work) and does not truly justify the rather strong conclusions that Satō draws from it. See *Tendai daishi no kenkyū*, pp. 135–136.

80. *Fa-hua san-mei ch'an-i*, T46.955b24–c1.
81. *Fa-hua san-mei ch'an-i*, T954b6–8.
82. Hui-ssu, *Fa-hua ching an-lo hsing i*, T46.702b8–15.
83. In his commentary Chan-jan gives the *Ch'i fo pa p'u-sa shen chou ching* ("Sūtra of the Divine Spells of the Seven Buddhas [of Antiquity] and the Eight Bodhisattvas," T#1332), translated during the Chin dynasty, as the possible source for the repentance of the seven Buddhas and eight bodhisattvas. He traces the discipline of eight hundred days of cleaning latrines [as taught by] the bodhisattva Ākāśagarbha to the *Kuan hsü-k'ung-tsang p'u-sa ching* ("Sūtra on the Visualization of the Bodhisattva Ākāśagarbha," T#409), which was translated the first half of the fifth century by the Khashimiran monk Dharmamitra. According to Chan-jan (who bases his account on this scripture), this latter practice involves secretly cleaning the latrines, meditating on the bodhisattva Ākāśagarbha, and repenting before the thirty-five Buddhas of confession every day for a period of eight hundred days. See *Chih-kuan fu-hsing ch'uan-hung-chüeh*, T46.196c8–197a19.
84. *KCPL, Chin Kuang-ming ch'an-fa*, T46.796a. The practice commences on one of the six monthly *uposatha* days. Over the course of the repentence (which lasts for one week) the participants bathe and purify themselves daily, as in the other repentances. The main worship and confessional ceremony comes just before the noon meal. The remainder of the day (and night) is occupied with reciting the *Suvarnaprabhāsa-sūtra*, meditating, and performing the invocations standardly used at the other five intervals of worship.
85. *Ch'ing kuan-shih-yin hsiao-fu tu-hai t'o-lo-ni ching*, T20.124.
86. *MHCK* states that this trinity of figures is to be enshrined on the western side of the hall (presumably because this is the direction of the Pure Land of *Sukhāvati*, where they reside). The manual of *Ch'ing Kuan-yin ch'an-fa* in the *KCPL*, however, stipulates that an image of Buddha (Śākyamuni?) is to be placed facing south, and a lone image of Avalokiteśvara is arranged (on the western side of the hall) facing east (T46.795b18–19).
87. The seven Buddhas are Vipaśyin, Śikhin, Viśvabhuj, Krakucchanda, Kanakamuni, Kāśyapa, and Śākyamuni.
88. The offering of a willow sprig and water derives from the sūtra itself: "The people of Vaiśāli thereupon prepared willow sprigs and purified water and presented them to the bodhisattva Avalokiteśvara" (T20.124c). Kuan-ting, in his commentary to this passage in the *Ch'ing Kuan-yin ching shu*, notes: "This is to encourage the acquiring of the two causes that act as the primary instigation [for enlightenment]. The willow sprig sweeps away, thereby symbolizing insight. Purified water is clear and cool, thereby symbolizing [the stability of the absorption of] samādhi" (T39.973a). Chan-jan notes in his commentary to this section of the *MHCK*: "As for setting out [the offering of] the willow sprig and so forth, because Kuan-yin holds a willow in her left hand and a vase for bathing *(kuṇḍikā?)* in her right, therefore the devotee must prepare these two items" (T46.193c). The term *yang-chih*, literally meaning "willow sprig," was used by the Chinese to translate the Sanskrit

term *dantakāṣṭa,* which designates a short piece of soft branch from a
banyan tree that was chewed by Indians to clean the teeth. Although the
original meaning of the vase and branch held by Avalokiteśvara would seem
to suggest the idea of purification (through bathing and cleansing the teeth),
the particular nuances that such images suggested to the Chinese seem to
have eventually obscured the original connotations.

89. *MHCK* adds the activity of ritual ablutions or bathing here (*T*46.15a6).
90. *MHCK* and the *Ch'ing Kuan-yin ch'an-fa* of *KCPL* both call for ritual reci-
     tation of the sūtra. The outline of the contents of an older text for the *ch'ing*
     Kuan-yin repentance that Kuan-ting lists in his *Ch'ing Kuan-yin ching shu,*
     however, does not mention recitation, but instead calls for seated medita-
     tion. Kuan-ting gives the entire ritual format as follows: "Formerly [Chih-i]
     devised a procedure for repentance based on the text of this scripture and
     stipulated ten points that were consistently to be put into practice. Eight [of
     these] points come from the text of the sūtra. [The ten] are: (1) preparations
     (self-inspection?), (2) adorning the sanctuary, (3) performing obeisance,
     burning incense, and scattering flowers, (4) fixing one's attention (in mind-
     fulness), (5) preparing the willow and water, (6) inviting the Three Jewels,
     (7) reciting the dhāraṇī, (8) exposing and confessing (sins), (9) doing pros-
     trations (and making obeisance), (10) sitting in meditation. These ten items
     are explained as containing both [the approaches of] Principle and phenom-
     enal activity" (*T*39.973a19–23).
91. *MHCK, T*46.15a24–25.
92. Kuan-ting, in his *Ch'ing Kuan-yin ching shu,* reverses the arrangement of
     the three dhāraṇī and the three obstructions, so that the dhāraṇī of six-sylla-
     ble phrases is matched with the obstruction of endowment, and the dhāraṇī
     for dispelling poison with the obstruction of vexation (*T*39.973a).
93. The *Ch'ing Kuan-yin ching* offers no clear explanation of why the third
     dhāraṇī is called dhāraṇī of six-syllable phrases. Chih-i, Kuan-ting, and
     Chan-jan offer various possible interpretations—the number six can refer to
     six syllables or phrases, or it can derive from a multiple of the Three Jewels
     —but the explanation they tend to favor is to equate the number six with the
     six realms of existence or the six senses. This is predominantly why Kuan-
     ting matches the dhāraṇī of six-syllable phrases with the obstruction of
     endowment—endowmnent being the six sense faculties and the six realms of
     existence into which one is born. Recitation of this dhāraṇī brings realiza-
     tion of the intrinsic purity of the six senses and realization of the interfusion
     of all realms of existence and their ultimate participation in the truth of the
     Middle.
94. *Ta-pan nieh-p'an ching, T*12.448b–c. A detailed discussion of the relation-
     ship of these twenty-five samādhis to the twenty-five states of existence (and
     their place in the course of bodhisattva training) appears in Chih-i's *Ssu-
     chiao i* (*T*46.755c29–758b28).
95. *MHCK, T*46.15b. These experiences are described in the sūtra as two among
     the various possible benefits that the practitioner can obtain from this prac-
     tice (*T*20.35c, 38a).
96. Hui-ssu's *Sui-tzu-i san-mei* (*ZZ*2/3/4.344a) is divided into six sections
     according to the six activities of walking, standing still, sitting, lying down,
     eating, and speaking. Each section gives explicit instructions (replete with
     various expedients) for cultivating samādhi, realizing emptiness, and per-
     fecting the Six Perfections at any moment one is engaged in these six activi-
     ties. At the beginning of the first section, which is concerned with cultivat-
     ing samādhi while walking, the following exchange occurs: "[Hui-ssu

remarks], 'When engaged in the deportment of walking, lifting his foot or lowering his foot thought after instant of thought, the bodhisattva is fully endowed with the Six Perfections.' [Someone] asked, 'What scripture does this idea come from?' [Hui-ssu] replied, 'It comes from the *Śūraṅgama-sūtra*' " (*ZZ*2/3/4.344d14–16). Hui-ssu's description of "lifting the foot and lowering the foot, thought after thought . . . being fully endowed with the Six Perfections" is taken directly from the *Śūraṅgamasamādhi-sūtra*. In that sūtra this line introduces a lengthy discussion wherein the Buddha explains to Dṛḍhamati how the bodhisattva who has realized *śūraṅgamasamādhi* is able to perfect each of the Six Perfections at any given instant and amidst any activity (*T*15.633b–634a). Hui-ssu appears to have modeled the basic structure of his text—fulfilling the Six Perfections in the midst of each of the six activities of walking, standing, and so forth—on this section of the *Śūraṅgama-sūtra*. However, yet another possible source for this scheme could be the chapter on "The Myriad Practices [Contained Within] One Mind" *(i-hsin wan hsing p'in)* of the *TCTL* (*T*25.670b), wherein very similar descriptions of perfecting the Six Perfections in an instant of activity can be found. Aside from the brief exchange in the opening lines of the section on cultivating samādhi while walking, the *Śūraṅgama-sūtra* is not mentioned anywhere else in Hui-ssu's text of *Sui-tzu-i san-mei*. Although the notion of eliciting the fundamental emptiness of all phenomena in any given instant of activity (and thereby realizing a kind of spiritual omniscience over all aspects of existence) is certainly a major theme of the *Śūraṅgama-sūtra*, no practice having either the name or the particular character of *sui-tzu-i* appears there. In fact, the sūtra itself is not so much concerned with describing the practice of *śūraṅgamasamādhi* as it is with describing the extraordinary spiritual powers and omniscience of one who has already obtained it. Hui-ssu himself seems to be aware of this fact. He sees a definite relationship between *sui-tzu-i* and *śūraṅgama-samādhi*, but he is careful to make the distinction that *sui-tzu-i* is the practice and *śūraṅgamasamādhi* is the result. "If this samādhi [of *sui-tzu-i*] is successful," Hui-ssu tells us, "then one will attain *śūraṅgamasamādhi*" (*ZZ*2/3/4.344d17–18). Therefore, although Hui-ssu may have looked to the *Śūraṅgama-sūtra* to lend an air of legitimacy to *sui-tzu-i*, it is difficult to claim that the practice was explicitly derived from this sūtra.

97. *Mo-ho po-jo po-lo-mi ching*, *T*8.251b.
98. *TCTL*, *T*25.401a25–26.
99. *MHCK*, *T*46.14b26–c1; *KHLS*, *T*46.603b22–26.
100. *KHLS*, *T*46.603b28–9.
101. The account of *sui-tzu-i* that appears in *KHLS* is brief, consisting of little more than the rudimentary definition of the terms *"sui-tzu-i," "chüeh-i san-mei,"* and *"fei-hsing fei-tso"* cited above. The scheme of classifying activities into wholesome, unwholesome, and neutral, as well as the lengthy discussions concerning meditation amidst such activities that appears in the *MHCK*, is not to be found in *KHLS* at all. Satō Tetsuei speculates that this material did not exist in the earlier recension of *MHCK* but was actually added by Kuan-ting when he edited the final version of *MHCK*. Given the close parallels between the meditations outlined here and those found in the manual of *Chüeh san-mei hsing-fa* (many passages being identical), it appears that the author relied heavily on this manual. See Satō, *Tendai daishi no kenkyū*, pp. 173–189, 393.
102. *Chüeh-i san-mei hsing-fa*, *T*46.623a12–14. The *Chüeh-i san-mei hsing-fa*

subsumes and classifies all the possible types of activity into a rubric of six (outer) activities—(1) walking, (2) standing, (3) sitting, (4) lying down, (5) miscellaneous functions, (6) speaking—and six (internal) activities of sense perception—(1) seeing, (2) hearing, (3) smelling, (4) tasting, (5) touching, (6) thinking. The text describes in detail the procedure for meditating while involved in each of these activities. The *MHCK* version of *sui-tzu-i* adopts this same twelvefold scheme, but adds the broader classification of activities into wholesome, unwholesome, and neutral. Although we do in fact find meditation amidst wholesome, unwholesome, and neutral dharmas mentioned in the passage from the *Chüeh-i san-mei hsing-fa* cited here, these three features are not given formal attention anywhere else in the text.

103. *Chüeh-i san-mei hsing-fa, T*46.623b25–24b11. The method of distinguishing the two phases of not-yet-thinking and being about-to-think, as well as the discernment of them according to the four alternatives, is based on the meditation for the activity of walking prescribed by Hui-ssu in his *Sui-tzu-i san-mei, ZZ*2/3/4.345a3–d4.

104. *Chüeh-i san-mei hsing-fa, T*46.624b13–28.

105. *MHCK, T*46.18c10–18.

106. *MHCK, T*46.18c19–20.

107. The treatment of various expedients in the *Chüeh-i san-mei hsing-fa* occurs in the following sections. The making of initial vows and the cultivation of the Six Perfections are treated in chapter three, "Expedient Practices" *(fang-pien hsing)*. Chapter four, "Clarifying the Distinguishing Characteristics of Mind" *(ming hsin hsiang)*, describes the features of the basic meditative object—the four phases. Chapter five, "Entering the Gate of True Discernment" *(ju cheng kuan men)*, describes the general procedure for discerning the four phases in terms of the four logical alternatives. It is here that Chih-i outlines the approach of first developing mental concentration (and an initial insight into emptiness of mind) through sitting, and then extending this to all other activities. Illuminating the mind through the practice of seated meditation is referred to as the general discernment *(tsung kuan)*. Carrying this insight to miscellaneous activities (i.e. the six external activities and the six internal activities of sense perception) is called the specific or distinct discernment *(pieh kuan)*.

108. *Chüeh-i san-mei hsing-fa, T*46.623b29–c3.

109. Chih-i's scheme of matching the six coverings *(liu pi)* with the Six Perfections appears to derive from the *TCTL, T*25.303c–304c.

110. *Chüeh-i san-mei hsing-fa, T*46.622c4–6.

111. *Chüeh-i san-mei hsing-fa, T*46.622c28–623a4.

112. Formal seated meditation was regarded as the posture most conducive to calming the mind and entering the Way. Chih-i makes this claim in his *Chüeh-i san-mei hsing-fa (T*46.624c5–9); Hui-ssu makes this claim in his *Sui-tzu-i san-mei (ZZ*2/3/4.347b).

113. *Chüeh-i san-mei hsing-fa, T*46.624c15–17.

114. Hui-ssu, *Sui-tzu-i san-mei, ZZ*2/3/4.346c. The final chapter of Chih-i's *Chüeh-i san-mei hsing-fa,* "Signs of Successful Realization" *(cheng hsiang),* is devoted entirely to describing the various stages of spirtual developmentat may come as a result of this practice. Chih-i's ideas in this regard conform fully to the description offered by Hui-ssu but are far more elaborate and technical in nature. For the sake of brevity and impact we have chosen to cite Hui-ssu's account.

115. *MHCK, T*46.19b27–c7.

The Concept of One-Practice
Samādhi in Early Ch'an

Bernard Faure

The term *"i-hsing san-mei,"* rendered throughout this volume as "one-practice samādhi," played an important role in the emergence of a particular early Ch'an discourse. The translation already embodies an interpretation of the meaning that the term had for the Chinese Buddhist meditation tradition. But what did an eighth-century Ch'an practitioner really understand by *i-hsing san-mei?* We have only textual evidence, and relatively little of that. On the basis of extant Ch'an materials, it seems clear that one-practice samādhi, even if it had been mediated through the T'ien-t'ai tradition, was not simply one of the four kinds of samādhi elaborated by Chih-i (538–597) in his masterwork, *Mo-ho chih-kuan* ("[Treatise on] the Great Calming and Discernment"). Rather, it appears as a kind of reaction against the T'ien-t'ai doctrine and its impressive, almost overwhelming, arsenal of meditation techniques or *upāyas.*

The first part of this chapter will show how this concept, in evolving from its canonical sources to its Sui and T'ang interpretations, acquired several different meanings within the T'ien-t'ai, Pure Land, and Ch'an traditions. Although each of these traditions employed this same term, the discursive contexts in which it functioned were sometimes quite different.

The second part of the chapter will focus on Ch'an, dealing mainly with the well-known chronicle of the so-called Northern School, *Leng-ch'ieh shih-tzu chi* ("Record of the Masters and Disciples of the *Laṅkā-vatāra*"). It will attempt to show how different concepts, the products of various social and historical circumstances, became identified with one-practice samādhi—or at least came to occupy an analogous position in the discourse of Northern Ch'an. By defining the semantic field to which "one-practice samādhi" belonged—that is, by examining all the contexts in which it occurred—this section will attempt to reveal dimensions of its meaning that are obscure in traditional interpretations.

In the third and last part, this concept will be placed in the context of the T'ang politico-religious situation, and the argument will be made that this context was a crucial factor in the formation of the sectarian branches of Chinese Buddhism as it was a link between some of those branches. The redefinition of "one-practice samādhi," like the claim for a "sudden awakening" *(tun-wu),* provided a convenient means for the Southern School to outbid its Northern rival. At the same time, it also provoked various reactions from other corners of the Buddhist world, namely from the T'ien-t'ai and Pure Land traditions.

This working hypothesis remains to be demonstrated in a less intuitive way. A more definitive demonstration would require an examination of how this concept, or this type of practice, related to other non-conceptual practices in T'ang society—in other words, what kinds of modifications in the political, economic, social, and linguistic realms accompanied its emergence in the seventh and eighth centuries, as well as its subsequent disappearance from the Chinese religious scene. But such an undertaking remains beyond the scope of the present chapter and must await future analysis.

I. Evolution of the Concept of *I-hsing San-mei*

1. CANONICAL SOURCES

According to Mochizuki's *Bukkyō daijiten,*[1] the Chinese term *"i-hsing san-mei"* was used to translate the Sanskrit *"ekavyūha-samādhi"* ("single magnificence samādhi") or *"ekākāra-samādhi"* ("single-mode samādhi"). The primary meaning was therefore not "one-practice samādhi." The *locus classicus* of this expression is found in the *Wen-shu-shih-li so-shuo po-jo po-lo-mi ching (Saptaśatikā-prajñāpāramitā-sūtra;* "Sūtra on the Perfection of Wisdom Spoken by Mañjuśrī"—hereafter *Wen-shu shuo ching):*

> Mañjuśrī asked: "World Honored One, what is *i-hsing san-mei?*" The Buddha answered: "The Dharmadhātu has only one mark *(i-hsiang; eka-lakṣaṇa).* To take this Dharmadhātu as an object is called *i-hsing san-mei.*"[2]

The *Wen-shu shuo ching* states two methods for entering *i-hsing san-mei.* The first consists of reading the Perfection of Wisdom sūtras and practicing the Perfection of Wisdom. The second is a kind of invocation of Buddha's name *(nien-fo; buddhānusmṛti)* in which one concentrates one's thought on a Buddha (not necessarily Amitābha) by unceasingly invoking his name while trying to avoid becoming attached to his appearance. One is thus able to visualize all Buddhas of the three periods.

These two approaches were later characterized by the Pure Land School as corresponding to "contemplation of Principle" *(li-kuan)* and "contemplation of phenomena" *(shih-kuan).* In the first case, one contemplates the absolute, the "Principle" of sameness *(samatā)* that is the mark of "suchness" *(tathatā).* In the second, one contemplates the "phenomenal" multiplicity of the Buddhas. Both contemplations lead eventually to a realization of the undifferentiated character of the Dharmadhātu. This is why this samādhi is also frequently called *i-hsiang san-mei,* or "one-mark samādhi," the "one mark" being precisely the absence of all marks.[3]

2. THE FIRST CHINESE INTERPRETATIONS

The definition of *i-hsing san-mei* given by the *Wen-shu shuo ching* refers to the metaphysical or ontological unity of truth rather than to the methodological singleness of practice. Even while pointing toward a merging of both subject and object, it remains centered on some kind of object (insofar as the absolute can be taken as an object), not on the human subject. This situation was changed during the sixth century by speculations on the meaning of śamatha-vipaśyanā *(chih-kua)* and in works like the *Awakening of Faith (Ta-sheng ch'i-hsin lun)* and the *Mo-ho chih-kuan,* the concept of *i-hsing san-mei* became integrated with the theory of śamatha-vipaśyanā to give it a Mahāyāna content.

According to Hirai Shun'ei,[4] the śamatha-vipaśyanā method typical of Indian dhyāna had fallen into disuse following the success of the Mahāyāna ideas introduced by Kumārajīva (344–413) and the subsequent development of the Mādhyamika School of the Three Treatises (San-lun). The stress laid on wisdom (prajñā) to the detriment of concentration (samādhi or dhyāna) found expression in a rejection of śamatha to the profit of vipaśyanā. This emphasis became prevalent in southern China, while northern China remained more attached to the traditional practice of dhyāna. This situation, however, eventually led to a reaction —already anticipated in the case of Buddhabhadra (359–429), the unlucky rival of Kumārajīva—that manifested itself as a search for a new balance between concentration and wisdom, a balance that was supposed to help reunify the Buddhist trends in northern and southern China. But since it was doctrinally impossible simply to return to the Hīnayāna practice of śamatha-vipaśyanā, some monks tried to redefine this practice in Mahāyāna terms. And the *Wen-shu shuo ching,* which had just been translated, helped greatly in the success of this undertaking. By adapting this sūtra's notion of *i-hsing san-mei,* the authors of the *Awakening of Faith* and the *Mo-ho chih-kuan* were indeed able to work out their new theory of śamatha-vipaśyanā. Let us now briefly examine the relevant positions of these works.

A. *According to the* Awakening of Faith

This Chinese apocryphal text, compiled toward the middle of the sixth century, gave the practice of śamatha the meaning of "samādhi of suchness" *(chen-ju san-mei)* or "one-mark samādhi" *(i-hsiang san-mei)*. In so doing, it transposed śamatha from the physical to the metaphysical level, making it a kind of contemplation of Principle. In Hīnayāna practice śamatha meant simply concentrating one's mind on an object, such as the body or the breath.[5] In contrast, the *Awakening of Faith* says:

> Through this samādhi, you understand that the Dharmadhātu has only one mark; in other words, that the Dharma-body *(dharmakāya)* of the Buddhas is the same as the body of sentient beings and that there is no duality between them. Hence this expression "one-mark samādhi" *(i-hsiang san-mei)*. You must know that suchness *(chen-ju; tathatā)* is the basis of the samādhis. If you practice it, you can gradually produce an infinity of samādhis.[6]

The apophatic concept of emptiness *(śūnyatā)*, as articulated in the Perfection of Wisdom sūtras, is here in the process of becoming a quasi-substantial suchness, a kind of metaphysical entity more intelligible to the Chinese mind. This interpretation, prefigured in the *Awakening of Faith*, was later promoted by Hua-yen philosophy. The originality of the *Awakening of Faith* on this point, however, seems to have been overlooked by its Hua-yen commentators.[7]

B. *According to the* Mo-ho chih-kuan

When Chih-i compiled the *Mo-ho chih-kuan* at the Yü-ch'üan Monastery in 594, he was attempting to realize a synthesis of the various kinds of Hīnayāna and Mahāyāna practices prevalent in his day. To achieve this, he grouped various meditation and devotional practices into four general types, the so-called four kinds of samādhi: (1) constantly sitting, (2) constantly walking, (3) partly walking and partly sitting, and (4) neither walking nor sitting. These samādhis are ably discussed by Daniel Stevenson in the previous chapter. There is, therefore, little need to say more about them here, other than to note some of the salient features of Chih-i's treatment of *i-hsing san-mei*. The first chapter of the *Mo-ho chih-kuan* states that these practices are collectively referred to as "samādhi" because one thereby "attunes, rectifies, and stabilizes [the mind]." Chih-i goes on to quote the *Ta-chih-tu-lun:* "Skillfully to fix the mind on one spot and abide there without shifting—that is called samādhi." He then adds: "The Dharmadhātu is a single spot, and through true contemplation you can abide there and never stray from it."[8] This is, *grosso modo*, the same ontological definition of śamatha *(chih, "calming")* as that given by the *Awakening of Faith*. But with Chih-i the *i-hsing san-mei* of the *Wen-shu shuo ching* is categorized as the first of the four kinds of samādhi, thus becoming at last a "one-practice" samādhi in the sense of one practice among several.

Chih-i notes that the constantly sitting samādhi derives from both the *Wen-shu shuo ching* and *Wen-shu wen ching (Mañjuśrī-paripṛcchā-sūtra)* and that it is also called "one-practice samādhi."[9] He writes that this type of meditation should be practiced without interruption for a ninety-day period. It includes invoking the Buddha's name, although this invocation seems to play a secondary role. Nevertheless, the expression *"i-hsing san-mei"* remains rather ambiguous as used by Chih-i. Those passages that deal with its function of taking the Dharmadhātu as its object emphasize the ontological aspect of this samādhi.

> Take the Dharmadhātu as an object and concentrate all your thought on it. To take it as an object is calming (śamatha) and to concentrate your thought is contemplation (vipaśyanā).[10]

In other passages, however, its modality as one practice—and, more concretely, as the sitting posture—is emphasized. A later commentator, the Japanese monk Shōshin (fl. 1164–1204), claims, in his *Shikan shiki,* that Chih-i achieved the synthesis of the two aspects of *i-hsing san-mei* (which we called earlier its ontological and methodological aspects), by borrowing from the *Wen-shu shuo ching* and *Ta-chih-tu-lun.*[11] Chan-jan (711–782), in his commentary to the *Mo-ho chih-kuan (Chih-kuan fu-hsing chuan-hung-chüeh),* inherits this ambiguity but seems to opt finally for the meaning of one-practice samādhi.[12] He argues that, if the term *i-hsing* referred simply to the oneness of truth, it should apply as well to the three other types of samādhi and could not reflect the specificity of seated meditation.[13] Although this interpretation marks a radical departure from previous ones, one-practice samādhi had already become identified with seated meditation in the *Mo-ho chih-kuan.* This meaning persisted for centuries in the T'ien-t'ai School[14] and, to a lesser degree, in the Ch'an School. Consequently, when the adepts of these two schools appeal to the *Wen-shu shuo ching* as scriptural evidence, they generally simply quote the *Mo-ho chih-kuan.*

C. Toward a Redefinition of I-hsing San-mei

The influence of both the *Awakening of Faith* and the *Mo-ho chih-kuan* made one-practice (or one-mark) samādhi a well-known practice, and this, in turn, contributed to the elaboration of a specifically Chinese type of Buddhism. Significantly, the appearance of the Pure Land and Ch'an schools was contemporaneous with the compilation of the *Mo-ho chih-kuan.* Although these two schools inherited the conception of *i-hsing san-mei* from these two works, they eventually modified its content considerably. From their soteriological outlook, the term *i-hsing san-mei* had to be understood quite literally: the one practice was superior

because it included all practices. It was no longer, as it had been in the
Mo-ho chih-kuan, one samādhi among others. The synthesis of contemplative and devotional practices realized by Chih-i came to be perceived
as too complex to be effective. Therefore, the Ch'an and Pure Land
adepts retained from this concept only what seemed to them appropriate.
Thus, one-practice samādhi became synonymous with seated meditation
(tso-ch'an) for the Ch'an School and with invoking the Buddha's name
(nien-fo) for the Pure Land School. The definition originally given by the
Wen-shu shuo ching, with its double valence, had left the door open for
such interpretations.

   In the Pure Land School, the *An-lo chi* of Tao-ch'o (562–645)
reduced one-practice samādhi to one of its initial components, invocation *(nien-fo; buddhānusmṛti).*[15] But this *nien-fo san-mei* was still a kind
of contemplation. Such was not the case with Shan-tao (613–681), who
gave one-practice samādhi the meaning of an "exclusive invocation of
Buddha's name" *(chuan ch'eng fo-ming).*[16] He thus emptied it of part of
its content as a samādhi. In a later commentary on Shan-tao's work, the
Ōjōraisan shiki, the Japanese monk Ryōchū (1199–1287) used the distinction between contemplation of Principle *(li-kuan)* and contemplation
of phenomena *(shih-kuan)* as it had been applied to the *Wen-shu shuo
ching's* double definition of *i-hsing san-mei.* But, in so doing, he transformed the *shih-kuan* into the invocation of Amitābha's name:

> Question: "The [*Wen-shu shuo*] *sūtra* says to concentrate all one's thought
> on the Dharmadhātu. T'ien-t'ai [Chih-i] quotes this passage as evidence for
> his contemplation of Principle. Now you speak of 'invoking the name.'
> What is the difference?" Answer: "The term *'i-hsing'* is applied equally to
> Principle and to invocation. This is why one starts from the point of view of
> contemplating Principle and ends by expounding exclusive invocation.
> Chih-i adopts the outlook of the beginning, Shan-tao the outlook of the
> end. This distinction between before and after, Principle *(li)* and phenomena
> *(shih),* can be explained by the diversity of circumstances."[17]

   If all the practices amount to invoking the name, Ryōchū concluded, they obviously lose their purpose, because none of them allows
rebirth as rapidly in the Pure Land, where one becomes a Buddha. This
line of argument led quite naturally to a criticism of seated meditation
(tso-ch'an) and was already found in Shan-tao's works. His *Nien-fo
ching,* for example, condemns the practice of "gazing at the mind" *(k'an-
hsin).*[18] Another of his later commentators, Gijō (1796–1858), in his *Ōjōraisan monki,* summarized the three positions considered earlier: whereas the *Awakening of Faith* understands *i-hsing san-mei* from the point of
view of Principle, the *Mo-ho chih-kuan* takes into account both Principle
and practice, and Shan-tao adopts only the "phenomenal" outlook.[19]

D. I-hsing San-mei *in the Ch'an School*

Let us now examine the different definitions given to one-practice samādhi within Ch'an. If we are to believe the *Leng-ch'ieh shih-tzu chi,* this one-practice samādhi came to the fore with Tao-hsin (580–651), the dhyāna master who later became the "Fourth Patriarch" of Ch'an. Tao-hsin quotes the *Wen-shu shuo ching's* definition, which leads him to admit the value of *nien-fo.* But recollecting the Buddha remains for him a secondary *upāya,* an accessory to seated meditation *(tso-ch'an),* and is ultimately negated for the sake of "spontaneity."[20] Despite the heavy influence of the T'ien-t'ai tradition, Tao-hsin's conception clearly goes beyond the constantly sitting samādhi of the *Mo-ho chih-kuan* to include all everyday acts, such as "lifting or lowering the foot."[21] We cannot be certain whether this conception belongs to Tao-hsin himself or to Ching-chüeh, the author of the *Leng-ch'ieh shih-tzu chi.* In any case, this samādhi is not purely "passive, static," as claimed by Suzuki, who contrasted it with the "active, dynamic" conception of Hui-neng (638–713), the "Sixth Patriarch" of Ch'an.[22]

According to Saichō's *Naishō buppō kechimyakufu* (hereafter *Kechimyakufu*), the "Fifth Patriarch" Hung-jen (601–674) inherited his interest in one-practice samādhi from Tao-hsin. But, in Hung-jen's case, the influence of the *Awakening of Faith,* already at work in Tao-hsin's thought, seems to outshine the influence of the *Mo-ho chih-kuan:*

> Hung-jen said to the Great Master [Tao-hsin]: "What is one-practice samādhi? It is realizing that the Dharmakāya of the Buddhas and the nature of sentient beings are identical." The Great Master [Tao-]hsin . . . understood then that Hung-jen had entered directly into the one-practice samādhi and had perfectly reached the deep Dharmadhātu. He therefore transmitted to him the secret words.[23]

Despite such influence of the *Awakening of Faith,* the *Wen-shu shuo ching* remained the scriptural authority for the East Mountain School, as can be seen from the following dialogue between Empress Wu Tse-t'ien and Shen-hsiu (606–706), the "founder" of the so-called Northern School:

> The Empress . . . Tse-T'ien asked: "The Dharma that you transmit, whose teaching is it?" [Shen-hsiu] said: "I inherited the Dharma-gate of the East Mountain (Tung-shan) in Ch'i-chou." Tse-t'ien [asked]: "Upon which scriptures does it rely?" Shen-hsiu [replied]: "It relies upon the one-practice samādhi of the *Wen-shu shuo po-jo ching.*" Tse-t'ien [said]: "If one is discussing cultivating the Tao, nothing surpasses the East Mountain Dharma-gate!"[24]

Shen-hsiu's *Kuan-hsin lun* ("Treatise on Contemplating the Mind") gives "mind-contemplation" *(kuan-hsin)* as the "single practice" that includes all others but does not connect it explicitly with one-practice samādhi. Although the *Kuan-hsin lun* still shows Chih-i's influence (as can be seen from the title itself, identical to one of Chih-i's works), it assimilates the theory of the *Awakening of Faith* concerning the two aspects of the mind—i.e., the pure and defiled.

With Shen-hsiu's coming to the capital at the beginning of the eighth century, the interest of Ch'an adepts in the metaphysical speculation of Hua-yen philosophy increased greatly. Nonetheless, the dhyāna master Shen-hsiu was not, as has been repeatedly claimed by Korean and Japanese scholars, the author of the two commentaries on the *Avataṁsaka,* fragments of which have been discovered recently in Korea and Japan. The real author of these commentaries was a later Hua-yen master, also named Shen-hsiu, as I have demonstrated elsewhere.[25] He was registered at the Hui-chi Monastery (in modern Chekiang) and was a contemporary of such third generation masters of the Northern School as Tao-hsüan (Dōsen, 702–760) and Shou-chih (var., Shou-chen, 700–770). These two monks may have been instrumental in giving a firm Hua-yen basis to the Northern School. The Japanese and Korean scholars are correct, however, in thinking that the ontological trend seen in this commentary was already prevalent at the time of the dhyāna master Shen-hsiu. The *Awakening of Faith,* which supposedly had just been "retranslated" by Śikṣānanda,[26] was very popular by then. A one-mark samādhi *(i-hsiang san-mei)* that has lost the methodological connotations of the T'ien-t'ai one-practice samādhi reappears in this pseudo-translation.

The Northern Ch'an text *Wu-sheng fang-pien men* ("Treatise on the Five Upāya"), though not explicitly referring to *i-hsing san-mei,* nevertheless lays constant stress on the necessity of realizing the one mark (i.e., the absence of all marks) of the ultimate reality. In so doing, it refers to the *Awakening of Faith:*

> The term "awakening" *(chüeh)* means that the mind-essence *(hsin-t'i)* is free from thought *(li-nien).* This detachment from thought is characterized as similar to space: it is universal. The Dharmadhātu has one mark. It is the Tathāgata's Dharmakāya of sameness. It is in reference to this Dharmakāya that one speaks of "fundamental awakening" *(pen-chüeh).* [27]

The pronounced taste of the Northern School for ontological ideas derived from the *tathāgatagarbha* tradition gave Ch'an a new direction, in which it turned away from Indian-style dhyāna. At the same time, the school also deviated from the Mādhyamika orthodoxy from which it had originally sprung. This transformation may have arisen from a misinterpretation, in substantialist terms, of the *Awakening of Faith.* But, whatever its origin, it directly affected the interpretation of one-practice samādhi.

Although both Hui-neng (or at least the author of the *Platform Sūtra*) and Shen-hui (684–758), the leading figures of the Southern School, borrowed the notion of one-practice samādhi from the *Leng-ch'ieh shih-tzu chi,* they reshaped it according to their own purposes, using it as the main instrument in their criticism of the Northern School and its seated meditation. The *Platform Sūtra* has a long passage on this one-practice samādhi, which begins thus:

> One-practice samādhi is straightforward mind at all times, walking, stand-ing, sitting, and lying. The *Vimalakīrti Sūtra* says: "Straightforward mind is the place of practice *(tao-ch'ang; bodhimaṇḍa);* straightforward mind is the Pure Land." Do not with a dishonest mind speak of the straightforwardness of the Dharma. If while speaking of one-practice samādhi you fail to prac-tice straightforward mind, you will not be disciples of the Buddha. Only practicing straightforward mind, and in all things having no attachments whatsoever, is called one-practice samādhi.[28]

A criticism of passive meditation that is clearly, if somewhat mis-takenly, directed at the Northern School follows this passage. This criti-cism will be more fully discussed later in this chapter. Suffice it to note for now that, in quoting the *Vimalakīrti*[29] as the source of this samādhi, the author seems to be consciously rejecting the *Wen-shu shuo ching* as well as any T'ien-t'ai influence.[30] The "straightforward mind" of the *Platform Sūtra* appears equally distant from the *Awakening of Faith* and its ontological concept of "essential mind."

On the other hand, an attempt at reconciling the various definitions is attributed to Hui-neng by the authors of the *Tsu-t'ang chi* (K. *Cho-dang chip):*

> The mind produces myriads of dharmas. . . . You must reach one-mark samādhi, one-practice samādhi. One-mark samādhi means, in all circum-stances, not to dwell in marks; even in the midst of marks, not to give rise to hatred or desire, neither to grasp nor to reject. . . . One-practice samādhi means that all circumstances, whether walking, standing, sitting, or lying, are for straightforward mind the place of practice *(tao-ch'ang; bodhi-maṇḍa);* all these are the Pure Land.[31]

Shen-hui's position can be interpreted as a reaction against the onto-logical tendencies of the Northern School by a return to the source of Ch'an in the Perfection of Wisdom tradition. This may be the reason why Shen-hui replaced the *Wen-shu shuo ching* (as well as the *Laṅkāva-tāra*), which had been excessively used by Shen-hsiu and his epigons, with the *Diamond Sūtra.* In his *Recorded Sayings,* for example, he declares:

If you want to gain access to the very deep Dharmadhātu and directly enter
one-practice samādhi, you must first read and recite the *Diamond Sūtra* and
cultivate and study the teaching of the Perfection of Wisdom.[32]

Reciting the *Diamond Sūtra* also effects the disappearance of all
past sins and all subsequent hindrances. Whereas the Northern School's
one-practice samādhi is criticized for its "voluntarist" aspect, Shen-hui's
practice is characterized as *wu-wei,* or "non-acting." In other words, it
involves non-intentionality *(wu-tso-i)* and non-thinking *(wu-nien):*

> Absence of thought *(wu-nien)* is the Perfection of Wisdom and this Perfec-
> tion of Wisdom is one-practice samādhi.[33]

Shen-hui also invokes the authority of the *Shen-t'ien wang po-jo
po-lo-mi ching (Devarājapravara-prajñāpāramitā-sūtra).* But neither in
these two Perfection of Wisdom sūtras nor in the *Vimalakīrti* quoted by
Hui-neng in the *Platform Sūtra* is there any mention of one-practice
samādhi. Therefore, it is clear that, on this point, Shen-hui and the
author of the *Platform Sūtra* remain dependent on the *Leng-ch'ieh shih-
tzu chi.*

Tsung-mi (780–841) inherited Shen-hui's criticism of the Northern
School but added certain nuances to the role of seated meditation. In his
*General Preface to the Collected Writings on the Sources of Ch'an
(Ch'an-yüan chu-ch'üan-chi tu-hsü*—hereafter *General Preface),* he dis-
tinguishes five kinds of dhyāna from the point of view of practice: (1)
heterodox dhyāna, (2) common-man dhyāna, (3) Hīnayāna dhyāna, (4)
Mahāyāna dhyāna, and (5) dhyāna of the Highest Vehicle—the last of
which he defines as follows:

> If one's practice is based on having suddenly awakened [to the realization
> that] one's own mind is from the very beginning pure, that the depravities
> have never existed, that the nature of the wisdom that is without outflows is
> from the very beginning complete, that this mind is Buddha, and that they
> are ultimately identical, then it is dhyāna of the Highest Vehicle. This type is
> also known as pure dhyāna of the Tathāgata, one-mark samādhi, and Tathā-
> gata samādhi. It is the root of all samādhis.[34]

Tsung-mi's conception of the one-practice samādhi is derived from
the *Awakening of Faith,* not from the *Diamond Sūtra.* Paradoxically,
Tsung-mi is in this respect closer to the Northern School[35] than to his
own master Shen-hui. He goes even further than Shen-hsiu's disciples in
interpreting the "originally pure mind" as an ontological reality. The
cleavage on the question of the one-practice samādhi thus does not
always conform to the doctrinal assertions of the two schools.[36]

Northern School influence also appears in the *Tun-wu yao-men*

("Essentials of Sudden Awakening") of Ta-chu Hui-hai (d.u.).[37] Hui-hai is traditionally considered a disciple of Ma-tsu Tao-i (709–788), but his biography is uncertain, and he may actually have lived earlier than Ma-tsu. Doctrinally, he certainly represents a less radical trend of Ch'an. Whatever the case, his concept of one-practice samādhi is obviously indebted to the *Leng-ch'ieh shih-tzu chi* and can be seen as another attempt at a doctrinal synthesis from a purely Ch'an point of view. But his synthesis, like Tsung-mi's, came too late and did not prevent Ch'an from moving in completely new directions, directions that soon rendered one-practice samādhi obsolete. But to understand how this concept lost its meaning, it is necessary to examine the significance that it initially had for Ch'an practitioners. And to this end it is appropriate to take a second look at the *Leng-ch'ieh shih-tzu chi.*

II. One-Practice Samādhi and Its Paradigms in Northern School Texts

Our argument so far has followed a traditional approach[38] in considering the evolution of the concept of one-practice samādhi in terms of its textual basis. We have thus found that its *Problematik* was framed by the definitions given to it in works such as the *Wen-shu shuo ching, Mo-ho chih-kuan,* and *Awakening of Faith.* Such an approach, however, does not allow us to understand the purport, to say nothing of the purpose, of one-practice samādhi. It is accordingly necessary to distinguish clearly the aims of an analysis that attempts to assess the theoretical role of one-practice samādhi in the religious (mainly Ch'an) discourse of the T'ang period from the decontextualized attempt to elucidate the meaning of *i-hsing san-mei* itself that has motivated traditional exegeses. The concern of this section is thus not the explication of *i-hsing san-mei* as such —a paradoxical task, after all, given that this type of practice is supposedly beyond the reach of words—but an examination of its theoretical role in the religious discourse of the T'ang period. On the one hand, the ambiguity, or polyvalence, of the canonical definition of *i-hsing san-mei* facilitated its assimilation with a range of practices and theories, as seen in the *Leng-ch'ieh shih-tzu chi.* On the other hand, the concept also provided the basis for a rejection of all other theories or practices. In what follows, we shall examine the more or less explicit equivalences given to one-practice samādhi by the *Leng-ch'ieh shih-tzu chi*—or, when appropriate, by other contemporary works.

A few words on the *Leng-ch'ieh shih-tzu chi* and its author, Ching-chüeh, may be helpful. Ching-chüeh was born in 683 and probably died around 750, before the An Lu-shan rebellion. He was the younger brother of Lady Wei, Emperor Chung-tsung's consort, who was killed in

710 after trying to seize power. Ching-chüeh apparently studied with the dhyāna masters Shen-hsiu and Hui-an (d. 708), the two great representatives of the East Mountain School, and inherited the Laṅkāvatāra tradition from his master, Hsüan-tse (d.u.). Ching-chüeh's work is an attempt to present the East Mountain School as the legitimate heir of the Laṅkāvatāra tradition supposedly initiated by Guṇabhadra and his "disciple" Bodhidharma. It enumerates eight generations of "masters of the Laṅkāvatāra [School]" and may be said to represent a marginal trend within the Northern School. In any case, it should be kept in mind that Ching-chüeh's position differs slightly from that of Shen-hsiu's main disciples.

1. The Fundamental Paradigm

The Hua-yen theory of the interpenetration of the one and the many (i.e., of the absolute [*li*] and the phenomenal [*shih*]) provided the theoretical basis of the *Leng-ch'ieh shih-tzu chi's* stress on one-practice samādhi. This idea of interpenetration, as is well known, is associated with the *Avataṁsaka Sūtra*—a text that Ching-chüeh quoted often, particularly in the section of the *Leng-ch'ieh shih-tzu chi* devoted to Hui-k'o—and the theory itself was developed in the section devoted to Seng-ts'an. The famous formula one is everything and everything is one, constituted, in fact, a double paradigm, and the Hua-yen and T'ien-t'ai traditions have each stressed a different one of its aspects.

For Hua-yen, "one is everything." In other words, since Principle or the absolute *(li)* manifests itself in each and every phenomenon *(shih),* one must start from the absolute to understand the phenomenal world. For T'ien-t'ai, on the other hand, "everything is one." Since all phenomena equally reflect the absolute, one can, from the phenomenal multiplicity of the human world, return to the absolute. This contrast, of course, has merely heuristic value and does not do justice to the doctrinal complexity of these two traditions. But it may prove useful as a general distinction between two attitudes also very common in Ch'an circles. Applied to the question of practice, it has important consequences. If one stresses the fact that "one is everything," then one practice equals all practices and consequently renders them obsolete. From this derives the exclusiveness of *i-hsing san-mei* and its claim to orthodoxy (or, strictly speaking, "orthopraxy").

If "everything is one," then all practices are equal and compatible, because all express the same truth. In other words, pacifying the mind *(an-hsin)* or realizing one-practice samādhi, far from representing a rejection of other practices, is their necessary presupposition. Otherwise, these practices would be merely gradual *upāyas* and would, as such, only

lead one astray from the goal. Another Ch'an text related to the Northern School, the *Wu-sheng fang-pien men,* makes this point clear by referring to the "unborn" (i.e., absolute) *upāya.* In this respect, one-practice
samādhi is not simply a practice selected from among others.[39] It is
rather the uninterrupted, unremitting practice (another connotation of *i-
hsing)* that pervades and sustains all others.[40] This conception of practice
may have been borrowed from the Hua-yen School. Chih-yen (602–668),
for example, argued that one-practice samādhi is a "pervasive contemplation" *(t'ung-kuan)* and corresponds to the Sudden Teaching *(tun-
chiao).*[41]

   The gradual shift of emphasis from the notion of one practice
(among others) to that of the one (absolute) practice (and therefore no
practice at all) can be inferred from Tao-hsin's criticism of the Taoist concept of unity. He quotes the apocryphal *Fa-chü ching:*

> The One itself is not the [number] one. It implies a denial of numbers. But
> those of shallow knowledge understand it to be a unity.[42]

   Ching-chüeh seems mainly preoccupied by the danger of hypostasiz-
ing *i-hsing san-mei*—either as "one" definite practice (methodological
aspect) or as one "object" of practice (ontological aspect). To avoid the
ontological deviation, he states repeatedly that "one mark is the absence
of all marks." As to the methodological aspect, he seems to hesitate
between two solutions: either the "real practice" corresponding to this
"real mark" is no particular practice—and can therefore be any practice
—or it is no practice at all. In fact, he has to give up his apophatic stand
and is led to admit that the absolute must be expressed "anyway in a certain way." His hesitation, however, concerns only the phrasing, not the
underlying meaning, of *i-hsing san-mei* itself. Any practice, being
grounded on "sudden" realization,[43] is "no-practice." The same logic
runs through a whole range of expressions: just as "one" comes to mean
"absolute" and therefore negates any relative number, one mark, or real
mark, is no-mark. Seeing it is, in fact, non-seeing; knowing it is non-
knowing—a kind of *docta ignorantia* in which both subject and object
have disappeared. Clearly, the Northern School's fundamental teaching,
as expressed by the *Leng-ch'ieh shih-tzu chi,* is "sudden"—and not
"gradual," as its opponents claimed. Moreover, it can be said that its
essence was contained in the term *"i-hsing san-mei."* In a sense, all these
terms, although they do not perfectly overlap due to their semantic evolution and their field of application (practice vs. realization), can be considered synonymous. They derive from the same play of meaning already
at work in the fundamental paradigm One/one, a paradigm that can be
broken down into the following set of polarities:

absolute	relative
metaphysical	methodological
exclusive	eclectic
apophatic	positive
sudden	gradual

Still, before one reaches the stage of one-practice samādhi or sudden awakening, some concrete, external practice appears, paradoxically, to be useful. Tao-hsin and his successors had to address themselves mainly to beginners who could not readily fulfill their elitist expectations. A compromise had to be found. This was accomplished by borrowing diverse meditative techniques from other Buddhist and non-Buddhist schools and reinterpreting them from a Ch'an "sudden" perspective. We will now consider some of these techniques and their background.

2. Equivalents of *I-hsing San-mei*

A. Shou-i

The first of the terms identified with one-practice samādhi is the practice of keeping the One *(shou-i)*. In the *Leng-ch'ieh shih-tzu chi,* this practice is attributed to Fu ta-shih (alias Fu Hsi, 497–569),[44] known also as the Chinese Vimalakīrti. Despite T'ang Yung-t'ung's claim that the Taoists borrowed *"shou-i"* from the Buddhists (who used the term to render the Sanskrit "dhyāna"),[45] it is clearly a borrowing from the Taoist tradition. The term *"shou-i"* had many connotations in a Taoist context, and we may wonder how many of these resonate in the Ch'an interpretation. The One in the *Lao Tzu* and *Chuang Tzu* was the absolute, the impersonal Tao itself.[46] "Keeping" or "embracing" the One meant a mystical union with the Tao and, therefore, an integration of all elements constituting the individual. But very early, along with the divinization of Lao-tzu, the One came to be considered as a personal divinity or even as a divine triad. In the *Pao-p'u-tzu,* for example, it "possesses names, uniforms, and colors."[47] "To keep the One," then, involves visualizing the "supreme One" and its hypostases so that they manifest themselves in the practitioner's body and bring him longevity. According to Ko Hung, the author of this text, "If men could know the One, everything would be accomplished."[48] A similar interpretation is given by T'ao Hung-ching (456–536) and the Mao-shan School, as well as later by the Double Mystery School (Ch'ung-hsüan tsung), a Taoist sect heavily influenced by Mādhyamika philosophy.[49] It also appears in a dialogue between Emperor Kao-tsung (d. 682) and P'an Shih-chen, a Taoist hermit living on Mount Sung (the cradle of the Northern School).[50]

Another interpretation of *shou-i,* reflecting a moralizing trend, was known in certain Taoist circles. It is found in a commentary on the *Lao Tzu* discovered in Tun-huang and attributed to Chang Lu, the third representative of the sect of the Celestial Masters (T'ien-shih). This commentary, the *Hsiang-erh,* goes against all anthropomorphic conceptions of the One. Here, "keeping the One" means first of all to follow the prescriptions ordained by the Tao, thereby contributing to the great harmony *(t'ai-p'ing).*[51] This amalgam between keeping the One and keeping the precepts has some affinities with the Buddhist conception of the Bodhisattva Precepts. According to a Taoist master named Chang Wang-fu:

> To keep the precepts means eventually to keep the mind-precept. This is what is called "keeping the One without losing it."[52]

At about the same time, the Northern School began to assert conformity with Buddha-nature as the one mind precept *(i-hsin chieh);* the main difference with the Taoist notion is that keeping the One aims at awakening, not simply longevity. As Paul Pelliot has said: "The resemblance and identity of terms did not entail the community of systems. . . . Often enough, the apparent identity of words hid certain oppositions of ideas."[53]

Were the early Ch'an adepts aware of these doctrinal incompatibilities? Tao-hsin's (or Ching-chüeh's) criticism of the Taoist tendency to hypostasize the One or the Mind might have been better addressed to some Ch'an followers than to adepts of the Taoist school of the Double Mystery.[54] In an apocryphal text, the *Chin-kang san-mei ching,* written toward the middle of the seventh century and closely related to the East Mountain School, the following definition of "keeping the One" can be found:

> The bodhisattva sees to it that sentient beings "preserve the three and keep the One" and thus enter into Tathāgata dhyāna *(ju-lai ch'an).* Owing to this dhyāna, the "panting" of the mind stops. What is "preserving the three and keeping the One" and what is "entering into Tathāgata dhyāna?" "Preserving the three" means "preserving the triple deliverance." "Keeping the One" means keeping the suchness of the one mind. "Entering into Tathāgata dhyāna" means contemplating the principle *(li-kuan)* that the mind is purity and suchness.[55]

Nevertheless, the "keeping the One" that Tao-hsin borrowed from Fu ta-shih remains a classical practice. It consists of examining the emptiness of the body and modes of consciousness *(vijñāna).* All mental phenomena that may appear during this process are rejected as illusory. Despite some possible allusions to Taoist techniques, the content of this meditation is obviously Buddhist.

The Taoist connotations of the expression "keeping the One" may have appealed to the eclectic backgrounds of many lay Ch'an adepts. Thus the Prime Minister Chang Yüeh (d. 730), although a disciple of Shen-hsiu, had very intimate Taoist friends; and his son, Chang Chün (d.u.), while following the Northern Ch'an master I-fu (658–736), continued to practice the Taoist techniques of longevity. The identification of "keeping the One" with one-practice samādhi must, in any case, have been widely acknowledged at the time, since it was still in use in such later Ch'an works as the *Tun-wu yao-men.*[56]

B. Kuan-hsin/K'an-hsin

Another term closely connected with one-practice samādhi was "contemplating" *(kuan)*—or "gazing at" *(k'an)*—the mind *(hsin)*. At first glance, Tao-hsin does not seem very consistent on this point, since he initially rejects "gazing at the mind," only to recommend it afterwards to beginners. Here again—unless it be some interpolation—the dual structure (sudden/gradual) of his teaching appears. In any case, "mind-contemplation" was certainly a prominent feature of the Northern School practice. Shen-hsiu himself dedicated what was probably his first work, the *Kuan-hsin lun,* to the subject. This interest seems to reflect a strong influence from T'ien-t'ai thought, where this type of contemplation was prevalent. But within the T'ien-t'ai tradition itself an argument later arose over which aspect of mind this contemplation should be directed toward. Was it the true mind *(chen-hsin)* or the illusory mind *(wang-hsin)?* This question became one of the stumbling blocks for the school, the orthodox branch, with Ssu-ming Chih-li (d. ca. 1023), holding that *kuan-hsin* meant the examination of the illusory mind, not the absolute mind *(li-hsin).* Guṇabhadra, the "First Patriarch" of Ch'an according to the *Leng-ch'ieh shih-tzu chi,* would probably have rejected such an argument, but his "heir" Tao-hsin seems ambivalent.[57] For Shen-hsiu, *kuan-hsin* is undeniably a kind of *visio spiritualis,* not merely a *visio mentalis.* Such seems to be his point when, according to the *Leng-ch'ieh shih-tzu chi,* he declares: "This mind, is it mental activity *(yu-hsin)?* What kind of mind is it?"[58] The implicit answer is that it is "no-mind" and that looking at it is like looking at space. Hung-jen, in the same work, defines "gazing at the mind" in terms reminiscent of the Latin etymology of the word "contemplation" (from *templum,* which, in the terminology of divination, meant a place from which one had an open view):

> After [the mind] is clarified, when one sits, it is like being on a solitary tall mountain in the midst of a distant field. Sitting on exposed ground at the top of the mountain, gazing off into the distance on all four sides—there are no limits.[59]

Now this state of mind is engendered, according to Hung-jen, by visualizing the letter "one" (or "one" character, *i-tzu*)[60] at the very bottom of space. The more advanced practitioner is told to visualize it in his mind. This practice may be related to the contemplation of the letter A *(a-tzu kuan)* used in Tantrism.

On the other hand, "gazing at the mind" is equated to "gazing at the unlocalized" *(k'an wu-so-ch'u)* by a later anthology of the Northern School, the *Shih-tzu ch'i-tsu fang-pien wu-men* ("The Five Types of Upāya [According to] the Seven Patriarchs").[61] But this notion was already in use during Shen-hsiu's lifetime, for it can be found in a work of his disciple Chih-ta (alias Hui-ta, or Hou-mo-ch'en Yen, d. 714). Because of its reference to "sudden awakening," this work, known as the *Yao-chüeh* ("Essential Teachings"), was believed to postdate the "sudden/gradual" controversy, but I have found evidence that its preface, dated 712, is authentic. Shen-hui and his school did not, therefore, "discover" the sudden teaching. Chih-ta defines, without naming it, the one-practice samādhi as follows:

> From moment to moment do not abide, and then you will realize the one uniform mark. . . . This is the unlocalized, . . . the pure Dharmadhātu, . . . Vairocana, the Pure Land.[62]

Like Ching-chüeh, Chih-ta affirms that true vision is "non-seeing" and admits that it must be preceded by "gazing." Nevertheless, this gazing itself is from the beginning "absence of thought" (and therefore "sudden"). This logically leads to the definition of *k'an-hsin* as "non-reflection, non-examination" *(pu-ssu pu-kuan)* given by the Chinese master Mo-ho-yen (Mahāyāna) during the so-called Council of Tibet.[63] The "mind-contemplation" of the Northern School was, from the outset, conceived as an "anoetism," an *excessus mentis.* By looking at his mind, the practitioner, so to speak, dissolves it. He certainly does not freeze it or hypostasize it, as Shen-hui and Tsung-mi's criticism of the Northern Ch'an would have us believe.

The funerary inscription for Chih-ta, written by an official named Ts'ui Kuan,[64] raises again the question of the Tantric influence on the meditation practice of the Northern School, especially in regard to its interpretation of one-practice samādhi. According to his epitaph, Chih-ta, having received from Shen-hsiu the oral (i.e., esoteric) teaching *(k'ou-chüeh)* and the secret *piṭaka (pi-mi tsang),* converted people in the Lo-yang region. He "directly showed the essentials of dhāraṇī and spread the principle of sudden awakening." Two of his works found in Tun-huang, *Hui-ta ho-shang tun-chiao pi-mi hsin-ch'i ch'an-men fa* ("The Secret Method of Master Hui-ta") and *Yao-chüeh,* show esoteric connotations in their titles. The first was originally believed by D. T. Suzuki to be a Tantric work, while the second has been copied, in one recension, together with *Kuan-shih-yin p'u-sa t'o-lo-ni ching* ("Dhāraṇī Sūtra of the Bodhisattva Avalokiteśvara"). We know the interest taken by Northern School adepts—such as I-hsing (683–727), I-fu, Ching-hsien (660–723), and Shou-chih (700–770)—in the teachings of the Tantric masters Śubhakarasiṃha (637–735) and Vajrabodhi (669–741). But Chih-ta's case shows that, even before the arrival of these two Indian monks in the years 716–719, Shen-hsiu's disciples were attracted to the esoteric teaching then in vogue in Loyang.[65]

Some passages of the *Leng-ch'ieh shih-tzu chi* might be interpreted in this light. The first that comes to mind is, of course, Hung-jen's injunction to "gaze at one letter." Could this letter or syllable be a dhāraṇī? Elaborating on the logic of the type "to understand one thing is to understand everything," Tao-hsin quotes a sūtra that says: "If only one sentence impregnates the mind, it will remain forever incorruptible."[66] In another passage he declares: "The ocean of the Dharma may be unlimited, but the practice of the Dharma is contained in one word."[67]

The *Ch'an-yao* ("Essentials of Dhyāna"), a record of Śubhakarasiṃha's talks with the Northern Ch'an master Ching-hsien, makes the following statement: "Whoever can explain one word can expound countless dharmas."[68] In the same vein, Shen-hsiu, quoting the *Nirvāṇa Sūtra*, declares: "Whoever understands perfectly one word deserves the title of 'Vinaya Master.'"[69] Still, Ching-chüeh does not give any evidence that this "one word" could be a dhāraṇī, and the question of the Tantric aspect of one-practice samādhi remains open. Possibly what drew Shen-hsiu's disciples to Śubhakarasiṃha was not his Tantric doctrine as such, but the question of the Bodhisattva Precepts.[70]

C. I-hsin Chieh

The importance of the Bodhisattva Precepts in the Northern School must be understood in relation to one-practice samādhi. These precepts, also known as the "formless" or "one-mind" precepts, developed in the Northern School with regard to classical Vinaya in the same way as one-practice samādhi had developed vis-a-vis traditional dhyāna. They are an application of the "sudden" theory. Yanagida Seizan thinks that the "formless precepts" *(wu-hsiang chieh)* found in the *Platform Sūtra* were specific to the Ox-head (Niu-t'ou) School,[71] but the same notion was used in a commentary on the apocryphal *Fan-wang ching*. This commentary was compiled by Tao-hsüan (Dōsen), the Northern Ch'an master who introduced Vinaya and Hua-yen (along with Ch'an) to Japan in 736. It is unfortunately not extant, but the relevant passage is quoted in the *Denjutsu isshin kaimon,* a work on the "one-mind precepts" *(i-hsin chieh)* written by a disciple of Saichō named Kōjō (779–858).[72] The theory of the one-mind precepts later played a key role in the Japanese Pure Land and Sōtō Zen sects.

Characteristic of these precepts is the "highest repentance," which consists of "sitting correctly and thinking of the true mark."[73] This famous passage from the *P'u-hsien kuan ching* is quoted in the *Leng-ch'ieh shih-tzu chi* by Tao-hsin to illustrate one-practice samādhi.[74]

D. Nien-fo

The canonical definition of one-practice samādhi included a recollection of the Buddha *(nien-fo)*. Tao-hsin, after quoting this definition, felt the need to clarify his position concerning the Pure Land doctrine. He admits *nien-fo* as an ancillary practice, but its meaning is very different from the "invocation of the name" recommended by Shan-tao and his disciples. It is based on the Perfection of Wisdom notion of emptiness, and, instead of leading to rebirth in the Pure Land, it aids in the realization that "to think of the Buddha is to think of the mind." The Buddha, like the mind, cannot be apprehended through forms. There is no need to turn westwards since "one direction is all directions" and the Pure Land is within oneself. The same point is repeatedly stressed in both Northern and Southern schools. In the *Tun-wu yao-men,* a naive practitioner asks Hui-hai:

> I wish to be reborn in the Pure Land, but I still wonder whether this Pure Land really exists or not?[75]

Hui-hai pretends to resolve this doubt with a quotation from the *Vimalakīrti Sūtra:* "If your mind is pure, all places will be pure." This kind of answer may miss the point, for it ignores the simple fact that the question was asked precisely because the practitioner's mind *is* defiled. The influence of Hua-yen philosophy gave Ch'an doctrine a kind of optimistic, irenist bias that was incapable of meeting the expectations of ordinary people, trapped in a world of suffering and desperately longing to find an escape. This may be one of the shortcomings of the "sudden" position advocated by Ch'an. Thus, in order to proselytize, Ch'an masters had to use "gradual" *upāyas.* Most of the time, they merely concealed this fact with their "sudden" terminology. By doing so, they could also maintain a fruitful dialogue with other Buddhist schools. This ambiguity is most clearly evident in the *Leng-ch'ieh shih-tzu chi* and its use of the one-practice samādhi—understood sometimes as one simple practice, but more often, or more fundamentally, as the one absolute or "sudden" practice, that is, no practice whatsoever, or pure spontaneity.

Our discussion so far has focused on the "eclectic" conception of one-practice samādhi that appears to be at the core of the *Leng-ch'ieh shih-tzu chi* and a number of other Northern Ch'an texts. The other conception, which can be characterized as "exclusive" or "purist," is by its very nature refractory to a discursive approach. It may be found in another trend of the Northern School, whose point of view is expressed in a chronicle entitled *Ch'uan fa-pao chi* ("Record of Transmitting the Jewel of the Dharma"). This trend stemmed from Fa-ju (d. 689), a co-disciple of Shen-hsiu. Its main representative was Yüan-kuei (644–716), traditionally considered a disciple of Hui-an (d. 708). Yüan-kuei's inscription contains the following passage:

> As to this one-practice samādhi, in India they transmitted its purport from mind to mind and, from the very beginning, never used written teachings.[76]

A parallel is found in Fa-ju's epitaph:

> Master Fa-ju, with the Dharma of one-seal, impressed secretly the multitude of meanings. . . .[77] In India they inherited it from each other, from the outset, without using written words. Those who enter this gate transmit only mind to each other.[78]

In the same way, the *Ch'uan fa-pao chi* opens with an assertion of the *siddhānta-naya* (or ultimate realization that cannot be expressed by words or induced by others). Apparently, one-practice samādhi is here understood as a rejection of the "joint practice" of Ch'an and doctrinal study and as an affirmation of what was later labeled the "special transmission outside the scriptures" *(chiao-wai pieh-ch'uan)*. This also may be the origin of the *shōbōgenzō* theory asserted by Dōgen (1200–1253).

In sum, the "sudden/gradual" controversy (which in the Chinese context of the eighth century revolved around the question of the value of *upāyas*) was already latent in the Northern School before it provoked the schism between the Northern and Southern schools. The controversy manifested itself in the various ways of interpreting one-practice samādhi. But this doctrinal debate itself was motivated by factors of an entirely different kind, to which we shall turn in the final section.

III. The Sectarian Background of One-Practice Samādhi in the Eighth Century

What was the real purport of one-practice samādhi? Shall we follow Hu Shih's line of argument and view the notion as a result of the Chinese tendency to simplify Buddhism because it was too complex for the Chinese mind? As Paul Demiéville remarks in a review of Hu Shih's thesis, this idea itself is too simplistic.[79] Obviously, the *Problematik* that gave rise to one-practice samādhi was more elaborate. This is not to say that, as Ch'an ideas became diffused among lower levels of Chinese society, there was no desire to simplify the hair-splitting analyses of meditative practices brought from India. But the Hua-yen logic of interpenetration that formed the doctrinal basis of one-practice samādhi also reflected the evolution of Ch'an as it became the ideology of the ruling class. It is no coincidence that the most striking praise of one-practice samādhi came from Empress Wu herself; some political interests were possibly at stake in what appeared at first to have been a merely doctrinal question.

Lack of sufficient textual evidence obscures a clear picture of these interests. Moreover, the controversy over one-practice samādhi—that is, over the "sudden/gradual" question—undoubtedly had its own logic and dynamics, whose workings lay hidden beyond the reach of the protagonists. Thus, given the inaccessibility of the political nuances that may have informed these discourses, we cannot hope to develop a wholly consistent picture, and the information necessary to establish alternative interpretations may be lacking. Nonetheless, the present analysis ought to be preferred if, as I think it does, it organizes in an intelligible framework a more encompassing set of issues and data.

One fact stands out: one-practice samādhi is in most cases discussed in works whose main purpose is to establish the orthodoxy of the Ch'an lineage. Moreover, it is often implicitly related to the transmission of the *Laṅkāvatāra Sūtra* and to the question of the six or seven Ch'an patriarchs. This is true, of course, of the *Leng-ch'ieh shih-tzu chi,* in which Tao-hsin is shown equating one-practice samādhi with the *Laṅkāvatāra's* assertion that "the mind of all Buddhas is what comes first."[80] Further, Ching-chüeh comments on the dialogue between Empress Wu and Shen-hsiu in the following manner: "Since [Shen-]hsiu was [Hung-]jen's disciple, this is the core of the oral [tradition]."[81] He thus seems to suggest that there was a transmission based on the one-practice samādhi.

The same point is made in Yüan-kuei's inscription, where we learn that one-practice samādhi is the hallmark of the Indian transmission.[82] Yüan-kuei himself, who succeeded Fa-ju and took the *Laṅkāvatāra Sūtra* as a "spiritual mirror," is given as representative of the seventh generation after Bodhidharma.

In his *Kechimyakufu,* Saichō gives his religious lineages as Ch'an, T'ien-t'ai, Vinaya (T'ien-t'ai Bodhisattva Precepts), and both "pure" and "mixed" esoteric teachings. Concerning his Ch'an lineage, he first quotes the *Ch'uan fa-pao chi,* proceeding with short notices on Bodhidharma, Hui-k'o, Seng-ts'an, Tao-hsin, Hung-jen, Shen-hsiu, P'u-chi, Tao-hsüan (Dōsen), and his own master, Gyōhyō (722–797).[83] Although he mentions the Ox-head lineage, he relies mainly on the Northern Ch'an tradition as he knew it through Tao-hsüan. His explanation of one-practice samādhi can be found in the notice on Hung-jen and refers to the

Wen-shu shuo ching.[84] In the notice on Tao-hsüan, P'u-chi is cited as the representative of the seventh generation.[85] This lineage continued to be accepted in much later texts (for example, Yosai's *Kōzen gokokuron*) and was closely connected to the one-mind precepts *(isshinkai).* One-practice samādhi is mentioned another time in the notice on I-hsing, a monk who first studied Northern Ch'an under P'u-chi and owed his religious name to his intent practice of *i-hsing san-mei.* He is cited here as a representative of the esoteric tradition.

In the case of Shen-hui's *Recorded Sayings* and the *Platform Sūtra,* the discussion of one-practice samādhi turned into a sharp criticism of Northern Ch'an practice. According to the *Platform Sūtra:*

> The deluded man clings to the characteristics of things, adheres to one-practice samādhi, [and thinks] that straightforward mind is sitting without moving and casting aside all delusions without letting things arise in the mind. This he considers to be one-practice samādhi. This kind of practice is the same as insentience and is the cause of an obstruction to Tao. . . . If sitting in meditation without moving is good, why did Vimalakīrti scold Śāriputra for sitting in meditation in the forest?[86]

But behind this doctrinal criticism we can discern Shen-hui's and the *Platform Sūtra's* real aim: establishing Hui-neng as Sixth Patriarch instead of Shen-hsiu, and Shen-hui himself as Seventh Patriarch instead of P'u-chi. Tsung-mi also states that one-practice samādhi is "precisely the dhyāna that has been transmitted down from Bodhidharma" and opposes it to the "gradual" practice of T'ien-t'ai (and Northern Ch'an).

Therefore, the semantic field encompassed by the notion of one-practice samādhi and its correlated terms can be considered from two perspectives: (1) as a kind of "space of discord" within the Ch'an School, within which each faction tried to outbid the others in a general struggle for orthodoxy and power; and, at the same time, (2) as a common ground for conciliation, permitting fruitful exchanges between Ch'an and the other schools.

But to arrive at this position, we must first "deconstruct" the artificial lineage trees that were imposed on an intricate reality by the later, fossilized tradition of each sect. These schools, at the beginning of the eighth century, were not yet monolithic. At that time, the rise of sectarianism was just beginning to alter the good relations between the various trends of Buddhist thought.

In the so-called Northern School of Ch'an, at least four currents are discernible, stemming respectively from Fa-ju, Hui-an, Shen-hsiu, and the *Laṅkāvatāra* tradition of Hsüan-tse and Ching-chüeh. One of them, Hui-an's group, remained somewhat peripheral, allowing its later redefinition as a representative of the early Southern School. The Southern School itself was never unified, and dissensions concerning the status of Seventh Patriarch may have arisen soon after Shen-hui's death, if not before. Tsung-mi's veiled criticism of the Hung-chou, Szechwan, and Ox-head schools echoes this sectarian polemic.

The Tantric School before Amoghavajra (705–774) and the Hua-yen School between the time of Fa-tsang (643–712) and Ch'eng-kuan (738–839) have been relatively neglected by Japanese scholars. The same can be said, as far as the T'ien-t'ai School is concerned, for the Yü-ch'üan ssu branch, which flourished at the time.[87] Hung-ching (634–692) and his disciple Hui-chen (673–751) were very close to Shen-hsiu's group, and their syncretic outlook probably influenced Northern School thought. This syncretism is best represented by I-hsing who, after studying Northern Ch'an on Mount Sung under P'u-chi, went to study T'ien-t'ai and Vinaya with Hui-chen and later received the Tantric teachings from Śubhakarasiṃha. His interest in one-practice samādhi must be placed in this context.

The other branch of the T'ien-t'ai School, centered on Mount T'ien-t'ai, also responded favorably at first to Shen-hsiu's disciples. Its main representative, Chan-jan, had friendly relations with Northern Ch'an monks and apparently even played a role in the erection of an epitaph for the third Ch'an patriarch, Seng-ts'an (d. 606), which supported the Northern School's lineage. His disciple Li Hua, in his inscription for Chan-jan's master, Hsüan-lang (673–754), also displayed partiality for the Northern School.[88] Several inscriptions by Li Hua stress the perfect harmony of Ch'an and T'ien-t'ai or Ch'an and Vinaya. On the other hand, some degree of rivalry between adepts of the various schools continued. A characteristic example is the controversy pitting Hui-ch'i and Hui-jen—two T'ien-t'ai nuns and blood sisters—against P'u-chi and his followers. This episode is revealed in the two nuns' epitaph, conserved in a work by the Korean monk Ŭich'ŏn (1055?–1101), the *Shih-yüan tz'u-lin*.[89] According to that document, I-hsing, chosen by the emperor Hsüan-tsung to decide who was right, sided with the T'ien-t'ai nuns.

In the Pure Land School, several trends can also be discerned. They are represented mainly by Shan-tao's disciples, such as Huai-kan (d.u.), and by Hui-jih (alias Tz'u-min, 680–748), a very popular and independent monk. In the same vein, another group, composed of monks such as Fei-hsi (d.u.), Ch'u-chin (698–759), Ch'eng-yüan (713–803), and Fa-chao (d.u.)—who descended from the Yü-ch'üan ssu branch of T'ien-t'ai and were adepts of the "joint practice" of Ch'an and *nien-fo*—also deserves mention.

One-practice samādhi was apparently an important topic in these T'ien-t'ai and Pure Land circles. Its significance may have been partly a reaction against the "sudden/gradual" controversy that was then dividing the Ch'an School. Consider, for instance, Chan-jan's statement about the *Wen-shu shuo ching:*

> This is why the dhyāna master [Tao-]hsin originally used this sūtra as the essentials of mind. But his epigons followed their own biases, and their opinions differed. This led the Ch'an schools in the Chiang-piao and Ching-ho [regions] to oppose each other.[90]

Chan-jan put the blame on both the Northern and Southern schools, but he still relied on the *Leng-ch'ieh shih-tzu chi's* account. By insisting that the textual basis of the one-practice samādhi was the *Wen-shu shuo ching,* he implied a criticism of the Southern (Ho-tse) School that rejected that scripture. But, despite his initial sympathy for the Northern School, he eventually rejected Ch'an completely. As "Sixth Patriarch" of the T'ien-t'ai tradition, he reasserted the T'ien-t'ai explanation of one-practice samādhi (as defined in the *Mo-ho chih-kuan).* While the *Leng-ch'ieh shih-tzu chi* tried to claim Fu ta-shih and his "keeping the One" for the Ch'an tradition, Ch'an-jan abruptly declared that this "Bodhi-sattva" Fu, the ancestor of his own master Hsüan-lang, was definitely superior to the Indian monk Bodhidharma.[91]

Pure Land masters interpreted one-practice samādhi as a samādhi of recollecting the Buddha *(nien-fo san-mei).* But several of them, like Ch'u-chin, were known for also practicing the Lotus samādhi *(fa-hua san-mei),* which appeared at that time as a variant of the "ontological" *i-hsing san-mei* (which took the Dharmadhātu as its object). The Lotus samādhi is mentioned in several inscriptions by Li Hua. Fei-hsi uses the same metaphor of archery as the *Leng-ch'ieh shih-tzu chi* to illustrate the constant succession of thoughts in one-practice samādhi.[92] But, despite the common ground offered by the notion of *i-hsing san-mei,* discussion of this topic frequently led to mutual criticism.[93] As David Chappell discusses more fully in his chapter later in this volume, the most famous criticism of Ch'an is found in Hui-jih's *Wang-sheng ching-t'u chi* ("Record of Rebirth in Pure Land"). This work, subsequently withdrawn from circulation during the Sung and preserved only by chance in Korea, speaks ironically of dhyāna masters who "recommend to monks and laymen to look within themselves for the Buddha and not to rely on an external Buddha." It goes on to argue that, in order to become a "good friend," one must also avoid relying on the instructions of such dhyāna masters and should know by oneself how to gaze at the mind *(k'an-hsin).*[94]

To whom was this criticism addressed? Certain parts of it seem valid for Ch'an as a whole. But seated meditation *(tso-ch'an)* is not denied as such. On the contrary, it is admitted as a "joint practice" as one of the

Six Perfections. The main target of Hui-jih appears to be the Southern School, with its insistence on emptiness *(śūnyatā)* and its rejection of all works. Is it just a coincidence that this criticism of Ch'an was made soon after Shen-hui's attack on the Northern School? Some monks from the Yü-ch'üan ssu branch of T'ien-t'ai, namely Fei-hsi and Ch'u-chin, were connected to the city of Nan-yang, whence Shen-hui had launched his offensive.[95] This fact may be a clue to their criticism of the Southern School. They were initially sympathetic to the Northern School; only later, with the intensification of the polemic within Ch'an, did they assert their own lineage and their own interpretation of one-practice samādhi on the basis of the *Wen-shu shuo ching.*

However, if the "exclusive/eclectic" aspect of *i-hsing san-mei* belonged to the same polemical discourse as the "sudden/gradual" paradigm, how could this one-practice samādhi be seen as a valid alternative? Before trying to answer this question, I should point out that, during the T'ang Dynasty, all Buddhist schools derived from Mahāyāna were—in theory at least—advocating a "sudden" doctrine; Northern Ch'an was certainly no exception. But, due to the success of Shen-hui's polemic, the term "sudden awakening" became the label of the Southern School. To be complete, Shen-hui's victory required that one-practice samādhi, synonymous as it was with "sudden awakening," also become the exclusive possession of the Southern School. He encountered unexpected resistance, however. On the one hand, one-practice samādhi was too closely associated with the Northern School—probably due to the *Leng-ch'ieh shih-tzu chi's* influence. On the other hand, the semantic field covered by this notion differed slightly from that of "sudden awakening," allowing other schools to reject Shen-hui's claim. Therefore, to support the Northern School and to assert their own "sudden teaching" against Shen-hui's "sudden awakening," the T'ien-t'ai and Pure Land schools chose to stress the canonical definition of the *i-hsing san-mei,* with its ontological and methodological *(nien-fo)* components.

The reaction of the Southern School to this polemical front is not known. Logically, it should have included the T'ien-t'ai and the Pure Land schools in its criticism of "gradualism." A passage in the *Ching-te ch'uan-teng lu* ("Record of the Transmission of the Lamp [Compiled in] the Ching-te [Period]") (1004) hints at this: the Sixth Patriarch Hui-neng criticizes a poem by the monk Wo-lun in a way reminiscent of his rejection of Shen-hsiu's poem on the "mind-mirror." The identity of Wo-lun is not clear, but he was obviously close to the Northern School and Ch'an/Pure Land circles. His original poem, found in Tun-huang manuscripts, expresses a conception akin to the one-practice samādhi of the *Leng-ch'ieh shih-tzu chi;* a passage of his *K'an-hsin fa* ("Method for Gazing at the Mind") also appears in the preface of the *Leng-ch'ieh shih-tzu chi* and in Fa-chao's *Ching-t'u fa-shen tsan* ("Praise to the Dharma-Body of the Pure Land"). His thought played an important role in China as well as in Tibet, and the amalgamation with Shen-hsiu made by the Southern Ch'an tradition may be significant.

Another example of such a compromise can be found in Tsung-mi's writings. In his *General Preface,* Shen-hui's disciple attempts to contrast the Southern School's superior type of one-practice samādhi to the poor practice summarized as "stopping the unreal and cultivating mind" *(hsi-wang hsiu-hsin).* He adds:

> The disciples of [Chih-]shen in the South, [Shen-]hsiu in the North, Pao-t'ang, Hsüan-shih, and others are all of this type. The techniques of advancement of Ox-head, T'ien-t'ai, Hui-ch'ou, Guṇabhadra, and others are much the same [as this type], but their understanding is different.[96]

In his conclusion to the same work, Tsung-mi incidently connects the names of Guṇabhadra (394–468), Hui-ch'ou (= Seng-ch'ou, 480–560), and Wo-lun.[97] We may, in this classification, detect a veiled criticism of contemporary trends in Ch'an and read the name of Ching-chüeh behind those of Guṇabhadra and Seng-ch'ou. The author of the *Leng-ch'ieh shih-tzu chi* had indeed become famous for claiming that Guṇabhadra was the first Ch'an patriarch, and he had presented himself as a spiritual heir of Seng-ch'ou, Bodhidharma's traditional counterpart. Ching-chüeh's conception of one-practice samādhi and the patriarchal lineage had a lasting influence. Almost one century after the "sudden/gradual" controversy, Tsung-mi still felt the need to usurp the *Leng-ch'ieh shih-tzu chi*'s claim of orthodoxy.

Nonetheless, Tsung-mi's attempt at a synthesis and his militant syncretism came too late. Already, in the Hung-chou School, a radically new type of Ch'an was developing, one that needed none of the old *Problematik* of one-practice samādhi. Even the "pure dhyāna of the Tathāgata"—in which Tsung-mi saw the "Highest Vehicle"—was judged too philosophical. It had to be pushed aside before the "Ch'an of the patriarcal masters" *(tsu-shih ch'an).* Saichō was correct in arguing that one-practice samādhi summarized the Ch'an tradition that stemmed from Bodhidharma. But this tradition, which he attempted to transplant to Japan, existed only precariously in China. The same could probably be said of the three other traditions—T'ien-t'ai, Vinaya, and Tantrism—studied by Saichō and his disciples during the ninth century.

The disappearance of one-practice samādhi as a topic of religious discourse should be interpreted as one of the signs of the epistemological break that took place between "early" and "classical" Ch'an. But one must not underestimate the importance of this notion; it permitted a fruitful dialectic between metaphysics and practice and thus facilitated the transition to "classical" Ch'an. Moreover, by giving a common referent to the T'ien-t'ai, Ch'an, and Pure Land schools, this concept greatly contributed to closing the gaps among these Buddhist trends of thought. It lost its interest precisely when the relationships among the three schools were turning antagonistic. And it was precisely to counterweight such an evolution that Saichō based his syncretic doctrine on this one-practice samādhi.

Notes

1. Mochizuki Shinkō, *Bukkyō daijiten* (Tokyo: Sekai seiten kankō kyōkai, 1958), vol. 1, p. 130a.
2. *T*8.731a. The entire passage is translated in the paper by David Chappell below.
3. See *Ratnakūṭa, T*11.655b–656a.
4. Hirai Shun'ei, "Ichigyōzammai to kūkan shisō," *Sōtōshū kenkyūin kenkyūsei kenkyū kiyō,* no. 3 (1971), pp. 5–12.
5. See Paul Demiéville, "La Yogācārabhūmi de Saṅgharakṣa," *Bulletin de l'École Française d'Extrême-Orient,* vol. 44, no. 2 (1954), pp. 409–410.
6. *T*32.582b.
7. Such as Wŏnhyo (617–686) and Fa-tsang (643–712). See *T*#1846 and *T*# 1847.
8. *T*46.11a22–23.
9. *T*46.11a25.
10. *T*46.11b22.
11. *Dainihon bukkyō zensho,* vol. 22 (Tokyo: Bussho kankōkai, 1978), pp. 285–287.
12. *T*46.182ab.
13. See *Chih-kuan ta-i, T*46.459c10.
14. See *Ssu-ming tsun-che chiao-hsing lu, T*46.868a26.
15. *T*47.14c.
16. See *Wang-sheng li-tsan chi, T*47.439a24.
17. *Jōdoshū zensho,* vol. 4 (Tokyo: Sankibō busshorin, 1973), p. 383.
18. *T*47.128c.
19. Mochizuki, *Bukkyō daijiten,* vol. 1, p. 131a.
20. *T*85.1287b. See David Chappell's chapter in this volume for further discussion of Tao-hsin's understanding of one-practice samādhi. See also David Chappell, "The Teachings of the Fourth Ch'an Patriarch Tao-hsin (580–651)," in Whalen Lai and Lewis R. Lancaster, eds., *Early Ch'an in China and Tibet* (Berkeley: Asian Humanities Press, 1983), pp. 89–129.
21. In some respects, it seems closer to the fourth samādhi expounded by Chih-i, "neither walking nor sitting." See the previous chapter by Daniel Stevenson.
22. In fact, Suzuki himself immediately tries to blur this opposition by judging it superficial: the two apparently opposite interpretations of Tao-hsin and Hui-neng would refer to the same "deep" religious experience. If this reasoning is admitted, one has to conclude that the Northern and Southern schools are, as far as their spirituality is concerned, fundamentally identical. Of course, Suzuki carefully avoids drawing this conclusion. See *Suzuki Daisetsu zenshū,* vol. 2 (Tokyo: Iwanami shoten, 1968), pp. 222 ff.

23. *Dengyō daishi zensho,* vol. 2 (Tokyo: Sekai seiten kankō kyōkai, 1975), p. 210.
24. *T*85.1290b1–4.
25. See my paper "Shen-hsiu et l'Avataṁsaka," *Memoirs of the Research Institute for Humanistic Studies,* no. 19 (1983), pp. 1–15.
26. *T*#1667.
27. *T*85.1273c23.
28. I have adapted the translation of Philip Yampolsky, *The Platform Sutra of the Sixth Patriarch* (New York: Columbia University Press, 1967), pp. 136–137 (cf. *T*48.338b). Yampolsky, following the "ontological" tradition, translates *i-hsing san-mei* as "the samādhi of oneness."
29. *T*14.538b, 542c.
30. The T'ien-t'ai influence is, however, strong in the *Platform Sūtra,* as was argued by Neal Donner in his paper "The Perfect and the Sudden: T'ien-t'ai Light on the Platform Sūtra," presented at the American Council for Learned Societies-sponsored conference "The Sudden/Gradual Polarity: A Recurrent Theme in Chinese Thought," held at the Kuroda Institute in 1981. A substantially revised version of this paper is to be published in the conference volume edited by Robert M. Gimello and Peter N. Gregory, forthcoming from the University of Hawaii Press.
31. Yanagida Seizan, ed., *Sōdōshū, Zengaku sōsho,* vol. 4 (Kyoto: Chūbun shuppansha, 1974), p. 48b.
32. Hu Shih, ed., *Shen-hui ho-shang i-chi,* (Taipei: Hu Shih chi-nien kuan, 1970), p. 181; cf. French translation by Jacques Gernet, *Entretiens du Maître de Dhyāna Chen-houei du Ho-tsö,* (Paris: Publications de l'École Française d'Extrême-Orient, 1949), pp. 99–100.
33. Hu Shih, p. 308.
34. *T*48.399b; I have adapted the translation by Jeffrey L. Broughton, "Kuei-feng Tsung-mi: The Convergence of Ch'an and the Teachings" (Ph.D. dissertation, Columbia University, 1975), pp. 93–94.
35. And in particular to a text like the *Wu-sheng fang pien men* (*T*#2834).
36. As in the case of the "sudden/gradual" controversy. This controversy, as is well known, started at the conference of Hua-t'ai in 734 when Shen-hui labelled the Northern School "collateral" (as to its lineage) and "gradual" (as to its practice). Although this criticism was hardly justified, it allowed the rival Southern School to rise as the orthodox representative of the Ch'an tradition. On this question, see Yampolsky's Introduction to *The Platform Sutra* and the forthcoming volume referred to in note 30 above. See also the sudden/gradual conference report published in *Journal of Chinese Philosophy,* vol. 9 (1982), pp. 471–486.
37. See Hirano Sōjō, ed., *Tongo yōmon, Zen no goroku,* vol. 6 (Tokyo: Chikuma shobō, 1970), p. 92.
38. For examples of the "traditional" approach, see the following articles of Kobayashi Enshō: "Zen ni okeru ichigyō-zammai no igi," *IBK,* vol. 9 (1961), pp. 160–161; "Ichigyō-zammai shikō," *Zengaku kenkyū,* vol. 51 (1961), pp. 176–186; "Ichigyō-zammai ron," *Nihon bukkyō gakkai nempō,* vol. 41 (1976), pp. 159–173. See also Hirai Shun'ei, "Ichigyō-zammai to kūkan shisō" and Fujiwara Ryōsetsu, "Ichigyō-zammai ni tsuite," *Ryūkoku daigaku ronshū,* no. 360 (1959), pp. 1–10
39. This idea was also, at the beginning, present in the Ch'an interpretation. See Yanagida Seizan and Umehara Takeshi, *Mu no tankyū: Chūgoku Zen* (Tokyo: Kadokawa shoten, 1969), pp. 104–108.

40. Such a conception seems very close to Dōgen's notion of *"gyōji;"* see *Shō-bōgenzō, T*82.127ff.
41. *T*45.550a.
42. *T*85.1289b3.
43. "Sudden awakening" is synonymous with *"an-hsin"* ("pacifying the mind") or *"li-ju"* ("entrance via Principle"). See Yanagida Seizan, "Hoku-shū Zen no shisō," *Zenbunka kenkyūjo kiyō,* vol. 6 (1974), pp. 67–104.
44. *T*85.1288a22.
45. T'ang Yung-t'ung, *Han Wei liang Chin nan-pei ch'ao fo-chiao shih* (T'ai-pei: Ting-wen shu-chu, 1975), pp. 71, 79.
46. See *Lao Tzu,* ch. 10; Kristofer Schipper, *Le corps taoïste* (Paris: Fayard, 1982), pp. 175–208; and Paul Andersen, *The Method of Holding the Three Ones: A Taoist Manual of Meditation of the Fourth Century* A.D. (London: Curzon Press, 1980).
47. *Pao-p'u-tzu,* ch. 18, *Tao-tsang,* 870 (Taipei: Chung-hua shu chu, 1974).
48. *Ibid.*
49. Concerning the Mao-shan School, see Michel Strickmann, "The Mao Shan Revelations: Taoism and the Aristocracy," *T'oung Pao,* vol. 63, no. 1 (1977), pp. 1–64; concerning the *Ch'ung-hsüan* school, see Isabelle Robinet, *Les commentaires du Tao tö king jusqu'au VIIe siècle* (Paris: Institut des Hautes Études Chinoises, 1977), pp. 96 ff.
50. See Yoshioka Yoshitoyo, *Dōkyō to bukkyō,* vol. 3 (Tokyo: Kokusho kankō-kai, 1976), p. 307.
51. Stein #6825, edited by Jao Tsung-i, *Lao-tzu Hsiang-erh chu chiao chien* (Hong Kong: Tong Nam, 1956), pp. 13 and 63–65; see also Anna Seidel, *La divinisation de Lao-tseu dans le taoïsme des Han* (Paris: Publications de l'École Française d'Extrême-Orient, 1969), p. 78.
52. See *Tao-tsang,* 77, and Yoshioka, *Dōkyō to bukkyō,* vol. 3, pp. 335–336.
53. Paul Pelliot, "Autour d'une traduction sanscrite du Tao Tö King", *T'oung Pao,* vol. 13 (1912), pp. 415–416.
54. Notice that Shen-hsiu himself, according to the *Leng-ch'ieh shih-tzu chi,* defined his doctrine by the same expression: *"ch'ung-hsüan"* ("double mystery"). See *T*85.1290c5.
55. *T*9.370a.
56. See Hirano, ed., *Tongo yōmon,* p. 92.
57. See *T*85.1288c–1289a.
58. *T*85.1290b.
59. *T*85.1289c–1290a.
60. Or "one" character, *i-tzu.* Cf. *ibid.*
61. See *Suzuki Daisetsu zenshū,* vol. 2, p. 454.
62. See ms. Pelliot #2799 (Fonds Pelliot, Bibliothèque Nationale, Paris). The *Yao-chüeh* is discussed more extensively in the paper by John McRae to be published in the sudden/gradual volume mentioned in note 30 above.
63. See Paul Demiéville, *Le concile de Lhasa* (Paris: Presses Universitaires de France, 1952), pp. 78 ff.
64. See *Mang-lo chung-mo i-wen* in *Shih-k'o shih-liao hsin-pien,* vol. 19 (Taipei: Hsin wen feng ch'u-pan kung-ssu), pp. 14263–14264.
65. See Osabe Kazuo, *Tō Sō mikkyō shiron kō* (Kyoto: Nagata bunshodō, 1982), pp. 1–33.
66. *T*85.1289a20.
67. *T*85.1288c10.
68. *T*18.948c.

69. *T*85.1290b28.
70. Of course both matters were intimately related, since, according to the *Ch'an-yao,* the Precepts of the True Dharma amounted to dhāraṇīs.
71. See Yanagida Seizan, "Daijōkaikyō to shite no *Rokuso dangyō,*" *IBK,* vol. 12, (1964), pp. 65–72.
72. *T*74.653a.
73. *T*85.1287a7.
74. The *Leng-ch'ieh shih-tzu chi* is, in turn, quoted in a Tibetan manuscript, Pelliot #116, under the name of Hsiang-mo Tsang ("Tsang the devil-subduer"), another famous disciple of Shen-hsiu. The same definition of the "highest repentance" is given by Chih-ta in his *Yao-chüeh.*
75. Hirano, ed., *Tongo yōmon,* p. 197.
76. Lu Tseng-hsiang, *Pa-ch'iung shih chin-shih pu-cheng, Shih-k'o shih-liao hsin-pien,* vol. 53, p. 4849.
77. Yanagida Seizan, *Shoki zenshū shisho no kenkyū* (Kyoto: Hōzōkan, 1967), p. 489.
78. *Ibid.,* p. 487.
79. See *Bibliographie bouddhique,* vols. 7–8 (1934–1936) (Paris: Adrien-Maisonneuve, 1937), p. 133.
80. *T*85.1286c22.
81. *T*85.1290b4.
82. See *Yüan-kuei chi te ch'uang* in *Pa-ch'iung shih chin-shih pu-cheng, Shih-k'o shih-liao hsin-pien,* vol. 53, pp. 4849–4850.
83. See *Dengyō daishi zenshū,* vol. 2, pp. 202–203.
84. *Ibid.,* p. 210. See also Hui-k'o's biographical notice, *ibid.,* p. 207.
85. *Ibid.,* p. 212.
86. I have adapted Yampolsky's translation, *The Platform Sutra,* pp. 136–137.
87. For a discussion of the Yü-ch'üan ssu branch, see Tsukamoto Zenryū, *Chūgoku jōdokyōshi kenkyū* (Tokyo: Daitō shuppansha, 1976).
88. See *Ch'uan T'ang wen,* 320 (Taipei: Hua-wen shu chu, 1965), p. 4101.
89. See Saitō Kōjun, "Shakuen shirin," in Kushida Yoshihiro hakushi shoju kinenkai, ed., *Kōsōden no kenkyū; Kushida hakushi shoju kinen* (Tokyo: Sankibō busshorin, 1973), pp. 839–840.
90. *T*46.184c.
91. See *Chih-kuan i-li, T*46.452c20–21.
92. *T*47.240a.
93. See *T*47.466c24.
94. *T*85.1237c–1238b.
95. See Ōkubo Ryōjun, "Tōdai ni okeru Tendai no denjō ni tsuite," *Nihon bukkyō gakkai nempō,* vol. 17 (1952), pp. 87–99.
96. *T*48.402b29–c3; I have adapted Broughton's translation, p. 148.
97. See *T*48.412c18; Broughton, p. 298.

Ch'ang-lu Tsung-tse's *Tso-ch'an I* and the "Secret" of Zen Meditation

Carl Bielefeldt

It is not entirely without reason that Zen Buddhism is known as the Meditation School. Visitors to the modern Zen monastery, even if they are prepared to find meditation there, cannot but be struck by the extent to which the practice dominates the routine. The novice monk spends his first days almost entirely within the meditation hall, and, although he is expected during this period to learn some rudimentary features of clerical decorum, it is primarily his willingness to submit to the discipline of long hours of meditation in the cross-legged posture that will determine his admission into the community. Once accepted, he can expect to pass much of his daily life in this posture. Although customs differ with the institution and the season, it is not uncommon for the community to spend four to eight hours a day in formal meditation and at regular intervals to hold prolonged sessions during which the hours of practice may be increased to twelve, sixteen, or even more. To be sure, there are usually other things to do—rituals and begging rounds, study and lectures, administrative duties and manual labor—but, in principle at least, the monk's main work is meditation. When he meets in private with his master, it is often about the progress of this work that they are likely to talk.

Yet there is another sense in which Zen Buddhism appears to be an "anti-meditation school." For, whatever Zen monks may talk about in private, when they discuss their practice in public, they often seem to go out of their way to distance themselves from the ancient Buddhist exercises of samādhi and to criticize the traditional cultivation of dhyāna. The two Japanese Zen churches, Rinzai and Sōtō, have their own characteristic ways of going about this: the former most often attacks absorption in trance as a mindless quietism—what it sometimes calls the "ghost cave" *(kikutsu)* of the spirit—and claims to replace it with the more dynamic technique of *kanna,* or kōan study; the latter rejects the utilitarian component of contemplative technique—the striving, as it says, to "make a Buddha" *(sabutsu)*—and offers in its stead what it considers the less psychologically limited, more spiritually profound practice of *shikan taza,* or "just sitting." Of course, these critiques of meditation are not simply modern Japanese developments; while the contemporary teachings of both schools may owe much to Edo sectarian ideology, both trace their positions back to the famous Southern Sung disputes between the advocates of *k'an-hua,* or concentration on the *hua-t'ou,* and the champions of *mo-chao,* or "silent illumination." Indeed, whatever their differences in psychological technique and interpretative strategy, both these positions can be seen as instances of a characteristic Zen polemic against contemplative practice that goes back much further, almost to the very origins of the religion itself. To this extent, the Meditation School seems never to have been entirely happy with its name.

The Zen ambivalence toward its own specialization is reflected not only in the record of its recurrent and sometimes bitter disputes over meditation but also in the fact that this record tells us surprisingly little about the actual content of Zen meditation practice. If the school's ideological doubts about the practice have not prevented Zen monks from engaging in it, they do seem to have made the tradition more loath than most to discuss the concrete details of its spiritual techniques. Still, we are not entirely without resources; for, in addition to what little we can glean from the vast corpus of biographies, sayings, essays, and other writings of the school, we also have recourse to a small but interesting body of texts specifically intended to guide the practitioner through the basics of Zen meditation. Most of them, as we might expect, seem to have been written with the neophyte in mind, a characteristic that, if it limits their usefulness in determining the full range of Zen practices, also probably makes them relatively faithful to the actual experience of the majority of Zen practitioners. Like the tradition as a whole, they tend to eschew the doctrinally tidy, suspiciously systematic accounts of meditation that we find in the scholastic treatises; unlike much of the tradition, they also tend to avoid philosophical obscurity and literary fancy—or at least to balance them with a healthy dose of plain talk.

Of these meditation manuals, the earliest and in some ways most influential is a brief tract from the Northern Sung entitled simply *Tso-ch'an i* ("Principles of Seated Meditation"), attributed to a monk named Ch'ang-lu Tsung-tse (d.u.). Since this text is not very well known, I would like to introduce it here, together with some reflections on its place in the history of the Zen meditation tradition. Along the way, I shall suggest that, in writing his little manual, Tsung-tse broke with what might almost be called a conspiracy of silence about meditation and thereby helped to touch off the Southern Sung discourse on the subject—a discourse that, in one form or another, is still with us today.

The origin of the *Tso-ch'an i* is not entirely clear. The work is usually thought to have been composed as a section of the *Ch'an-yüan ch'ing-kuei* ("Pure Regulations of the Zen Preserve"), the earliest extant Zen monastic code, compiled by Ch'ang-lu Tsung-tse in 1103. The best-known version of this code does indeed contain the manual in fascicle 8, but this version represents a revised and enlarged edition published in 1202 by a certain Yü Hsiang (d.u.).[1] A variant text of the *Ch'an-yüan ch'ing-kuei,* produced in Korea from blocks carved in 1254 and based on a Northern Sung text printed in 1111, does not include the *Tso-ch'an i.* By far the earliest extant version of Tsung-tse's code, dated within a decade of the composition of the work, this variant strongly suggests that the original text of the *Ch'an-yüan ch'ing-kuei* lacked the manual of meditation.[2]

If the *Tso-ch'an i* was not in fact written as a part of Tsung-tse's monastic code, we cannot be certain of its date or, indeed, of its authorship. Still, there is reason to think that it belongs to the period, around the turn of the twelfth century, in which Tsung-tse flourished. We know that the manual was in circulation well before the publication of Yü Hsiang's edition, for an abbreviated version of the text already appears in the "Dhyāna" section of the *Ta-tsang i-lan* ("Compendium of the Canon"), the lengthy collection of scriptural passages compiled by Ch'en Shih (d.u.) sometime prior to 1157.[3] Ch'en Shih's quotation does not identify the author, but it does provide us with a *terminus ad quem* probably within a few decades of Tsung-tse's death. Yü Hsiang's version, moreover, contains a quotation from the Zen master Fa-yün Fa-hsiu (1027–1090), the presence of which indicates that the text cannot be earlier than mid eleventh century. This quotation is particularly significant because, as Yanagida Seizan has pointed out, it lends some credence to the tradition of Tsung-tse's authorship of the *Tso-ch'an i.* Although we have few details on Tsung-tse's life, we do know that he originally entered the order under Fa-hsiu. Hence, the appearance here of this master's saying—words not recorded elsewhere—would seem to provide circumstantial evidence for the work's ascription to his student Tsung-tse.[4]

However the *Tso-ch'an i* originated, it quickly became a well-known work after its publication in the *Ch'an-yüan ch'ing-kuei.* The early and enduring reputation of the text among Zen students was no doubt considerably enhanced by its association with Tsung-tse's monastic code, for the *Ch'an-yüan ch'ing-kuei* was widely regarded by the tradition as an expanded version of the original Zen regulations established by Po-chang Huai-hai (720–814). Hence, some who used its meditation manual may have done so in the belief that it preserved an ancient rite set down by the founder of Zen monasticism.[5] In this, they were probably mistaken. Though Tsung-tse himself claims that his *Ch'an-yüan ch'ing-kuei* represents a revision of Po-chang's rules to fit the circumstances of his day, it is by no means clear that he knew what those rules were. Despite Po-chang's fame as the creator of an independent Zen monastic system, and despite repeated references in the literature to the "Pure Regulations of Po-chang" *(Po-chang ch'ing-kuei),* there is little evidence that this monk actually produced a written code and still less that it survived to Tsung-tse's time.[6] In any case, given the radical changes in the Zen monastic system that had taken place in the centuries between the mid T'ang and the Sung, we may be sure that much in the *Ch'an-yüan ch'ing-kuei* would have been unfamiliar to Po-chang. Particularly when we turn to our text, the *Tso-ch'an i,* the connection with Huai-hai seems remote indeed. There is no evidence whatsoever that this T'ang master wrote a meditation manual; and especially if—as appears likely—Tsung-tse's own manual was not originally intended for the *Ch'an-yüan ch'ing-kuei,* there is no reason to think that it was based on Po-chang's teachings.

In the absence of any evidence that Po-chang authored the prototype for the *Tso-ch'an i,* Tsung-tse's manual represents the earliest known work of its kind in the Zen tradition. This does not, of course, by any means make it entirely without precedent in the Chinese Buddhist literature; indeed, Tsung-tse himself calls our attention to several earlier accounts of meditation on which he drew. In a passage of the *Tso-ch'an i* warning against the "doings of Māra" *(mo-shih),* which can afflict the higher stages of meditation practice, he advises the reader who seeks further information to consult the *Śūraṅgama-sūtra,* T'ien-t'ai's *Chih-kuan,* and Kuei-feng's *Hsiu-cheng i.* Of these, the first presumably refers to the T'ang text in ten fascicles traditionally attributed to Paramiti, a work quite popular with Tsung-tse's Sung contemporaries, which contains a detailed discussion of fifty demoniacal states of mind into which the practitioner may fall.[7] Apart from this particular discussion, there is nothing in the *Śūraṅgama* text that would serve as a basis for Tsung-tse's description of meditation. Such is not the case, however, with the other two works he mentions, which clearly have more intimate connections with his own manual.

We cannot say with certainty which text Tsung-tse intends by his reference to the *Chih-kuan.* One thinks first of the famous *Mo-ho chih-kuan* ("Greater [Treatise on] Calming and Discernment") by T'ien-t'ai Chih-i (538–597), a work that includes two lengthy sections on the various morbid and demoniacal states to which the meditator is susceptible.[8] Similar discussions, however, appear in other meditation texts by Chih-i, and it would seem that a more likely candidate here is the so-called *Hsiao chih-kuan* ("Lesser [Treatise on] Calming and Discernment"). Not only does this work contain an explanation of *mo-shih,* but, more importantly, it provides a concrete description of the preparation for, and practice of, meditation, several of the elements of which are reflected in the *Tso-ch'an i.* Moreover, it is the basis for the discussion of meditation practice in the *Hsiu-cheng i,* the other work to which Tsung-tse refers us.[9]

The *Yüan-chüeh ching hsiu-cheng i* ("Cultivation and Realization According to the *Perfect Enlightenment Sūtra"*) by Kuei-feng Tsung-mi (780–841) represents an extended explication of Buddhist practice according to the *Yüan-chüeh ching.* It consists of three major divisions dealing with the conditions for practice, the method of worship, and the method of meditation. As Sekiguchi Shindai has shown, large sections of the text, especially of the first and third divisions, are taken directly from the *Hsiao chih-kuan.* Indeed, when these sections are assembled and rearranged, it appears that Tsung-mi has quoted Chih-i's work almost in toto. It is passages from these same sections, in which the *Hsiu-cheng i* is relying on the *Hsiao chih-kuan,* that have parallels in our text.[10]

Although we can assume from Tsung-tse's reference to the *T'ien-t'ai chih-kuan* that he was familiar with Chih-i's manual and may, indeed, have consulted it in the writing of his own, the question of its direct influence on his text remains problematic. Sekiguchi, in his several studies of the *Hsiao chih-kuan,* has called attention to the parallels between the two texts and has emphasized the degree to which not only Tsung-tse's work but also many of the subsequent meditation manuals of Zen have relied, at least indirectly, on Chih-i. Such emphasis, it may be noted, is but an extension of this Tendai scholar's general argument for the T'ien-t'ai influence on the Zen tradition.[11] Whatever the merits of that argument as it applies to the early history of the school, its significance in this case would seem to have some real historical and textual limitations.

The *T'ien-t'ai hsiao chih-kuan,* as Sekiguchi has emphasized, probably represents the first practical manual of meditation available to the Chinese. Although it draws on material from several Indian and Chinese sources, it differs from earlier works in being expressly intended to introduce the practice of seated meditation to the beginning student.[12] Except for a brief final section, therefore, it omits discussion of the kind of technical T'ien-t'ai doctrine characteristic of most of Chih-i's writings and emphasizes instead the concrete description of the actual techniques of mental and physical discipline. For this reason, the work—and especially its "T'iao-ho" chapter on the control of body, breath, and mind—could serve as a handy, nonsectarian guide to the basics of Buddhist mental discipline; in fact, not only Tsung-mi but also many other Buddhist writers, from Tao-hsüan (596–667), Shan-tao (613–681), and Fa-tsang (643–712) on, referred to this chapter in their own presentations of seated meditation. It is hardly surprising, therefore, that by the Northern Sung a brief text like Tsung-tse's *Tso-ch'an i,* itself intended as a meditation primer, should reflect something of this popular guide. Yet such reflection should not blind us to the fact that, unlike the *tso-ch'an* section of Tsung-mi's

Hsiu-cheng i, Tsung-tse's manual is essentially a new work, original in both its language and the focus of its treatment.[13]

The *T'ien-t'ai hsiao chih-kuan's* discussion of meditation practice is divided into ten chapters covering, in addition to the morbid and demoniacal states, such topics as control of desire and abandonment of the *nivaraṇa,* development of *kuśula-mūla,* practice of śamatha and vipaśyanā, and so on. Tsung-tse ignores most of this technical material: not only, as might be expected, is there nothing in the *Tso-ch'an i* comparable to Chih-i's concluding chapter on the T'ien-t'ai dogma of the three truths *(san-ti),* but even on the central practice of *chih-kuan* itself we find not a word. Of the five chapters devoted to Chih-i's standard list of twenty-five spiritual techniques *(fang-pien),* only the first, on fulfilling the conditions for meditation, and (especially) the fourth, on regulating physical and mental activities in meditation, find significant parallels in our text. These parallels, moreover, aside from certain standard Buddhist admonishments, are limited almost wholly to the concrete description of the meditation posture—material that, by Tsung-tse's time, was surely the common lore of Chinese Buddhist monks and precisely the sort in which one would expect to find the least innovation. Under the circumstances, the question of influence, if it still remains relevant, becomes too vague to sustain much interest.[14]

Tsung-tse's *Tso-ch'an i,* then, is probably neither an elaboration of an earlier manual by Po-chang nor an abbreviation of Chih-i's work. Instead, it combines a portion of the kind of material found in the T'ien-t'ai text with a dash of the particular approach to meditation characteristic of some earlier Zen writings. The resulting mix—and the simple, colloquial style in which it is presented—gives Tsung-tse's Buddhism a very different flavor from Chih-i's sixth-century scholastic version. At the same time, it gives his meditation teachings a conservative, matter-of-fact quality that contrasts with much of the intervening Zen literature on the subject. This quality may, in fact, have been an important factor in the popularity of his manual, but it also makes the work—for all its seeming innocuousness—rather controversial. For if the text itself is new, its teachings, from the perspective of Sung Dynasty Zen, appear as something of a throwback to an earlier, less ideologically developed treatment of Buddhist practice—a treatment in some ways more akin to that of the *Hsiao chih-kuan* than to the received position of the school. Despite the widespread acceptance of the *Tso-ch'an i,* this heterodox character of the work was not entirely lost on its early readers, some of whom were prompted to react. To see why they were concerned, we shall need to recall the way in which the tradition had dealt with meditation. But first, let us look at what Tsung-tse himself has to say, and how his teaching compares with that of Chih-i.[15]

The *Tso-ch'an i* is a very brief text of no more than some 600–700 characters. Addressed to "the bodhisattva who studies prajñā," it opens with a reminder that the meditation to be described here should be cultivated for the benefit not just of the practitioner but of all living beings. Tsung-tse then mentions some preliminary conditions for the practice: the meditator should renounce worldly activities and seek quiet quarters, and he should regulate his eating and sleeping habits, avoiding either deprivation or indulgence. After these brief prefatory remarks, the text proceeds directly to the description of the meditation posture: one is to sit erect on a mat in the classic yogic cross-legged position *(chieh chia-fu tso)* or the variant semi-cross-legged position *(pan chia-fu tso),* with hands in the traditional meditation mudrā of the Dharmadhātu *(fa-chieh ting-yin);* the tongue rests against the palate, and the lips and teeth are closed; the eyes are kept slightly open; the breath is regulated. Having thus composed himself, the meditator is to relinquish all judgments and simply observe his thoughts as they arise; once observed, thoughts will cease, and eventually the mind will become unified.

Having completed his description of the practice, Tsung-tse praises it as "the Dharma-gate of ease and joy." When properly performed, it is easy to do and good for both body and mind. Still, he warns, when done improperly, it can lead to illness and, as we have seen, can generate various undesirable experiences, against which one should brace oneself. The text goes on to advise that, on leaving samādhi, one should arise slowly and calmly and, at all times, should try to maintain a meditative calm in order to develop the ability to enter samādhi at will *(ting-li).* Finally, the *Tso-ch'an i* closes with an appreciation of meditation and an admonition to put it into practice: without it, one will simply drift aimlessly in the sea of saṃsāra, at the mercy of death; with it, the surface waves of the mind will subside, and the pearl of liberating wisdom beneath will appear of its own accord. Therefore, we are reminded, the sūtras have recommended it, and the great sages of the tradition have practiced it. We should cultivate this meditation without delay, lest death intervene before its benefits are realized.

Such, in outline, is our text. Most of it is rather standard Buddhist fare, and those familiar with Chih-i will indeed recognize echoes of his presentation of meditation. The opening admonition to the bodhisattva is, of course, a constant refrain of the Mahāyāna literature and echoes a similar passage in the *Hsiao chih-kuan:* "The practitioner beginning to study *tso-ch'an* and intending to cultivate the dharmas of the Buddhas of the Ten Directions and three realms should first produce the great vow to lead all beings to liberation and to seek the supreme enlightenment of a Buddha."[16] The suspension of worldly activities and the retirement to secluded quarters, besides being obvious good advice, are items on an ancient list of five conditions for meditation discussed in the "Chü-yüan" chapter of the *Hsiao chih-kuan:* purity in keeping the precepts,

provision of food and clothing, retirement to a quiet place, cessation of
worldly involvements, and contact with good friends.[17] Moderation in
food and sleep corresponds to the first two of the five kinds of regulation
given in Chih-i's "T'iao-ho" chapter: food, sleep, body, breath, and
mind.[18]

Similarly, of course, the description of the meditation posture has
antecedents in the *Hsiao chih-kuan,* though Tsung-tse's passage is considerably abbreviated and, in fact, departs from Chih-i's model on some
basic points: where the latter prefers to sit with the right leg crossed over
the left, Tsung-tse opts for the position, more often seen in Zen, with the
left on top; where Chih-i recommends that the eyes be closed, Tsung-tse
goes out of his way to criticize this practice.[19] Again, as we have seen, the
subsequent warning on perverse states explicitly invokes Chih-i, and the
remarks on remaining mindful on leaving samādhi recall advice in the
closing section of his "T'iao-ho" chapter.[20]

If these passages in the *Tso-ch'an i* resemble material in the *Hsiao
chih-kuan,* more interesting are the passages that have no close equiva-
lents. Of these, the most important and problematic is the teaching on
the mental aspect of meditation. The "T'iao-ho" chapter follows the
description of the meditation posture with a discussion of the techniques
for regulating the mind to avoid the twin obstacles of torpor and agitation;[21] and in other chapters Chih-i recommends various mental antidotes for different spiritual problems. But the core of his meditation is,
of course, the traditional exercises of śamatha and vipaśyanā, from
which his manual takes its name. In the "Cheng-hsiu" chapter, which is
devoted to these exercises, he divides them into five types, depending on
the purposes for which they are practiced. Of these, the first, intended to
overcome the rough fluctuations of the mind at the outset of meditation,
is basic. There are essentially two types of śamatha exercises for this purpose: one is more or less mechanical, involving fixation on an object or
conscious suppression of random thoughts; the other is intellectual, in
which the practitioner is to understand as each thought occurs that its
object arises from conditions and has no nature of its own. This understood, the mind will not grasp the object, and deluded thoughts will
cease. A somewhat more complicated technique is recommended for the
vipaśyanā practice: if the meditator has failed to put an end to deluded
thoughts through śamatha, he should reflect on these thoughts, asking
himself whether they exist or not. Chih-i then supplies a set of arguments
that the practitioner can rehearse to convince himself that neither the
mind nor its object can be grasped; thus convinced, the mind will break
off discrimination and become still.[22]

Tsung-tse's meditation does not quite correspond to any of
these techniques. What he calls the "essential art" of meditation is simply this:

Do not think of any good or evil whatsoever. Whenever a thought occurs, be aware of it *(nien ch'i chi chüeh);* as soon as you are aware of it, it will vanish. If you remain for a long period forgetful of objects *(wang yüan),* you will naturally become unified *(i-p'ien).*

This passage has no parallel in the *Hsiao chih-kuan;* as we shall shortly see, it probably derives from Zen sources. If it has any analog in Chih-i's teachings, it is not in the *chih-kuan* techniques described in his manual, but rather in the simple mindfulness practice recommended as one of the famous four kinds of samādhi in the *Mo-ho chih-kuan*—the practice referred to there as neither walking nor sitting *(fei-hsing fei-tso)* and otherwise known as the samādhi of awareness of mind *(chüeh-i san-mei):*

The master Nan-yüeh [i.e., Hui-ssu] called this [practice] "to follow one's own mind" *(sui-tzu-i)*—that is, to cultivate samādhi whenever the mind arises *(i ch'i chi hsiu san-mei).* The *Ta-p'in ching (Pañcaviṃśati)* refers to it as the samādhi of awareness of mind—that is, [a state in which] wherever the mind may be directed, one is conscious of, and clear about, it. . . . "Awareness" *(chüeh)* here means luminous understanding *(chao-liao);* "mind" *(i)* means the mental dharmas *(hsin-shu; caitasika).* . . . In practicing this, when a mental dharma arises, one reflects on, and contemplates, it, without attending to its development—its source or outcome, its point of origin or destination.[23]

Whatever the antecedents of Tsung-tse's practice, it differs in one important respect from the vipaśyanā meditations recommended in the *Hsiao chih-kuan.* In these meditations, as is characteristically the case in vipaśyanā, the practitioner is expected to engage the object actively, contemplating it in terms of some Buddhist doctrine until he has brought about a change in the way the object occurs to him. In contrast, Tsung-tse's meditation seems to involve no such discursive activity; instead, the practitioner is to relinquish judgments and passively observe his thoughts as they come and go. In this sense, his practice is more akin to such common śamatha techniques as following the breath, observing the activities of the body, and so on. The difference is worth noting because the active-passive dichotomy is a recurrent theme in Zen discussions of meditation and one source of internecine dispute. Some of the dispute is no doubt engendered by the linkage of this theme with the somewhat similar but separable dichotomy of clarity and calm, a matter quite vexing to the Zen meditation tradition. On this latter issue as well, it is instructive to compare the *Tso-ch'an i* with the *Hsiao chih-kuan.*

It will be recalled that the *chih-kuan* practice I summarized earlier is expressly recommended for the control of the gross fluctuations of the mind; it is intended to put an end to the stream of deluded thoughts characteristic of ordinary consciousness and to bring about the calm, concentrated state of samādhi. This same state would seem to be the goal of Tsung-tse's meditation: one is to observe one's thoughts so that they will cease; one is to continue observing them until they no longer occur and the mind becomes unified. This agreement on the goal of the practice is hardly surprising: no doubt most Buddhists would hold with Tsung-tse that the unified state of samādhi, or dhyāna, is indeed the essential art of meditation. They would also hold, however, that this state is not an end in itself. Whether or not it is a necessary condition for enlightenment, it is not a sufficient one but must be supplemented by the generation of insight, or wisdom. On this point Chih-i would surely concur, as his entire *chih-kuan* system makes quite clear. Whether Tsung-tse would also agree is much less clear, at least from the text of the *Tso-ch'an i*. His silence on this matter makes it possible to interpret the work as recommending the elimination of thought for its own sake. A tendency toward some such understanding of yogic discipline is probably endemic to the Buddhist meditation teachings, from the early dhyāna and *samāpatti* systems on, and the religion has repeatedly been obliged to counter it with an emphasis on the need for doctrinal study. Zen Buddhism, with its focus on meditation and its characteristic dismissal of theoretical studies, has probably been particularly susceptible to this tendency and has often struggled mightily against it. Hence, if only by omission, the *Tso-ch'an i* account of meditation touches a sensitive nerve in the tradition.

In fairness to Tsung-tse, it must be pointed out that he is not entirely oblivious to the question of wisdom. In his opening remarks he recommends the cultivation of samādhi for one who has taken the Bodhisattva Vows and seeks to study prajñā. This passage undoubtedly reflects the traditional formula of the three disciplines *(san-hsüeh)* and suggests that, like most Buddhists, Tsung-tse understood the three as a series, such that meditation is based on ethics and somehow leads to wisdom. Unfortunately, he does not pause to discuss the question of just how it leads to wisdom, although later on he does give at least a hint of what he may have had in mind. In his rather rambling discussion of the benefits of meditation, he seems to offer three: it will make one happy, healthy, and peaceful; it will prepare one to face death; and it will lead to wisdom. This last is expressed through of a well-known metaphor:

> To seek the pearl, we should still the waves; if we disturb the water, it will be hard to get. When the water of meditation is clear, the pearl of the mind will appear of itself. Therefore, the *Perfect Enlightenment Sūtra* says, "Unimpeded, immaculate wisdom always arises dependent on meditation."[24]

As Tsung-tse uses it, the metaphor itself may have become somewhat opaque, but we can still discern the outlines of the model behind it:

wisdom rests deep within the mind, obscured only by the surface fluctuations of thought; once these fluctuations are calmed, it is automatically made manifest. Hence, meditation leads to wisdom not in the usual sense that it prepares the mind to undertake the discipline of prajñā, but in the sense that it uncovers a preexistent prajñā inherent in the mind. In this sense, it is possible to speak of the calm of meditation, if not as an end in itself, at least as a sufficient condition for that end. The theory behind this way of speaking—the model of the pure, enlightened mind covered by discursive thinking—is by no means, of course, an uncommon one, not only in Zen texts but also in Chih-i's writings and other versions of Mahāyāna. Whatever we may say of it as a theory, from the perspective of practice it offered Buddhism a handy way of dealing with the difficult question of the relationship between samādhi and prajñā and provided a meaningful rationale for the cultivation of meditation. These virtues notwithstanding, the theory was questioned by some of the most influential figures of the early Zen movement—figures whose teachings became the basis for orthodoxy in the later tradition. On this point too, then, the *Tso-ch'an i* could raise the eyebrows (if not the hackles) of its more thoughtful readers.

Tsung-tse's approach to Buddhism may not be quite that of sixth-century T'ien-t'ai treatises, but neither is it quite what we are familiar with from the recorded sayings of the great Zen masters of the late T'ang and Five Dynasties—sayings so popular among Tsung-tse's Sung contemporaries. If anything, he seems rather to take us back to an earlier phase of the school, when the Zen movement was still seeking to articulate its basic doctrinal positions and define a form of religious practice consistent with them. Indeed, of all the preceding Zen literature, his manual is perhaps most reminiscent of the kind of material one sometimes finds in the texts associated with the seventh-century East Mountain tradition of the patriarchs Tao-hsin (580–651) and Hung-jen (601–674). In the teachings of these men and their immediate successors in the so-called Northern School of the eighth century, we find the most explicit descriptions of Zen meditation prior to the *Tso-ch'an i* itself. In their teachings also we find the beginnings of the doctrines that, in the hands of their rivals in the Southern School, would render Zen meditation peculiarly problematic and help to silence, for some three centuries, the open discussion of its techniques.

This is not the place to explore in detail the early Zen meditation literature, a job in any case better left to those more expert in this matter than I. But it is worth recalling here several general features of this literature that help to explain some of the attitudes of the later tradition. Of the East Mountain corpus, we may take as examples the teachings of Tao-hsin in the *Leng-ch'ieh shih-tzu chi* ("Record of the Masters and Disciples of the *Laṅkāvatāra*") and the *Hsiu-hsin yao lun* ("Essentials of the Cultivation of the Mind"), attributed to Hung-jen. Whether or not this material represents accurate reports of the Buddhism of the Fourth and Fifth Patriarchs, it does preserve for us the understanding of their Buddhism current among influential factions of Zen in the eighth century. Both texts are highly practical in approach and provide fairly concrete instructions on a range of spiritual techniques. These seem to fall into three general types. One is a contemplation on emptiness roughly of the sort we have seen in Chih-i's meditations. We find this type, for example, in the Tao-hsin section of the *Leng-ch'ieh shih-tzu chi,* where it appears in conjunction with the famous practice of "guarding the one without moving" *(shou-i pu-i).* Here we are told to contemplate all dharmas of both body and mind—from the four elements and five *skandhas* to the dharmas of *pṛthagjana* and *ārya*—recognizing that they are all empty and quiescent, without origination or cessation, and so on. We should continue this practice in all activities, day and night, until we can see our own existence as but a reflection, a mirage, an echo. Should random thoughts intrude on the meditation, we are to see whatever occurs as ultimately not occurring, as coming from nowhere and going nowhere; when thoughts are seen thus, the mind becomes stabilized.[25]

More commonly encountered, and probably more characteristic of the tradition, are two other types of meditation. One recommends the observation of some symbol of what, for want of a better term, we may call the ultimate principle. Such, for example, is the popular one-practice samādhi *(i-hsing san-mei; ekavyūha-samādhi),* introduced at the outset of the Tao-hsin section of the *Leng-ch'ieh shih-tzu chi.* Here (following the instructions of the *Wen-shu shuo ching)* the practitioner is to focus on the image of a single Buddha, recognizing therein the identity of that Buddha with the entire Dharmadhātu and with the practitioner's own mind.[26] In the Hung-jen section the same text, we find a meditation on the numeral one, either projected onto the horizon or visualized internally; in this meditation one experiences a sense of unlimited space analogous to the dharmakāya.[27] Similarly, the *Hsiu-hsin yao lun,* using the sun as a metaphor for the true, enlightened mind within us all, recommends (following the *Kuan wu-liang-shou ching*) the contemplation of an image of the disk of the sun.[28]

The other type of technique involves some sort of simple concentration exercise, which would seem to be the practical import of Tao-hsin's most basic description of "guarding the one without moving." This technique is defined simply as maintaining the concentrated observation of one thing *(kuan i wu)* until the mind becomes fixed in samādhi. If the mind wanders, it is to be brought back to the object, as the saying goes, like a bird held by a string. Just as the archer gradually narrows his aim to the very center of the target, so too the meditator should learn to focus his attention until the mind remains fixed on its object in each moment, and right mindfulness *(cheng-nien)* is present without interruption.[29] Closest, perhaps, to Tsung-tse's description of meditation are some of the accounts of Hung-jen's practice of "guarding the mind" *(shou-hsin)* given in the *Hsiu-hsin yao lun.* In the most explicit of these, we are told to abandon the seizing of objects, to regulate body, breath, and mind, and then gently to focus on the fluctuations of consciousness *(hsin-shih liu-tung)* until they disappear of their own accord. When they do so, they take with them all the obstacles to complete enlightenment.[30]

The distinction among these types of meditation is not always clear, and such catchphrases as "guarding the one" or "guarding the mind" could, in practice, denote a variety of contemplative techniques. Whatever their differences, they seem to share a common theoretical context— the characteristic East Mountain doctrine of the pure, radiant consciousness inherent in every mind—and a common purpose—the detachment from, and eventual suppression of, the stream of discursive thoughts that obscures this consciousness. Perhaps most significantly, on the basis of these common elements, each of the techniques is typically presented as at once readily accessible to the beginner and yet leading directly to enlightenment.

This abrupt leap from a seemingly rather pedestrian psychophysical exercise to the rarified reaches of the spiritual path is well expressed in a passage from the *Leng-ch'ieh shih-tzu chi* attributed to Tao-hsin. There we are told that, when one first sets out to practice meditation and observe the mind, he should seek solitude. Sitting erect, he should loosen his robe and belt, relax his body, stretch himself several times, and exhale fully; then he will have a sense of expanding to his true nature and will become clear and vacant, tranquil and still. When he has thus regulated body and mind and settled his spirit, his breathing will be calm; as he gradually controls his mind, it will become clear and bright. When his contemplation becomes clear, and both inside and out become empty and pure, the mind itself will be quiescent, and the *ārya* mind *(sheng-hsin)* will appear. The text then goes on to tell us that the nature of this mind, always functioning within us, is the Buddha-nature, and that one who experiences this nature is forever released from saṃsāra and has transcended this world; he has, as the *Vimalakīrti Sūtra* says, suddenly regained his original mind *(pen-hsin).*[31]

Though this passage tells us little about the mental technique involved, its concrete description of some of the physical elements reminds us of both the *Hsiao chih-kuan* and the *Tso-ch'an i.* Indeed, the passage has been singled out by Sekiguchi as the first extant Zen account of meditation techniques.[32] What is perhaps most striking from a doctrinal perspective is its apparent identification of the calm, clear state of samādhi with the attainment of the *ārya* path, and the impression it gives that the beginning meditator, simply by quieting his mind, can in a single sitting attain this samādhi and propel himself onto that path. Such hyperbolic praise of meditation is not, of course, unusual in Buddhist literature; in fact, the message here is quite similar to the direct identification of śamatha with the attainment of nirvāṇa that we sometimes find in the *Hsiao chih-kuan* itself.[33] Nor is the recommendation of a single, simple practice for exclusive cultivation without ample precedent: it is a characteristic of some of the very Mahāyāna sūtra literature on which both Chih-i and the East Mountain teachers like to draw for their accounts of meditation. Unlike more conservative interpretations of such literature, the East Mountain teachings tend to ignore the various graded hierarchies of vehicles, paths, stages, and the like that provide the traditional contexts for specific meditations. In effect, then, they seem to reduce the panoply of Buddhist spiritual exercises to a single practice and the perpetuity of the bodhisattva path to a single experience. In this, they are presenting one form of a "sudden" version of Buddhist practice.

The Zen tradition may look to its own Sixth Patriarch for its doctrine of sudden enlightenment, but by his day, of course, notions of a sudden approach to practice had been current in Chinese Buddhism for some time. One such notion was basic to the early T'ien-t'ai discussion of meditation and is well expressed in Kuan-ting's oft-quoted introduction to the *Mo-ho chih-kuan*. There we are told that, unlike the gradual cultivation of śamatha-vipaśyanā, which proceeds through the *mārga* by overcoming in turn the obstacles characteristic of each of the stages of the path, the "perfect sudden" *(yüan-tun)* practice takes from the start the ultimate reality of the Dharmadhātu itself as the sole object of meditation. Such a practice is based on what T'ien-t'ai considers the highest version of Buddhism—the one Buddha vehicle, in which, as the text says, every sight and every smell is the ultimate Middle Way, in which ignorance is identical with enlightenment, saṃsāra is identical with nirvāṇa, and there is no religious path leading from one to the other. In such a practice, śamatha is nothing but the quiescence of *dharmatā* itself *(fa-hsing chi-jan),* and vipaśyanā is but its constant luminosity *(ch'ang-chao).*[34]

In one sense, the distinction here between "gradual" and "sudden" practices can be seen as one between antidotal meditations, which are intended to counteract specific spiritual obstacles, and what we might call wisdom meditations, which, like the venerable *nirvedha-bhāgīya* exercises, take the metaphysical doctrines of Buddhism as their theme and lead directly (and, by necessity, quite suddenly and inexplicably) to an insight into the truth of these doctrines. The model here seems clearly to be the last of such meditations, the mighty *vajropamasamādhi,* in which the bodhisattva vaults, in one moment of trance, to supreme, perfect enlightenment. For his part, Chih-i is ever careful to hedge around such moments of ecstatic vision with the drudgery of traditional Buddhist training and to find room on his one great vehicle for even the humblest forms of *upāya*. Ever the scholar, he never forgets the distinction between theory and practice or the various levels of philosophical discourse and spiritual maturation. Yet for those impatient to taste the fruits of his supreme Buddha vehicle, the prospect of a sudden meditation beyond the old practices of the *bodhisattvamārga* was too tempting to postpone to the final course.

The most obvious problem with the "sudden" meditation, of course, is that, taken in itself, its radical nondualism undermines the rationale for its practice. Chih-i's ample Buddhism could easily live with this problem, for its catholic embrace of *upāya* allowed him room to discuss the practical methods of even this most mysterious and metaphysical of meditations—hence the *Mo-ho chih-kuan*'s detailed presentation of the practice of contemplation of the mind, in which the "sudden" meditation is effected through the recognition of the three thousand dharmas in every thought *(i-nien san-ch'ien)*. Similarly, the early Zen movement, though no doubt inspired by the notion of a perfect Buddha vehicle, still tended to operate within a model—of the Buddha-nature obscured—that retains what T'ien-t'ai would call the relative *(hsiang-tai)* understanding more characteristic of the separate *(pieh)* bodhisattva vehicle. Though its vision of meditation may have narrowed to the single, sudden practice that leads directly to enlightenment, it still takes for granted the kind of distinctions—between theory and practice, *hetu* and *phala,* meditation and wisdom—that allow it to speak frankly of the *upāya* through which this practice is implemented. But as the movement, perhaps in the heat of sectarian competition, began to focus more and more narrowly on the supreme vehicle *(wu-shang sheng),* on the one true teaching *(chen-tsung),* on the meditation of the Tathāgata *(ju-lai ch'an),* and so on, the metaphysics of the absolute, nondual truth became the norm. Thus, the radiant Buddha-nature became ever brighter, its obscurations ever emptier, and the contradiction inherent in any description of a method for inducing the "sudden" practice ever more obvious.

It is this contradiction, of course, that so tickled the fancy of the movement known to us as the Southern School and inspired the severe criticisms of meditation that we find in texts like the *Platform Sūtra* and Shen-hui's *T'an yü* ("Platform Teachings") and *Ting shih-fei lun* ("Determination of the Truth"). Taking its stand in the uncompromised cardinal principle *(ti-i i)* of the Perfection of Wisdom alone, the movement delighted in pointing out the folly of methods to overcome what was, after all, not really real. Now the "sudden" practice was to be precisely that which sees through the unreal and abandons all *upāya*—that which is without attributes *(wu-hsiang),* without intentionality *(wu-wei),* without artifice *(wu-tso),* and so on. Since it was without characteristics, this practice could not be described; since it was without artifice, nothing could be done about it: it was enough to recognize this fact and leave off misguided attempts to cultivate Buddhism. Meditation, as Buddhist cultivation *par excellence* (and the forte of the Northern masters), was particularly to be avoided: any effort to control or suppress thoughts was *ipso facto* a "gradual"—and, hence, at best a second-rate—form of Buddhism. In first-rate Buddhism, the true meaning of sudden meditation was simply that the mind was inherently calm, inherently without any deluded thoughts *(wu-nien)* that might disturb it. In this way, the practical thrust of early Zen meditation was overwhelmed by its own logic: religious prescription was sublated in metaphysical description, and samādhi was liberated from its earthly burdens, to join prajñā in the higher realm of pure Principle.

Thus, by the mid eighth century, even as the movement was becoming known as the Meditation School, it was beginning to find itself unable openly to advocate the practice of meditation. This predicament is well reflected in the writings of Shen-hui himself: hemmed in by his doctrine of no-thought and its rejection of contemplative practices, he is left with little room for cultivation and can only hint shyly at how one might go about practicing his Buddhism. Not surprisingly, perhaps, what he hints at turns out to be a version of the mindfulness technique we have seen in Hung-jen—the same practice recommended much later by Tsung-tse.

In the *Ting shih-fei lun,* when asked about no-thought *(wu-nien),* Shen-hui replies that it is not thinking about being or nonbeing, about good or evil, *bodhi* or nirvāṇa, and so on; it is nothing but the Perfection of Wisdom, which is itself one-practice samādhi. He then describes this samādhi.

> Good friends, for those at the stage of practice, whenever a thought occurs to the mind, be aware of it *(hsin jo yu nien ch'i chi pien chüeh-chao).* When what has occurred to the mind disappears, the awareness of it vanishes of its own accord. This is no-thought.[35]

Similarly, in the *T'an yü,* in warning against the misguided attempt to purify the mind of delusion, he says,

> Friends, when you correctly employ the mind, if any deluded [thought] occurs and you think about things either near or far, you should not try to constrain it. Why? Because, if the putting forth of a thought is a sickness, the constraint of it is also a sickness. . . . If any deluded [thought] occurs, be aware of it *(jo yu wang ch'i chi chüeh).* When awareness and delusion have both disappeared, this is the non-abiding mind of the original nature.[36]

In keeping with his "sudden" doctrine, Shen-hui seems to be trying here to close the gap between the spiritual exercise and its goal—to offer a unified practice of samādhi and prajñā and provide an account of this practice that will be no more (and no less) than a description of the enlightened state itself. Since that state is our natural state of mind, and meditation and wisdom are both inherent, clearly only the most passive, most minimal of meditations will do—hence his rejection of formalized contemplation and visualization techniques in favor of a simple mindfulness. Yet for all his doubts about dhyāna and suspicions of samādhi, his description of practice still seems to suggest (though he is careful to keep this ambiguous) that no-thought, or the original, non-abiding nature of the mind, is to be discovered when thoughts have been extinguished. In this, he is not so different from the earlier tradition or from Ch'ang-lu Tsung-tse. In fact, Shen-hui's Buddhism remains rather conservative: while he argues ardently for the Sudden School, he acknowledges here and there that his "sudden awakening," though it launches one directly onto the path, must still be followed by a gradual cultivation of that path.[37] As is well known, this teaching of sudden enlightenment and gradual practice *(tun-wu chien-hsiu)* was fixed in its classic form by his self-styled descendant in the fifth generation, the Hua-yen master Kuei-feng Tsung-mi.

Tsung-mi sought to check the Zen School's rapid drift toward a radical rejection of works and to steer its practice back onto a more traditional Buddhist course. To this end, he tried to align its teachings with scholastic categories and confine its definition of "sudden awakening" to an initial insight attained at the early stages of the path.[38] Thus freed from the need for a single, "sudden" meditation, he could, as we have seen, advocate the frankly gradual techniques of Chih-i's *Hsiao chih-kuan.* Yet as heir to the supreme vehicle of the Southern School, even Tsung-mi had to bite his tongue. Such techniques belonged, after all, only to the very lowest form of Zen, that which teaches "the stopping of delusion and cultivation of mind" *(hsi-wang hsiu-hsin).* As we learn in his *General Preface (Ch'an-yüan chu-ch'üan chi tu-hsü),* this form of Zen, though it recognizes the Buddha-nature inherent in all beings, still believes that in ordinary beings the nature is obscured by ignorance, and, hence, that there is a real difference between *pṛthagjana* and *ārya.* On these grounds, it encourages the contemplation of the mind *(kuan-hsin),* in order to wipe away deluded thoughts. Thus it emphasizes techniques for entering samādhi, teaching one to "dwell in a quiet place, avoiding the hustle and bustle of the world, to regulate body and breath, to sit in silent meditation with the legs crossed, the tongue pressed against the palate, and the mind fixed on a single object." Such is the Zen of Shen-hui's notorious enemy, the benighted Northern master Shen-hsiu; Shen-hsiu's understanding, says Tsung-mi, may differ somewhat from that of T'ien-t'ai, but his techniques are basically the same.[39]

The highest form of Zen, in contrast, "directly reveals the nature of

the mind" *(chih-hsien hsin-hsing).* Here all dharmas are just the true
nature, which is without attributes *(wu-hsiang)* and without conditions
(wu-wei), beyond all distinctions of *pṛthagjana* and *ārya,* cause and
effect, good and evil, and so on. In this teaching, deluded thoughts are
inherently quiescent, and mental objects inherently empty: there is only
the numinous awareness *(ling-chih)* that is one's own true nature, without thought *(wu-nien)* and without form *(wu-hsiang).* The practice of
this Zen is simple and, by now, quite familiar.

> If one is aware that all attributes are empty, the mind will naturally be with-
> out thought *(wu-nien).* As soon as a thought occurs, be aware of it *(nien ch'i
> chi chüeh);* as soon as you are aware of it, it will cease to exist. The pro-
> found gate of practice lies precisely here.[40]

If even Tsung-mi was thus constrained by the "sudden" doctrine to
relegate the meditation teachings of his own *Hsiu-cheng i* to the lowest
rank of Zen, it is hardly surprising that his more radical contemporaries
would be reluctant to associate their Buddhism with meditation. And
though his catholic vision would be preserved by men like Yung-ming
Yen-shou (904–975) and others who sought to integrate Zen and the scholastic systems, already by his day the mantle of the Sixth Patriarch had
passed to the radicals. In their style of Zen, the emphasis shifts, as is
sometimes said, from "substance" *(t'i)* to "function" *(yung)*—from the
glorification of the calm, radiant Buddha-nature latent in every mind to
the celebration of the natural wisdom active in every thought. Now the
everyday mind is the Way, and the suppression of that mind is a mistake.
In such a setting, to talk of sitting calmly in meditation is in poor taste;
rather, one must be ever on one's toes, vitally engaged in the object.
Thus, the great masters of the second half of the T'ang—especially those
of the dominant Hung-chou School of Tsung-mi's adversary Ma-tsu Tao-
i (709–788)—turned their often remarkable energies to the creation of
new techniques more appropriate to the new spirit of the "sudden" practice. The old forms of cultivation were superseded—at least in the imagination of the tradition—by the revolutionary methods of beating and
shouting or spontaneous dialogue, and formal discussion of Buddhist
doctrine and praxis gave way to suggestive poetry, enigmatic sayings, and
iconoclastic anecdotes. In the process, the philosophical rationale for
Zen practice, not to mention its psychological content, became part of
the great mystery of things.[41]

For all this, it is doubtful that many Zen monks, even in this period,
actually escaped the practice of seated meditation. We may recall, for
example, that the Sixth Patriarch himself, in the *Platform Sūtra,* leaves
as his final teaching to his disciples the advice that they continue in the
practice of *tso-ch'an,* just as they did when he was alive; that in the *Li-tai*

fa-pao chi ("Record of the Generations of the Dharma Treasure") the radical Pao-t'ang master Wu-chu (714–777), whom Tsung-mi saw as negating all forms of Buddhist cultivation, still admits to practicing *tso-ch'an;* that Hui-hai's *Tun-wu ju-tao yao men* ("Essential Teaching of Entering the Way Through Sudden Awakening") begins its teaching on "sudden awakening" by identifying *tso-ch'an* as the fundamental practice of Buddhism; that Ma-tsu himself, though he is chided by his master for it, is described by his biographers as having constantly practiced *tso-ch'an;* and that, according to the *Ch'an-men kuei-shih* ("Zen Regulations"), Po-chang found it necessary to install long daises in his monasteries to accommodate the monks in their many hours of *tso-ch'an.*[42] Such indications of the widespread practice of meditation could no doubt be multiplied severalfold. Indeed, the very fact that Wu-chu, Huai-jang, Lin-chi, and other masters of the period occasionally felt obliged to make light of the practice can be seen as an indication that it was taken for granted by the tradition. It is probably safe to assume that, even as these masters labored to warn their disciples against fixed notions of Buddhist training, the monks were sitting with legs crossed and tongues pressed against their palates. But what they were doing had now become a family secret. As Huai-jang is supposed to have said to the Sixth Patriarch, it was not that Zen monks had no practice, but that they refused to defile it.[43]

In one sense, then, the style of classical Zen can be seen as the culmination of the efforts of the early movement to liberate Buddhism from its monastic confines and to open the religion to those unequal to, or unattracted by, the rigors of the traditional course of yogic discipline. In another sense—a sense, I think, too rarely recognized—its style represented the termination of such efforts, brought about in part by the very success of the school itself. The earlier meditation texts of the East Mountain tradition, like most of the Tun-huang Zen materials, were written by men who were striving to promote a new brand of Buddhism attractive to the new society of the mid T'ang. To this end, they sought, among other things, to articulate a practical approach to Buddhist training accessible to the ordinary man and to advertise that approach as a distinctive asset of the school. By the turn of the ninth century, however, the public promotion of Zen was no longer an issue, for by then the school was comfortably established as a legitimate institution. Now it could remain ensconced on its famous mountains and wait for its followers to come; and now it could revert to the esoteric style of the cloister, where meditation practice was taken for granted and its techniques transmitted orally within the community. In the context of this community, where the monk enjoyed intimate contact with the meditation master, the radical new devices of shouting, beating, riddles, and repartee undoubtedly served to invigorate the practice and inspire the practitioner with a more vivid sense of his goal. But outside this context, these devices offered few clues to how the ordinary believer might gather himself spiritually for the leap to nirvāṇa. Ironically enough, then, the practical effect of the new doctrine of "sudden awakening" was to reseal the doors of the meditation hall and reopen the traditional gap between clerical and lay Buddhist practice.

In any case, from the establishment of Zen as a separate Buddhist tradition and the recognition of the "sudden" doctrine as its distinctive teaching, it was over three centuries before the school began to discuss its meditation practices in public. By this time, of course, the Zen movement had undergone considerable change. From a loose network of independent meditation communities surrounding prominent masters, it had grown to become the central monastic organization of Chinese Buddhism, rapidly coming under control of the state. As its ranks swelled and its social, political, and economic responsibilities broadened, the school was forced to turn its attention to the formalization and regulation of its institutions and practices. At the same time, in their new position of prominence, Zen monks were mingling with the lay political and intellectual elite and, in the process, finding themselves participating in, and reacting to, secular Sung culture. In response, the school began to sharpen its poetic skills, develop a proper history of the church, and produce a body of literature on the sayings of its masters that would advertise the tradition through the new medium of printed books and would appeal to the new classicism of a resurgent Confucian scholarship. The school also began to consider ways in which its monastic practices might be translated into forms accessible to a wider segment of the community, so that it could assume its rightful place in the nascent Sung religious reformation. Hence, for the first time in a long time, the school was obliged to face the fact that it had such practices and to set about explaining them in public.

Tsung-tse stands, at the close of the eleventh century, near the beginning of some of these tendencies, tendencies that would soon yield the new Zen of the Southern Sung. He seems to have been a man of his time, and in several ways his Buddhism both reflects and contributes to the emerging reformation. Unfortunately, we know little of his life: though the school's histories make note of him and preserve a few of his sayings, they record no dates and almost no biographical information. For the most part, they simply repeat the brief notice in the *Chien-chung ching-kuo hsü teng lu* ("Further Record of the Lamp, from the Chien-chung Ching-kuo Era"), the first of the histories in which he appears. Since this work was compiled during his lifetime by Fo-kuo Wei-po, a fellow disciple of Tsung-tse's first master, Fa-hsiu, what little it does record is no doubt to be trusted. There we are told that Tsung-tse was from Yung-nien, in Lo-chou (modern Honan), and that his family name was Sun. As a youth, he excelled in Confucian studies. He was encouraged to study Buddhism by Yüan-feng Ch'ing-man, a Yün-men monk in the lineage of the influential T'ien-i I-huai (993–1064), and, as we have seen, subsequently entered the order under I-huai's disciple Fa-yün Fa-hsiu. Thereafter, he studied with another of I-huai's disciples, Ch'ang-lu Ying-fu (d.u.), under whom he attained a sudden awakening to the way. He was favored with the patronage of the Lo-yang official Yang Wei (fl. 1067–1098) and was honored by the court. Fo-kuo identifies him as a monk of the Hung-chi ch'an-yüan in Chen-ting, the monastery where, as we know from its colophon, the *Ch'an-yüan ch'ing-kuei* was composed in 1103.[44]

This is all that the Zen histories have to tell us, but Tsung-tse is also remembered in the literature of Pure Land. As early as the *Lo-pang wen-lei* ("Texts on Sukhāvatī"), the miscellany of Ching-t'u material published in 1200 by Shih-chih Tsung-hsiao, he is listed as the last of the five great patriarchs who carried on the tradition of the Lotus Society. A brief notice there informs us that he was given the honorific title Tz'u-chüeh, "Compassionate Enlightenment" (which also appears in the colophon of the *Ch'an-yüan ch'ing-kuei*), and that he was living at Ch'ang-lu during the Yüan-yu era (1086–1093). There he was active in proselytizing and, apparently in 1089, founded a Lotus Assembly *(lien-hua sheng-hui)* to promote the universal cultivation of the *nien-fo* samādhi. His practice was to seek rebirth in the Western Pure Land by reciting the name of Amitābha up to ten thousand times a day, recording each recitation with a cross.[45] P'u-tu's *Lu-shan lien-tsung pao-chien* ("Precious Mirror of the Lotus School of Lu-shan"), of 1305, also contains a brief biography, which gives Tsung-tse's place of origin as Hsiang-yang and adds the information that he lost his father as a boy and took vows at the age of twenty-nine. Even as abbot of Ch'ang-lu, we are told here, he remained a deeply filial son and guided his mother in the *nien-fo* practice, so that she passed on in beatitude. He is said to have written a *Ch'üan hsiao wen,* a work in 120 sections "promoting filial piety," as well as a *Tso-ch'an chen* (sic), or "Lancet of Meditation."[46] Tsung-hsiao's collection of Pure Land writings, the *Lo-pang i-kao* ("Documents on Sukhāvatī"), also reports on Tsung-tse's *Ch'üan hsiao wen* and provides a short extract; and the *Lo-pang wen-lei* preserves a few minor pieces by Tsung-tse, including a preface to the *Kuan wu-liang-shou ching,* some verses, and several brief tracts.[47]

Tsung-tse's Pure Land writings seem, in one sense, to present another side of his religion, a side quite different from that of the Zen abbot who composed the monastic code and the meditation manual. For in these writings, and especially in the piece called *Lien-hua sheng-hui lu wen* ("Record of the Lotus Assembly"), apparently written for his *nien-fo* congregation, he emphasizes the difficulty of actually practicing monastic Buddhism in this Sahā world and encourages his readers to turn to Amitābha and to call upon him to take them up to the next world, where they may enjoy the purity and bliss of Sukhāvatī. Whereas in the Sahā world the practitioner is plagued by demons and assailed by sexual and other sensory temptations, in Sukhāvatī he is bathed in the radiance of Amitābha, everything around him proclaims the Dharma, and his karma is purified; there are no demonic experiences there, and no women.[48]

In another sense, Tsung-tse's Pure Land piety seems of a piece with his approach to Zen. For, as is clear from his regimen of multiple recitations, Tsung-tse was no protestant ideologue of pure grace, seeking to deny the efficacy of works. Like other Zen masters who sought conciliation with the Ching-t'u teachings, he held that "Amitābha is our own nature, and the Pure Land our own mind," and that "the cardinal principle [of these teachings] is to think [on him] without thought *(wu-nien),* and to be born [therein] without birth *(wu-sheng).*"[49] Hence, elsewhere he could claim that "*nien-fo* and the study of Zen do not interfere with each other: they are but two methods based on the same principle."[50] And as in his Zen writings, so too here it is less the principle than the method of the Pure Land faith—perhaps especially its power to overcome spiritual obstacles—that seems to have most attracted him. He recommends the *nien-fo* practice in particular to beginners, as a means of developing *kṣānti,* and also to those near death, as a means of relieving pain and calming the mind.[51]

Tsung-tse, it seems, was a practical and a compassionate man. Undistracted by dogmatic niceties, he directly addressed the everyday problems of spiritual cultivation; undaunted by the weight of tradition, he sought to open up the mystery of Zen practice and to share with others, both inside and outside the cloister, some of the techniques and institutions that might aid them in that cultivation. On the one hand, deploring the confusion and corruption of monastic tradition that accompanied the rapid growth of the school, he tried to rationalize the training of monks by setting out, in his *Ch'an-yüan ch'ing-kuei,* a detailed code of the bureaucratic structure, administrative procedures, and ritual forms of the Zen institution. On the other hand, lamenting the isolation of that institution from the Pure Land faith of the lay community, he sought—like his Yün-men predecessors I-huai and Ying-fu—to encourage interaction, bringing Ching-t'u practices into the ritual of his monastery and taking the Zen emphasis on mental cultivation out to his *nien-fo* society. It was probably for the sake of both these goals that he took it upon himself to make available, for the first time, a practical guide to the procedures of Zen meditation.[52]

Tsung-tse may not have left us many profound Zen sayings, but what he did leave had a profound impact on subsequent Zen literature. His *Ch'an-yüan ch'ing-kuei* became the inspiration and often the model for a new body of monastic codes. Whereas before its publication there had apparently been—if we discount the elusive *Po-chang ch'ing-kuei*—no detailed written rule, in the centuries following its appearance we find a steady stream of such texts in both China and Japan. Though some of these codes would, in time, come to supplant his own, many of the practices and institutions first set down by Tsung-tse endured. And though Zen monasteries would change considerably after his day, Tsung-tse's basic principle that they should be governed by written regulations remained a permanent fixture of the school.[53]

Similarly, although the Zen tradition had managed to survive for half a millennium without producing a meditation manual, once Tsung-tse's *Tso-ch'an i* appeared, it seems to have found a ready market and soon spawned a new genre of practical guides to mental cultivation. We have already seen that an abbreviated version of the text was quickly picked up by the layman Ch'en Shih for inclusion in his *Ta-tsang i-lan,* a work intended to make available a digest of the basic teachings of Buddhism for popular consumption. Following the publication of Yü Hsiang's edition of the *Ch'an-yüan ch'ing-kuei,* the full text of the manual circulated within the monastic community as well; and, in 1338, it was incorporated, with only minor variations, in Te-hui's important *Ch'ih-hsiu Po-chang ch'ing-kuei* ("Imperial Recension of the Pure Regulations of Po-chang"). This work—compiled by order of the last Mongol emperor, Shun-tsung—became the standard code for the Zen monasteries of the Ming. Shortly after its publication, it was taken to Japan, like the *Ch'an-yüan ch'ing-kuei* before it, where it provided a model for the regulation of the monasteries of the *gozan* system. In this way, Tsung-tse's *Tso-ch'an i* spread its influence throughout the lay and clerical communities of both China and Japan and became a basic source for the description of Zen meditation.[54]

It is perhaps a measure of the success of Tsung-tse's manual that it was soon imitated. Although there had long been a genre of brief poetic appreciations of meditation—texts known as "meditation lancets" *(tso-ch'an chen),* "meditation inscriptions" *(tso-ch'an ming),* and so on—the popularity of the *Tso-ch'an i* soon inspired others to try their hands at the new, more explicit style of text. This seems to have been particularly true in Japan, where, of course, during the thirteenth and fourteenth centuries, the school was earnestly seeking to explain itself to both the lay and clerical communities and to promote itself as a legitimate and attractive alternative to the established sects of Buddhism. In later Japanese Zen, the *Tso-ch'an i* was probably best known through its inclusion—together with the *Hsin-hsin ming* ("Inscription on Trusting the Mind"), *Cheng-tao ko* ("Song of Realization of the Way"), and K'uo-an's *Shih-niu t'u* ("Ten Oxherding Pictures")—in the extremely popular collection called the *Shibu roku* ("Fourfold Record"). Exactly when these four texts were first collected—and whether in China or Japan—is not known, but it is likely that the Japanese were already familiar with Tsung-tse's manual before the *Shibu roku* appeared. As early as 1198, the *Ta-tsang i-lan* version was quoted by Yōsai (or Eisai, 1141–1215) in his *Kōzen gokoku ron* ("Treatise on the Promotion of Zen for Defense of the Nation"); and soon thereafter, in 1233, the Sōtō master Dōgen (1200–1253) incorporated most of the *Ch'an-yüan ch'ing-kuei* text into his own meditation manual, the *Fukan zazen gi* ("Universal Promotion of the Principles of Meditation").[55]

This last work is undoubtedly the most famous attempt to improve on the *Tso-ch'an i,* but it was by no means the only one. Perhaps the earliest such text is the *Ju-ju chü-shih tso-ch'an i* ("Layman Ju-ju's Principles of Meditation"), attributed to the Yang-ch'i lay follower Yen Ping (d. 1212?) and preserved in the Kanazawa bunko. Yen Ping quotes from Tsung-tse but goes on to offer his own explanation of meditation, reflecting the *k'an-hua* practice popular in his day. We do not know when this work was introduced into Japan, but we do know that it was only one of a considerable number of similar meditation texts that circulated in the Kamakura period.[56] Dōgen, for example, wrote no less than four descriptions of zazen, and his descendent Keizan (1268–1325) added his own, relatively lengthy contribution, the *Zazen yōjin ki* ("Admonitions on Meditation"). Similarly, we have a *Zazen gi* by Muhon Kakushin (1207–1297), founder of the Hottō branch of Rinzai, and a *Zazen ron* by Enni Ben'en (1202–1280), written for his patron, the Regent Kujō Noriie. In the same period, the important Lin-chi missionary Lan-ch'i Tao-lung (Rankei Dōryū, 1213–1278) composed a well-known *Zazen ron* and also a brief *Zazen gi.* In addition to such meditation tracts, the masters of this period produced an abundance of informal writings—homilies, epistles, and so on, often in Japanese—that taught the basic techniques of Zen mental discipline to monk and layman alike.[57]

If the rather sudden proliferation of such writings, both in Japan and on the continent, bears witness to the historical significance of Tsung-tse's manual in pioneering a new genre of meditation literature, it also probably indicates that the authors of these writings were not wholly satisfied with his account of meditation practice. In fact, almost none of the texts that succeeded it retains the *Tso-ch'an i*'s core passage on the venerable concentration exercise that Tsung-tse calls the essential art of *tso-ch'an,* and almost all of them seek, in one way or another, to supplement (or replace) his rather humble, frankly utilitarian interpretation of the practice with the higher insights of Zen wisdom. For, by the time the first of these texts appeared, the school had already moved to stop the leak in the one true vehicle and right the alarming list toward samādhi that seemed to follow from his approach. If the Sung discourse on meditation opens with Tsung-tse's gentle advice on how to calm the mind, it also begins with his contemporary Hui-hung's stern reminder that the practice of Bodhidharma should not be confused with the cultivation of dhyāna *(hsi-ch'an)* or his tradition with those misguided quietists who would turn the mind into "dead wood and cold ashes" *(k'u-mu ssu-hui)*.[58] These two poles marked out once again the old field of discourse within which the new teachings of *mo-chao* and *k'an-hua* would be debated.

The Southern Sung teachings of *mo-chao* and *k'an-hua* are regularly understood as two opposing approaches to Zen mental training: the former seeking to identify it with the primal nature of the mind itself—what is sometimes called the practice "before the aeon of annihilation" *(k'ung-chieh i-ch'ien);* the latter preferring to focus it on the insight into the nature of the mind *(chien-hsing)* that comes through the power of the *kung-an*. These two approaches dominate the new meditation literature that succeeds the *Tso-ch'an i* and set the terms of the subsequent Japanese debates between Sōtō and Rinzai. Yet, whatever their differences, there is an obvious sense in which each represents a reaffirmation of the traditional Zen preference for the "sudden" practice of the supreme wisdom—whether it be through the metaphysical elevation of meditation to the nondual realm revealed by such wisdom or through the psychological reduction of meditation to the act of wisdom that reveals this realm. To this extent, each must also reassert the classical Zen doubts about yogic technique and distance itself from Tsung-tse's mechanical method of concentration. In fact, even as the new meditation literature was carrying on the work (begun by Tsung-tse) of disseminating Zen methods, Tsung-tse's own method—and the method of the early patriarchs of the school —was being dismissed as mere "toying with the spirit" *(lung ching-hun)* and as leading to the "deep pit" *(shen-k'eng)* of quietude. The Meditation School was once again closing the doors on its practice and moving to preserve the ancient secret of Zen meditation.[59]

Notes

1. See *Chung-tiao pu-chu Ch'an-yüan ch'ing-kuei, ZZ2/16/5.438–471.* For the original date of Tsung-tse's compilation, see his preface, *ibid.,* 438a. The *Zoku zōkyō* text is based on eighteenth-century Japanese printings; earlier, somewhat variant traditions of Yü Hsiang's edition are preserved in a Southern Sung printing from 1209 and a mid-Kamakura manuscript in the collection of the Kanazawa bunko. (See Kagamishima Genryū, "Kanazawa bunko bon *Zen'en shingi* ni tsuite," *Kanazawa bunko kenkyū,* vol. 14, no. 3 [1968], pp. 1–6.) An annotated modern edition can be found in Kagamishima et al., *Yakuchū Zen'en shingi* (Tokyo: Sōtō-shū shūmuchō, 1972). My discussion here of the texts of the *Tso-ch'an i* is indebted to Kagamishima's

introduction to this work, pp. 1–25, and to Yanagida Seizan's "Kaisetsu," in Kajitani Sōnin et al., *Shinjin mei Shōdō ka Jūgyū zu Zazen gi, Zen no goroku,* vol. 16 (Tokyo: Chikuma shobō, 1974), pp. 225–238.

2. Discussion of the Korean text and comparison of its contents with the Yü Hsiang edition can be found in Kozaka Kiyū, "*Zen'en shingi* no hen'yō katei ni tsuite: Kōrai bon *Zen'en shingi* no kōsatsu o kaishite," *IBK,* vol. 20 (1972), pp. 720–724; and in Kagamishima's *Yakuchū Zen'en shingi,* pp. 5–11.

3. See *Shōwa hōbō sōmokuroku* 3.1305a–b. On the date of this work, see Yanagida Seizan, "Zenseki kaidai," in Nishitani Keiji and Yanagida Seizan, *Zenke goroku,* vol. 2, *Sekai koten bungaku zenshū,* vol. 36B (Tokyo: Chikuma shobō, 1974), p. 496. The *Ta-tsang i-lan* text is quite similar to Yü Hsiang's version but lacks several more or less parenthetical amplifications. (Major variants are indicated in the notes to my translation, appended below.) It is possible, of course, that this earliest extant text of the *Tso-ch'an i* is closer to the original and that the longer version represents a later expansion. Given the character of Ch'en Shih's digest, however, it is more likely that he quoted only the basic material of the manual.

4. See Yanagida's "Kaisetsu," in Kajitani et al., *Shinjin mei,* pp. 232–233. The *Ta-tsang i-lan* version does not include the reference to Fa-hsiu; however, since this version is quite abbreviated, its absence there, although it does not help Prof. Yanagida's argument, does not detract from it. We shall come back later to what little is known of Tsung-tse's biography; for the reference to his association with Fa-hsiu (Yüan-t'ung ch'an-shih), see *Chien-chung ching-kuo hsü teng lu,* ZZ2B/9/2.133c11–12.

5. So, for example, the Japanese Zen master Dōgen (1200–1253) justifies his own revisions of Tsung-tse's manual on the grounds that, "though it follows Po-chang's original intentions *(ko i),* it adds several new clauses by I Shih [i.e., Tsung-tse]" and, therefore, suffers from various sorts of errors. See his so-called "Fukan zazen gi senjutsu yurai," in Ōkubo Dōshū, *Dōgen zenji zenshū,* vol. 2 (Tokyo: Chikuma shobō, 1970), p. 6.

6. For Tsung-tse's reference to the Po-chang code, see Kagamishima, *Yakuchū Zen'en shingi,* p. 3. Our earliest source for Po-chang, the epitaph by Ch'en Hsü, written in 818 just after his death, makes no reference to a *Po-chang ch'ing-kuei* ("T'ang Hung-chou Po-chang shan ku Huai-hai ch'an-shih t'a-ming," *Ch'üan T'ang wen,* fasc. 446, pp. 4b–7a.); in fact, the tradition's knowledge of Po-chang's famous rule seems to have been limited to brief notices attached to his biography in the *Sung kao-seng chuan* (*T*50.770c–771a) and *Ching-te ch'uan-teng lu* ("Ch'an-men kuei-shih," *T*51.250c–251b). It is no doubt because the information contained in these sources is all he had on Po-chang's regulations that Tsung-tse felt it worth including the appended notices on Po-chang's rule, under the title "Po-chang kuei-sheng sung," at the end of his own code (Kagamishima, *Yakuchū Zen'en shingi,* pp. 340–352).

7. *Shou-leng-yen ching, T*19.147a–155a. This work is now generally thought to be of Chinese origin. (See Mochizuki Shinkō, *Bukkyō kyōten seiritsu shi ron* [1946; repr., Tokyo: Hōzōkan, 1978], pp. 493–508; Paul Demiéville, *Le Concile de Lhasa* [Paris: Impremerie Nationale de France, 1952], pp. 43–52, n. 3.) Sekiguchi Shindai suggests that the reference here is to the earlier *Śūraṅgamasamādhi-sūtra* (*Shou-leng-yen san-mei ching, T*#642), translated by Kumārajīva (see his *Tendai shikan no kenkyū* [Tokyo: Iwanami shoten, 1969], p. 323); but this text, though it contains a discussion of Māra, does

not provide explicit information on his obstructions of meditation. Kagami-shima, *Yakuchū Zen'en shingi,* p. 282, appears to have the two sūtras con-fused.

8. *T*46.106a–111c, 114c–117a.
9. For the *Hsiao chih-kuan* discussion of *mo-shih,* see *Hsiu-hsi chih-kuan tso-ch'an fa yao, T*46.470b–472b. This work, in one (or two) fascicles, summa-rizes Chih-i's earlier and much longer *Shih ch'an po-lo-mi tz'u-ti fa-men* (*T*#1916; see Sekiguchi, *Tendai shō shikan,* Iwanami bunko 33-309-3 [Tokyo: Iwanami shoten, 1974], pp. 203–207). *T*#1915 is based on the vulgate version; another, widely variant text entitled *Lüeh-ming k'ai-meng ch'u-hsüeh tso-ch'an chih-kuan yao-men* is preserved in Japan. For a study and comparison of all extant versions, see Sekiguchi, *Tendai shō shikan no kenkyū* (1954; repr., Tokyo: Sankibō busshorin, 1961).
10. See Sekiguchi, *Tendai shō shikan no kenkyū,* pp. 29–32. The text of the *Hsiu-cheng i* can be found at ZZ2B/1/4–5.361–498; for a summary of its contents, see Kamata Shigeo, *Shūmitsu kyōgaku no shisō shi teki kenkyū* (Tokyo: Tōkyō daigaku shuppankai, 1975), pp. 499–521. Tsung-mi also quotes extensively from the *Hsiao chih-kuan* in his *Yüan-chüeh ching ta-shu ch'ao* (ZZ1/14/5.454aff). Sekiguchi, *op. cit.,* pp. 285–302, provides a table comparing the "Cheng-hsiu" section of the *Hsiao chih-kuan* with the *Hsiu-cheng i, the Ta-shu ch'ao,* and Chih-i's *Ch'an-men yao-lüeh* (ZZ2/4/1.35–37); Kamata, *op. cit.,* pp. 524–608, gives a similar table of the first three of these works covering the first and third divisions of the *Hsiu-cheng i.*
11. Sekiguchi's general argument goes back at least to his *Tendai shō shikan no kenkyū* and *Daruma daishi no kenkyū* (1957; rev. ed., Tokyo: Shunjūsha, 1969); he has reviewed many of the points of that argument in *Tendai shikan no kenkyū,* pp. 271–281. This last work (pp. 328–335) provides an elaborate table comparing the relevant sections of the *Hsiao chih-kuan* and *Hsiu-cheng i* with parallel passages in the *Tso-ch'an i* and several other Zen texts.
12. See Chih-i's introduction, Sekiguchi, *Tendai shō shikan no kenkyū,* p. 322. There is a tradition that the work was composed for Chih-i's brother, the layman Ch'en Chen, who had been diagnosed as terminally ill; after he practiced the repentence recommended in the book, his health was fully restored. (For a discussion of the story, see Sekiguchi, *op. cit.,* pp. 51–62.)
13. For a list of early texts affected by the *Hsiao chih-kuan,* see Sekiguchi, *Ten-dai shikan no kenkyū,* pp. 343–344.
14. Prior to Sekiguchi's publication of his table of the texts, Yamauchi Shun'yū did his own comparison and analysis of the *Hsiao chih-kuan* and *Tso-ch'an i;* he also concludes that Chih-i's influence is largely limited to the descrip-tion of the meditation posture (see *"Zazen gi to Tendai shō shikan," Shū-gaku kenkyū,* vol. 8 [1966], pp. 29–50).
15. The following summary is based on the text in Kagamishima, *Yakuchū Zen'en shingi,* pp. 279–283, a full translation of which appears in the Appendix, below.
16. *T*46.465b. This passage occurs in the vulgate version as the introduction to the "T'iao-ho" chapter, but it seems originally to have represented an intro-duction to the discussion of śamatha and vipaśyanā in the "Cheng-hsiu" chapter (see Sekiguchi, *Tendai shō shikan no kenkyū,* pp. 150–151).
17. *T*46.462c–463b.
18. *T*46.465b–466c.
19. For the *Hsiao chih-kuan* description of the *tso-ch'an* posture, see *T*46.465c7ff.

20. *T*46.466b.
21. *T*46.466a.
22. *T*46.466c–469b.
23. *T*46.14b28–c4; see also Chih-i's *Chüeh-i san-mei, T*46.621–627. The interesting interpretation here of the term *"chüeh-i"* (usually *"bodhyaṅga"*) is discussed at some length in Neal Donner, "The Great Calming and Contemplation of Chih-i," (Ph.D. dissertation, University of British Columbia, 1976), pp. 252–253, n. 249. See also the chapter in this volume by Daniel Stevenson.
24. The metaphor of water and waves is best known in Zen from the *Laṅkāvatāra Sūtra* (e.g., *T*16.538c); Tsung-tse's line on the pearl here is probably from Tung-shan Liang-chieh (see *T'ien-sheng kuang teng lu,* ZZ2B/8/4.353d). The passage from the *Yüan-chüeh ching* occurs at *T*17.919a21.
25. The *Leng-ch'ieh shih-tzu chi* appears at *T*85.1283ff; here I am using the edition in Yanagida, *Shoki no zen shi,* vol. 1, *Zen no goroku,* vol. 2 (Tokyo: Chikuma shobō, 1971), pp. 248–249.
26. Yanagida, *Shoki no zen shi,* vol. 1, p. 186. Though Chinese tradition, both inside and outside of Zen, tends to interpret the term *i-hsing* as "single practice," it seems clear that here, as in the sūtra itself, the emphasis is on the original sense of "single array"—i.e., the entirety of the Dharmadhātu manifest in the samādhi.
27. *Ibid.,* p. 287.
28. *Tsui-shang sheng lun, T*48.378a–b.
29. Yanagida, *Shoki no zen shi,* vol. 1, p. 241.
30. *Tsui-shang sheng lun, T*48.379a.
31. Yanagida, *Shoki no zen shi,* vol. 1, p. 255.
32. See, e.g., his *Tendai shikan no kenkyū,* p. 346.
33. So, for example, this passage on "śamatha through comprehension of the truth" *(t'i-chen chih):*

    If the practitioner knows that the mind is without [its own] nature, why should there be reality to the dharmas [that arise from the mind]? . . . Being empty and without substance, they cannot be grasped. If they are not grasped, the mind of deluded thoughts *(wang-nien hsin)* will cease; if the mind of deluded thoughts ceases, it is quiescent and unconditioned *(wu-wei).* This unconditionedness is the original source of all dharmas. If one rests one's mind in this original source, it is without defilement; if the mind is without defilement, then all karmic activity of saṃsāra ceases. When the karmic activity of saṃsāra ceases, this is itself nirvāṇa. (See Sekiguchi's edition, *Tendai shō shikan no kenkyū,* pp. 339–340.)

34. *T*46.1c–2a.
35. Hu Shih, *Shen-hui ho-shang i-chi* (rev. ed., Taipei: Hu Shih chi-nien kuan, 1970), pp. 308–309.
36. *Ibid.,* p. 249; reading *cheng* for *fei* in line 8 and supplying *wang chü* before *mieh* in line 11.
37. See, e.g., *Ting shih-fei lun,* Hu Shih, *op. cit.,* p. 287.
38. Hence his distinction (following Ch'eng-kuan) between the awakening of understanding *(chieh-wu),* which is to be followed by gradual cultivation, and the awakening of realization *(cheng-wu),* which represents the culmination of the Path. (See, e.g., his *Yüan-chüeh ching ta shu ch'ao,* ZZ1/14/3.280b.) The structure here clearly recapitulates the classical progression of the *mārga* from *darśana,* through *bhāvanā,* to *aśaikṣa.* See the concluding

chapter in this volume by Robert Buswell for a detailed discussion of Tsung-mi's theory of the Path.

39. *T*48.402b–c.
40. *Ibid.*, 403a4–6. This passage is repeated under the section on Shen-hui's Ho-tse School in Tsung-mi's *Zenmon shishi shōshū zu* (**Ch'an-men shih-tzu ch'eng-hsi t'u*), *ZZ*2/15/5.436c. Note that, for all its "higher wisdom," the first sentence here could be used to summarize the description of śamatha through comprehension of the truth that we have seen in the *Hsiao chih-kuan*.
41. The basic theoretical position of this "classical" style of Zen is already depicted in Tsung-mi himself. Thus, for example, in the *Tu-hsü* passage we have just seen, he distinguishes between two versions of the highest Zen: one (the Southern position), based on the true nature of "numinous awareness" and the cultivation of no-thought; the other (the Hung-chou position) iden-tifying the Buddha-nature with the totality of human states. According to this latter view, there is no point in rousing the mind to cultivate the Path: true awakening, cultivation, and verification lie only in the free expression of one's natural mind in all circumstances (*T*48.402c).
42. *T'an ching*, *T*48.345a20–21; *Li-tai fa-pao chi*, *T*51.191a1–2; *Tun-wu ju-tao yao men*, *ZZ*2/15/5.420c14–15; *Ching-te ch'uan teng lu*, *T*51.240c18ff; *ibid.*, 251a13.
43. *Ching-te ch'uan teng lu*, *T*51.240c. Huai-jang's famous criticism of Ma-tsu's meditation appears at the same location; for an example of Wu-chu's denial that he enters samādhi or abides in meditation, see *Li-tai fa-pao chi*, *ibid.*, 195a29; Lin-chi's dismissal of those who "sit motionless with tongue pressed against the palate" appears in *Lin-chi lu*, *T*47.501a.
44. *ZZ*2B/9/2.133c. The table of contents of the *Hsü teng lu* (*ibid.*, 12a) gives the graph *i* rather than *tse* as the second element of Tsung-tse's name, and in fact a number of other early sources follow the form "Tsung-i." The prob-lem has been discussed in Kondō Ryōichi, "Chōro Sōsaku ni tsuite," *IBK*, vol. 14 (1966), pp. 280–283. There is some uncertainty about Tsung-tse's place of residence. The Chen-ting district is in modern Hopei, but the Hung-chi monastery there has not been identified. The Hung-chi ssu known in Zen records is at Ch'ang-lu, in modern Kiangsu.
45. *T*47.193c.
46. *T*47.324c. P'u-tu goes on to report that Tsung-tse once had a dream in which he was approached by a man named P'u-hui, who sought member-ship in the Lotus Assembly for himself and his brother P'u-hsien. After awakening, Tsung-tse realized that these were the two bodhisattvas who appear in the *Hua-yen ching* (*T*10.279bff). The story of the dream is found among Tsung-tse's writings in the *Lo-pang wen-lei*, *ibid.*, 178a–b; the source of the other information here is unknown.
47. *Lo-pang i-kao*, *T*47.249a; the notice is taken from the *Lung-shu ching-t'u wen*, *T*47.271a. Tsung-tse's preface appears at *T*47.167a–b; see also his "Lien-hua sheng-hui lu wen" (dated 1089), "Nien-fo fang t'ui fang-pien wen," "Nien-fo hui-hsiang fa-yüan wen," *ibid.*, 177b–178c; and his verses, *ibid.*, 219c–220a.
48. *Lo-pang wen-lei*, *T*47.177b–178b; the same text is preserved in the *Lung-shu ching-t'u wen* under the title "Ch'üan ts'an-ch'an jen chien hsiu ching-t'u" ("Promotion of the Combined Cultivation of Pure Land Among Zen Prac-titioners," *T*47.283c–284c).
49. *T*47.177b23, 178a20.

50. "Nien-fo tsan ch'an chiu tsung-chih shuo," *Lu-shan lien-tsung pao-chien,* T47.318b25–26.
51. "Lien-hua sheng-hui wen," *T*47.177c; "Nien-fo hui-hsiang fa-yüan wen," *ibid.,* 178c.
52. Tsung-tse's *nien-fo* practice appears several times throughout the *Ch'an-yüan ch'ing-kuei* and clearly represented a major element in the ritual of his monastery. His combination of Zen tradition with Sung popular religion is perhaps nowhere better symbolized than in his saying "The one word 'filial' is the gateway to all mysteries," an expression that gives a homey, ethical twist to Tsung-mi's famous metaphysical dictum, "The one word 'awareness' is the gateway to all mysteries" (quoted in *Lu-shan lien-tsung pao-chien, T*47.306c26).
53. For the history of the early literature on the monastic rule in China and Japan, see Imaeda Aishin, *Chūsei zenshū shi no kenkyū* (Tokyo: Tōkyō daigaku shuppankai, 1970), pp. 56–72; Martin Collcutt, *Five Mountains: The Rinzai Zen Monastic Institution in Medieval Japan* (Cambridge: Harvard University Press, 1981), pp. 133–170.
54. For Te-hui's text of the *Tso-ch'an i,* see *T*48.1143a–b. The manual also appears in the *Tzu-men ching-hsün,* a compendium of practical advice for Zen monks compiled in 1313 by Yung-chung (d.u.) (*T*48.1047b–c). However, since the extant text of this work is a much later, greatly expanded version, we cannot be entirely certain that the *Tso-ch'an i* was included in the original.
55. For the *Shibu roku* text, the earliest extant version of which is a *gozan* printing from the fourteenth century, see Ōmori Sōgen, *Kunchū Zenshū shibu roku* (Kyoto: Kichūdō, 1962), pp. 1–18. For Yōsai's quotation, see *T*80.12a14–17. As Yanagida has pointed out, the fact that Yōsai often quotes the *Ch'an-yüan ch'ing-kuei* but uses the *Ta-tsang i-lan* as his source for the *Tso-ch'an i* provides additional evidence that, when he visited China in 1187, the manual was still not included in Tsung-tse's code (see Yanagida's additional notes to the *Kōzen gokoku ron,* in Ichikawa Hakugen et al., *Chūsei zenke no shisō, Nihon shisō taikei,* vol. 16 [Tokyo: Iwanami shoten, 1972], p. 398; and his "Yōsai to *Kōzen gokoku ron* no kadai," *ibid.,* pp. 471–476). Dōgen's *Fukan zazen gi* can be found at Ōkubo Dōshū, *Dōgen zenji zenshū,* vol. 2, pp. 3–5.
56. The Kanazawa manuscript of Yen Ping's text has been edited by Ishii Shūdō, in *Kanazawa bunko shiryō zensho,* vol. 1 (Yokohama: Kanazawa bunko, 1974), pp. 155–161. Yen Ping's biography does not appear in the Ch'an histories, but the *Hsü ch'uang teng lu* (*T*51.701a) identifies him as a follower of Ta-hui's disciple Hsüeh-feng Hui-jan.
57. For Dōgen's descriptions of meditation, all of which reflect Tsung-tse's text, see (in addition to the *Fukan zazen gi* mentioned above) his *Eihei kōroku* (Ōkubo, *Dōgen zenji zenshū,* vol. 2, pp. 165–166), *Shōbō genzō zazen gi* (*ibid.,* vol. 1 [Tokyo: Chikuma shobō, 1969], pp. 88–89), and *Bendō hō* (*ibid.,* vol. 2, pp. 317–318). The *Zazen yōjin ki* can be found in *Sōtō shū zensho, Shūgen,* vol. 2 (1930; repr., Tokyo: Sōtō-shū zensho kankōkai, 1971), p. 423–427; see also Keizan's *Sankon zazen setsu, ibid.,* 428–429. For Kakushin's *Zazen gi,* see *Dai Nihon bukkyō zensho,* vol. 96, pp. 211–212; more explicit instruction on meditation appears in his *Hottō kokushi hōgo, ibid.,* pp. 220–222. Enni's *Zazen ron* appears as *Shōichi kokushi hōgo,* in *Zenmon hōgo shū,* vol. 2, pp. 411–424. For Lan-ch'i's *Zazen ron,* see *Daikaku zenji zazen ron, Kokuyaku zengaku taisei,* vol. 23

(Tokyo: Nishōdō shoten, 1930), pp. 1–8; his *Zazen gi* is preserved in a manuscript of the Kanazawa bunko (see *Kanazawa bunko shiryō zensho,* vol. 1,
pp. 161–168).
58. In the *Lin-chien lu, ZZ2/21/3.*295d.
59. "To indulge yourself by forgetting objects *(wang yüan)* is to fall into the
deep pit. . . . To be aware of your thoughts as soon as they occur *(nien ch'i
chi chüeh)* is [the practice of] one who toys with his spirit." ("Lancet of
Zen" [*Ch'an chen*], appended to the *Wu-men kuan, T*48.299b1–3.)

Appendix

The following translation of the *Tso-ch'an i* is based on the *Ch'an-yüan
ch'ing-kuei* text appearing in Kagamishima Genryū et al., *Yakuchū Zen'en shingi*
(Tokyo: Sōtō-shū shūmuchō, 1972), pp. 279–284. Notes in the translation refer to
variants in the *Ta-tsang i-lan* text (*Shōwa hōbō sōmokuroku* 3.1305a–b). A fully
annotated Japanese translation is provided in Kajitani Sōnin et al., *Shinjin mei
Shōdō ka Jūgyō zu Zazen gi, Zen no goroku,* vol. 16 (Tokyo: Chikuma shobo,
1971), pp. 145–164.

PRINCIPLES OF SEATED MEDITATION

The bodhisattva who studies prajñā should first arouse the thought of great
compassion, make the extensive vows, and vigorously cultivate samādhi. Vowing
to save sentient beings, you should not seek liberation for yourself alone.
   Now cast aside all involvements and discontinue the myriad affairs. Body
and mind should be unified, with no division between action and rest. Regulate
food and drink, so that you take neither too much nor too little; adjust sleep, so
that you neither deprive nor indulge yourself.
   When you sit in meditation, spread a thick mat in a quiet place. Loosen your
robe and belt, and assume a proper posture.[1] Then sit in the cross-legged position: first place your right foot on your left thigh; then place your left foot on
your right thigh.[2] Or you may sit in the semi-cross-legged position: simply rest
your left foot on your right foot. Next, place your right hand on your left foot,
and[3] your left hand on your right palm. Press the tips of your thumbs together.
Slowly raise your torso and stretch it forward. Swing to the left and right; then
straighten your body and sit erect. Do not lean to the left or right, forward or
backward. Keep your hips, back, neck, and head in line, making your posture
like a stūpa. But do not strain your body upward too far, lest it cause your
breathing to be forced and unsettled.[4] Your ears should be in line with your
shoulders, and your nose in line with your navel. Press your tongue against your
palate, and close your lips and teeth. The eyes should remain slightly open, in
order to prevent drowsiness. If you attain samādhi [with the eyes open], it will be
the most powerful. In ancient times, there were monks eminent in the practice of
meditation who always sat with their eyes open. More recently, the Ch'an master
Fa-yün Yüan-t'ung criticized those who sit in meditation with their eyes closed,
likening [their practice] to the ghost cave of the Black Mountain. Surely this has a
deep meaning, known to those who have mastered [meditation practice].[5]
   Once you have settled your posture and regulated your breathing, you
should relax your abdomen. Do not think of any good or evil whatsoever. Whenever a thought occurs, be aware of it; as soon as you are aware of it, it will van-

ish. If you remain for a long period forgetful of objects, you will naturally become unified. This is the essential art of seated meditation.[6]

Honestly speaking, seated meditation is the Dharma-gate of ease and joy; if, nevertheless, people often become ill [from its practice], it is because they do not take proper care. If you grasp the point of this [practice], the four elements [of the body] will naturally be light and at ease; the spirit will be fresh and sharp; thoughts will be correct and clear; the flavor of the Dharma will sustain the spirit; and you will be calm, pure, and joyful.[7] One who has already developed clarity may be likened to the dragon gaining the water or the tiger taking to the mountains. Even one who has not yet developed it, by letting the wind fan the flame, will not have to make much effort: if you just assent to it, you will not be deceived.[8] Nevertheless, as the path gets higher, demons flourish, and agreeable and disagreeable experiences are manifold. Yet, if you just keep right thought present, none of them can obstruct you. The *Śūraṅgama-sūtra,* T'ien-t'ai's *Chih-kuan,* and Kuei-feng's *Hsiu-cheng i* give detailed explications of these demonic occurrences, and those who would be prepared in advance for the unforeseen should be familiar with them.[9]

When you come out of samādhi, move slowly and arise calmly; do not be hasty or rough. After you have left samādhi,[10] always employ appropriate means to protect and maintain the power of samādhi, as though you were protecting an infant; then your samādhi power will easily develop.

This one teaching of meditation is our most urgent business. If you do not settle [the mind] in meditation, or dhyāna, then, when it comes down to it, you will be completely at a loss.[11] Therefore, [it is said,] "To seek a pearl, we should still the waves; if we disturb the water, it will be hard to get." When the water of meditation is clear, the pearl of the mind will appear of itself. Therefore, the *Perfect Enlightenment Sūtra* says, "Unimpeded, immaculate wisdom always arises dependent on meditation." And the *Lotus Sūtra* says, "In a quiet place, he practices control of the mind, abiding motionless like Mt. Sumeru."[12] Thus, we know that transcending the profane and surpassing the holy are contingent on the condition of dhyāna; shedding [this body] while seated and fleeing [this life] while standing are dependent on the power of samādhi. Even if one devotes oneself to the practice one's entire life, one may still not be in time; how then could one who procrastinates possibly overcome karma? Therefore, an ancient has said, "Without the power of samādhi, you will meekly cower at death's door." Shutting your eyes, you will return [to the earth] in vain; just as you are, you will drift [in saṃsāra]. Friends in Ch'an, go over this text again and again. Benefiting others as well as ourselves, let us together achieve perfect enlightenment.[13]

NOTES TO APPENDIX

1. "When you sit . . . proper posture": lacking.
2. "Then sit . . . right thigh.": "For the cross-legged position, first place your left foot on your right thigh; then place your right foot on your left thigh."
3. "your right hand on your left foot, and": lacking.
4. "But do not . . . unsettled.": lacking.
5. "If you attain . . . [meditation practice].": lacking.
6. "This is the essential art of seated meditation.": lacking.
7. "Honestly speaking . . . calm, pure, and joyful.": "If you grasp the point of this [practice], the four elements [of the body] will naturally be light and at ease: thus it is called the Dharma-gate of ease and joy."

8. "by letting the wind fan the flame, will not have to make much effort.":
    lacking.
9. "Nevertheless, . . . familiar with them.": lacking.
10. "do not be . . . samādhi,": lacking.
11. "This one teaching . . . at a loss.": lacking.
12. "The *Lotus Sūtra* . . . Mt. Sumeru.": lacking.
13. "Even if one . . . perfect enlightenment.": "[Meditation] is our most urgent
    business."

From Dispute to Dual Cultivation: Pure Land Responses to Ch'an Critics

David W. Chappell

Although the eighth century falls within the so-called golden age of Chinese Buddhism, the very vitality of Buddhism at that time was marked by the strong and competing religious claims of various new sectarian movements. This chapter will explore the conflict that split two of these groups, Pure Land and Ch'an, beginning with the evolution of Ch'an criticisms of Pure Land devotionalism in the seventh and early eighth centuries. Separate sections will be devoted to three different Pure Land responses to Ch'an—those of Tz'u-min Hui-jih (680–748), Fei-hsi (d.u.), and the *Wu fang-pien nien-fo men* ("The Gateway of the Five Expedient Methods for Contemplating the Buddha"). These three responses represent different patterns, ranging from opposition to Ch'an to integration with it. The implications of these options will be discussed in the final section.

Pure Land and Ch'an are often described as the two major poles of Buddhist practice in East Asia. Pure Land devotees emphasize the inadequacies of their own capacities and the futility of their times; salvation can only be achieved at another time (in the next rebirth), in another place (the Western Pure Land), and through another power (Amitābha Buddha). By contrast, Ch'an affirms the completeness of the present moment and human capacities, collapsing the space-time distinctions of Pure Land symbolism into an existential challenge by arguing for the nonduality of oneself and the Buddha, as well as the identity of this realm and the Pure Land. Whereas Pure Land devotionalism calls upon an external power, Ch'an affirms self-reliance and rejects dependence upon external religious objects. The dramatic contrast between these two religious options is strikingly revealed in their artistic styles. Amitābha Buddha is portrayed in vivid concreteness and the Pure Land drawn with precise detail, whereas Ch'an art takes this present world as its subject but treats it with a lack of formal detail to emphasize freedom and tranquility and to dissolve static concreteness and separation.

It is not surprising, therefore, that Pure Land and Ch'an became distinct and competing denominations in Japan. In China, however, the break was never institutionalized in such a final form. Instead, the two were joined in a dialectical balance expressed architecturally in recent centuries by having both a Ch'an meditation hall and a recitation hall for Pure Land devotionalism in the same monastery. This was possible in China because by the end of the eighth century larger frames of reference had been devised to reconcile Pure Land and Ch'an. But at the beginning of the eighth century, instead of a pattern of living together harmoniously, Pure Land and Ch'an were in open conflict with each other.

I. Ch'an Attacks on Pure Land Devotionalism

Pure Land devotionalism entered China in a wide variety of Mahāyāna texts recommending rebirth in Amitābha's Western Paradise as the most effective way to gain a favorable rebirth leading to eventual enlightenment.[1] Visualization techniques, mantra chanting, methods for attaining rebirth with a compassionate Buddha figure, and other devotional practices shared by the Amitābha movement were also an integral part of the Perfection of Wisdom *(prajñāpāramitā)* tradition. Since this tradition, established by Kumārajīva (344–413), was accepted by Chinese Buddhists as authoritative in questions of doctrine and practice from the sixth century on, Pure Land ideas therefore became a part of Buddhist orthodoxy in China. And since Ch'an often turned to Perfection of Wisdom texts as a scriptural basis, one would not have expected an eighth-century Ch'an attack on Pure Land devotionalism as an inferior and misguided practice. Thus, in order to understand the historical setting for the eighth-century conflict between the two traditions, we must first review briefly the relation between the Perfection of Wisdom texts and Pure Land devotionalism.

It is not surprising that the encyclopedic commentary on the Perfection of Wisdom, the *Ta-chih-tu-lun,* should have a major section on the Pure Lands.[2] Supported by the prestige of Nāgārjuna as its alleged author, the *Ta-chih-tu-lun* came to be accepted by Chinese Buddhists as a definitive authority on questions of doctrinal orthodoxy. At the other extreme was the *Heart Sūtra,* which condensed the Perfection of Wisdom insights into a short form for liturgical use. Indeed, the *Heart Sūtra* became the most popular liturgical text in all East Asian Buddhism— most likely because it so clearly embodied the dialectical harmony between the philosophy of emptiness and explicitly devotional practices. After proclaiming that the five *skandhas,* the eighteen *dhātu,* the Twelvefold Chain of Causation, the Four Noble Truths, and various other key Buddhist ideas are all empty, the text offers a simple mantra to be recited to cure all ills. This device of sweeping away all religious structures and then offering them back again (but supposedly with a new awareness) is also a frequent theme in the *Diamond Sūtra*. Conveniently summarizing this Perfection of Wisdom atttitude is the *Vimalakīrti Sūtra*, which asserts that, "although he knows that the various Buddha Lands and sentient beings are empty, at the same time [the bodhisattva] is always cultivating a Pure Land to save all beings."[3]

By the seventh century the passage that was invariably cited to show how the philosophy of emptiness and devotional practices functioned together came from the *Wen-shu shuo ching* (*Saptaśatika-prajñāpāramitā-sūtra;* "Sūtra on the Perfection of Wisdom Spoken by Mañjuśrī"). The key passage from this text was quoted again and again by all parties throughout the T'ang Dynasty. The chapters by Daniel Stevenson and Bernard Faure have already noted that the account of one-practice samādhi outlined in the *Wen-shu shuo ching* contains two distinct approaches to practice: a radical approach that takes the Dharmadhātu itself as its "object" as well as an expedient approach that concentrates on the idealized image or name of a particular Buddha—what the later Pure Land tradition referred to as the contemplation of Principle *(li-kuan)* and contemplation of phenomena *(shih-kuan)*. The double valence of the *Wen-shu shuo ching* passage came to serve as a doctrinal litmus test, revealing the religious orientation of the interpreter by which aspect of the practice he selected for emphasis. The passage was thus used by various groups in the early separation of Ch'an and Pure Land to support their particular sectarian claims. A translation follows:

Mañjuśrī asked: "World-Honoured One, what is one-practice samādhi?" The Buddha replied: "The Dharmadhātu has a single characteristic. Taking the Dharmadhātu as the object [of contemplation] is called one-practice samādhi. If sons and daughters of good families want to enter one-practice samādhi, they should first listen to the Perfection of Wisdom and then practice as instructed. Only then will they be able to enter one-practice samādhi, and just like the Dharmadhātu itself they will not slide back, will not be destroyed, will be inconceivable, will be without obstructions, and will be without characteristics. Sons and daughers of good families who want to enter into one-practice samādhi should take up residence in an untrammeled spot, give up all confused thoughts, and, without adhering to any characteristic, concentrate their mind on a particular Buddha and single-mindedly recite his name. By properly facing in the direction of that Buddha, keeping their body upright, and being able to maintain uninterrupted concentration on a single Buddha, thought after thought, then, within that very mindfulness, they will be able to see all the Buddhas of the past, present, and future. Why? Because being mindful of the boundless infinity of the merit of one Buddha is the same as [being mindful of] the merit of infinite Buddhas—they are nondual and inconceivable. The Buddha Dharma is equal and without distinctions. All [Buddhas] achieve supreme perfect enlightenment by relying on [this] one suchness. They all thereby become endowed with incalculable merit and boundless eloquence. Those who enter one-practice samādhi thus fully know that the Dharmadhātu of Buddhas as numerous as the sands of the Ganges is free from any mark of difference.[4]

This passage is quoted prominently at the beginning of the section on the fourth Ch'an patriarch in the *Leng-ch'ieh shih-tzu chi* ("Record of the Masters and Disciples of the *Laṅkāvatāra*"), where one-practice samādhi is said to be one of the cornerstones of the teaching of Tao-hsin (580–651). It is important not only to notice the primacy given to the formless, nondualistic state of one-practice samādhi emphasized by Ch'an, but also to recognize the positive role given to devotionalism, ritual, and recitation of a Buddha's name *(nien-fo)* as a method to attain this state. The classic balance between these two aspects of one-practice samādhi had been struck by T'ien-t'ai Chih-i (538–597) in his *Mo-ho chih-kuan* ("[Treatise on] the Great Calming and Discernment"). As Daniel Stevenson discusses in detail in his chapter earlier in this volume, Chih-i cites this passage from the *Wen-shu shuo ching* as canonical support for his constantly sitting samādhi,[5] in which the practitioner is to remain seated in meditation for ninety days. If his mind should wander, he is to recite the Buddha's name as recommended by the sūtra. Chih-i's emphasis is not just on recitation, but on cultivating one-practice samādhi in order to overcome all duality. In an eloquent description bordering on the ecstatic, Chih-i describes the ultimate Mahāyāna awareness in which the duality of defilements and purity is transcended, all living beings are no different from the Buddha, evil is not separate from nirvāṇa, and true cultivation is non-cultivation and vice versa. This is the Perfection of Wisdom and appears at first glance to be the highest attainment.

The interpretation of this passage by the *Leng-ch'ieh shih-tz'u chi* echoes Chih-i's nondualistic emphasis. Immediately after quoting this passage, the *Leng-ch'ieh shih-tzu chi* repeats a statement from the *Vimalakīrti Sūtra* that all modes of activity are the place of enlightenment *(tao-ch'ang, bodhimaṇḍa),* even lifting or lowering one's foot. It then quotes from a scripture especially valued by T'ien-t'ai, *P'u-hsien kuan ching* ("Meditation on Samantabhadra Sūtra"), to recommend the repentance and meditation on true reality that eradicates all illusions. To achieve lucidity and serenity, one should constantly be mindful of a Buddha or recite his name *(nien-fo),* a practice that the *Leng-ch'ieh shih-tzu chi* explains according to the *Ta-p'in ching (Pañcaviṃśatisāhasrikā-prajñāpāramitā-sūtra,* "The Sūtra of the Perfection of Wisdom in Twenty-five Thousand Lines"), which claims that, since the Buddha has no form, there is no object of meditation but only mindfulness of the non-substantiality and interpenetration of all things. This awareness of non-duality pacifies the mind *(an-hsin)*. The *Leng-ch'ieh shih-tzu chi* goes on to illustrate nondualistic thinking by asserting that the Pure Land, Buddha-nature, enlightenment, the Tathāgata, nirvāṇa, and so on are identical, while acknowledging that the methods for realizing nonduality are endless. According to the *Leng-ch'ieh shih-tzu chi,* Tao-hsin emphasizes that all activities can be agents for enlightenment, since for those with insight there is nothing that is apart from the one true suchness, there is nothing that is not enlightenment.

The *Leng-ch'ieh shih-tzu chi* then presents Tao-hsin as turning to answer a number of specific questions relating mostly to practice. The stage is set by affirming that true reality is formless yet contains all forms and so is serene yet diverse. The Ch'an practitioner is to be aware like a mirror, but like a plant he does not grasp or seek anything in particular. Accordingly, he is urged to identify with the natural rhythm of things *(chih-jen-yun)*. Some may be able to do this by themselves, some may need a teacher, and some may need three to five years of practice. Those with keen abilities can appreciate the interpenetration of all phenomena, but those less gifted may find it helpful to follow specific practices. According to the *Leng-ch'ieh shih-tzu chi,* Tao-hsin saw these as involving the use of expedient methods (like the Pure Land practices) in the light of the Perfection of Wisdom teaching. Nevertheless,

> if we know our mind originally neither is born nor dies but is ultimately pure and is identical to the Pure Buddha Land, then it is not necessary to face toward the West. . . . The Buddha causes beings who have dull capacities to face toward the West, but he does not teach people with keen abilities to do so.[6]

We do not know if the *Leng-ch'ieh shih-tzu chi* account of Tao-hsin's ideas is wholly accurate; therefore, we cannot be certain that Tao-hsin classified Pure Land devotionalism as a practice for the dull-witted, as this passage claims. Doubt over the reliability of the *Leng-ch'ieh shih-tzu chi* in this regard is raised by the fact that Tao-hsin's disciple Hung-jen (601–674) produced various Ch'an followers who advocated Pure Land practices: (1) Fa-chih (635–702) and his disciple Chih-wei (d. 680); (2) Chih-shen (609–702), his disciple Ch'u-chi (d. 730s), and Ch'u-chi's disciple Wu-hsiang (K. Musang; 694–762); and (3) Hsüan-shih (d.u.) and his disciples.[7] Furthermore, this portion of the text is stylistically very different from the first section, which quotes the *Wen-shu shuo ching,* thus giving rise to the suspicion that it may have been interpolated later when the *Leng-ch'ieh shih-tzu chi* was compiled in the eighth century by an advocate for Northern Ch'an.[8]

In any case, whether or not Ch'an criticism of Pure Land devotionalism appeared in the seventh century, it definitely was present by the early eighth century, when the *Leng-ch'ieh shih-tzu chi* was compiled. In addition, such criticism was also clearly evident in sections 35–37 of the Tun-huang text of the *Platform Sūtra*. In neither case, however, is it clear precisely who is being attacked, since the early development of Pure Land devotionalism as a self-sufficient movement took place in a different area of China, beginning in Shansi Province.[9] Indeed, Philip Yampolsky proposes that the *Platform Sūtra* might have been reacting to the type of Ch'an advocated by the Szechwan school that derived from Chih-shen.[10] In any event, by the early eighth century, when the *Leng-ch'ieh shih-tzu chi* and possibily the *Platform Sūtra* were compiled, both the Northern Ch'an of the *Leng-ch'ieh shih-tzu chi* and the Southern Ch'an of the *Platform Sūtra* had rejected Pure Land devotionalism as an inferior path practiced by those of dull capacities.

The *Platform Sūtra* teaches that there are not only two grades of beings, those with dull capacities and those with keen capacities, but also two corresponding forms of practice, "gradual" and "sudden."[11] Those with keen capacities, "by making the mind pure, are without crime." The Perfection of Wisdom teaching "has nothing to do with recitations." "The deluded person merely recites; the wise man practices with his mind."[12] The text claims that it is wrong to try to accumulate merit for the sake of a better rebirth, the extinction of bad karma, and enlightenment in the future:

> The ignorant person practices seeking future happiness, does not practice the Way,
> And says that to practice seeking future happiness *is* the Way.
> Though he hopes that alms-giving and offerings will bring boundless happiness,
> As before, in his mind the three karmas are created.[13]

This Ch'an emphasis on the inner practice of the mind called for the transcendence of temporal distinctions in a sudden realization in the immediate present. It also served to dissolve spatial distinctions, since for the enlightened "the Western [Pure] Land can be seen here in China." "If inside and outside are clear, this will be no different from the Western Land." One should not look for the Buddha outside of oneself as do the devotees of Amitābha. "The sūtras say to take refuge in the Buddha within yourselves; they do not say to rely on other Buddhas."[14] Indeed, "separation from form on the outside is ch'an; being untouched on the inside is meditation *(ting)*."[15] One should avoid all dualism between self and the Buddha.[16]

In contrast to Ch'an, the vitality of Pure Land devotionalism, and the source of its later attack on Ch'an, was based upon the usefulness and validity of conventional space-time distinctions. It is within this framework that Pure Land thinkers interpreted the *Wen-shu shuo ching*. For example, Tao-ch'o (562–645) quoted the text to justify the spread of vocal recitation of Amitābha's name, since the text implies that meditation on and recitation of the name of one Buddha involves all Buddhas.[17] Later, the systematizer of Pure Land thought, Shan-tao (613–681), quoted this passage to show that, if one is having difficulty in attaining undistracted meditative insight, solitary recitation of the name of the Buddha is more effective than the more difficult practice of visualization.[18] As these references make clear, Pure Land devotionalism had a totally different motivation from Ch'an in its use of Perfection of Wisdom materials. Instead of emphasizing formlessness and mental clarity, the Pure Land masters used the doctrine of nonduality to justify the cosmic significance of specific practices. This divergence of Pure Land interpretation from Ch'an practice is most vividly illustrated by the writings of Tz'u-min Hui-jih.

II. The Counterattack of Tz'u-min Hui-jih

By the middle of the seventh century, Pure Land devotionalism in North China had developed sufficient momentum and self-awareness to produce its first historian, Chia-ts'ai (d.u.).[19] The strength of the Pure Land movement can also be seen by the fact that Shan-tao developed his religious thought almost totally within a Pure Land framework. Unlike his teacher, Tao-ch'o (562–645), he made very few references to other sources, and what opponents he had were from the Yogācāra tradition. The arguments of these opponents emphasized the high requirements for entering the Pure Land and the incompleteness of the benefits of rebirth there. Although Shan-tao personally preferred visualization techniques, he argued for low entrance requirements to the Pure Land—namely, that the use of vocal recitation of the Buddha's name with sincere intent was a sufficient means for rebirth there for the most humble devotee.

The first Pure Land thinker to feel the full brunt of Ch'an criticisms of Pure Land was Tz'u-min Hui-jih (680–748). That his ideas continue the emphasis of Shan-tao can be seen clearly in the three Pure Land hymns he composed (which are preserved in the writings of Fa-chao recovered at Tun-huang). In addition, Hui-jih launched a vigorous counterattack to Ch'an criticisms in his major writing, the *Lüeh chu-ching-lun nien-fo fa-men wang-sheng ching-t'u chi* ("A Collection Outlining Various Scriptures and Treatises Regarding Methods of Contemplating the Buddha and Rebirth in the Pure Land").[20] Originally in three fascicles and believed to be lost, the text was partially restored earlier in this century when Ono Gemmyō discovered the first fascicle in Korea.[21] Hui-jih had organized the text into three parts, beginning, in the first, with a refutation of the errors of Ch'an. Fortunately for us, it is this section of the text that has survived; the other two sections—which set forth the "correct teachings *(cheng-tsung)* of the Pure Land *nien-fo*" and try to resolve various doctrinal problems—remain lost.

Because Hui-jih moved to Kuang-chou (Canton) in South China, it is quite possible that he directly encountered the disciples of Hui-neng/ Shen-hui and their attack on Pure Land devotionalism. In describing the views of Ch'an leaders, Hui-jih first attributes to them the idea that the world is empty and tranquil and that there is not a single thing that has real existence. "All the various dharmas are like hairs on a tortoise or horns on a rabbit; they originally have no substance. Although they are born and die, there is no good that can be cultivated and no evil that can be cut off." Yet, according to Hui-jih, these people "only cause their inner mind to be pacified and dwell in emptiness, understanding that the world is false and the ten thousand dharmas are nonexistent."[22] Thus, after attaining meditative concentration *(ch'an-ting),* they discard the remaining external practices as empty—including all the usual Pure Land practices, such as "*nien-fo,* reciting scripture, seeking rebirth in the Pure Land, plus practicing the Six Perfections of a bodhisattva, copying scriptures, making images, establishing temples, worshipping in a temple, being filial to one's parents, serving one's teachers and elders, and so on." Hui-jih charges that, according to Ch'an, these are all causes for birth-and-death, not liberation, because they entail "attachment to form and empty distinctions." Hui-jih concludes that this viewpoint of the Ch'an masters is totally in error, being contrary to the scriptures, the truth, and the Buddha.[23]

Not only have Ch'an masters distorted and rejected the Buddhist teachings, Hui-jih continues, they are also guilty of arrogance by falsely believing themselves to be wise. He condemns their path to enlightenment, the cultivation of emptiness *(hsiu-k'ung),* because it is difficult, lengthy, and filled with suffering. Having upbraided Ch'an masters at length for their arrogance and the difficulty their teachings cause others, Hui-jih boldly charges them with not even achieving adequate meditative concentration *(ch'an-ting).* If they had, they would at least have achieved the stage of concentration with defilements *(yu-lou ting),* with its five supernatural powers *(wu-t'ung),* to say nothing of the Mahāyāna achievement of undefiled concentration, with its sixth power of "supernatural consciousness of the waning of vicious propensities." As one who had spent seventeen years travelling in India, Hui-jih expresses no little arrogance himself in remarking that this Ch'an method, "coming from the East [China], had not yet heard about realizing these five powers, to say nothing of the six powers!"[24]

Indeed, Hui-jih claims that Ch'an masters are often guilty of committing the Buddhist offense of claiming to have achieved enlightenment in this body. Masters and disciples praise each other, saying that they have already attained enlightenment, but they are wrong, he concludes. They teach their disciples to look for the Buddha not outside but inside. "Don't rely on the teachings of these Ch'an masters," warns Hui-jih. "They are common men, and none of them has realized true understanding."[25]

In response to the Ch'an criticism of Pure Land practice as being attached to form and false methods,[26] Hui-jih appeals to scriptural authority by quoting passages from eight scriptures recommending *nien-fo*. The last passage Hui-jih cites is the one from the *Wen-shu shuo ching* translated earlier; in doing so, however, he significantly omits the first part, which recommends cultivation in terms of the Perfection of Wisdom.[27] Instead, he concludes by saying: "All these scriptures say that *nien-fo* is the cause for enlightenment. How can one abruptly have true understanding based on common emotions? This is a rejection of the holy teaching. It is to speak falsehoods and is not the cause for attaining Buddhahood. How can anyone be so reckless!"[28]

Of course, such an appeal to scriptures was destined to meet with little success among Ch'an practitioners, whose teachings "repeatedly say that to read aloud the Mahāyāna scriptures is attachment to the falseness of form and is not a cause for achieving Buddhahood." All that Hui-jih could do was attack this position as "meaningless" and "worse than a raging fire that burns the Buddha's teachings and injures the good capacities of people."[29] Hui-jih finally appeals to the *Diamond Sūtra,* which recommends its own reading and recitation,[30] and goes on to quote other practices from other scriptures. He concludes:

> Various practices are broadly taught in the scriptures as a cause for becoming a Buddha, not merely the Six Perfections [of a bodhisattva]. How can Ch'an masters be so strongly attached to meditative concentration *(ch'an-ting)* as the correct cause of Buddhahood, and not [realize the importance of] the remaining [five] perfections? Rather, all the holy teachings say that wisdom is supreme, and the correct cause for Buddhahood, while the remaining practices are all supplementary conditions. . . . How can they praise meditative concentration as supreme?[31]

Next Hui-jih goes on to defend the practice of making Buddhist images, which Ch'an masters repeatedly say "has merit but is not a cause for Buddhahood."[32] This is followed by a defense of copying scriptures as beneficial preparation for enlightenment. "Although all this is attachment to form," acknowledges Hui-jih, "it is not false. It is necessary as a cause and is not empty."[33] To prove this, he then outlines four kinds of falseness[34] to show that the ten thousand practices are not false but are "marvellous causes that should produce the fruit of enlightenment and nirvāṇa."[35] These four kinds of falseness are:

1. The essential unreality of conditioned phenomena *(shih)*, in comparison with Principle *(li)*, which is true reality
2. The cause and effect of birth-and-death, which is impermanent and unreal, in comparison to the cause and effect of transcending attachments, which is true, enduring enlightenment and nirvāṇa
3. The profane mind, which is dualistic and attached to distinctions, in comparison to the holy mind, which understands names as temporary and is free of attachment
4. The unreality *(wu)* of all things produced by delusions and attachments, such as perceiving a rope to be a snake, in comparison to the existence *(yu)* of everything as causally produced

Thus, when properly understood, conditioned practices can be used to reach the unconditioned. One can only practice using forms, but those forms must not obstruct one's quickly leaving birth-and-death and rapidly attaining liberation.[36] Accordingly, he criticizes the "unrecorded mind" *(wu-chi hsin;* also criticized in the East Mountain School[37]) which is balanced, never wavers to left or right, and does not conform to distinctions. How can we benefit ourselves and others, asks Hui-jih, or find an impetus to transcend the world, if we are in agreement with the natural rhythm of things? Being without an effective cause, nothing can be accomplished, let alone the fruit of liberation.[38]

Hui-jih advocates Pure Land devotionalism in the remaining sections of our text:

> When the ten thousand practices are quickly completed, then we quickly attain Buddhahood. Although the Pure Land is only one gateway, if we exhaustively and single-mindedly cultivate and study this one form, with the vow to be reborn in that land, then in this manner all the dharmas will be completed. How do I know? Because we will attain rebirth in the Pure Land and there all dharmas will be perfected.[39]

Hui-jih then contrasts the Pure Land devotee with the Ch'an practitioner. It is interesting that the standard he uses is not the lowest of the nine ranks of the *Kuan wu-liang-shou ching* ("Meditation on the Buddha of Infinite Life Sūtra"), but the highest.[40] Whereas the Shansi movement of Pure Land (associated with T'an-luan [ca.488–ca.554], Tao-ch'o, and Shan-tao) was concerned to guarantee a minimal method for salvation, Hui-jih emphasizes its high requirements in order to offset what he considers to be the pernicious reductionism and false extremism of Ch'an. Accordingly, the Pure Land practice he advocates involves: (1) being compassionate, not killing, and maintaining all the precepts; (2) upholding, reading, and reciting the Mahāyāna scriptures; and (3) cultivating the six forms of mindfulness and dedicating the merit of that cultivation to being reborn in the Pure Land. By following these practices for up to seven days, one is assured of rebirth in the Pure Land. The six forms of mindfulness are: mindfulness of (1) the Buddha, (2) the Dharma, (3) the Sangha, (4) charity, (5) the precepts, and (6) the heavens, plus mindfulness of the bodhisattvas Kuan-yin (Avalokiteśvara) and Ta-shih (Mahāsthāmaprāpta) as advised in the *Kuan wu-liang-sheng ching.* Basically, these practices entail *nien-fo,* scripture chanting, and invocation of the bodhisattvas, in addition to vegetarianism. Those who drink and eat meat, Hui-jih warns, will have bad luck and be reborn in hell. The text ends with an extended appeal against alcohol and meat-eating.[41]

In considering the virulence of Hui-jih's criticisms, we should not forget the major life experiences that informed his religious orientation. He left for India in 702 at the age of twenty-two and returned to Ch'ang-an in 719, when he was thirty-nine. On his return journey he began fasting in a mountain retreat and prayed to Kuan-yin, who immediately appeared and revealed the teachings of rebirth in the Pure Land. Thus, having spent the formative years of his adult life seeking the "authentic" tradition at its source in India, he understandably objected to the Buddhist tradition's being shunned or dangerously abbreviated by Ch'an. In addition, the Ch'an demotion of Pure Land devotion to the status of ancillary or even deluded and obstructive practice was in direct contradiction to his own religious experience. Finally, his move into Kuang-chou in South China during his mature years placed him in direct contact with the full force of the rising Southern School of Sudden Enlightenment, which contrasted dramatically with his lifetime of search.

In summary, his main objections to Ch'an masters were:

1. They distort and deny basic Buddhist teachings.
2. They are arrogant.
3. They cause suffering to others through their distorted and difficult teachings.
4. Their own achievements in *ch'an* practice fall far short of Mahāyāna teaching.
5. They claim to have achieved enlightenment when they have not.
6. They reject the scriptures and what the scriptures teach and are thus a scourge to Buddhism.
7. They injure human capacities for learning by misleading people.
8. They mistakenly reject *nien-fo,* even though many scriptures recommend it.
9. They mistakenly elevate *ch'an* (i.e., dhyāna) as the supreme practice, but among the Six Perfections of a bodhisattva it is traditionally considered less important than wisdom.

10. External practices like making images and reciting scriptures are not empty but are recommended by the scriptures and have temporary use as an efficient cause to help stimulate enlightenment.

11. Ch'an emphasis on an open and harmonized mind lacks any means to stimulate transcendence and compassion.

12. Their disregard for basic precepts is unorthodox and harmful, and those who break precepts are in danger of being reborn in hell.

The great Japanese Pure Land figure Hōnen (1133–1212) divided Chinese Pure Land into three branches, those of (1) Lu-shan Hui-yüan (344–416); (2) Tao-ch'o and Shan-tao; and (3) Tz'u-min Hui-jih, who is seen as reconciling the practice of scripture learning, precepts, *nien-fo,* and *ch'an.* Although Hui-jih did want to reconcile *nien-fo* and *ch'an,* we must remember that he does this by taking *ch'an* as the Chinese word for samādhi or dhyāna. He was thus recommending meditation *(ch'an-ting)* in its classical Buddhist forms, not the teachings and practices of the Chinese Ch'an movement, which, on the contrary, he thoroughly condemned. The vehemence of his polemic put Hui-jih in direct opposition to the Southern School of Ch'an. In life experience, teachings, and temperament, he contrasts sharply with Shen-hui and Hui-neng, and he differs from Shan-tao in the breadth of his perspective.

Hui-jih is a fitting model for Pure Land in the T'ang Dynasty. His influence was strong; he converted Ch'eng-yüan (713–803) to Pure Land devotionalism, even though Ch'eng-yüan began his Buddhist practice as a disciple of the Ch'an master Ch'u-chi (himself a disciple of Chih-shen, one of the ten main disciples of the fifth Ch'an patriarch, Hung-jen). Ch'eng-yüan[42] became the teacher of Fa-chao, perhaps the most influential Pure Land teacher of the ninth century in China.[43] Furthermore, Hui-jih's writings were current in the tenth century, and Yung-ming Yen-shou (904–975) quoted Hui-jih as well as Southern Ch'an patriarch Hui-neng with approval.[44] Yüan-chao (1048–1116) reprinted his work in the Sung Dynasty, but its sharp criticisms of Ch'an provoked a complaint by Ssu-ming Pao-ying to the secular authorities, who stopped its circulation and destroyed the printing blocks.[45] This marked the end of Hui-jih's role as a Pure Land critic of Ch'an in China.

III. The Dialectics of Fei-hsi

During the eighth century, the Southern School of Ch'an emerged partially by defining itself over against various Pure Land practices. This development precipitated the strong reaction seen in the writings of Hui-jih and marked the point of greatest controversy between Pure Land and

Ch'an. Nevertheless, these extremes did not represent all practitioners, and various theoretical and practical methods were available for integrating Pure Land and Ch'an into a common world view. Representative of the attempt to accommodate the different approaches of the two schools was the position put forward by Fei-hsi. Although an important Pure Land thinker of the eighth century, Fei-hsi was less aggressive in his approach to Ch'an than Hui-jih.[46] In his *Nien-fo san-mei pao-wang lun* ("Treatise on the Contemplation of the Buddha as the Jewel King of Meditation"), he responded to a variety of issues by offering support and guidance rather than criticism. Not only was he less assertive than Hui-jih,[47] he also offered a balance between the Lotus samādhi practice of non-despising and the *nien-fo* samādhi teaching of beholding all the Buddhas of the present age *(pan-chou; pratyutpanna).*

Fei-hsi's *Nien-fo san-mei pao-wang lun* comprises twenty sections, which are divided into three parts dealing with (1) future Buddhas, (2) the present Buddha Amitābha, and (3) the past Buddha Śākyamuni. Part one, consisting of the first seven sections,[48] focuses on future Buddhas and is based on chapter twenty of the *Lotus Sūtra,* in which Bodhisattva Sadaparibhuta-parivarta (Never Disparaging) venerates everyone, whether laity or clergy, as a future Buddha. Even if some people break the precepts or are in hell, they should never be disparaged or held in contempt, since that creates duality in the mind and shows a lack of respect for their future destiny as Buddhas. Fei-hsi also quotes the same passage from the *Leng-ch'ieh pao-chi ching* that Hui-jih had used[49] to argue for vegetarianism and for respecting living beings by not killing them for food.

The second part of the text, consisting of the next six sections,[50] is devoted to the present Buddha, Amitābha, who is now abiding in the Western Pure Land. In contrast to part one, which draws on the Lotus and T'ien-t'ai traditions, part two contains Fei-hsi's major Pure Land teachings. It strongly advocates chanting the Buddha's name with a loud voice[51] and recommends group recitation after the practice of Lu-shan Hui-yüan's group.[52]

However, it is part three (sections fifteen to twenty)[53] that deals with the relation of Pure Land and Ch'an. Fei-hsi begins with an affirmation of the essential unity of the Buddha and the devotee. They differ only because the devotee is still in the state of preparation *(yin),* whereas Śākyamuni Buddha represents the fruition *(kuo).* Nevertheless, when seen together, the preparation and fruition have the same attributes *(hsiang-t'ung).*[54]

This unity in diversity is then analyzed more closely in section fifteen in terms of two categories made famous in Hua-yen thought: Principle *(li)* and phenomena *(shih).* The gateway of Principle is an awareness of emptiness: Buddha and mind do not exist in themselves. Nor is the Buddha produced from the mind, or the mind from the Buddha. Rather, their mutuality and interrelatedness enable both to appear. When both are tranquil *(shuang-chi),* there is calmness (*chih;* śamatha). When there is mutual illumination *(shuang-chao),* there is insight (*kuan;* vipaśyanā). Calmness and insight are not identical. Illumination (insight), which is always tranquil, is the mind without an object of mindfulness; whereas tranquility (calmness), which is always illuminating, is the cultivation of *nien-fo.* The Tathāgata realizes the samādhi of both tranquility and illumination.[55]

Although Principle involves emptiness and a mind without an object of contemplation, this is balanced by its manifestation in the realm of phenomena *(shih)* and the use of objects of contemplation to accomplish this goal. "Just as a wedge is used to remove a wedge, . . . so mindfulness *(nien)* is used to calm the mind."[56] Fei-hsi then quotes the famous reference to methods for obtaining one-practice samādhi found in the *Wen-shu shuo ching* to support the use of reciting the name of the Buddha. With this method one becomes just like an archer who practices to such a degree that, "after he has no-mind *(wu-hsin),* everywhere is the target for the arrow to hit."[57] Fei-hsi is concerned with the maturation of mindfulness,[58] which involves "using the mind of *nien-fo* to enter into the patience based on the insight of non-arising."[59] Fei-hsi argues that this assumes an accessible Buddha who responds, who appears, and whose activity is not just a temporary skillful means, but involves an automatic opening of the mind. Thus, Fei-hsi presents a reasoned argument for the "dual cultivation of no-mind and mindfulness of the Buddha, of Principle *(li)* and phenomena *(shih).*"[60] This use of Principle and phenomena pioneers an important new vehicle for conceptualizing dual cultivation of Ch'an and Pure Land, which was quoted later in the *Nien-fo ching* ("A Mirror of Devotion to [Amitābha] Buddha")[61] and which became an essential device in the thought of Yung-ming Yen-shou.

In section sixteen Fei-hsi elaborates further on this theme of "the middle path of no-mind and no-Buddha," by which he means transcending both the conceptualizing mind and the Buddha who is conceptualized.[62] Continuing at the level of emptiness *(li* rather than *shih),* he posits the fundamental identity of all activities. Contemplating the true reality of the Buddha is like contemplating the true reality of the body (oneself); there is no difference.[63] Echoing T'ien-t'ai and Ch'an expressions, Fei-hsi says that delusions are identical to nirvāṇa and that sentient beings are identical to the various Buddhas.[64] Moreover, *nien-fo* is not different from true no-thought *(wu-nien),* and rebirth in the Pure Land is true no-birth.[65] This interpretation of Pure Land teachings and practices in terms of Perfection of Wisdom doctrine places Fei-hsi in the mainstream of Chinese Buddhism and connects him with T'an-luan and Tao-ch'o, who interpreted Pure Land devotionalism in similar terms.

Fei-hsi continues by quoting from the account of Hui-k'o (recognized by then as the Second Patriarch of Ch'an) in the *Hsü kao-seng chuan* ("Continued Biographies of Eminent Monks") in which Hui-k'o teaches that delusion and nirvāna are related as form to shadow or as sound to its echo: one is the root of the other. To try to be free of sentient beings in order to seek Buddha-nature is like dampening the sound in order to search out the echo. Therefore, one should realize that they are a single path. Stupidity and wisdom are not different.[66] Fei-hsi then invokes Bodhidharma to say that one "must not abandon mindfulness *(nien)* existing in no-thought, nor abandon birth established in no-birth. . . . Delusions are identical to nirvāna, sentient beings are identical to the various Buddhas. . . . Thus, mindfulness of the Buddha *(nien-fo)* is true no-mind *(chen wu-nien)*. Rebirth in the Pure Land is at the same time no-birth *(wu-sheng*, i.e., non-arising)."[67] Again, similar statements can be found in the writings of T'an-luan, Chih-i, and Tao-ch'o from the sixth and seventh centuries and are based on the Perfection of Wisdom dialectic.

In section seventeen Fei-hsi presents his view of *nien-fo* as the king of all the other samādhis.[68] *Nien-fo* is the jeweled king samādhi because it does not abide anywhere. Rather, it is like a dream wherein one experiences vastness without coming or going anywhere.[69] Nevertheless, even though it does not abide in good or evil, *nien-fo* is always in accord with Principle *(li);* it is a mental practice involving good elements, not evil or uncertain ones.[70]

Fei-hsi moves to the concrete level of daily practice in the eighteenth section of *Nien-fo san-mei pao-wang lun.* Having adopted the dialectic of Principle *(li)* and phenomena *(shih),* of *nien-fo* as no-thought *(wu-nien),* and having accepted the supremacy of *nien-fo* as non-abiding, he raises the question of what kinds of offerings can be made now that the Buddha has passed away. Fei-hsi acknowledges that any of the ten thousand practices (since they all participate in the Dharmadhātu and can purify our body, mind, and speech) can be called an offering. How could one think that the true realm itself would not also be an offering! Indeed, since all dharmas, whether permanent or impermanent, cannot be acquired (because they are empty), neither can offerings to the Buddha be acquired (as Principle, *li*).[71] However, having said all this, Fei-hsi then comments that, when the Buddha was in the world, clouds of flowers or oceans of incense were not sufficient offerings to express proper devotion. People today do little but think of themselves and neglect ceremonies, yet they consider themselves reverential. How arrogant! Today to offer a single flower with sincerity is very rare, but such an act is the beginning of holiness.[72] Thus, while affirming the level of Principle *(li),* Fei-hsi is also anxious to establish the obligations of practice in the phenomenal realm *(shih).*

Now Fei-hsi comes to his criticism of Ch'an. How does just offering flowers with the mind or "burning mental incense to worship a mental Buddha" differ from "monkey business" or looking at a plum forest from the outside but not entering to taste its fruit? It is hard to survive when one uses only mental clothes and food! How can one neglect the Six Perfections and the ten thousand practices simply because one's mind has a view of nonbeing? We must not be so careless, Fei-hsi admonishes. Rather, we must learn from the practices of Esoteric Buddhism (Chen-yen) that reverence cannot be merely mental but must express itself in form according to the realm of phenomena *(shih)*. Adornments, incense, and flowers must always be offered unceasingly during the six daily times of worship.[73]

In section nineteen Fei-hsi echoes the *Heart Sūtra,* stating that, just as form is identical to emptiness, so flowers are not just phenomena *(shih)* but also Principle *(li)*.[74] He then moves back into the realm of phenomena, the realm of cause and effect, with a long passage on the good retribution for faith *(hsin)* and the bad retribution for disbelief. He asserts that doing evil to others, such as slandering them or looking at them maliciously, will result in defective speech or sight for aeons to come. Moreover, cultivation of good qualities will surely bring benefits; for example, a king who practices the bodhisattva ideal of relinquishing attachment to his body, head, eyes, bone marrow, and brain, even though he is ignorant at the time, will completely fulfill all of the Six Perfections in the future. Thus beings pass on their own defects or merit. If one wants to keep sentient beings from having their carts overturned in the crooked ruts of their predecessors, one should offer a flower. Making images of earth and wood, copying scriptures on bamboo and silk, shaving one's head and becoming a monk or nun, all such practices uphold the Three Jewels and the threefold discipline of morality, meditation, and wisdom. They all express reverence and give beings access to true reality. As the *Lotus Sūtra* says:

> Those people who, with reverence, make an offering of flowers, incense, or banners at a temple or before a jeweled image or a picture and utter even a single word [of praise], their future Buddhahood is already assured.[75]

This is possible, Fei-hsi claims, not just because evil is balanced with good, but because such offerings invoke the true formlessness of the wisdom that uses evil to grasp emptiness. One can break evil karma by establishing the perfection of giving *(dānapāramitā)* by making offerings of flowers.[76] Thus the section on "worshipping true reality with perfect sincerity of mind, body, and speech" ends by reaffirming traditional religious practices in the face of Ch'an iconoclasm.

In the last section Fei-hsi uses a parable to introduce a new doctrine.[77] When an emperor goes on tour, he is preceded by chariots, officials, and foot soldiers, who carry an imperial banner and announce with a loud voice the coming of the emperor. People who do not clear the way but intrude onto his pathway will receive the punishment of heaven and be killed immediately. On the other hand, when these same soldiers return to their home villages, if they speak the emperor's name, they will be killed immediately. The soldiers are the same, and their action is the same, but the context and purpose are entirely different *(yüan-ch'i chih shu).*[78] Thus, if we offer flowers without knowing the *Lotus Sūtra,* the reward will simply be rebirth in heavenly palaces. However, if we join the samādhi jeweled king (the *Lotus Sūtra*), we are like officials in the emperor's retinue, and even offering a flower will achieve Buddhahood. Such an offering is the Buddha-seed, but it must conform to the situational principle *(yüan-ch'i li)* illustrated by this parable. It is like birds that fly to Mt. Sumeru—all have the same color—or waters that flow into the ocean—none returns to its individual identity.[79]

After discussing how a word (i.e., the emperor's name) used in two different contexts can bring about either glory or death, Fei-hsi draws on a Buddhist scripture to say that all elements (beings, forms, etc.) can be either mundane or marked by samādhi, just as the ocean is contained in a hair or Mt. Sumeru in a mustard seed.[80] He argues that how we understand a situation is what is most important.[81] As his conclusion, he asserts that the Lotus samādhi is identical to the *nien-fo* samādhi. Thus, if we have this understanding when we offer a flower, we are offering it to the Buddha-essence in the past, present, and future. It is like shooting an arrow at the earth—no matter where one shoots, one cannot miss the target![82] Or, as the title of this section states, "the ten thousand virtuous practices are all the same *(wan-shan t'ung-kuei)* and can complete the gate of samādhi."[83] Fei-hsi summarizes his position with the eight character phrase:

The dual illumination of movement and tranquility;
The perfect interfusion of Principle *(li)* and phenomena *(shih).*[84]

IV. Developmental Models

Another text that relates to our theme is the short eighth-century *Wu fang-pien nien-fo men* ("The Gateway of the Five Expedient Methods for Contemplating the Buddha"),[85] which offers a different perspective on *nien-fo* than those texts we have examined so far in tracing the controversy between the Pure Land and Ch'an schools.

This text is an expanded version of a shorter text discovered by Satō Tetsuei entitled *Wu fang-pien men* ("Five Expedient Methods"), which

survives in a ninth-century copy in the Shōsoin of Tōdaiji.[86] The expanded text consists of four sections:

1. Five kinds of dhyāna *(ch'an)*
2. Five methods of *nien-fo* samādhi
3. Questions and answers
4. *Nien-fo* contemplation according to the T'ien-t'ai fourfold teachings

Only sections one and four are included in the shorter text,[87] which is less
than one third the length of the expanded version. The parallel sections
are virtually identical in the two texts, except that the expanded text
omits the title for section four that is included in the shorter version.
Although both the shorter and expanded versions are attributed to T'ien-
t'ai Chih-i, the expanded version must have been compiled after 713, and
even the shorter version was probably written after Chih-i's death. Whatever its authorship, the shorter version is definitely in the T'ien-t'ai tradition. Even though the longer version shows clear Hua-yen influence,
both texts have a coherent view that offers a significant alternative to the
nien-fo controversy as it developed between Pure Land and Ch'an advocates. The shorter text will be outlined first, followed by an analysis of its
expanded version.

The five kinds of dhyāna discussed at the beginning of both versions
of the text are: (1) freezing the mind dhyāna *(ning-hsin ch'an),* (2) subduing the mind dhyāna *(chih-hsin ch'an),* (3) true essence dhyāna *(t'i-chen
ch'an),* (4) expedient methods for conforming to circumstances dhyāna
(fang-pien sui-yüan ch'an), and (5) eliminating the distinctions of the two
extremes dhyāna *(hsi erh-pien fen-pieh ch'an).* As these are briefly
explained, the first and second involve contemplating an image (such as
in the more traditional *nien-fo* practice); the third involves realizing the
true nature of things as empty; the fourth moves from emptiness to enter
the realm of temporary existence; and the fifth transcends the two extremes of emptiness and expediency. The last three echo the three truths
and three views at the heart of T'ien-t'ai thought.

The first section of the text concludes with the observation that one
can distinguish five kinds of dhyāna in the progression from the superficial to the profound. However, from the point of view of perfect discernment *(yüan-kuan),* there is no distinction as to superficial and profound,
although the superficial and profound are still evident. Accordingly, the
text is called "Five Expedient Methods."

Various configurations of these five kinds of dhyāna can be found in
Chih-i's writings. For example, the first three appear as a group and the
last four appear as a group, but the five never occur together as a
group.[88] On the other hand, a century after Chih-i the northern line of

Ch'an organized its doctrines in terms of five scriptures, which were interpreted under the rubric "five expedient methods" *(wu fang-pien).*[89] Since T'ien-t'ai and Northern Ch'an Buddhists mingled in the same geographical area with students practicing under masters from both traditions, the *Wu fang-pien men* may have evolved within that milieu as a new packaging of Chih-i's ideas.

The other section of the shorter text (section four of the longer version) is entitled "Achieving Detachment from Thought *(li-nien)* by Means of the Fourfold Teachings concerning *Nien-fo* Meditation." The fourfold teachings—i.e., tripiṭaka *(tsang),* shared *(t'ung),* distinctive *(pieh),* and complete *(yüan)*—constitute Chih-i's major arrangement of Buddhist teachings in terms of four ascending stages of spiritual understanding. Each of the four is subdivided into numerous other stages, which, when taken together, constitute the fifty-two stages of the bodhisattva's career. The brief discussion of the fourfold teachings in our text, however, focuses on the way the mind that practices *nien-fo* should be viewed in relation to the aim of being detached from thought *(li-nien),* a central aim of Northern Ch'an practice.[90] Our text's attempt to reconcile *nien-fo* with *li-nien* by making use of the progressive stages of understanding represented by the T'ien-t'ai fourfold teachings reveals how it tries to recast T'ien-t'ai ideas within the context of Northern Ch'an teachings.

First, the rise of thinking *(nien)* is analyzed according to the tripiṭaka teaching as a cooperative activity between mental intent and dharmic conditioning. When one thinks of Buddha *(nien-fo),* the thought that arises is identical to the dharma that is produced so that the three forms (i.e., perceptual awakening, perceptual faculties, and perceived object) are seen to be in constant process. Thus there is no (separate and substantial) Buddha and no (separate and enduring) thought.

Next, the mind that practices *nien-fo* is analyzed according to each of the remaining three teachings and correlated with the T'ien-t'ai three truths of emptiness, expediency, and the middle. Both the tripiṭaka and shared teachings involve a movement from seeing form to being aware of emptiness, initially through analysis and subsequently by seeing the emptiness of the essential nature of Buddha and mind. The distinctive teaching involves adopting an expedient use of terms in the bodhisattva path. Finally, the complete teaching avoids extremes and embraces both emptiness and expediency in the Middle Way. The last level always contains, balances, reconciles, and completes all the previous stages in the T'ien-t'ai world view. Even though each teaching is shown to contain no Buddha and no thought, one must nevertheless "not relinquish thought distinctions but seek to be detached from thought *(li-nien).*"[91]

The central theme in the two sections of the shorter text is an examination of the contemplation of the Buddha *(nien-fo)* in terms of (1) progressive stages of spiritual insight (the five dhyānas and the fourfold teachings) based on (2) the recognition of the dialectic between form and emptiness and the dynamic relationship of the mind to its object of cognition and (3) their resolution in the three truths. The first section concludes that the distinction between superficial and profound dhyāna practices is still evident although empty, whereas the last section emphasizes that one must not relinguish thought even while one transcends it. This text mounts a powerful defense of *nien-fo* practice consistent with T'ien-t'ai principles. Satō Tetsuei concludes that it agrees with Chih-i's mature thought and that there is no reason to deny that the text was written by Chih-i, although there is also no binding reason to attribute it to him. Based on the late date of the first catalog reference to the text (805)[92] and the key role of the two Northern Ch'an terms around which the text is organized *(wu fang-pien* and *li-nien),* an early eighth-century date would seem most plausible; in all probability, it was written by a T'ien-t'ai follower influenced by Northern Ch'an.

The expanded version of the text inserts a section on five methods of *nien-fo* samādhi (section two) and a section of questions and answers (section three). This last section must have been added after 713, as the answers consist of lengthy quotations from the *Ta-pao-chi ching*[93] translated by Bodhiruci in 706–713. The last quotation deals with the visualization of the Buddha, whose body and images are not different from the letters of his name in that all are empty of any essential nature. The proper way to view a picture of the Buddha is to see it as the body of suchness/Tathāgata: it is beyond realization and attainment; neither comes nor goes; transcends birth-and-death, purity and form, the three poisons of greed, anger, and ignorance; and is without beginning, middle, or end. The first quotation is another version of the *Wen-shu shuo ching* passage explaining one-practice samādhi.

The main portion of the expanded text[94] is a list of five methods of *nien-fo* samādhi that became so central to the work that the text's name was changed to emphasize the five expedient methods of *nien-fo* instead of the five expedient methods of dhyāna. Although the earliest catalog reference to this new title is in 839 by Ennin (794–864),[95] the source for this section is much older. The fourth Hua-yen patriarch, Ch'eng-kuan (738–839), quotes this same list in his subcommentary to the *Avataṁsaka (Hua-yen ching sui-shu yen-i-ch'ao),* saying that it was taught by "a man of old" *(ku-jen).*[96] He could not have been too ancient, however, since the fifth and culminating method of *nien-fo* is based on "the perfect understanding of nature origination" *(hsing-ch'i yüan-t'ung),* a doctrine first formulated by the second Hua-yen patriarch, Chih-yen (602–668).[97]

The five expedient methods of *nien-fo* samādhi are:

1. Calling the Buddha's name to attain rebirth in the Pure Land
2. Visualizing the form of the Buddha to eradicate sins

3. Realizing that all items of perception are mind-only
4. Transcending both the mind and its objects of perception
5. The perfect understanding of nature origination

The first method of *nien-fo* is basic to the Shansi Pure Land movement of T'an-luan, Tao-ch'o, and Shan-tao: "When one vocally recites 'Nan-wu O-mi-t'o-fo,' the mind must vow to be born in [Amitābha's] land."[98] The second method, involving the visualization of Amitābha to eradicate past sins, was perfected by Shan-tao.[99] In their role of calming and redirecting the mind by focusing on a Buddha image, both of these methods parallel to some degree the first two forms of dhyāna listed at the beginning of the text. The third method of *nien-fo* is used to prevent harmful stagnation and substantialization. In the fivefold dhyāna scheme of the first section, attention is given in the third stage to the true nature of things as empty. The *nien-fo* scheme, however, emphasizes understanding all phenomena as mind-only *(wei-hsin)* and empty of enduring distinctions. The contrast between the two schemes becomes even greater when the fourth method of *nien-fo* directs attention to the mind and its objects as equally nonsubstantial; the practitioner is to return from emptiness to reenter the expedient manifold phenomena with penetrating understanding according to the dhyāna scheme.

The fifth level of the *nien-fo* scheme moves beyond the state of deep objectless and subjectless meditation to the perfect understanding of nature origination. This is a transcendent level of nirvāṇa beyond birth-and-death, beyond mind and its objects, in which the merit achieved in the previous four levels is inapplicable. This description echoes Hua-yen's use of the *tathāgatagarbha* tradition to affirm a transcendent dimension in the midst of the phenomenal realm—something very different from the fifth stage of dhyāna which was concerned to reconcile the dialectic of emptiness and temporary existence in typical T'ien-t'ai fashion. The two schemes are similar insofar as the fifth stage represents the consummation of the previous stages, but the different terminology reflects the different doctrinal legacies of T'ien-t'ai and Hua-yen. In both cases, however, *nien-fo* is viable as a metaphor and is given new interpretations as a practice. In the dhyāna scheme the superficial and profound, the expedient and empty, are perfectly interfused, and *nien-fo* practice is thereby made meaningful. In the *nien-fo* scheme the perfect understanding of nature origination involves the completion of all vows, the perfection of all beings in the Pure Land, the unity of all merits, and the taking of one body as an infinite number of bodies. In this transcendent level, where all interfuses in the rise of true nature, mundane *nien-fo* meditation is maintained as a metaphor while having been freed from specific reference to Amitābha to include all Buddhas and all wisdom.

The *Wu fang-pien nien-fo men* betrays no evidence of the rivalry between Southern Ch'an and Pure Land devotionalism. Instead, there is a harmonious use of devotional practices within T'ien-t'ai and Northern Ch'an doctrinal categories in the shorter text as well as within Hua-yen doctrinal categories in the expanded text. The shorter text provides the rationale that legitimizes the spiritual validity of expedient methods *(fang-pien; upāya)* at each level without discussing expediency per se. On the other hand, the new Hua-yen-influenced scheme of five methods of *nien-fo* in the expanded text discusses the use of numerous expedient devices—including the fivefold, step-by-step arrangement—used by the Buddhas to facilitate enlightenment in beings. But this and all other lists —such as the ten degrees of faith, the ten stages of the bodhisattva, etc. —never go beyond *nien-fo,* which the expanded text claims gives birth to them all.

All of these sections of the text illustrate principles that were important features of T'ien-t'ai. First, the five levels of dhyāna and *nien-fo* echo the *p'an-chiao* schemes—such as the five periods *(wu-shih)* and five flavors *(wu-wei)*—used by T'ien-t'ai to classify the Buddha's teachings. The basic assumption behind these schemes is that the Buddha taught different things at different times because the needs and capacities of people were different. People are thought to be at different levels of spiritual growth, and expedient devices are considered necessary for those at lower levels. However, beyond these principles of growth, stages, and expendiency lies the recognition that the most elementary contains the ultimate and vice versa. Each element has a range of levels. Thus one-practice samādhi can consist in recitation of the Buddha's name *and* at the same time be ultimate, formless reality. Similarly, an image of the Buddha can be viewed as a picture *and* as beyond distinctions of space and time. In the expanded text this idea is expressed by the presence of *nien-fo* at all levels of spiritual growth.

The *Wu fang-pien nien-fo men* outlines an alternative Pure Land response to Ch'an. Instead of offering a counterattack (as did Hui-jih) or a corrective to restore a balanced dialectic (as did Fei-hsi), it interprets both Pure Land and meditative practice *(ch'an)* in terms of progressive levels of spiritual attainment. In this way it utilizes a pattern of coping with diversity that harks back to the *p'an-chiao* schemes of earlier Chinese Buddhism and beyond that to early Mahāyāna classification as exemplified by the *Lotus Sūtra*.[100] In the eighth century a variety of schemes were current, most notably the "five periods and eight teachings" of Chan-jan (717–782) and the fivefold scheme of Fa-tsang (643–712), both of which had been evolved to integrate and prioritize the vast array of conflicting Indian Buddhist sources that had been introduced to China. In contrast to such efforts to organize Indian materials, the schemes offered in the *Wu fang-pien nien-fo men* were guides for spiritual growth using ideas and practices, particularly *nien-fo* devotionalism, that had become deeply rooted in China.

The organization of Pure Land devotionalism and Ch'an in terms of stages of spiritual growth was a natural one for T'ien-t'ai and Hua-yen thinkers, but it was not accepted among Pure Land and Ch'an advocates until a century or two later. Ch'eng-kuan reflects some of the stages in this process. In his commentary on the twenty-one types of *nien-fo* samādhi listed in the chapter on the practice and vows of Samantabhadra from the *Gaṇḍavyūha (Hua-yen ching hsing-yüan p'in shu)*, he writes that they can be grouped into five categories:

1. Recitation of the Buddha's name in reference to an externally perceived Buddha and Pure Land
2. Mind-only *nien-fo* in which one is aware that "this mind is Buddha, this mind becomes a Buddha"
3. Extinction of both the mind and the object of its visualization as nonsubstantial
4. The non-obstruction of mind and its object of perception based on mutual interpenetration, and the mutual embrace of Principle *(li)* and phenomena *(shih)*, existence and emptiness
5. The inexhaustible identity of oneself with all things[101]

However, as we have seen in his subcommentary to the *Avataṁsaka*, Ch'eng-kuan also quotes without comment a different list of five categories of *nien-fo* from "a man of old"—a list that is equivalent to the one in our expanded text. Nevertheless, this list is lost in an ocean of other lists and technical detail and seems to have had little importance in his work.

In any event, these are not merely lists of various kinds of *nien-fo*, they represent ascending levels of spiritual growth. The simple recitation of the Buddha's name and the use of visual forms is not rejected, but expanded and transformed, as one moves to higher levels. Hence a ladder was built between those of inferior and those of superior capacities, laying the foundation for the dual cultivation of Pure Land and Ch'an.

This ladder becomes clearer when we look at Tsung-mi (780–841), who is already famous as a bridge figure since he is revered as a patriarch in both the Hua-yen and Ch'an traditions. In his subcommentary to Ch'eng-kuan's commentary on the chapter on the practice and vows of Samantabhadra *(Hua-yen ching hsing-yüan p'in shu-ch'ao)*,[102] Tsung-mi reworked Ch'eng-kuan's five categories of *nien-fo* into four:

1. Vocally calling on the name of the Buddha, which he illustrates by quoting the passage from the *Wen-shu shuo ching* cited earlier.
2. Visualizing the form of the Buddha as an image in a painting, etc.; he quotes the *Ta-pao-chi ching* to say that since the visualization of an image of the Buddha is identical to the Buddha itself,

one will receive the five spiritual powers and attain the all-pervading light samādhi to see all Buddhas in the Ten Directions.

3. Visualizing the major and minor marks of the Buddha, which will eradicate the karma of countless kalpas of past wrongs.

4. Contemplation of the absolute (*shih-hsiang* or dharmakāya), viewing the true self-nature within one's own body and within all dharmas; he again quotes from the *Wen-shu shuo ching:* "Non-arising and non-extinction, neither coming nor going, nameless and formless—this is what is called Buddha. By viewing the absolute within one's own body, one views the Buddha. . . . Focusing on the one mark of the Dharmadhātu is called one-practice samādhi." Tsung-mi then quotes the *Ta-chih-tu-lun* to say not to fix attention on the physical form or on the marks of the Buddha, for there is nothing that his body has. "Therefore, use no-thought *(wu-i)* as contemplation of the Buddha *(nien-fo)."*

It is interesting to note how frequently Tsung-mi uses the *Wen-shu shuo ching.* Moreover, the passages he draws from it and from the *Ta-pao-chi ching* (which contains the *Wen-shu shuo ching* as one of its texts) to illustrate the first two kinds of *nien-fo* are the same passages used as illustrations in the *Wu fang-pien nien-fo men.* However, the list of the five dhyānas in the *Wu fang-pien nien-fo ching* ends with the T'ien-tai three views, and the list of the five methods of *nien-fo* of the expanded text ends with Hua-yen, whereas Tsung-mi replaced these T'ien-t'ai and Hua-yen categories with categories more compatible with Ch'an. Tsung-mi's position thus culminates in the *dual cultivation* of Pure Land and Ch'an: "Therefore, no-thought *(wu-i)* can be considered as contemplating the Buddha."[103]

The final practice of contemplating the Buddha as the absolute *(shih-hsiang nien-fo)* is related to Tsung-mi's doctrine of mind, which is derived from the *Awakening of Faith.* He considers the mind in terms of two aspects: the absolute *(t'i)* and the phenomenal *(hsiang).* The phenomenal aspect includes the physical mind *(ju-t'uan hsin),* the object-perceiving mind *(yüan-lü hsin;* i.e., the eight modes of consciousness), and the accumulating and generating mind *(chi-ch'i hsin;* i.e., the ālaya-vijñāna). Following the *tathāgatagarbha* tradition, Tsung-mi then defines the absolute mind *(chien-shih hsin)* as including both purity and impurity while being beyond phenomenal change. It is One Mind, suchness, Buddha-nature, the *tathāgatagarbha,* true nature.[104] It is interesting that Tsung-mi has three aspects of the phenomenal mind, much as he had three phenomenal aspects of *nien-fo,* whereas all is unified in the *nien-fo* on the absolute, which is also the goal of Ch'an.

Besides his classification of different levels of *nien-fo,* Tsung-mi also offers a convenient organization of Ch'an into three teachings: (1)

stopping of the false and cultivation of the mind *(hsi-wang hsiu-hsin);* (2) complete emptying *(min-chüeh wu-chi);* and (3) direct revelation of the mind-nature *(chih-hsien hsin-hsing).*[105] These categories are used by Yen-shou in his *Tsung-ching-lu,* where he quotes from Tsung-mi at length.[106] In addition, Yen-shou adopts from Tsung-mi a similar arrangement for classifying all of Buddhism (and the myriad practices involved in dual cultivation), namely, (1) the teaching of form *(hsiang),* (2) the teaching of emptiness *(k'ung),* and (3) the teaching of true nature *(hsing).*[107] In these terms, the historical practice of Pure Land inclines to the first category, iconoclastic Ch'an to the second, whereas the truth lies in the last category where both can meet.

V. Patterns of Pure Land Responses to Ch'an

Many of the twelve criticisms levied at Ch'an by Hui-jih are not merely defenses of Pure Land. Other people also criticized Ch'an because it had broken a dialectical balance inherent in the Perfection of Wisdom tradition. For example, the *Śūraṅgamasamādhi-sūtra,* one of the earliest and most often translated Perfection of Wisdom texts in China, says that the bodhisattva neither urges nor avoids upholding morality; rather, he appears to be devoted to morality in order to save other beings.[108] Thus, the bodhisattva maintains all traditional religious behavior and distinctions for the sake of perfecting others, even though he knows that both good and bad eternally dwell in true reality *(fa-hsing)* and transcend the actions of body, speech, and mind.[109]

On the other hand, like Vimalakīrti, the bodhisattva of the tenth stage is said to be able to make himself blind, dumb, and lame to save beings and to disport with female musicians while maintaining inner purity and concentration.[110] This behavior, which violates traditional Buddhist morality, is undertaken by a bodhisattva of the highest stage, one who has already fulfilled all of the conventional religious practices. Thus two of the major dialectical balances in the Perfection of Wisdom tradition involved: (1) practicing conventional Buddhism for the sake of others, even though one has the awareness that there is nothing to be achieved, that there is neither good nor bad, and that all things are ultimately nirvāṇa;[111] and (2) not practicing conventional Buddhism while inwardly dwelling in the highest level of Buddhist attainment just short of Buddhahood.

Hui-jih criticizes Ch'an practitioners for violating both of these dialectics. They did not maintain standard Buddhist morality, practices, and beliefs for the sake of others—especially those associated with Pure Land—and their unconventional behavior was accompanied not by high inner attainment but by arrogance, ignorance of the tradition, and even a lack of meditative attainment. Carl Bielefeldt's chapter in this volume highlights the bind that Ch'an had created for itself by the mid eighth century when its affirmation of sudden enlightenment as a nondiscursive state of inner tranquility inhibited any open discussion of training and teaching. That this resulted in unconventional behavior unsupported by knowledge of the tradition or by true wisdom is reported not just by Hui-jih, but by Ch'an documents as well. Although he may have had additional reasons (such as the inundation of Ch'an monasteries with insincere and unprepared monks in flight from war and famine), Kuei-shan Ling-yu (771–853) offers a number of criticisms of Ch'an monks that echo those of Hui-jih. This fact is striking—especially since Kuei-shan was the dharma heir of Po-chang and thus stood squarely in the Hung-chou lineage of Ma-tsu and Huang-po, perhaps the most iconoclastic of all Ch'an traditions. In his *Kuei-shan ching-ts'e* ("Kuei-shan's Admonishing Stick"), he criticizes Ch'an monks for their arrogant, undisciplined, and uninformed behavior:

> Not yet versed in the rules of the order, you have absolutely no self-discipline. Sometimes you talk big, with a loud voice, spewing forth words without constraint. And as you have no respect for your seniors, peers, or subordinates, you are no different from a gathering of [haughty] Brahmans. Making a racket with your dishes, you get up to leave as soon as you have finished eating. With your daily activities all awry you have absolutely nothing of the appearance of a monk. You rise from your seat in agitation and disturb the thoughts of others. As you have not taken in even a bit of the rules, you have not even the slightest hint of dignified manners. Therefore on what basis do you discipline later generations, since to the new learners you present nothing they can depend upon to emulate? Even when others caution you in return, you simply reply, "I am a mountain [backwoods/Ch'an iconoclast] monk." As you have not yet heard of the unremitting practice of Buddhism, up to now you have only been coarse and rude. Seen in this way, because your initial resolve has turned into negligence and avariciousness, in the long run you dilly-dally in the secular world and thus end up rude and vulgar. [Later,] not realizing that you are stumbling along old and decrepit, in all matters you touch you will end up facing a wall. [Now] when young learners consult you, you have no words of guidance, or if you do discuss and explain, it is not in accord with the scriptures. But if someone speaks to you rudely, you then carry on about the rudeness of the younger generation and become so thoroughly enraged that your words alarm them.[112]

Based on this self-criticism from within Ch'an, many of Hui-jih's criticisms can be deflected away from Ch'an itself and levied at those who only claimed to be Ch'an monks but had no Ch'an attainment. Nevertheless, it is safe to say that Ch'an iconoclasm and slogans of sudden attainment removed many traditional safeguards and often encouraged unconventional and undisciplined behavior. Furthermore, Ch'an's "non-reliance on words and letters" was unorthodox and could be taken to entail the rejection of many external religious practices. Thus, as we have seen, the first pattern of Pure Land response to Ch'an is essentially a rejection and counterattack condemning Ch'an theory and practice as arrogant, distorted, unorthodox, harmful, and basically non-Buddhist.

Although Ch'an found some support for its practice in the Perfection of Wisdom tradition, Pure Land thinkers also based themselves on that tradition but understood it in terms of the first dialectical balance outlined earlier; namely, they cultivated devotionalism for themselves and others even though at a fundamental level they were aware that all was empty and there was nothing to attain. For example, two of the issues that T'an-luan addresses in his *Wang-sheng-lun chu* ("Commentary on the Treatise on Being Reborn in the Pure Land") are (1) how can rebirth in the Pure Land be recommended when the Buddha teaches a solution to the bondage of rebirth? and (2) how can focusing on one Buddha and rebirth in one place be recommended, since that involves attachment to distinctions *(fen-pieh;* Skt. *vikalpa)?* T'an-luan responds that such problems can only be resolved by recognizing that there are two levels of meaning. Rebirth implies a physical level, although really there is no rebirth. To be unborn means that "all dharmas are mutually dependent."[113] Second, discriminating beings assume that there is being and nonbeing, negation and affirmation, good and evil. "Because of discrimination, one wallows in the three stages of existence and receives the pain of the various discriminations, the pain of selecting and rejecting: this is an extended sleep in a long night, with no hope of escape. These beings, on meeting Amitābha Tathāgata's unchanging glory, . . . obtain release from the various bonds of mental activity."[114]

These same issues of rebirth, discrimination, and attachment to form were also faced by Tao-ch'o. According to him, the Pure Land of Amitābha includes both form and non-form. Although he held that the formless Amitābha was superior to Amitābha as form, he endeavored to defend the latter as a legitimate and necessary temporary manifestation for those still dependent on form. Tao-ch'o found it hard to accept that devotion to the Buddha could involve harmful attachment to form. To support his belief, he appealed to the authority of scripture and quoted passages from the *Nirvāṇa Sūtra* and the *Ching-t'u-lun* ("Treatise on the Pure Land") that advocated worship and love of the True Dharma. Tao-ch'o concludes: "Therefore, although this is grasping onto form, such grasping does not correspond to binding attachment. In addition, the form of the Pure Land that we are discussing is identical to form without defilements, form that is true form."[115]

In Indian Buddhism there were different attitudes toward the relative legitimacy of using particular phenomena as expedient aids *(upāya).*

Tao-ch'o justified the practice in terms of the concept of two truths: conventional *(saṃvṛti)* and ultimate *(paramārtha)*. The Mādhyamika tradition as represented in India by Candrakīrti understood "conventional truth" as a purely negative term. Nagao Gadjin points out that Candrakīrti interpreted *saṃvṛti* as "(1) falsehood through ignorance, (2) contingent existence without substance, and (3) conventional terminology, manner of speaking, and name."[116] On the other hand, the Yogācāra tradition interpreted conventional truth in positive terms. Sthiramati radically differed with Candrakīrti's interpretation of *saṃvṛti,* glossing the term as *udbhavana-saṃvṛtti* ("manifestation"): "*Saṃvṛtti* is thus an utterance, attempting to express the inexpressable Absolute. . . . Such a state of being may be appropriately compared with the notion of *mārga,* the way which leads to the Absolute on the one hand, and which emerges from the Absolute on the other."[117] It is this latter sense of *saṃvṛti,* as manifestation, that reverberates throughout those Chinese Buddhist traditions based on the *tathāgatagarbha* doctrine. Ching-ying Hui-yüan's (523–592) positive interpretation of conventional truth is adopted by Tao-ch'o, who invokes the *Wu-shang-i ching* ("Sūtra Concerning the Ultimate Foundation") from the *tathāgatagarbha* tradition.[118] This acceptance of the validity of conventional truth reinforces the idea of the nonduality of the phenomenal and the absolute *(shih* and *li),* form and non-form, knowing and not-knowing, passion and enlightenment, advocated by such influential thinkers as Seng-chao, T'ien-t'ai Chih-i, and later Hua-yen masters. The interrelationship of the absolute and the phenomenal was to be a major emphasis of Fei-hsi.

In defending Pure Land devotionalism, Fei-hsi has a two-stage argument. From the *li-shih* perspective, all things *(shih)* are not different from nirvāṇa, and conventional life (whether it involves religious practices or the passions) cannot be avoided in the pursuit of enlightenment. To avoid it would be like dampening the sound to seek the echo or removing the form to find the shadow. Nevertheless, even though from the point of view of ultimate truth *(li)* all things are not different from nirvāṇa, all things are not equally good. Rather, at the level of conventional truth *(shih)* there are practical consequences, some better than others. Hence, instead of criticizing Ch'an behavior in terms of ignorance of the Buddhist tradition as Hui-jih had done, Fei-hsi expresses his concern in terms of reaping bad karma and evil rebirths on the conventional/phenomenal level. For example, he comments that those who speak with slander or look with malicious intent will suffer defective speech or sight for aeons to come. In contrast, traditional religious and moral practices bring future rewards and Buddhahood. The point is clear: Ch'an practitioners who reject these religious activities are in danger of reaping future punishments. Of course, some Ch'an thinkers did speak in this way—for example, Ta-hui (1089–1163) in his sermons to laity.[119] But in most Ch'an teaching this point was either understated or ignored.

Accordingly, an important concern of Fei-hsi is to teach beneficial attitudes and devotional practices at the conventional level. He ridicules the Ch'an tendency toward "burning mental incense to worship a mental Buddha" and advocates concrete offerings of flowers, incense, banners, images, and scriptures as recommended to disciples by the *Lotus Sūtra*. Yet Fei-hsi also criticizes mindless religiosity. *Nien-fo* may be the king of all samādhis, but to speak the emperor's name carelessly when not in his entourage may lead to death; to offer flowers to the Buddha without understanding the *Lotus Sūtra* can only bring minimal rewards, not Buddhahood. Fei-hsi accordingly emphasizes not only correct bodily actions, but also proper understanding. Rote recitation of the Buddha's name is not adequate. Thus cultivation should be practiced both inwardly and outwardly. *Li* and *shih* should be perfectly interfused.

Fei-hsi strongly advocates Pure Land devotionalism while also affirming Ch'an masters and their teaching. Unlike Hui-jih, who launched a counterattack against Ch'an, Fei-hsi, because of his background in the Lotus tradition, was committed to seeing all people as future Buddhas. In this sense he implicitly criticized every Pure Land and Ch'an thinker who rejected the other practices as wrong or inferior. All Buddhists share the same attributes as the Buddha, they just have not yet achieved complete fruition. This approach spells an end to sectarian rivalry.

Fei-hsi recognizes the difference between Pure Land and Ch'an practices but reconciles them by identifying them as two poles in a dialectic of mutual interdependence. His application of the *li-shih* polarity was innovative and argued for a balance between Ch'an, which emphasized Principle *(li)*, and Pure Land, which taught specific practices *(shih)*. However, his contribution did not end with his use of the *li-shih* polarity; he also made use of the dialectic of śamatha (*chih* or *ting*) and vipaśyanā (*kuan* or *hui*). On the one hand, Pure Land calms, settles, and removes distractions (śamatha) through devotional practices to Amitābha *(nien-fo)*. On the other hand, the Ch'an tenet of no-thought *(wu-nien)* brings wisdom (vipaśyanā) to the practice. Thus, Fei-hsi takes two key terms from the heart of Ch'an and Pure Land and, rather than opposing them, unites them as the two functions that Buddhism has always claimed were interrelated. This adoption of the dialectic combinations of *li* and *shih* in doctrine and of śamatha (i.e., *nien-fo*) and vipaśyanā (i.e., *wu-nien*) in practice became the classic Chinese resolution for the tension between the two religious orientations of Ch'an and Pure Land. Appropriately, Fei-hsi concludes his treatise with a couplet reaffirming this dialectic of tranquility and movement, *li* and *shih*.

These last two points are developed further in the *Wu fang-pien nien-fo men*. Fei-hsi argues that people are not to be rejected because of their present limitations but are to be affirmed because of the attributes they share in their common destiny, which culminates in Buddhahood. Similarly, the *Wu fang-pien nien-fo men* sees *nien-fo* and dhyāna *(ch'an)* not as two opposing and static religious options, but as multidimensional practices that change at different levels of spiritual development and lead to Buddhahood. Fei-hsi sees *nien-fo* and *ch'an* as fulfilling different roles that are mutually supportive and in some ways can be identified. In the *Wu fang-pien nien-fo men* the juxtaposition of the two schemes of *nien-fo* and dhyāna *(ch'an)* implies some relationship, although its exact nature is never spelled out. Only with Tsung-mi and Yen-shou do Pure Land and Ch'an become integrated into a unified vision of spiritual growth.

The *Wu fang-pien nien-fo men* and the related passages from Ch'eng-kuan and Tsung-mi have a very different tone from the writings of Hui-jih and Fei-hsi. Instead of offering commentary and criticism in response to competing religious movements, as Hui-jih and Fei-hsi did, these later writings are more theoretical and detached. They often treat *nien-fo* and *ch'an* as dimensions of our inner world of meditation rather than as the slogans of externally contending religious groups. Thus their aim is to outline stages of religious growth within an overall scheme rather than to defend Pure Land devotionalism against Ch'an criticisms. Moreover, the *Wu-fang-pien nien-fo men* and related writings provide a doctrinal basis that is compatible with the Ch'an emphasis on mind as the arena where one's religious destiny is decided. This also echoes Fei-hsi's emphasis that the meaning of any act is determined by the context— the primary context being one's understanding. Thus, in both the devotionalism of the Pure Land/Lotus tradition and the formless practices of Ch'an, mind can be seen as a central element. This idea will be of growing importance in later centuries as a basis for dual cultivation of Pure Land and Ch'an.

The specific contribution of the *Wu fang-pien nien-fo men* and related writings is the means for transcending the Pure Land/Ch'an rivalry by asserting that both can and should be multidimensioned and that they both need one another and are interrelated. The sources of these views were the Lotus, T'ien-t'ai, Perfection of Wisdom, *tathāgata-garba*, Hua-yen, and meditative traditions found in Chinese Buddhism, which provided perspectives broader than either Pure Land or Ch'an. At least five basic principles were invoked from these traditions.

1. All beings are at various stages of religious growth, which are not mutually exclusive or absolute, but are interrelated and share a common destiny.

2. Thus, mutual respect should be engendered between Buddhists as fellow travellers on the same path and equal participants in the final goal.

3. All practices are temporary and none is absolute; yet some practice is always necessary, since there is no *li* without *shih,* no emptiness without form, and since all beings are living in a conditioned body in a world of dependent origination.

4. From the point of view of the ultimate *(li)* all things are not different from nirvāṇa, true nature, mind, and Buddhahood. Thus, one's view of particular practices and people should always see both the space-time particulars and their ultimate true nature as expressions of the absolute.

5. Ultimate truth always involves the interplay and balance of emptiness and expediency, *li* and *shih,* as expressed in the three truths of T'ien-t'ai, the five expediencies of the *Wu fang-pien nien-fo men,* and the three stages of Tsung-mi.

While these principles provided a basis for defending Pure Land devotionalism against Ch'an attacks, they also transcended any sectarian rivalry by showing religion as a process. In the thought of T'an-luan, Tao-ch'o, Chi-tsang, Chih-i, and Shan-tao, sixth-and seventh-century Pure Land devotionalism had been multidimensioned and incorporated views of emptiness, two truths, an absolute dharmakāya, temporary expediencies, and stages of religious growth.[120] Still, not all Pure Land devotees were as knowledgeable as those sixth- and seventh-century thinkers, and the Ch'an criticisms of Pure Land devotees probably had more than a grain of truth to them. At the same time, criticisms were also leveled against Ch'an practices by Ch'an masters themselves, revealing that ignorant Ch'an practitioners existed who did not represent the highest levels of their movement. Apparently, then, both Pure Land and Ch'an movements involved some emotionally charged, simplistic, and uninformed groups that gained momentum not only through the salvific nature of their own religious experiences, but also through the development of a false sense of their own uniqueness and superiority. Although these rival groups expressed a less than adequate or comprehensive awareness of their own tradition, their rivalry arose at a time when Buddhism was vigorous and popular, and to some degree the Ch'an-Pure Land rivalry is an expression of this vitality.

The wide range of responses by advocates of Pure Land devotionalism to Ch'an attacks during the eighth century reminds us how strong the sectarian rivalry had been at one time in China between Ch'an and Pure Land. It also shows that affirmation of a shared Perfection of Wisdom tradition was no guarantee of unanimity. Insofar as the Perfection of Wisdom dialectical balance reemerged, it did so as a new synthesis arising from Chinese experimentation with a variety of Buddhist forms. The Chinese Buddhist dialectical and developmental models of religious growth that emerged to resolve the conflict eventually became the classic methods for interpreting and propagating Pure Land practices in China. Thus, the creativity of the period expressed itself not only in the formation of new groups and new rivalries, but also by the development of new and enduring methods of religious integration.

Notes

1. This conclusion was reached by Gregory Schopen, "Sukhāvatī as a Generalized Religious Goal in Sanskrit Mahāyāna Sūtra Literature," *Indo-Iranian Journal,* vol. 19 (1977), pp. 177–210.
2. See *T*25.108a–114c.
3. *T*14.550a1–2; cf. 545c26–27.
4. *T*8.731a–b.
5. *T*46.14c22–29.
6. *T*85.1287c8–12.
7. See Ui Hakuju, *Zenshūshi kenkyū,* vol. 1 (Tokyo: Iwanami shoten, 1935; repr., 1966), pp. 171–192.
8. For a recent study of the *Leng-ch'ieh shih-tz'u chi,* see Tanaka Ryōshō, *Tonkō zenshū bunken no kenkyū* (Tokyo: Daitō shuppansha, 1983), pp. 23–60.
9. See my article "The Formation of the Pure Land Movement in China: Tao-ch'o and Shan-tao," in James Foard, ed., *The Pure Land Tradition: History and Development* (Berkeley: Asian Humanities Press, forthcoming).
10. Philip Yampolsky, *The Platform Sutra of the Sixth Patriarch* (New York: Columbia University Press, 1967), p. 119, where Chih-shen is romanized as Chih-hsien.
11. *Ibid.,* sec. 16, p. 137; sec. 19, p. 163.
12. *Ibid.,* secs. 24–26, pp. 146–147.
13. *Ibid.,* sec. 33, p. 154.
14. *Ibid.,* sec. 23, p. 146.
15. *Ibid.,* sec. 19, pp. 140–141.
16. *Ibid.,* secs. 45–46, pp. 170–173.
17. *T*47.14c22–29.
18. *T*47.439a.
19. The first historian of early Pure Land is Chia-ts'ai, who wrote a three fascicle work in the mid seventh century entitled *Ching-t'u-lun* (*T*#1963) to clarify the doctrines and practices of Pure Land devotionalism and to set down the biographies of twenty of the early devotees. Thus for Chia-ts'ai Pure Land already constituted a clearly evolving movement *(i-tsung)* mostly centered in Shansi province (see *T*47.83b).
20. *T*#2826.
21. For an account of this discovery, see Ono Gemmyō, "On the Pure Land Doctrine of Tz'u-min," *Eastern Buddhist,* vols. 2–3 (1930), pp. 200–210.
22. *T*85.1236b13–17.
23. *Ibid.,* 1236b21–c1.
24. *Ibid.,* 1237b20–29.

25. *Ibid.*, 1237c17–25.
26. *Ibid.*, 1238a11–12.
27. *Ibid.*, 1238b16–23.
28. *Ibid.*, 1238b23–25.
29. *Ibid.*, 1238b25–28.
30. *Ibid.*, 1238c.
31. *Ibid.*, 1239b21–28.
32. *Ibid.*, 1239c4–5.
33. *Ibid.*, 1240b18–19.
34. *Ibid.*, 1240b23–1241a18.
35. *Ibid.*, 1241a22.
36. *Ibid.*, 1241a18–29.
37. *T*48.378b22–26.
38. *T*85.1241a19–b19.
39. *Ibid.*, 1241c1–4; cf. 1242a13–20.
40. *Ibid.*, 1241c4; 1242a13, 24, 25; 1242b2.
41. *Ibid.*, 1242b4–27.
42. See the study by Tsukamoto Zenryū, "Nangaku Shōon den to sono Jōdokyō," *Tōhō Gakuhō,* no. 2 (1931), pp. 186–249.
43. See the study by Tsukamoto Zenryū, *Tō chūki no Jōdokyō: Toku ni Hosshō Zenshi no kenkyū* (Kyoto: Tōhō bunka gakuin Kyoto kenkyūsho, 1933).
44. See *T*48.963c and 973c; 959a18–19 for Hui-neng.
45. Ono reports that Chih-p'an's *Fo-tsu t'ung-chi* gives an account of this censorship by the government ("Tz'u-min," p. 202).
46. Although Fei-hsi's age and date of death are unknown, there are several references to his activities between 740 and 780 (see Mochizuki Shinkō, *Chūgoku Jōdokyōrishi* [Kyoto: Hōzōkan, 1946; repr., 1964], pp. 282–283), and the *Nien-fo san-mei pao-wang lun* must have been written during that time. However, Morimoto Shinjun dates the text precisely at 742, but does not give his evidence (see Ono Gemmyō, ed., *Bussho kaisetsu daijiten* [Tokyo: Daitō shuppansha, 1932], vol. 8, p. 421).
47. Fei-hsi comments in his preface that he searched for thirty years and that, although he does not have all the answers, he offers these twenty methods outlined in his text (*T*47.134a5–14).
48. *T*47.134a–137c.
49. *T*85.1242b.
50. *T*47.138a–141a.
51. *Ibid.*, 139c–140a.
52. *Ibid.*, 140b.
53. *Ibid.*, 141b–144c.
54. *Ibid.*, 141b14.
55. *Ibid.*, 141c8–23.
56. *Ibid.*, 142a26–27.
57. *Ibid.*, 142a16–20.
58. *Ibid.*, 142a27–b1.
59. *Ibid.*, 142b22.
60. *Ibid.*, 141c3.
61. *T*47.128b17–18.
62. *T*47.142c2.
63. *Ibid.*, 142c4–5, 23–24.
64. *Ibid.*, 142c27–28.
65. *Ibid.*, 142c29–143a.

66. *Ibid.,* 142c11–16.
67. *Ibid.,* 142c26–143a1.
68. *Ibid.,* 143a29.
69. *Ibid.,* 143a28–b5.
70. *Ibid.,* 143a7–25.
71. *Ibid.,* 143b14–18.
72. *Ibid.,* 143b23–c1.
73. *Ibid.,* 143c5–12.
74. *Ibid.,* 143c15.
75. Leon Hurvitz, trans., *Scripture of the Lotus Blossom of the Fine Dharma* (New York: Columbia University Press, 1976), pp. 39–40; cf. *T*9.9a10–11 and 16.
76. *T*47.143c15–144a14.
77. *Ibid.,* 144a15–b29.
78. *Ibid.,* 144a22.
79. *Ibid.,* 144a15–16.
80. *Ibid.,* 144a26–29.
81. *Ibid.,* 144b1–4.
82. *Ibid.,* 144b5–13.
83. It is interesting that the classic work on dual cultivation by Yen-shou used the name of this last section as its title: *Wan-shan t'ung kuei* (see *T*#2017).
84. *T*47.144b17–18.
85. *T*47.81c–83a.
86. For Satō Tetsuei's account and analysis of his discovery of this ninth-century version of the text, see his article *"Tendai daishi go hōben men ni tsuite,"* *IBK,* vol. 2, no. 2 (1954), pp. 396–403. A photocopy of the shorter text is available in Satō Tetsuei, *Tendai daishi no kenkyū* (Kyoto: Hyakkaen, 1961), p. 645.
87. *T*47.81c25–82a9 and 83a10–25.
88. Satō, *Tendai daishi no kenkyū,* pp. 652–654.
89. See the section on "The Method of 'Five Upāya' in Northern Ch'an" by Robert Zeuschner in his "Awakening in Northern Ch'an," in David Chappell ed., *Buddhist and Taoist Practice in Medieval Chinese Society* (Honolulu: University of Hawaii Press, forthcoming).
90. See Robert Zeuschner, "The Concept of *Li-nien* ('Being Free from Thinking') in the Northern Line of Ch'an Buddhism," in Lewis Lancaster and Whalen Lai, eds., *Early Ch'an in China and Tibet* (Berkeley: Asian Humanities Press, 1983), pp. 131–148.
91. *T*47.83a24.
92. *Dengyō daishi shōrai taishū roku, T*55.1056a15.
93. *T*11.655b–c and 513b–514a.
94. *T*47.82a9–b29.
95. *Jikaku daishi zai tō sō shin roku, T*55.1077a29.
96. *T*36.667b.
97. For a discussion of the first use of the phrase "nature origination" *(hsing-ch'i)* as a technical term, see Robert M. Gimello, "Chih-yen (602–668) and the Foundations of Hua-yen Buddhism" (Ph.D. dissertation, Columbia University, 1976), pp. 442–445. For further references see note 56 in the following chapter by Robert Buswell.
98. *T*47.82b16–17.
99. See, for example, *T*47.22–30.
100. For discussion of the *p'an-chiao* schemes, see Leon Hurvitz, *Chih-i (538–*

597), Mélanges chinois et bouddhiques, vol. 12 (1960–1962), pp. 214–244. This is not a purely Chinese invention; it can be seen in such Indian texts as the *Wu-liang-i-ching* (*T*9.386a28–b28), translated in 481 and partially quoted by Chih-i in his *Fa-hua hsüan-i* (*T*33.807b28–c8); the *Nirvāṇa Sūtra* (*T*12.691a3–5), which Chih-i also quotes (*T*33.807b1–3); and the *Saṃdhinir-mocana Sūtra* (*Shen-mi chieh-t'o ching,* *T*16.673c17–674a1), translated by Bodhiruci in 514. These three texts distinguish (1) different teachings of the Buddha (2) intended for different levels of understanding and (3) taught at different times, (4) but taught in an identical and consistent way (5) in a sequential and (6) progressive order. Similarly, the *Avataṁsaka Sūtra* (*T*9.616b14–19) refers to the progressive reception of the Buddha's wisdom in terms of the capacities of the hearers. Of course, the idea is implicit throughout the *Lotus Sūtra.*

101. *T*35.924b; cf. discussion by Mochizuki Shinkō, *Chūgoku Jōdokyōrishi,* pp. 306–309.
102. *ZZ*1/7/5.457a–c.
103. *T*11.513b–514a.
104. *Ch'an-yüan chu-ch'üan-chi tu-hsü,* *T*48.401c; cf. the translation by Jeffrey Broughton, "Kuei-feng Tsung-mi: The Convergence of Ch'an and the Teachings" (Ph.D. dissertation, Columbia University, 1975), pp. 133–138; cf. also Jan Yün-hua, "The Mind as the Buddha-nature: The Concept of the Absolute in Ch'an Buddhism," *Philosophy East and West,* vol. 31 (1981), pp. 471–472.
105. See *Ch'an-yüan chu-ch'üan-chi tu-hsü,* *T*48.402b15ff.
106. See *T*48.614a19ff.
107. See *T*48.440b14–15 and 959a13–18.
108. *T*15.632a15–17.
109. *Ibid.,* 632b5–10.
110. *Ibid.,* 631c16–17, 21–22.
111. *Ibid.,* 636b8–9.
112. *ZZ*2/16/2.144), translated by Melvin Takemoto, "The *Kuei-shan ching-ts'e:* Morality and the Hung-chou School of Ch'an" (M.A. thesis, University of Hawaii, 1983), pp. 81–82.
113. *T*40.827b18ff; 831b13ff; and 838c10ff.
114. *Ibid.,* 839c8–15, translated by Roger Corless, "T'an-luan's Commentary on the Pure Land Discourse: An Annotated Translation and Soteriological Analysis of the *Wang-sheng-lun chu*" (Ph.D. dissertation, University of Wisconsin, 1973), p. 268.
115. *An-lo-chi, T*18c15–17.
116. Nagao Gadjin, "An Interpretation of the Term 'Saṃvṛti' (Convention) in Buddhism," *Silver Jubilee Volume of the Zinbun-Kagaku-Kenkyu-syo* (Kyoto: Zinbun-kagaku-kenkyu-syo, 1954), p. 553.
117. *Ibid.,* p. 555.
118. *T*47.8b15ff.
119. See Miriam Levering, "Ta-hui and Lay Buddhists: Ch'an Sermons on Death," in David Chappell, ed., *Buddhist and Taoist Practice in Medieval Chinese Society.*
120. For the use of these principles in Pure Land thought, see David Chappell, "Chinese Buddhist Interpretations of the Pure Lands," in Michael Saso and David Chappell, eds., *Buddhist and Taoist Studies,* vol. 1 (Honolulu: University of Hawaii Press, 1977), pp. 23–53.

Chinul's Systematization of Chinese Meditative Techniques in Korean Sŏn Buddhism

Robert E. Buswell, Jr.

In any attempt to assess the Chinese contributions to Buddhist meditative culture, we must not forget that what was "Chinese" about Chinese Buddhism was not restricted to the Han national, cultural, or racial group. To the contrary, there was in fact a remarkable homogeneity between the Buddhist tradition of China and those that developed in neighboring countries, in particular Korea, and to a somewhat lesser extent, Japan and even Vietnam. Because of these congruities, it is more valuable to refer to a comprehensive "East Asian" Buddhism than to separate national traditions. This is not to deny that distinct regional traits did develop in the Buddhism of East Asia; nevertheless, we should not allow this admission to obscure the overall continuity of concern to be found in all of these traditions. Hence, by treating Chinese Buddhism as the pan-East Asian tradition it truly was, we will gain a much more comprehensive and accurate view of it than we would by limiting our investigation arbitrarily to national boundaries.[1]

In the case of the Korean branch of the East Asian Buddhist tradition, which is the focus of this chapter, examples of this homogeneity abound. We know, for instance, that Korean exegetes working in their native country made significant contributions to the development of such seminal "Chinese" schools as Hua-yen and Ch'an. By the same token, Korea had numerous organic links with the Buddhism of the Chinese mainland, which makes it virtually impossible to treat Korean Buddhism without making constant reference to Chinese developments. Korea was also a crucible in which many of the Chinese insights into Buddhist theology were fused into new forms, unknown as such in China, but no less

"Chinese" than other mainland developments. Hence, Korean Buddhism serves as a simulacrum of the greater Chinese tradition, within which the problematics of the Chinese church may be profitably evaluated and analyzed.

Perhaps the monk who best represents this tendency among the Koreans to assimilate representative themes of the Chinese tradition is Chinul (1158–1210), the charismatic reformer of the Buddhist church during the Koryŏ Dynasty (918–1392) and the systematizer of the native Korean Sŏn (Ch. Ch'an) tradition. Since the Unified Silla (668–935) period, Korea had experienced a series of often hostile interactions among the different traditions of Buddhism introduced from China— especially between the Hwaŏm (Ch. Hua-yen) School and the Nine Mountains Sŏn School, which came to represent, respectively, the scholastic *(kyo)* and meditative *(sŏn)* concerns of Buddhism. Some years before Chinul, Ŭich'ŏn (1055–1101) attempted to unite both branches of the tradition into a rejuvenated Ch'ŏnt'ae (Ch. T'ien-t'ai) School, but his efforts simply added one more school to what was already a crowded sectarian scene.[2] Chinul was able to see the value and utility in each of the two major aspects of Buddhist spiritual endeavor—doctrinal study and meditation practice—and to develop an approach to religious cultivation that drew upon both.

Chinul's fusion of the Hua-yen philosophy of Li T'ung-hsüan (635–730) with the Ch'an teachings of Kuei-feng Tsung-mi (780–841) placed Korean Buddhism on a firm ontological and soteriological foundation that restored the vitality of the decadent mid-Koryŏ tradition and sustained the church through the difficult centuries of Confucian persecution during the Yi Dynasty (1392–1910). The system of doctrinal training combined with Sŏn practice championed by Chinul—and the approach of sudden awakening/gradual cultivation that epitomized this system— outlined for Koreans an approach to spiritual training that would remain the hallmark of its tradition down to the present. Indeed, it is with Chinul that we can first speak of a truly native Korean Sŏn tradition that developed in ways influenced by, but nevertheless independent of, the Ch'an schools of China. Finally, the emphasis in Chinul's later thought on *hwadu* (Ch. *hua-t'ou*) meditation was to augur the subsequent eclipse of Tsung-mi's influence over the formal practices of the Korean Sŏn School by the "shortcut" meditative approach of Ta-hui Tsung-kao (1089–1163). This shift adumbrates the ultimate fusion of Tsung-mi's soteriology and Ta-hui's praxis that characterizes the later Sŏn tradition. Hence, an examination of the synthesis Chinul forged in Korea between different trends within Chinese Buddhism should provide insights into the doctrinal perspectives of the Chinese church itself, as well as into ways in which those outlooks could be adapted in a different culture with novel, and sometimes decisive, results.

I. Chinul's Rapprochement Between Sŏn and Hwaŏm: Biographical Considerations

As a Sŏn adept, Chinul is rightly renowned for his accommodating attitude toward the scholastic schools; indeed, his attempts to demonstrate the correspondences between Sŏn and *kyo* constitute one of his most important contributions to Korean Buddhist thought and certainly helped to restore the credibility of both of the tradition's two major branches. At the same time, however, his eclecticism should not obscure the fact that Chinul considered himself to be ultimately an adherent of Sŏn, and, especially in his later works, his sympathies are clearly with that school rather than with *kyo*. He was ordained into the Nine Mountains Sŏn School of Sagul-san, which was reputed to have derived from the Nan-yüeh lineage of Southern Ch'an, and passed his Sangha entrance examinations in the Sŏn sector.[3] Hence, it could be expected that Chinul would take a tack to the problem of ecclesiastical reconciliation opposite from that of Ŭich'ŏn, who had attempted to merge Sŏn into *kyo*.

Despite his penchant for Sŏn, however, Chinul's funerary stele tells us that he did not train for an extended period under any Sŏn master, and there is no evidence that he ever received formal transmission from an orthodox successor in the Nine Mountains lineages.[4] As one of the few important Korean teachers who also never made the requisite pilgrimage to China, Chinul was compelled to look for his information from the sources readily available to him: Indian sūtras, East Asian commentaries, and the records of earlier Ch'an and Sŏn masters. For this reason, Chinul was fervently eclectic from early on in his vocation, never hesitating to draw upon the scholastic teachings when he found their instruction to be of benefit. Throughout his life, all of his spiritual progress and each of his three enlightenment experiences were catalyzed by insights gleaned from passages in the canon, not through the direct instruction of Sŏn masters.[5] Hence, despite the classic Ch'an adage that the school "does not establish words and letters,"[6] it is hardly conceivable that Chinul, despite his strong Sŏn allegiance, would have denied the efficacy of the written teachings in religious cultivation.

Based on his readings and practice, Chinul developed a vision of the basic unity of Sŏn and the sūtras. In the preface to his *Excerpts from the Exposition of the New* [*Translation of the*] *Avataṁsaka Sūtra (Hwaŏmnon chŏryo),* he notes his confusion over Hwaŏm's rejection of the efficacy of Sŏn and its claim that the only valid meditation technique was contemplation of the Dharmadhātu.[7] Chinul, who was then following orthodox Sŏn techniques, decided to return to his ultimate refuge in all cases of doubt—the texts of the Tripiṭaka—to see whether the sūtras would substantiate the claims of the Sŏn School that Buddhahood could be achieved by simply contemplating the mind. After three years of reading, he discovered passages first in the *Ju-lai ch'u-hsien p'in* ("Appearance of the Tathāgatas" chapter) of the *Avataṁsaka Sūtra*[8] and later in the *Exposition of the New [Translation of the] Avataṁsaka Sūtra (Hsin Hua-yen ching lun)* by Li T'ung-hsüan[9] that confirmed for him the veracity of the Sŏn teachings and outlined an approach to Buddhist practice that he felt would be appropriate for the majority of his fellow-cultivators. Setting the texts aside, Chinul concluded:

> What the World Honored Ones said with their mouths are the teachings *(kyo)*. What the patriarchs transmitted with their minds is Sŏn. The mouths of the Buddhas and the minds of the patriarchs certainly cannot be contradictory. How can [students of both Sŏn and *kyo*] not plumb the fundamental source but, instead, complacent in their own training, wrongly foment disputes and waste their time?[10]

Based on this inspiration, Chinul developed an approach to Buddhism in which the ontological speculations of the scholastic doctrine—especially as presented in Li T'ung-hsüan's interpretation of Hua-yen philosophy—could be used to support Sŏn soteriological techniques, initially as outlined by Tsung-mi for the Ho-tse School of Ch'an and, later in his life, as taught by Ta-hui Tsung-kao for the Lin-chi lineage. Both of these aspects came to function symbiotically in Chinul's system. As Chinul declares:

> I say to men who are cultivating the mind that first, through the path of the patriarchs, they should know the original sublimity of their own minds and should not be bound by words and letters. Next, through the text of [Li T'ung-hsüan's] *Exposition,* they should ascertain that the essence *(ch'e)* and functions *(yong)* of the mind are [identical to] the nature *(sŏng)* and characteristics *(sang)* of the Dharmadhātu. Then, the quality of the unimpeded interpenetration between all phenomena and the merit of the wisdom and compassion that has the same essence [as that of all the Buddhas] will not be beyond their capacity.[11]

This combination of two seemingly disparate approaches to Buddhist doctrine and practice constitutes one of the most distinctively Korean contributions to East Asian Buddhist thought.[12]

II. Chinul's Methods of Meditation: General Outline

Three primary types of meditation practice are taught in Chinul's works, each of which reflects the direct influence of one of Chinul's enlightenment experiences: (1) the simultaneous cultivation of samādhi and prajñā, deriving ultimately from Chinul's reading of the *Platform Sūtra of the Sixth Patriarch;* (2) faith and understanding (*sinhae;* Skt. *śraddhādhimukti)*[13] according to the Complete and Sudden teachings of the Hwaŏm School, from Li T'ung-hsüan's *Exposition;* and (3) the shortcut approach of *hwadu* (Ch. *hua-t'ou*) investigation, from the *Records of Ta-hui (Ta-hui yü-lu).*[14] These techniques were intended respectively for adepts of inferior, average, and superior spiritual capacities and were supplemented by two additional types of meditation, for people of highest and lowest capacity respectively: (4) the approach of no-mind or no-thought *(mu'nyŏm;* Ch. *wu-nien)* and (5) recollection of the Buddha's name *(yŏmbul;* Ch. *nien-fo).*[15] Each of these techniques was a characteristic practice of independent schools in China, and Chinul's presentation of the methods themselves is heavily dependent on earlier interpretations; some of it, in fact, harkens back to Hīnayāna sources. However, Chinul did not view any one of these methods as an orthodox technique. Instead, he saw them all as expedient instructions adapted to the different needs and capacities of unique individuals according to their level of spiritual development; and, despite popular judgements about the relative ease or difficulty of the various practices, he insisted that any one of them would lead to the same result for the adept who cultivated the one suitable to him with sincerity and vigor. Further demonstrating his flexibility concerning meditation methods, Chinul also allowed the student to follow a progressive approach from simpler techniques to the more advanced, should the student find such an approach beneficial. Hence, Chinul's attitude toward meditation was quite pragmatic, and one of his major accomplishments was to demonstrate how all these divergent practices could function together to guide Buddhist students toward the same goal of liberation *(mokṣa).*

III. Sudden Awakening/Gradual Cultivation: The Process of Spiritual Development

Chinul was greatly influenced in many areas by Tsung-mi, traditionally considered to be the Fifth Patriarch in both the Ho-tse lineage of Middle Ch'an and the Hua-yen scholastic tradition.[16] Chinul's outline of spiritual development was based on Tsung-mi's own proposal concerning the processes governing praxis and gnosis—the approach of sudden awakening/gradual cultivation *(tono chŏmsu;* Ch. *tun-wu chien-hsiu)*—which was subsequently adopted by Yung-ming Yen-shou (904–975), another Chinese Ch'an master frequently cited by Chinul.[17] According to the analyses of Tsung-mi and Chinul, the teachings of the Ho-tse School offered a uniquely balanced approach toward Dharma *(pŏp;* Ch. *fa)* and person *(in;* Ch. *jen).* Dharma refers to the nature of reality: the ontological factors of immutability *(pulbyŏn;* Ch. *pu-pien)* and adaptability *(suyŏn;* Ch. *sui-yüan).* Person refers to the soteriological process followed in the spiritual development of the individual: the two ventures of sudden awakening and gradual cultivation.[18] In this approach, the sudden awakening to the mind-essence—the absolute, immutable aspect of Dharma—lays a firm foundation for the refinement of the phenomenal qualities innate in that essence. This refinement takes place through the gradual cultivation of all the myriads of practices incumbent upon the bodhisattva. In such an approach, both the absolute and phenomenal aspects of reality and the ultimate and conventional approaches to practice are kept in harmony, and relatively consistent progress in spiritual development can be expected.

> Through these two aspects of Dharma, they will be able to understand the doctrine to which all the sūtras and śāstras of the entire Tripiṭaka return: the nature and characteristics of their own mind. Through the two approaches concerning person they will be able to see the tracks of all the sages and saints—which are the beginning and end of their own practice. This clear assessment of the process of practice will help them to free themselves from delusion, move from the provisional toward the real, and realize bodhi quickly.[19]

The quality of other types of Buddhist practice was weighed according to how well they emulated this ideal approach. As Chinul notes, this focus on the Ho-tse approach was intended

> primarily so that people who are practicing meditation will be able to awaken first to the fact that, whether deluded or awakened, their own minds are numinous, aware, and never obscured and that their nature is unchanging. If, at the beginning, [you students] do not get to the source of all these different approaches [i.e., the numinous awareness], you will be lured by the traces of the words used in the teachings of those schools and wrongly give rise to thoughts of either acceptance or rejection. Then how would it be possible for you to develop a syncretic understanding *(yunghoe)* [that recognizes the value in all teachings] and take refuge in your own minds?[20]

Chinul covers the approach of sudden awakening/gradual cultivation in several of his works, including an extremely detailed treatment of all the possible combinations of sudden and gradual practice and enlightenment in his *Excerpts from the Dharma Collection and Special Practice Record with Personal Notes (Pŏpchip pyŏrhaeng nok chŏryo pyŏngip sagi).*[21] Perhaps Chinul's most accessible and inspiring treatment of the theory, however, appears in one of his best-known works, *Secrets on Cultivating the Mind (Susim kyŏl).*[22] There he explains that sudden awakening is the vision that one's own original nature is no different from that of all the Buddhas. The person realizes the noumenal wisdom *(i chi)* that exposes the essential voidness of all dharmas and the individual's own lack of ego.[23] But this awakening is not simply intellectual awareness engendered through study or learning; it is, instead, an experience that makes use of doctrinal explanations concerning the void, calm, and numinous awareness *(kongjŏk yŏngji)* to develop the student's own practice of introspection *(panjo).*[24] This is the understanding-awakening *(haeo;* Ch. *chieh-wu)* in which one gains the initial comprehension of one's own true nature; because this awakening is not achieved through gradual progress in practice, it is called sudden.[25]

Even after a person has awakened to the fact of his incipient Buddhahood, however, his forces of habit *(sŭpki;* Skt. *vāsanā),* which have been acquired over a "beginningless" *(musi)* period of time, are not so easily removed. Hence, even after this initial experience, the student must continue on to develop all of the various meritorious qualities of mind required of the bodhisattva. This is called gradual cultivation. Nevertheless, because this cultivation is based on an initial sudden awakening, it is completely different from the inferior gradual practices that East Asian adepts of Ch'an have traditionally attributed to the Northern School of Ch'an or the Hīnayāna teachings.[26] Since the student has already awakened to the fact that deluded thoughts are originally void and the mind-nature is originally pure, he continues to eliminate negative states of mind while recognizing that there is actually nothing real that needs to be eliminated; by the same token, he continues to develop wholesome states of mind while realizing that there is nothing that truly needs development. Hence, the gradual cultivation that follows sudden awakening is true cultivation and true purification.[27]

Chinul uses several similes, many of which are adopted from Tsung-mi, to describe the process of initial enlightenment followed by subsequent cultivation. For example, he says that it is like the maturation of an infant who, at the moment of birth (sudden awakening), is endowed with all of the potential of an adult but will not be able to achieve that potential until after many years of growth (gradual cultivation).[28] It is also like the sun rising in the morning (sudden awakening), which only gradually evaporates the morning dew or frost (gradual cultivation).[29] As these similes make clear, cultivation does not even become possible until the initial sudden awakening catalyzes those processes. Indeed, Chinul explicitly states that it would be virtually impossible for a bodhisattva to continue on through the three incalculable kalpas of cultivation necessary to consummate the path toward Buddhahood without an initial sudden awakening:

> It is clear that if at first a person does not awaken to the mind-nature, does not attain the [noumenal] wisdom that knows the voidness of dharmas, and

does not leave behind any sign of self or person, then how would it be possible, on this sea of immeasurable, incalculable kalpas, to maintain in this way the practice of the difficult to practice and the endurance of the difficult to endure? Deluded and ignorant people of today are not aware of this idea and, from the beginning, are depressed that they have to face the difficulties of the manifold supplementary practices *(manhaeng)* of the bodhisattva.[30]

Such difficult practices have been consummated in the past only because of the efficacy of this approach of sudden awakening/gradual cultivation; for this reason, it is the approach that has been followed by all the sages and saints of past and present.

The principal challenge to sudden awakening/gradual cultivation came from an approach to practice advocated by teachers in the Hung-chou lineage of Middle Ch'an, which became the standard of the Lin-chi branch of the mature Ch'an School: sudden awakening/sudden cultivation *(tono tonsu;* Ch. *tun-wu tun-hsiu).* Chinul admitted the validity of such an approach to Ch'an meditation, in which a sudden realization of the mind-nature was assumed to bring about the instant consummation of all the myriad wholesome qualities inherent in that mind-nature, thereby obviating the need for any subsequent cultivation.[31] Chinul, however, also recognized the limitations of the Sŏn adepts of his time and apparently considered this approach to be inappropriate for the great majority of Sŏn practitioners. There were two reasons for this. First, cultivators could become attached to an insouciant attitude. Because all things are innately perfect and completely indistinguishable from the noumenal Buddha-nature, such adepts might wrongly assume that no wholesome practices need be cultivated and no defilements need be eradicated. In addition, since all practices will be perfected and all defilements overcome immediately upon enlightenment, only awakening need be stressed. Second, students might end up grasping at the mere verbal description of the innate perfection of the Buddha-nature, thereby hindering their own capacity to awaken personally to that nature. Hence, while the Hung-chou/Lin-chi doctrine of sudden awakening/sudden cultivation might contain useful expedients, "[it] is the practice engaged in by those whose faculties are mature; it does not apply to the majority of ordinary men."[32]

Indeed, Chinul goes so far as to say that, if one examines the practice of even those superior cultivators who seem to have a sudden awakening requiring no further cultivation, one will find that they too in fact have had an initial awakening in a previous life that sustained their present sudden cultivation:

> Although sudden awakening/sudden cultivation has been advocated, this is the entrance for people of the highest faculties. If you were to probe their

pasts, you would see that their cultivation has been based for many lives on the insights gained in a previous awakening. Now, in this life, after gradual permeation, these people hear the Dharma and awaken: in one instant their practice is brought to a sudden conclusion. But if we try to explain this according to the facts, then sudden awakening/sudden cultivation is also the result of an initial awakening and its subsequent cultivation. Consequently, this twofold approach of sudden awakening and gradual cultivation is the track followed by thousands of saints. Hence, of all the saints of old, there were none who did not first have an awakening, subsequently cultivate it, and finally, because of their cultivation, gain realization.[33]

Thus, in Chinul's comprehensive outline of Buddhist soteriology, there is always first an initial understanding-awakening *(haeo;* Ch. *chiehwu),* followed by gradual cultivation of that awakening, which ultimately concludes with a final realization-awakening *(chŭngo;* Ch. *cheng-wu).*[34]

IV. The First Approach to Meditation: The Cultivation of Samādhi and Prajñā

The method of meditation taught by Chinul that is most closely associated with the Ho-tse School and its sudden awakening/gradual cultivation approach is the balanced development of samādhi and prajñā. Chinul's use of this method can be directly traced to his first enlightenment experience, catalyzed through his reading of the *Platform Sūtra.*[35] Chinul's principal instructions on this approach appear in such earlier works as *An Encouragement to Practice: The Compact of the Samādhi and Prajñā Community (Kwŏnsu Chŏnghye kyŏlsa mun)* and *Secrets on Cultivating the Mind,* where he focuses on the need to "cultivate samādhi and prajñā as a pair" *(chŏnghye ssangsu)* and to "maintain alertness and calmness equally" *(sŏngjŏk tŭngji).*[36] These are both common dictums that can be found in everything from the Pāli Canon[37] to Yogācāra[38] materials. They also epitomize the approach of the syncretic San-lun/Ch'an masters, such as the Koguryŏ monk Sŭngnang (ca. 494) and his later successor Fa-lang (507–581), who attempted to integrate philosophical and meditative practices.[39]

Samādhi and prajñā, as they figure in Chinul's thought, are closely related to the term *sŏn* (Ch. *ch'an,* J. *zen),* which was eventually taken as the name of the meditation school in East Asia. *Sŏn* is the Chinese transliteration of the Indian term "dhyāna" (absorption), which is virtually equatable, for our purposes, with the word "samādhi" (concentration).[40] Its use as a designation for the Ch'an and Sŏn schools, however, carries a somewhat different connotation. As Tsung-mi explains, Ch'an is a comprehensive term for both samādhi and prajñā (wisdom), and Ch'an practice is intended to lead to the rediscovery of the original enlightened source of all sentient beings: the Buddha-nature *(fo-hsing;* K. *pulsŏng)* or mind-ground *(hsin-ti;* K. *simji).* The awakening to this source is called prajñā; the cultivation of this awakening is called samādhi.[41] Chinul himself, expanding on this explanation, declares instead that samādhi and prajñā are themselves the abbreviation of the threefold training in *śīla* (morality), samādhi, and prajñā, the basic constituents of the Buddhist path of practice.[42] Consequently, Ch'an and Sŏn training is intended to involve the full range of Buddhist spiritual endeavor, from the beginning stages of morality to the highest stages of wisdom.

According to Chinul, the simultaneous cultivation of samādhi and prajñā can be interpreted from both relative and absolute standpoints. The relative types of samādhi and prajñā involve the more conventional approach to their cultivation and attempt to deal with objects in the conditioned realm in order to remove impurities gradually. Samādhi, in its guise of calmness, is used to counter the inveterate tendency of the mind toward distraction. Prajñā, in its guise of alertness, is employed to stimulate the mind from the occasional dullness that obscures its natural, incisive quality. In their relative form, samādhi and prajñā are instruments for counteracting ignorance and defilements; they are to be used until enlightenment is finally achieved and, consequently, represent a gradualistic approach to realization.

In the sudden awakening/gradual cultivation approach followed by Chinul, in which awakening precedes cultivation, the interpretation of samādhi and prajñā changes dramatically. This absolute form, which involves the cultivation of samādhi and prajñā as inherent in the selfnature, was first propounded in the Ch'an School by Shen-hui (684–758)[43] and is, of course, a major focus of the *Platform Sūtra,* the text so influential in Chinul's own spiritual development. In this approach, samādhi and prajñā are viewed as two aspects of the same self-nature; although each might have its own specific characteristics, they cannot be absolutely differentiated. While still characterized as calmness, samādhi is now considered to be the essence *(ch'e)* of the self-nature; while still characterized as alertness, prajñā is now the function *(yong)* of the selfnature. Although the ways in which they manifest may be distinguishable, both are ultimately based upon the nondual self-nature; hence, samādhi is actually the essence of prajñā, and prajñā is the functioning of samādhi. Because of this mutual identification, samādhi no longer implies detached absorption removed from ordinary sense experience; it is, rather, that same absorption during contact with sense-objects—i.e., a dynamic samādhi. Prajñā is not simply a discriminative faculty that critically investigates phenomena and exposes their essential voidness; it carries, rather, a more passive sense, in that it operates as the calm essence of phenomena and manifests as radiance[44] or bare awareness. In this conception, both samādhi and prajñā are centered in the unmoving self-nature and are, consequently, always identified with this absolute, non-dual state. Even when the two faculties are operating as calmness and alertness in the conditioned sphere—activities that would seem to parallel those of the relative samādhi and prajñā—they never leave their unity in the unconditioned mind-nature.

Even after the initial sudden awakening to the self-nature reveals the identity of samādhi and prajñā, however, residual habits *(vāsanā)* will continue to lead the student into defiled activities. These defilements could disturb the original harmony of the self-nature in such a way that one of its aspects, either essence or function, could become distorted. If essence were to predominate, dullness might result from excessive calmness; if function were to be exaggerated, distraction might develop from excessive alertness. In such an instance, "he should borrow the relative samādhi and prajñā that adapt to signs and not forget the counteractive measures *(taech'i;* Skt. *pratipakṣa)* that control both dullness and agitation. Thereby he will enter the unconditioned."[45] Because samādhi and prajñā remain centered in the self-nature throughout the application of such conventional techniques, however, they eventually become implicit in all of one's conduct, which is their true perfection:

> When both activity and stillness disappear, the act of counteraction is no longer necessary. Then, even though there is contact with sense-objects, thought after thought returns to the source; regardless of the conditions he meets, every mental state is in conformity with the path. Naturally samādhi and prajñā are cultivated as a pair in all situations until finally the student becomes a person with no concerns *(musain).* When this is so, one is truly maintaining samādhi and prajñā equally. One has clearly seen the Buddha-nature.[46]

Chinul, however, is quick to point out that samādhi and prajñā are actually integral parts of a person's spiritual cultivation at all stages of his development. Although samādhi and prajñā might be distinguished as separate practices, they are, in fact, the qualities that vivify all types of meditative endeavor. As Chinul quotes Tsung-mi with approval:

> From the initial activation of the *bodhicitta* until the attainment of Buddhahood, there is only calmness and only awareness, unchanging and uninterrupted. It is only according to their respective positions [on the bodhisattva path] that their designations and attributes differ slightly. At the moment of awakening they are called noumenon and wisdom. (Noumenon is calmness; wisdom is awareness.) When one first activates the *bodhicitta* and begins to cultivate, they are called śamatha-vipaśyanā. (Śamatha brings external conditioning to rest and hence conforms with calmness; vipaśyanā illuminates nature and characteristics and hence corresponds to awareness.) When the practice continues naturally in all situations, they are called samādhi and

prajñā. (Because of its effect of stopping all conditioning and fusing the
mind in concentration, samādhi is calm and immutable. Because of its
effect of illuminating and giving rise to wisdom, prajñā is aware and undis-
criminative.) When the defilements are completely extinguished and the
consummation of meritorious practices has led to the attainment of Buddhahood, they are called bodhi and nirvāṇa. ("Bodhi" is a Sanskrit word
meaning enlightenment; it is awareness. "Nirvāṇa" is a Sanskrit word
meaning calm-extinction; it is calmness.) Hence it should be known that
from the time of the first activation of the *bodhicitta* until the final achievement of Buddhahood, there is only calmness and only awareness. (Here
"only calmness and only awareness" is equivalent to alertness and calmness.)[47]

Hence, regardless of the technique the student might be cultivating,
he must always stay attentive to the equilibrium between these two elements if that technique is to be successful. And it is precisely because of
the equilibrium that samādhi and prajñā bring to any practice that
Chinul regards their balanced cultivation as being so well suited to a sudden awakening/gradual cultivation approach to Buddhist soteriology.

V. The Second Approach to Meditation: Faith and Understanding According to the Complete and Sudden School

The types of correspondences that Chinul attempted to draw between Sŏn and Hwaŏm were, of course, by no means unique to him.
Both Ch'eng-kuan (738–839) and Tsung-mi before him had explored
points of convergence between the two schools, but their analyses had little long-term effect on the subsequent development of Ch'an in China.
Ultimately, it was the reclusive Li T'ung-hsüan who had the greatest
effect of any Hua-yen exegete on the Ch'an tradition in East Asia. A
contemporary of Fa-tsang (643–712), the eminent third patriarch of the
Chinese Hua-yen school, Li T'ung-hsüan was perhaps better known during his lifetime for his thaumaturgic talents than for his exegetical skills.
Li's major work was his *Exposition of the New* [*Translation of the*]
Avataṁsaka Sūtra, a forty-fascicle commentary to Śikṣānanda's eighty-
fascicle translation of the sūtra, which had been completed in 699.[48]
Although Li's *Exposition* achieved some measure of renown following its
appearance, it seems to have soon dropped from circulation and exerted
little formal influence on the evolution of orthodox Hua-yen philosophy.
Centuries later, however, after Hua-yen scholasticism had ossified, Li's
thought enjoyed a resurgence of interest throughout East Asia. Ta-hui
Tsung-kao, the renowned Sung Dynasty systematizer of the *hua-t'ou* (K.
hwadu) method of meditation, was an avid student of Li's writings and

played an important role in rediscovering his works and popularizing them among a new generation of East Asian Buddhists. Chinul himself was profoundly affected by his own reading of Li's commentary—so much so, in fact, that the text is said to have catalyzed his second major awakening in 1188.[49] Chinul found considerable merit in Li's outline of Hua-yen doctrine and practice, using Li's thought as one of the cornerstones of his own system of meditation.[50] This influence can be seen in Chinul's second major meditative approach: "faith and understanding according to the Complete and Sudden Teaching" *(wŏndon sinhae mun),* the practice Chinul considered to be appropriate for the average capacity of the majority of practitioners.

In contrast to the metaphysical orientation of Fa-tsang's interpretation of Hua-yen, Li T'ung-hsüan presented an approach to Hua-yen more explicitly oriented toward practice.[51] Unlike Fa-tsang's, which had concentrated on a description of the state of enlightenment, Li's interpretation of Hua-yen centered on Sudhana's personal realization of the Dharmadhātu[52]—i.e., his pilgrimage in search of instruction, which would enable him to enter directly into the Dharmadhātu, as detailed in the *Ju fa-chieh p'in* ("Entering the Dharmadhātu" chapter, or *Gaṇḍavyūha*) of the *Avataṁsaka.*[53] Even more radically, Li proposed that Buddhahood could be achieved immediately in this very life[54] at the preliminary level of the bodhisattva path, that of the ten faiths *(shih-hsin;* K. *sipsin).*[55]

Li justified this proposal by abandoning Fa-tsang's focus on the unimpeded conditioned origination of the Dharmadhātu *(fa-chieh wu-ai yüan-ch'i;* K. *pŏpkye muae yŏn'gi)* in favor of the theory of nature origination *(hsing-ch'i;* K. *sŏnggi).*[56] In *The Complete and Sudden Attainment of Buddhahood (Wŏndon sŏngbullon),* his synopsis of Li T'ung-hsüan's Hua-yen thought, Chinul carefully compares the two theories, coming out in support of Li's theory of nature origination because "nature origination is more appropriate for contemplation and attaining the path."[57] As Chinul interprets Li's thought, nature origination provides the conceptual justification for the realization that

> Buddhas and sentient beings manifest illusorily from the nature-sea of the fundamental wisdom of universal brightness *(po'gwangmyŏng chi).*
> Although the forms and functioning of sentient beings and Buddhas seem to be different, they are entirely the form and functioning of the fundamental wisdom of universal brightness. Therefore, while they are originally of one essence, they still can give rise to functioning at many different levels.[58]

To bring about this understanding of the fundamental identity of ignorant sentient beings and fully enlightened Buddhas, Chinul taught the approach of faith and understanding. As Chinul interpreted Li's thought, the unmoving wisdom of Buddhahood *(pudong chi)*, which is based on the wisdom of universal brightness *(po'gwangmyŏng chi)*,[59] is the source of all dualistic phenomena, including both Buddhas and sentient beings.[60] Through faith in and understanding of the premise that this unmoving wisdom is identical to the discriminative thoughts of sentient beings, ordinary men of great aspiration *(taesim pŏmbu)*[61] are able "to look back on the radiance of the one true Dharmadhātu, which is their own mind's fundamental wisdom of universal brightness. . . . As the measure of their own wisdom of universal brightness is as great as space or all of the Dharmadhātu, there is neither a single Buddha who does not arise from this original wisdom nor a single sentient being who is not born from the fundamental wisdom."[62] Hence, the internal reflection initially induced by faith and understanding helps to ensure that the student's own faith and understanding remain genuine.[63] The understanding-awakening *(haeo)* engendered through that internal reflection clarifies that

> your own physical, verbal, and mental states and all your different impulses arise from the Tathāgatas' physical, verbal, and mental states and from all their different impulses. They are all without essence or nature, without self or person. Since they all arise from the nonproductive conditions of the own-nature of the Dharmadhātu, you cannot find a place where their roots were originally planted. Their nature itself is the Dharmadhātu.[64]

By understanding this fact right at the very inception of practice—at the first of the ten levels of faith—the student comes to be endowed with the wisdom and compassion of Buddhahood in potential form:

> One who relies on the complete and sudden approach of the one vehicle attains the fruition-sea of the fundamental wisdom at the first level of the ten faiths; it is clearly not achieved upon completion of the ten levels of faith after ten thousand kalpas of constant cultivation [as the Yogācārins had advocated]. The *Exposition* [of Li T'ung-hsüan] explains only that the work is finished after one life; there is no mention whatsoever of ten thousand kalpas.[65]

By knowing this fundamental wisdom, the student establishes nonretrogressive faith, which assures his continued progress on the bodhisattva path and naturally brings about the perfection of the expedient techniques of śamatha-vipaśyanā and the other constituent practices of the ten stages of faith. Through these expedients, samādhi and prajñā are correspondingly perfected, and one enters the initial abiding stage *(vihāra)* of the arousing of the thought of enlightenment *(bodhicittotpāda)*.[66] Through the direct experiential validation of the knowledge that one is a Buddha, the bodhisattva gains the tremendous potential inherent in the state of Buddhahood, and the subsequent stages of the bodhisattva path are automatically perfected:

> If one enters the first stage of the ten faiths, one naturally arrives at the first level of the ten abidings. If one enters the first level of the ten abidings, one naturally arrives at the ultimate stage *(ku'gyŏng chi).* In this wise, it is most essential for the bound ordinary man *(kubak pŏmbu)* to arouse the initial thought of right faith.[67]

Consequently, from the beginning of one's vocation until its consummation in the full enlightenment of Buddhahood, one actually never strays from the fundamental wisdom of universal brightness.

The utility of correct faith and understanding in consummating samādhi and prajñā and many of the other constituents of practice also helps to clarify how this approach can be integrated with Chinul's system of sudden awakening/gradual cultivation:

> A sentient being of great aspiration who relies on the supreme vehicle approach to Dharma has firm faith and understanding that the four great elements are like a bubble or a mirage, that the six sense-objects are like flowers in the sky, that his own mind is the Buddha-mind, and that his own nature is the Dharma-nature. Since the beginning, he has left behind the nature of defilements. His alertness is instantly alert; his clarity is instantly clear. Although a man who cultivates while relying on this understanding still has beginningless habit-energies *(vāsanā),* if he controls them with the unabiding wisdom they become the original wisdom; they need be neither suppressed nor removed. Although he knows how to use expedient samādhi to expel the influences of dullness and scatteredness, since he recognizes that mental projections and discrimination arise according to conditions from the true nature, he utilizes the purity of that nature while remaining free from any form of attachment. . . . Hence, despite all the hardships of the world, there is no danger that he will backslide.[68]

VI. Tracing Back the Radiance: The Fundamental Constituent of Meditation Practice

Passing mention has already been made of the idea of tracing the radiance emanating from the mind back to its essence *(hoe'gwang panjo).* This concept is an essential element of the processes governing all types of meditation practice as Chinul interprets them; because of its particular importance in the consummation of the faith and understanding approach, however, it is most appropriate to treat it here. Chinul employs a variety of complementary designations for this aspect of contemplation: "trace the radiance back to one's own mind" *(panjo cha-*

sim); "trace the radiance back to one's own nature" *(panjo chasŏng);* "in one thought-moment, trace the light back and see one's own original nature" *(illyŏm hoe'gwang kyŏn chabonsŏng);* "trace back and observe the qualities and functions of your own mind" *(pan'gwan chasim chi tog'yong);* "to observe and reflect on your own mind" *(kwanjo chasim);* "reflect on and view your own mind" *(cho'gyŏn chasim);* "mirror your own mind" *(kyŏng chasim);* or simply "trace back the radiance" *(panjo),* "contemplative reflection" *(kwanjo),* or "introspection" *(naejo).*[69] Although the term *hoe'gwang panjo* can be interpreted as "reflection," "introspection," or even "meditation," the more dynamic renderings given here better convey a sense of the actual process this aspect of contemplation involves.

Chinul's Yi Dynasty commentator, Yŏndam Yuil (1720–1799), has given perhaps the most succinct and precise definition of the term:

> To trace the radiance back [to one's own mind] means to trace the radiance back to the numinous awareness *(yŏngji)* of one's own mind; for this reason, it is called "trace back the radiance." It is like seeing the radiance of the sun's rays and following it back until you see the orb of the sun itself.[70]

The justification for this practice harkens back to the celebrated *Aṅguttara-nikāya* passage where the Buddha declares that the mind is inherently luminous but dimmed by adventitious defilements.[71] This luminous quality of mind is called by Chinul either "numinous awareness" or "void and calm, numinous awareness" *(kongjŏk yŏngji).* Adopted by Chinul from Tsung-mi, "numinous awareness" refers to the fundamental quality of sentience, which, perhaps not so figuratively, "shines" on sense-objects, illuminating them and allowing them to be cognized.[72] This view that the mind illuminates the sense-realms is found frequently in the writings of more orthodox Ch'an masters also; witness, for instance, the comments of Lin-chi I-hsüan (d. 866): "You, followers of the Way, right now vividly illumining all things and taking the measure of the world, you give the names to the three realms."[73] This inherent radiance of the mind does not merely illuminate the world of sense-phenomena, however; as the mind's natural brightness is restored through meditation practice, it comes virtually to shine *through* objects, exposing their inherent voidness *(śūnya).*[74] Hence, numinous awareness is the quality, common to all "sentient" beings, that constitutes their ultimate capacity to attain enlightenment;[75] it serves both as the inherent faculty that allows meditation to develop and the quality of mind consummated and brought to perfection through that meditation.

"Awareness" *(chi;* Ch. *chih)* in this term refers to the capacity of the void and calm mind-essence to remain "aware" of all sensory stimuli. Chinul provides various descriptions of this capacity: it is "that mind of outstanding purity and brilliance, . . . that enlightened nature that is the original source of all sentient beings;"⁷⁶ "the mind that has been transmitted successively from the Buddha through the patriarchs;"⁷⁷ or, simply, "your original face."⁷⁸ Other scholars have interpreted the term as "knowledge" or "prajñā-intuition," but neither translation properly conveys the sense that "awareness" is that fundamental quality through which all mental qualities, be they "knowledge" or otherwise, are able to manifest.⁷⁹ This property of awareness is itself formless and free of thoughts *(mu'nyŏm;* Ch. *wu-nien)* and, consequently, is able to adapt without limitation to the various inclinations of sentient beings, whether toward greed and hatred or toward wisdom and compassion. In all such cases, the noumenal source itself is forever unaffected and remains simply "aware."⁸⁰ To describe the adaptability of this faculty, Chinul uses a phrase that ultimately derives from the *Lao Tzu:* "This one word 'awareness' is the source [or gateway] of all wonders."⁸¹ As the foundation of sentience, this awareness is fundamentally nondual but remains dynamic enough to manifest its "wonders" in any dualistic form. In looking back on the radiance of the mind, one is starting at the level of these "wonders"—the phenomenal manifestations of the nondual mind-essence—and then tracing back those manifestations to their perceptual source: sentience itself, or "bare awareness."

For Chinul, regardless of the specific meditation technique being developed, tracing the radiance back to the mind is the function that illuminates the path through which the discriminative mind can rediscover its original, nondual source, which is free of thought.⁸² In discussing Li's treatment of Hua-yen practice, for example, Chinul determines that his purpose is solely to induce students "to look back on the radiance of the one true Dharmadhātu, which is their own mind's fundamental wisdom of universal brightness."⁸³ In this context, to reflect or look back on one's own mind refers to the immediate realization that one is originally a Buddha and that ignorance and its concomitants are all the products of the Tathāgatas' wisdom of universal brightness:

> If [ordinary men of great aspiration] can trace back the light and look back on the mind, then the defilements that have abided on the ground of ignorance for vast numbers of kalpas become the wisdom of universal brightness of all the Buddhas. Since the defilements, ignorance, and the illusory guises of sentient beings have all arisen from the Tathāgatas' wisdom of universal brightness, if they look back on the mind today they will find that these are all entirely their own essence and not external things. They are like waves that arise on still water: the waves are the water. They are like phantom flowers that appear in the sky: the flowers are only the sky.⁸⁴

Tracing the radiance back to the mind's source plays a vital role in Chinul's Sŏn thought as well. In his treatment of sudden awakening/

gradual cultivation, for example, it is tracing the radiance back to the mind-nature that functions as the sudden awakening constituent of the path and that opens the individual to a vision of his own enlightened nature: "If in one thought he then follows back the light [of his mind to its source] and sees his own original nature, he will discover that the ground of this nature is innately free of defilement and that he himself is originally endowed with the non-outflow wisdom-nature, which is not a hair's breadth different from that of all the Buddhas."[85] After the re-cognition of that nondiscriminating awareness, which is uninterrupted throughout all conscious moments, the student then must continue on to discipline his mind through gradual cultivation so that only salutory and beneficial manifestations of that awareness will appear. It is this process that all specific meditation techniques are intended to catalyze.

VII. The Third Approach to Meditation: *Hwadu* Meditation

If meditation practice were to be brought to consummation, Chinul assumed, the average student would require the doctrinal teachings of Buddhism to outline for him the course and goal of practice and to encourage him along that path. For these reasons, in most of his writings Chinul stressed the need for following the approach, outlined by Tsung-mi, in which the student develops understanding of the two aspects of Dharma (immutability and adaptability) and the two approaches concerning person (sudden awakening and gradual cultivation) while continuing to rely on the teachings. Because of the clarity and comprehensiveness of this approach, it was appropriate for the majority of people of average ability.[86]

Nevertheless, Chinul remained concerned lest the conceptualization inherent in this sort of approach eventually hinder the student's progress toward bodhi. Particularly in his later writings, Chinul seems to have moved away from the doctrinally based approach of Tsung-mi to a more exclusive focus on uniquely Sŏn practices. Based ultimately on his final enlightenment experience, which was engendered through his reading of the *Records of Ta-hui,* Chinul's third major meditative technique, the "shortcut" approach *(kyŏngjŏl mun)* of observing the *hwadu* (K. *kan-hwa sŏn;* Ch. *k'an-hua ch'an*), eschewed all scriptural explanations in favor of a radical disentanglement of the mind from its conceptual processes.

Hwadu (Ch. *hua-t'ou*) practice was the product of a long process of development in the Ch'an schools of the later T'ang period in China. After the mid 800s, Ch'an masters such as Nan-yüan Hui-yung (d. 930), Fen-yang Shan-chao (947–1024), and Yüan-wu K'o-ch'in (1063–1135) had begun to use stories concerning earlier Ch'an teachers as a systematic way of instructing their students and had begun to collect these anecdotes in large anthologies.[87] These stories came to be called *kung-an* (K. *kong-an;* J. *kōan*), or "public test-cases," because they put an end to private understanding *(kung)* and were guaranteed to accord with what the Buddhas and patriarchs would say *(an)*.[88] In the word's earliest usages in Ch'an and Sŏn texts, *hwadu* (lit., "head of speech") meant simply "topic," being virtually synonymous with such terms as *hwaje* ("theme of speech"), *hwabyŏng* ("handle, or topic, of speech"), and *hwach'ŭk* ("rule of speech").[89] In this non-technical sense, *hwadu* can be considered the primary topic or critical phrase of the entire situation set out in the complete *kung-an,* or test case. We may take, for example, the popular *kung-an* attributed to Chao-chou Ts'ung-shen (778–897): "Does a dog have Buddha-nature or not?" "No! (Ch. *wu;* K. *mu*)."[90] The entire exchange is the *kung-an;* the *hwadu* is "dog has no Buddha-nature" or simply "no."

An account found in the *Leng-ch'ieh shih-tzu chi* ("Record of the Masters and Disciples of the *Laṅkāvatāra*"), by the Northern Ch'an adept Ching-chüeh, suggests that practices similar to the *kung-ans* of later centuries may have been first employed by Hung-jen (601–674), traditionally considered to be the Fifth Patriarch of the Ch'an School. While we cannot assume that Ching-chüeh presents a verbatim account of Hung-jen's teachings, his statements could very well refer to teachings that might have ultimately derived from Hung-jen's time. At any rate, Hung-jen is presumed to have told his disciples: "Within the mind, observe the one word" (or, "the word 'one' ") *(hsiang hsin-chung k'an i-tzu)*[91]—a phrase that resonates with the *k'an-hua ch'an* of the later Ch'an and Sŏn schools.

It is, however, to Ta-hui Tsung-kao, a disciple of Yüan-wu K'o-ch'in in the lineage of the Lin-chi School, that credit must be given for popularizing the *hua-t'ou* technique throughout East Asia. Chinul was the first Korean Sŏn teacher to be influenced by Ta-hui's approach, and Chinul's adoption of the *hwadu* technique brought him into the mainstream of Ch'an's development on the mainland. That Ta-hui and Chinul were only one generation apart indicates that Chinul may have heard about Ta-hui early in his vocation, during his stay (ca. 1183–1185) at Ch'ŏngwŏn-sa (a monastery in the southwest of the peninsula near ports catering to trade with the Chinese mainland), when he may well have contracted with Sung or Koryŏ traders to import the first copy of the *Records of Ta-hui* to Korea.[92] Chinul was profoundly affected by Ta-hui's approach and, after his third and final awakening, which was induced through a reading of his *Records,*[93] *hwadu* practice came to play a major, and later an overriding, role in the ensemble of his thought. Chinul's adoption of the *hwadu* technique augured the stronger Imje (Ch. Lin-chi) orientation of later Korean Sŏn teachers like his disciple

Chin'gak Hyesim (1178–1234), who in 1226 compiled the first Korean collection of *kongan* stories, the *Sŏnmun yŏmsong chip* ("Collection of the Sŏn School's Verses of Critique").[94] This posture of Korean Sŏn became more striking as the centuries passed; it was particularly pronounced after the return from China of T'aego Pou (1301–1382), who brought the orthodox Lin-chi lineage to Korea; other of his contemporaries, such as Naong Hyegun (1320–1376), also stressed the efficacy of the *hwadu*.[95] Today in Korea the *hwadu* continues to be the primary technique employed in meditation halls, and virtually all masters advocate its use for students at any level of spiritual development.

Chinul's earlier works, such as *An Encouragement to Practice, Secrets of Cultivating the Mind,* and *Straight Talk on the True Mind (Chinsim chiksŏl),* had not even mentioned *hwadu* practice; indeed, only in his most comprehensive treatise, *Excerpts from the Dharma Collection and Special Practice Record with Personal Notes* (completed in 1209, one year before his death), does he recognize *hwadu* as a separate system and give it extensive coverage. Even there, however, Chinul remains markedly hesitant to prescribe the *hwadu* to any except the most exceptional of meditators. Even after penetrating the *hwadu,* Chinul notes, such adepts might still give rise to defilements when in contact with sense-objects because of their lack of correct understanding of the nature and characteristics of the mind. "For such a person," he declares,

> it is better to rely on the words and teachings of Master Tsung-mi, which accord with reality, and put all one's effort into investigation. This will enable one to subdue the thoughts of liking and disliking, anger and joy, others and self, success and failure. Since it is only through this sort of knowledge and vision of the Buddha Dharma, which accords with reality, that one will find a way out of saṃsāra, the mystery in the mystery [i.e., nondual comprehension] . . . will naturally come to exist within that conceptual knowledge and vision.[96]

Hence throughout most of his career, Chinul clearly favored an approach in which *hwadu* practice remained closely associated with doctrinal understanding as prescribed by Tsung-mi.

Late in his life, however, Chinul's views rapidly began to crystalize around Ta-hui's interpretation of *hwadu* practice, and this interpretation eventually eclipsed even Tsung-mi's influence over Chinul. This tendency to exalt Ta-hui is particularly prominent in *Resolving Doubts About Observing the Hwadu (Kanhwa kyŏrŭi ron),* a treatise found among Chinul's effects and published posthumously by his successor, Hyesim, in 1215.[97] As Chinul notes, most students of his time were still bound by the passions and so had first to purify their views and conduct through correct understanding of the doctrinal teachings before they could enter into realization. But the Ch'an approach of Ta-hui "transcends all standards. Consequently, it is not only students of the scholastic teachings who will find it difficult to have faith and enter into it; even those of lesser faculties and shallow comprehension in the Sŏn School are perplexed and cannot understand it."[98] Quoting with approval an anonymous Ch'an master, Chinul remarks, "The separate transmission outside the teachings far excels the teaching vehicle *(kyosŭng).* It is not something with which those of shallow intelligence can cope."[99] But he is equally adamant himself about the ultimate superiority of Sŏn: "The separate transmission [of Sŏn], which is outside the teachings, is not subject to the same limitations [as the Complete and Sudden Teaching]."[100] In such statements, the liberal attitude toward the scholastic sects and the restrained discussion of Sŏn, which characterized much of his earlier writing, are not as prominent. No longer does he act as the Sŏn apologist, attempting to vindicate the Sŏn outlook by demonstrating its parallelisms with the doctrinal descriptions of the canonical texts. Rather, he has accepted with few qualifications the preeminence of Ta-hui's interpretation of Ch'an, pointing out that in matters of spiritual technique, speed of consummation, and purity of view, the "shortcut" *hwadu* approach is clearly superior to the sudden awakening/gradual cultivation approach advocated by Tsung-mi. Although in *Excerpts from the Dharma Collection and Special Practice Record with Personal Notes,* Chinul had called the shortcut approach the "one living road that leads to salvation,"[101] this exclusivity was considerably vitiated by Chinul's concluding remarks in that text, which placed *hwadu* practice clearly within the soteriological scheme originally outlined by Tsung-mi.[102] In *Resolving Doubts About Observing the Hwadu* there is little such vacillation, and unadulterated Ta-hui Ch'an is stressed. This trend in Chinul's thought probably accounts for the pervasive influence of Ta-hui in the writings of Chinul's successor, Hyesim, surpassing even that of Tsung-mi. Hence, the focus on the Lin-chi interpretation of Ch'an that is prevalent in late Koryŏ Sŏn was in fact probably initiated late in life by Chinul —one more instance of the debt the Korean tradition owes him.

Hwadu, which means "head of speech," is best taken metaphorically as the "apex of speech" or the "point at which (or beyond which) speech exhausts itself." Since speech is initiated by thought, speech in this context includes all the discriminative tendencies of the mind itself, in accordance with the Indian Abhidharma formula that speech *(vācisaṃskāra)* is fundamentally intellection and imagination *(vitarkavicāra).*[103] By leading one to the very limit of speech—or, more accurately, thought —the *hwadu* acts as a purification device that sweeps the mind of all its conceptualizing activities, leaving it clear, attentive, and calm. As Chinul says, quoting Ta-hui, in true *hwadu* practice "you need only lay down, all at once, the mind full of deluded thoughts and inverted thinking *(vipa-*

ryāsa), the mind of logical discrimination, the mind that loves life and hates death, the mind of knowledge and views, interpretation and comprehension."[104] Cessation of the discriminative processes of thought strips the mind of its interest in the sense-experiences of the ordinary world and renders it receptive to the influence of the unconditioned. Hence, as Chinul explains at length in *Resolving Doubts About Observing the Hwadu* and *Excerpts from the Dharma Collection and Special Practice Record with Personal Notes,* the *hwadu* produces a "cleansing knowledge and vision *(jñānadarśana)*" that "removes the defects of conceptual understanding so that you can find the living road that leads to salvation."[105] As this approach allows none of the conventional supports for practice, it was intended principally either for "those patched-robed monks in the Sŏn lineage today who have the capacity to enter the path after leaving behind words"[106] or for those who have first matured themselves through another technique.

I. TWO TYPES OF *HWADU* INVESTIGATION

While accepting the unique features of *hwadu* practice, however, Chinul was able to turn it into a comprehensive meditative approach appropriate for students at all levels of advancement. This is accomplished by differentiating between two distinct types of *hwadu* investigation: investigation of the idea or meaning of the *hwadu (ch'amŭi)* and investigation of the word itself *(ch'amgu).*[107] Going back to Chao-chou's *mu hwadu,* investigating the idea means to look into the question: "With what intent in mind did Chao-chou make the statement *mu?*" Since this investigation involves more "taste" *(mi)*—that is, intellectual interest—it is comparatively easy for beginners in *hwadu* practice to undertake. Although such investigation may be of provisional value in prompting the student toward a more intense inquiry into the question, it will not permit him to abandon theoretical understanding or the discriminative processes of thought. Students who remain at this level

> are the same as those following the complete and sudden approach who have been enlightened through right understanding [i.e., they have achieved the understanding-awakening]. They still retain views and learning, understanding and conduct. They are no better than those scholar-monks of today who are attached to words and letters and, in their contemplation practice, speculate that internally the mind exists but still search externally for truth.[108]

If the student is to progress, he must eventually abandon his concern with Chao-chou's motives in making this statement and look directly into the word *mu* itself. At that point he is investigating the word, which is said to provide no conceptual support for the investigation. As this sort of investigation is thus free from the obstacle of understanding *(jñeyāvarana)*, it results in the realization-awakening *(chŭngo)*, which is the consummation of the gradual cultivation that follows the initial sudden experience of the understanding-awakening *(haeo)*.[109]

These two types of investigation are described respectively by Chinul —following a distinction traditionally attributed to Yün-men's disciple Tung-shan Shou-ch'u (?–990)—as "live words" *(hwalgu;* Ch. *huo-chü)* and "dead words" *(sagu;* Ch. *ssu-chü)*.[110] The *hwadu* investigated via its meaning is the dead word, for it can only clarify one's understanding, never bring true realization: "In the Sŏn approach, all these true teachings deriving from the faith and understanding of the Complete and Sudden School, which are as numerous as the sands of the Ganges, are called dead words because they induce people to create the obstacle of understanding."[111] The "tasteless" *hwadu* investigated via the word is the live word, for it guides one to the "living road that leads to salvation."[112] The live word allows no understanding through concepts and offers nothing at which the deluded mind may grasp. As it has been described by Ta-hui and Chinul, "this one word is the weapon that smashes all types of wrong knowledge and wrong conceptualization."[113] This live word is the true shortcut approach because it helps to free the mind from the fundamental activating-consciousness *(ŏpsik;* Skt. *karmajāti* [*lakṣaṇa*] *vijñāna)*, as Chinul's successor, Hyesim, had intimated.[114] As the *Awakening of Faith (Ta-sheng ch'i-hsin lun)* explains, the activating-consciousness represents the point at which subject and object are bifurcated and dualistic patterns of thought are generated.[115] As the origin of the deluded mind, it ultimately provides the impetus that drives the hapless individual toward ignorance and craving. Only through continued attention to the live word, engendered through investigation of the word itself, can the activating-consciousness be shattered and true realization achieved.[116]

These two types of investigation are also associated with two distinct functions served by *hwadu* investigation: that of an expression that removes the defects of conceptual understanding *(p'abyŏng)* and that of a complete expression in itself *(chŏnje)*.[117] In investigation of the meaning, the *hwadu* is used as a palliative to counteract the discriminative tendencies of mind by focusing the intellect on one logically indefensible question. By removing the obstacle of understanding, it ultimately leads to the sort of acquired-understanding that allows the student to enter onto the first stage of faith *(ch'osinji)* via the understanding-awakening *(haeo)*—Chinul's "sudden awakening." Investigation of the word is the *hwadu* as a complete expression *(chŏnje)*—that is, the ultimate state of realization summing up all aspects of the great matter *(taesa)* of awakening. It engenders the state of no-thought *(mu'nyŏm)*, which allows the access to realization *(chŭngip)* at the first stage of the ten abidings *(sipchu).*[118]

The distinctive feature in Ta-hui's "shortcut" approach to *hwadu* practice is that it is supposed to enable the practitioner to dispense with the initial investigation of the meaning and enter directly into the investigation of the "tasteless" *(mumi) hwadu*—that is, investigation of the word. "Straight off," says Chinul, "[the followers of the shortcut approach] take up a tasteless *hwadu* and are concerned only with raising it to their attention and focusing on it. For this reason, they remain free of ratiocination. . . . Unexpectedly, in an instant they activate one moment of realization concerning the *hwadu* and, as discussed previously, the Dharmadhātu of the One Mind becomes perfectly full and clear."[119] The motive force that impels the mind toward this realization is "doubt" *(ŭisim; ŭijong),* which may be better rendered "puzzlement," "wonder," or simply "questioning." Chinul, following Ta-hui, defines doubt as a state of mental perplexity "where the intellect cannot operate and thought cannot reach; it is the road through which discrimination is excised and theorizing is ended."[120] It makes the mind "puzzled, frustrated, and 'tasteless'—just as if you were gnawing on an iron rod."[121] Continued attention to the tasteless *hwadu* creates a sense of doubt that allows neither thought nor conceptual understanding to arise in the mind. Through this state of no-thought, the student is then primed for access to realization, the previously mentioned realization-awakening. Once the doubt "disintegrates" *(p'a),*[122] the student comes into direct conformity with the Dharmadhātu of the One Mind.[123] Thus, through investigation of the *hwadu,* the student can forgo all the gradual stages of spiritual development and get to the very root of the problem of saṃsāra: the inveterate conceptualizing tendency of the mind.

Doubt itself has various degrees of intensity, which are related to whether investigation of the *hwadu* is done via the meaning or via the word. Doubt developed through investigation of the meaning can only lead to the understanding-awakening of the first level of the ten faiths, for it does not free the mind from its acquired-understanding. Doubt achieved via investigation of the word, however, produces the realization-wisdom, allowing one to display prajñā and engage in dissemination of the teachings of Buddhism to all types of people.[124]

Drawing upon Chinul's ideas, Sung-bae Park has recently given a provocative accounting of the soteriological underpinnings of Sŏn practice, which helps to clarify the role of doubt in Korean Sŏn thought. As Park explains in his *Buddhist Faith and Sudden Enlightenment, hwadu* practice engenders an existential conflict in the adept's psyche between acquired knowledge in the truth of one's ultimate Buddhahood (faith) and the obvious fact of one's present delusion (doubt). The dialectical tension between doubt ("I am an ignorant sentient being") and faith ("I am a Buddha") ultimately results in the experience of "brokenness" *(kkaech'im)*—that is, the annihilation of the dualistic intellectual framework and all sense of personal ego—which, in turn, results in the rediscovery of the "ground of absolute nothingness."[125] The symbiotic relationship between faith and doubt in Sŏn thought helps to clarify why Chinul focused both on Hwaŏm "faith and understanding" and Sŏn investigation, as well as why these need not be antithetical.

2. THE THREE MYSTERIOUS GATES

Chinul seems ultimately to have despaired about the prospects of ordinary men in his time succeeding in their contemplation of the *hwadu* via investigation of the word. Even at the end of his *Resolving Doubts About Observing the Hwadu,* which is strongly supportive of Ta-hui's "shortcut" approach, he says: "Those who have manifested such realization-wisdom [through the investigation of the word] are seldom seen and seldom heard of nowadays. Consequently, these days we should value the approach that investigates the meaning of the *hwadu* and thereby produces right knowledge and vision."[126] Hence, while Chinul may have emphasized the importance of *hwadu* practice later in his life, it would be an exaggeration to say that it ever completely supplanted the role of Tsung-mi's gnoseology in his own synthesis of Sŏn thought.

This conclusion is especially borne out by the fact that Chinul provided a scheme for incorporating *hwadu* practice into his more conventional outline of meditative development based on Tsung-mi. This scheme employed the three mysterious gates *(samhyŏn-mun;* Ch. *san-hsüan men),* adopted from Lin-chi I-hsüan and other predecessors in the Ch'an School.[127]

The Ch'an and Sŏn schools are well known for their innovations in all areas of Buddhist exploration, from epistemology to praxis. Such doctrinal experimentation was especially prominent in the period of Middle Ch'an: the period after the six orthodox patriarchs of the school, but before the emergence of the five schools of the mature tradition, dating roughly from the early eighth to middle ninth centuries.[128] Although there is a paucity of extant literature concerning these schools, summaries of some of the sects appearing in later accounts indicate a truly remarkable variety of views and practices.[129] Later Ch'an theoreticians attempted to ascertain the general features of the various schools of the tradition and to delineate a comprehensive outline of the types of descriptions used in Ch'an. Chinul assumes that there are various levels of description used in the Sŏn teachings, each of which is correlated with a particular style of doctrinal description and spiritual capacity. He refers to these levels as three mysterious gates: the mystery in the essence *(ch'e-jung-hyŏn),* the mystery in the word *(kujung-hyŏn),* and the mystery in the mystery *(hyŏnjung-hyŏn)*. In addition to outlining Chinul's general attitude toward Sŏn practice, a description of these three stages will help to clarify the differences Chinul saw between more conventional Sŏn approaches and the "shortcut" approach of Ta-hui. Basically, these three stages involve (1) conceptual descriptions of doctrinal tenets, which are intended to engender correct understanding in the student; (2) the conventional use of the *hwadu,* a terse phrase relatively devoid of conceptual content, which is a more direct expression of the philosophical and metaphysical truths expressed on the first stage; and (3) gestures, pauses, and other nonverbal forms of expression, which were considered to come as close as possible to absolute truth itself, for they are in no way vitiated by conceptualization.[130]

The first level of explication is the mystery in the essence. This description of the process of awakening, appropriate for those of average capacity, involves expedient accounts of the ultimate goal of practice and the approach to be followed in consummating that goal. For the majority of Sŏn students, some grounding in doctrinal understanding is necessary if they are to avoid the inevitable pitfalls on the path of practice. As Chinul remarks, "Since the acquired-understanding of meditators in the present day is still involved with the passions, they must first develop views and learning and then develop understanding and conduct; afterward, they can enter into realization. At the moment of entering into realization, they slough off their former acquired-understanding and, through absence of thought, come into conformity [with the Dharmadhātu]."[131] This first mysterious gate is accordingly designed to instill correct view in beginning cultivators and to overcome the obstacles to understanding in the more advanced. Descriptions closely resembling those used in the scholastic schools are employed to demonstrate the essential identity of ignorant sentient beings and enlightened Buddhas. These would include such statements as: "One word is bright and clear and contains all the myriad images"[132] or "Throughout boundless world systems, oneself and others are not separated by as much as the tip of a hair; the ten time periods, from beginning to end, are not separate from the present thought-moment."[133] Such statements, of course, recall the Hwaŏm theory of the unimpeded interpenetration of all phenomena *(shih-shih wu-ai)* and help to break down the adept's attachment to his or her own individuality *(ātman)* by inducing an awareness of the pure nature of the mind and the relationship inherent therein between its immutable and adaptable qualities. Nevertheless, although such statements may seem similar to the outlook of the complete teachings, they are actually made with completely different purposes in mind. Whereas such descriptions in the doctrinal schools are designed to provide the conceptual understanding that will enable the Buddhist religion to survive unchallenged, parallel Sŏn descriptions are intended solely to prompt the student to direct, personal awakening. As Chinul notes:

[Tsung-mi says:] "The teachings of the Buddha are intended to support tens of thousands of generations; hence their principles have been demonstrated in detail. The admonitions of the patriarchs involve an immediate crossing-over to liberation; they aim at producing mysterious penetration." [134] [This statement means that] since mysterious penetration is predicated upon the elimination of words, the student should not dwell on the traces of a master's words. When these traces are eliminated from the ground of the mind-consciousness, the noumenon manifests in the fountainhead of the mind. For this reason, the instructions given by the masters of the school according to the capacities of their listeners about the doctrine of the unimpeded interpenetration of all phenomena are extremely terse. They are intended, above all else, to produce an access to awakening through a direct shortcut; they do not sanction knowledge through descriptive explanations. [135]

This sort of treatment is beneficial in instructing beginners of less than superlative spiritual capacity—that is, people who would have difficulty in grasping the purpose of practice if they were to start out directly with investigation of the *hwadu,* which has less intellectual content.

In the Sŏn school as well there are those who find it difficult to cope with the secret transmission and need to rely on the doctrine in order to awaken to the Sŏn school's teachings; for such people, the school has also explained the teaching of the unimpeded interpenetration of all phenomena, . . . and, with complete descriptions which accord with the nature, they instruct beginning students who are not yet able to investigate the live word of the shortcut approach and help to ensure that they have nonretrogressive faith and understanding. . . . [In the absence of such explanations,] how can the student expect to understand that principle unless he has superior faculties and great wisdom? How else can he expect to penetrate it? [136]

Accordingly, the majority of students must have a strong foundation in doctrinal understanding before they can proceed to investigate the *hwadu,* the second mysterious gate:

You must know that men who are cultivating the path in this present degenerate age of the Dharma should first, via conceptual understanding that accords with reality, discern clearly the mind's true and false aspects, its arising and ceasing, and its essential and secondary features. Next, through a word that splits nails and cuts through iron, you should probe closely and carefully. [137]

This word that "splits nails and cuts through iron" (K. *ch'amjŏng chŏlch'ŏl;* Ch. *chan-ting chieh-t'ieh*) [138] is the *hwadu.* With the maturation of the student's understanding through the expedient descriptions employed on the first mysterious gate, a further step must be taken to ensure that he does not stagnate at a purely intellectual level of understanding. This proclivity toward conceptualization is an inveterate tendency of the mind, which vitiates the unique experiential content of sensory experience.[139] The first stages of this tyranny of concepts are eliminated through the mystery in the word, as discussed earlier. That technique provides a "cleansing knowledge and vision" that helps to purify the mind from attachment to, or identification with, conceptual descriptions that might have developed through the use of doctrinal expedients at the first stage of the three mysterious gates.

Even though its very formulation involves some condescension to linguistic convention, the *hwadu* offers the practitioner further help in becoming free from the limitations of the conditioned realm. As the *hwadu* is "terser" *(saengnyak)*[140] and, hence, less dependent on conceptual delineation than the doctrinal descriptions that characterized the first mysterious gate, it is closer to being an authentic description of the unconditioned, which is beyond concepts. Nevertheless, even its "cleansing knowledge and vision" ultimately must be transcended if dualistic modes of thought are to be overcome. This transcendence is achieved through the mystery in the mystery, which includes such techniques employed in the Sŏn school as pregnant pauses, beatings, shouting, and other non-conceptual modes of expression, which provide no substratum upon which even cleansing knowledge and vision can subsist. Such catalysts shock the student out of the complacency engendered by the mind's normal conceptual processes, inducing a sudden realization of the full glory of the Dharmadhātu.[141] Hence this third mystery comes as close as any relative expression to conveying a sense of the unconditioned realm.

Chinul, then, envisions Sŏn instruction as progressing from kataphatic statements about the innate purity of the mind in the first gate, to more apophatic descriptions designed to free the mind from conceptualization in the second gate, and finally to nonverbal expressions in the third gate.[142] Hence, despite the Sŏn School's claim that it is a "separate transmission outside the teachings," Chinul compels it to accept expedient instructions that are virtually parallel to the types of descriptions generally considered characteristic of the doctrinal schools. Through these three gates, therefore, Chinul effects both an incorporation of *hwadu* meditation into Tsung-mi's Ch'an soteriology and an accommodation between Sŏn and *kyo*.

VIII. The Fourth Approach to Meditation: No-thought

As noted earlier in connection with *hwadu* meditation, access to realization *(chǔngip)*—that is, direct experiential validation of the student's innate Buddhahood—is achieved through investigation of the word. Chinul, in turn, defines this access to realization as a state of no-thought, which he also refers to as "no-mind" *(musim)*.[143] No-thought has considerably wider ramifications than its role in *hwadu* meditation, however. Regardless of whether one's realization is achieved via the "faith and understanding" of the Hwaŏm teachings, the "shortcut" approach of Sŏn, or the recollection practices of Pure Land, the thought processes and the conceptual apparatus that sustains those approaches are finally annihilated only in that moment of realization engendered by no-thought.[144] Even adherents of the complete teachings of the *kyo* schools, Chinul states, "must first pass through their views and learning, their understanding and conduct; only then can they enter into realization. At the time of the access of realization, their experience will correspond to the no-thought of the Sŏn approach."[145] Indeed, for all practices, no-thought is their consummation and serves as the factor that initiates the student into direct realization.

The cultivation of no-thought constitutes the primary element of practice following the initial sudden awakening. After the cultivator has achieved incipient understanding of his innate Buddhahood, he continues on to develop all the manifold practices of the bodhisattva *(manhaeng)*, which will help to mature his comprehension. However, because of his initial awakening, the student is able to continue with this gradual cultivation without retaining any sense that there is something wholesome that he must cultivate or something unwholesome that he must eliminate; rather, he cultivates all of these practices in a state of no-thought.[146] Chinul often quotes Tsung-mi in this regard: "Although one prepares to cultivate the manifold supplementary practices [of the bodhisattva], no-thought is the origin of them all."[147] Hence, a central feature of any true cultivation is the element of no-thought.

In most of his works, Chinul accepted no-thought as an integral part of all types of meditation practice and did not give it any particular emphasis. In *Straight Talk on the True Mind,* however, Chinul does attempt to outline a method whereby no-thought could be practiced as a meditative method in its own right. This is Chinul's approach of "no-mind that conforms with the path" *(musim hapto mun)*,[148] a method of practice intended for only the most spiritually adept cultivators. In that treatise, ten methods of practicing "no-mind" are outlined, which involve various combinations of overcoming one's identification with external sense-objects and with the internal activities of thought.[149] Once all one's mistaken conceptions of both internal and external are annihilated, the world is seen as it truly is *(yathābhūta)* and delusion can never arise again. Hence, the cultivation of no-thought is not to be construed as an absence of conscious activity. Rather, it refers to the cultivation of a state of mind that restores the original objectivity of sense-perception by bringing an end to the impulsion of the defilements *(kleśa)* during that perception; ultimately it enables the mind to interact spontaneously with the world by freeing it from its conceptual presumptions about the objects in that world.

IX. The Fifth Approach to Meditation: Recollection of the Buddha's Name

The importance of no-thought as the catalyst of realization is indicated quite explicitly in Chinul's discussion of a meditative technique that received little overall attention in his works: the recollection of the Buddha's name *(yŏmbul;* Ch. *nien-fo).* This technique, the hallmark of the Pure Land schools of East Asia, received little sympathy from Chinul in his earlier works, such as *An Encouragement to Practice,* where he condemned the practice for instilling complacency in the meditator. In that text, Chinul criticizes those Pure Land adepts who, convinced of their own inability to cultivate such presumably difficult practices as samādhi and prajñā, decide simply to recite Amitābha's name in the hopes of gaining admission to his Pure Land. By copious quotations from several sūtras and śāstras, Chinul attempts to convince such adherents that the process of seeking rebirth in the Pure Land "is never separate from one's own mind. Apart from the source of one's own mind, where else would one be able to enter?"[150] After citing a passage from the *Ta-fang-kuang fo ju-lai pu-ssu-i ching-chieh ching* ("The Expanded Scripture on the Inscrutable State of the Buddhas, the Tathāgatas") declaring that a bodhisattva who understands the teaching of mind-only is instantly reborn into the Pure Land,[151] Chinul concludes: "Even though a person does not recollect the Buddha in order to seek rebirth [in the Pure Land], if he understands that everything is only mind and investigates accordingly, he is naturally reborn there."[152] Hence, Chinul follows his predecessors in the Sŏn School in interpreting the Pure Land as being, in fact, the purified mind.[153] Chinul accepts that such recollection is valid for those people who are least talented in spiritual matters. However, he insists the technique, if it is to be brought to consummation, must be performed with as much care as is necessary for developing more sophisticated meditative techniques such as balancing samādhi and prajñā, understanding that everything in the Pure Land is grounded in the suchness of the mind, and remaining centered in the calm and and radiant nature. When that recollection is performed with such careful attention to one's mental state, "the inspiration of the adept and the response of the Buddha are then merged: it is like the moon that appears when the water is purified or the images reflected when a mirror is polished."[154]

The importance of developing appropriate meditative qualities even in Pure Land practice is made quite explicit in Chinul's own outline of recollection of the Buddha's name given in his *Essential Approaches to Recollecting the Buddha (Yŏmbul yomun).*[155] In this scheme, which is heavily indebted to the Pure Land interpretations of Ch'eng-kuan and Tsung-mi,[156] Chinul outlines ten stages of that recollection, from recollection performed while restraining the defiling tendencies of one's body, speech, and mind, through recollection maintained during all of one's daily activities. The process culminates in recollection of the Buddha in a state of no-thought, during which time the recollection is involuntarily sustained during all conscious moments. Once this mode of recollection is perfected, the adept then passes to the final stage, the recollection of the Buddha in suchness, wherein the practitioner understands the one true Dharmadhātu.[157] Although Chinul obviously intended this practice of recollection for the lay cultivator who still must continue with everyday activities, his interpretation of that practice brings it explicitly into line with his own interpretation of meditation practice in general. Hence, although Chinul might accept that there are relative degrees of sophistication in the particular methods of Buddhist meditation practice, he insists that they all must develop according to general criteria and, if cultivated correctly, will ultimately culminate in identical experiences.

X. Chinul's Synthesis of The Meditative Techniques of Sŏn and *Kyo*

From Chinul's analysis, it should now be clear that, despite the unique propensities of Sŏn and *kyo,* he does not consider their fundamental attitudes, goals, and practices to be ultimately opposed. Indeed, Chinul states repeatedly that the adherent of either school who practices sincerely and diligently can be assured of enlightenment:

> Thus we know that, whether Sŏn adepts or scholastics, all men past or present whose contemplation practice is satisfactory have penetrated to their own minds, where false thoughts and mental disturbances never originate. In the functioning of their noumenal wisdom and phenomenal wisdom there is never an interruption, and they realize the Dharmadhātu. . . . Consequently, we know the teachings are established according to the differences in individual capacities; in their broad details the teachings might differ slightly, but their source is one. . . . The thousands of different ways of explaining the holy teachings are adaptations made according to people's faculties and none of them fails to point the way to return to the Dharmadhātu of your own mind.[158]

His focus on introspection provides Chinul with a practical tool for effecting his vision of the unity of Sŏn and *kyo*. By advocating doctrinal reconciliation rather than simply another conceptual position from which to deal with the problem, Chinul effectively raises the conflict to an entirely different level. Theological descriptions intended to provide consistent theoretical interpretations of truth are inherently incapable of expressing an all-embracing position that could accommodate all viewpoints. The restrictions implicit in doctrinal perspectives, and the grasping at those teachings that ignorance and craving engender, inevitably involve the proponent in contention instead of leading him to realization. As Chinul remarks, "When those of lesser faculties grasp at words, everything becomes different. When those who are accomplished understand properly, everything becomes the same."[159] Hence, one of the primary results of speculative views is that they involve the advocate in conflict with people of differing beliefs.[160] Chinul, affirming this, says that even if one were to debate all day long, it would only increase pride and a sense of competitiveness, until the person would end up passing his whole life in vain. Hence, the mind that revels in argumentativeness must be conquered forever.[161]

Only by abandoning the conceptualization inherent in the scholastic teachings can one bring introspection into play:

> If you can suddenly forget the differences in the theoretical interpretation of the established verbal teachings and, while sitting quietly in a private room, empty your heart and cleanse your thoughts, trace back the radiance of your own mind, and return to its source, . . . the myriad images [will] then appear together.[162]

This type of reflection turns the mind, which is usually propelled outward into the sense-spheres, back in upon itself, until its fundamental source is seen. Accordingly, Chinul proposed a new criterion for the assessment of doctrinal points, one that demanded direct experiential confirmation rather than mere intellectual speculation. Finally, it was direct, personal realization of the unitary mind-essence through introspection that effected a true syncretic vision.

In Chinul's systematization of meditation practice as well, a combination of the theoretical and practical stances characterizing these two branches of Buddhism are considered to provide the most effective means of promoting spiritual development in the majority of practitioners.[163] In this formulation, both Sŏn and Hwaŏm meditation are completely synthesized into a single, unified system, as is readily apparent in the unusual fusion of Sŏn and Hwaŏm techniques found in Chinul's *Excerpts from the Dharma Collection and Special Practice Record with Personal Notes.*[164] Citing the explanations on the four Dharmadhātus given in the *Hua-yen chin-kuan* ("Embroidered Cap of the *Avataṁsaka*"), a lost work by Ch'uan-ao ta-shih (d.u.),[165] a disciple of

Tsung-mi, Chinul notes that these different Dharmadhātus, which are the subjects of separate contemplations in standard Hwaŏm practice, are in reality only the one true Dharmadhātu *(ilchin pŏpkye)*. Although the four Dharmadhātus might be valuable heuristically for explaining the attributes and functions of the mind, Chinul feels that meditation will come to naught if a person attempts to perform each of the four contemplations independently, as he explained in his *Excerpts from the Exposition of the New [Translation of the] Avataṁsaka Sūtra.*[166] In fact, says Chinul, the "capital" *(tu)* of this one true Dharmadhātu is the mind of each and every sentient being. One who wishes to rediscover this "capital" need only trace the radiance emanating from the mind back to the numinous awareness, its very source, until conceptualization is finally exhausted; then that Dharmadhātu will appear in all its fullness. This synthesis of formal Sŏn and Hwaŏm practices is thus considered to consummate both Hwaŏm Dharmadhātu meditation and the contemplative techniques of Sŏn.

Notes

1. For further discussion on this point, see Robert E. Buswell, Jr., *The Korean Approach to Zen: The Collected Works of Chinul* (Honolulu: University of Hawaii Press, 1983; hereafter abbreviated as *KAZ*), Introduction, pp. 1–2; idem, "The Biographies of the Korean Monk Wŏnhyo (617–686): A Study in Buddhist Hagiography," in John C. Jamieson and Peter H. Lee, eds., *Biography as a Genre in Korean History* (Berkeley: Institute of East Asian Studies, forthcoming).

2. This early conflict between Sŏn and *kyo* in Korea and Ŭich'ŏn's attempts to combine the two sects are summarized in *KAZ*, Introduction, pp. 12–17.

3. The successorship of the Sagul-san School is discussed in *KAZ*, pp. 82–83, n. 104. For an outline of the Korean ecclesiastical examination system as well as extensive references to relevant secondary studies, see *KAZ*, Introduction, pp. 80–81, n. 88.

4. *Sŭngp'yŏng-bu Chogye-san Susŏn-sa Puril Pojo kuksa pimyŏng* in Yi Nŭnghwa, *Chosŏn Pulgyo t'ongsa* (1918; repr., Seoul: Poryŏn'gak, 1976; hereafter cited as *Pojo pimyŏng*), p. 377.12. Chinul's lack of a legitimate transmission from a recognized master as well as the fact that he did not leave the customary enlightenment poem are often mentioned by present-day Sŏn masters, who raise doubts about the validity of Chinul's approach to Sŏn practice. (In Chinul's defense, however, it should be noted that such a poem might well have been included in his *Pŏbŏ kasong* ["Dharma Talks, Gāthās, and Verses"], which is no longer extant.) For this reason some Koreans consider T'aego Pou (1301–1382), whose Imje (Ch. Lin-chi) credentials are impeccable, to be the ancestor of the Korean Sŏn lineage. However, a careful reading of the works of such important later teachers as Taegak Hyesim, T'aego Pou, Naong, and Sŏsan Hyujŏng (1520–1604) shows clearly that Korean Sŏn thought—in particular, sudden awakening/gradual cultivation ideology and *hwadu* meditation—finds its source in Chinul.

For a discussion of the problems involved in ascertaining the lineage of the Korean Chogye School, see the study by Sŏk Sŏngch'ŏl, *Han'guk pulgyo ŭi pŏmmaek* (Kyŏngsang namdo, Korea: Haein ch'ongnim, 1975), which displays the author's wide knowledge of scriptural and epigraphical materials; see also Chang Wŏn'gyu, "Chogye chong ŭi sŏngnip kwa palchŏn e taehan koch'al," *Pulgyo hakpo*, vol. 1 (1963), pp. 311–351; Yi Chong'ik, *Chogye chonghak kaeron* (Seoul: Tongguk University, 1973); Yi Chi'gwan, *Chogye chong sa* (Seoul: Tongguk University, 1976); Ko Hyŏnggon, *Haedong Chogye-chong ŭi yŏnwŏn mit kŭ choryu: Chinul kwa Hyesim ŭi sasang ŭi chungsim ŭro* (Seoul: Tongguk University, Tongguk yŏkkyŏng wŏn, 1970), pp. 6–11; and other references in Yi Kibaek, *Han'guk-sa sillon* (Seoul: Ilcho'gak, 1967), pp. 179–180.

5. For Chinul's three enlightenment experiences see *Pojo pimyŏng*, pp. 377–338; *KAZ*, pp. 21–28 and summary on pp. 28–29.

6. This is the last line of a stanza summing up Ch'an practice that is traditionally attributed to Bodhidharma; the passage has been traced to *Ta pan-nieh-p'an ching chi-chieh* ("A Collection of Commentaries to the *Mahāparinirvāṇa-sūtra*"), *T*37.490c26. See discussion in Isshū Miura and Ruth Fuller Sasaki, *Zen Dust: The History of the Koan and Koan Study in Rinzai (Linchi) Zen* (New York: Harcourt Brace and Jovanovich, 1966), pp. 228–230.

7. Kim Chi'gyŏn, ed., *Hwaŏmnon chŏryo* (Tokyo: Seifū gakuen, 1968), pp. 1–3; the passage is quoted in *KAZ*, pp. 24–25.

8. *Ta-fang-kuang fo hua-yen ching*, *T*10.272c23–25 and 272c7–17. "Ju-lai hsing-ch'i p'in" is an abbreviation for "Pao-wang ju-lai hsing-ch'i p'in," the thirty-second chapter of Buddhabhadra's sixty-fascicle translation of the *Avataṃsaka Sūtra*, and is equivalent to the "Ju-lai ch'u-hsien p'in" of Śikṣānanda's later translation. The "Hsing-ch'i p'in" circulated independently before being incorporated into the *Avataṃsaka* compilation and was known as the *Tathāgatotpattisambhavanirdeśa*; it was translated into Chinese by Dharmarakṣa in 292 as the *Ju-lai hsing-hsien ching* (*T*#291). For a discussion of the text and its important implications for the development of *tathāgatagarbha* theory, see Takasaki Jikidō, *A Study on the Ratnagotravibhāga (Uttaratantra): Being a Treatise on the Tathāgatagarbha Theory of Mahāyāna Buddhism, Serie Orientale Roma*, vol. 33 (Rome: Istituto Italiano per il medio ed estremo oriente, 1966), p. 35 ff.; Takasaki Jikidō, "Kegon kyōgaku to nyoraizō shisō," in Nakamura Hajime and Kawada Kumatarō, eds., *Kegon shisō* (Kyoto: Hōzōkan, 1968), pp. 275–322; see also discussion in Kim Ingsok, *Hwaŏm-hak kaeron* (Seoul: Pŏmnyunsa, 1974), pp. 214–215, where he demonstrates that Fa-tsang also knew that this chapter was originally an independent sūtra.

9. *Hsin Hua-yen ching lun*, *T*36.815a3–8; 819a29–b.2; 862a7–8.

10. *Hwaŏmnon chŏryo*, p. 3. Chinul is here alluding to a statement in Tsung-mi's *Ch'an-yüan chu-ch'üan-chi tu-hsü* (*T*48.400b10–11): "The sūtras are the Buddha's words. Ch'an is the Buddha's mind."

11. *Hwaŏmnon chŏryo*, p. 3.

12. See Pak Chonghong, *Han'guk sasang sa: Pulgyo sasang p'yŏn, Sŏmun mun'go*, no. 11 (Seoul: Sŏmun mun'go, 1972), p. 193; Yi Chong'ik, *Taehan pulgyo Chogye chong chunghung non* (Seoul: Poryŏn'gak, 1976); *KAZ*, pp. 89–90, n. 178.

13. I use the *dvandva*-compound *śraddhādhimukti* for *sinhae* (Ch. *hsin-chieh*), rather than the more common Sanskrit equivalent *adhimukti*, because it helps to clarify that, in the interpretation of Li T'ung-hsüan and Chinul,

this quality of mind leads to the "understanding-awakening" through "faith" in one's fundamental Buddhahood. This *dvandva* is attested to in Vasubandhu's *Abhidharmakośabāṣyam,* edited by Prahlad Pradhan (Patna, India: K. P. Jayaswal Research Institute, 1967), pp. 372.12, 373, 380.9.

14. *Pojo pimyŏng,* p. 339.4–5.
15. Noted by Yi Chong'ik, *Chogye chong,* p. 89.
16. The last few years have seen the burgeoning of a secondary literature on Tsung-mi. The most comprehensive discussion of his thought is found in Kamata Shigeo, *Shūmitsu kyōgaku no shisōshi teki kenkyū* (Tokyo: Tokyo University Press, 1975); Tsung-mi's important role in the development of Korean and Japanese Buddhism has been covered in Kamata Shigeo, "Chōsen oyobi Nihon bukkyō ni oyoboshita Shūmitsu no eikyō," *Komazawa daigaku bukkyōgakubu ronshu,* vol. 7 (1976), pp. 28–37. Yoshizu Yoshihide offers an insightful treatment of Tsung-mi in his reappraisal of the Hua-yen tradition in *Kegonzen no shisōshi teki kenkyū* (Tokyo: Daitō shuppansha, 1985). Jan Yün-hua has contributed a useful series of articles on various aspects of Tsung-mi's life and thought; see "Tsung-mi: His Analysis of Ch'an Buddhism," *T'oung Pao,* vol. 58 (1972), pp. 1–54; "Conflict and Harmony in Ch'an and Buddhism," *Journal of Chinese Philosophy,* vol. 4 (1977), pp. 287–302; "*K'an-Hui* or the 'Comparative Investigation': The Key Concept in Tsung-mi's Thought," in Chai Shin Yu, ed., *Korean and Asian Religious Tradition* (Toronto: Korea and Related Studies Press, 1977), pp. 12–24; "Antagonism Among the Religious Sects and the Problem of Buddhist Tolerance," *International Buddhist Forum Quarterly,* nos. 1–4 (1979), pp. 62–69; "Tsung-mi's Questions Regarding the Confucian Absolute," *Philosophy East and West,* vol. 30 (1980), pp. 495–504; "Two Problems Concerning Tsung-mi's Compilation of *Ch'an-tsang,*" *Transactions of the International Conference of Orientalists in Japan,* vol. 19 (1974), pp. 37–47; "Tsung-mi chu *Tao-su ch'ou-ta wen-chi* te yen-chiu," *Hua-kang fo-hsüeh hsüeh-pao,* vol. 4 (1980), pp. 132–166. For an adequate general survey of Tsung-mi's philosophy, see Li Shih-chien, "Tsung-mi ssu-hsiang te t'e-chih," in Chang Man-t'ao, ed., *Hua-yen-hsüeh kai-lun, Hsien-tai fo-chiao hsüeh-shu ts'ung-k'an,* vol. 32 (Taipei: Ta-sheng wen-hua ch'u- pan-she, 1978), pp. 359–371. Peter N. Gregory has paid special attention to the important role of Tsung-mi's hermeneutics in the development of the mature Chinese scholastic tradition; see "Tsung-mi's *Inquiry into the Origin of Man:* A Study of Chinese Buddhist Hermeneutics" (Ph.D. dissertation, Harvard University, 1981); "The Teaching of Men and Gods: The Doctrinal and Social Basis of Lay Buddhist Practice in the Hua-yen Traditon" in Robert M. Gimello and Peter N. Gregory, eds., *Studies in Ch'an and Hua-yen* (Honolulu: University of Hawaii Press, 1983), pp. 253–319; "Sudden Enlightenment Followed by Gradual Cultivation: Tsung-mi's Analysis of Mind" in Robert M. Gimello and Peter N. Gregory, eds., *The Sudden/ Gradual Polarity in Chinese Thought* (Honolulu: University of Hawaii Press, forthcoming); "The Place of the Sudden Teaching Within the Hua-Yen Tradition: An Investigation of the Process of Doctrinal Change," *Journal of the International Association of Buddhist Studies,* vol. 6 (1983), pp. 31–60; "Chinese Buddhist Hermeneutics: The Case of Hua-yen," *Journal of the American Academy of Religion,* vol. 51 (1983), pp. 231–249; "Tsung-mi and the Single Word 'Awareness' *(Chih),*" *Philosophy East and West,* vol. 35 (1985), pp. 249–269; "What Happened to the Perfect Teaching? Another Look at Hua-yen Buddhist Hermeneutics" in Donald S. Lopez, Jr., ed.,

Buddhist Hermeneutics (Honolulu: University of Hawaii Press, forthcoming). Tsung-mi's *Ch'an-yüan chu-ch'üan-chi tu-hsü,* so important in the Korean Buddhist doctrinal scheme, has been translated in Jeffrey L. Broughton, "Kuei-feng Tsung-mi: The Convergence of Ch'an and the Teachings" (Ph.D. dissertation, Columbia University, 1975). Valuable insights on Tsung-mi's syncretic attitudes can also be found in Takamine Ryōshū, *Kegon to Zen to no tsūro* (Nara: Nanto bukkyō kenkyūkai, 1956), pp. 22–35; Huan-sheng, "Tsung-mi Chiao-Ch'an i-chi ssu-hsiang chih hsing-ch'eng," in Chang Man-t'ao, ed., *Hua-yen-hsüeh kai-lun,* pp. 305–358. I have attempted to determine the relationship between Tsung-mi's *Chung-hua ch'uan-hsin-ti Ch'an-men shih-tzu ch'eng-hsi t'u* ("Chart of the Successorship in the Chinese Ch'an School That Transmits the Mind-ground") and his *Pŏpchip pyŏrhaeng-nok* ("Dharma Collection and Special Practice Record") in my article "The Identity of the *Pŏpchip pyŏrhaeng-nok* (Dharma Collection and Special Practice Record)," *Korean Studies* (Michael Rogers Festschrift), vol. 6 (1982), pp. 1–16; see also *KAZ,* pp. 375–384.

17. Tsung-mi's descriptions of sudden awakening/gradual cultivation are quoted extensively in *KAZ,* passim; the theoretical issues have been treated in Peter Gregory, "Sudden Enlightenment Followed by Gradual Cultivation: Tsung-mi's Analysis of Mind." For the treatment by Yung-ming Yen-shou (904–975), see *Wan-shan t'ung-kuei chi,* T48.987b–c (quoted in *KAZ,* pp. 304–305).

18. These two important concepts are discussed at length by Chinul in *KAZ,* pp. 312, 334. For Tsung-mi's description, see *Chung-hua ch'uan-hsin ti Ch'an-men shih-tzu ch'eng-hsi t'u,* ZZ2/15/5.436c10–14. Yŏndam Yuil's descriptions appear in *Pŏpchip pyŏrhaeng nok chŏryo kwamok pyŏngip sagi* (Taehŭng-sa xylograph, dated 1916, in the Tongguk University archives; hereafter *CYKM*), fol. 1a4–5, and in his *Sŏnwŏn chip tosŏ so,* reprinted in Kamata, *Shūmitsu,* p. 277.

The distinction between *jen* and *fa* is one of the four refuges *(pratisāraṇa)* of the bodhisattva: "One should take refuge in the Dharma, not in the person [who teaches it]" *(dharmapratisāraṇena bhavitavyam na pudgala-pratisāraṇena);* see *Wei-mo-chieh so-shuo ching (Vimalakīrtinirdeśa-sūtra),* T14.556c10, interpreted by Thurman as "relying on reality and not insisting on opinions derived from personal authorities" (Robert A. F. Thurman, trans., *The Holy Teaching of Vimalakīrti: A Mahāyāna Scripture* [University Park: Pennsylvania State University Press, 1976], p. 99); *P'u-sa shan-chieh ching (Bodhisattvabhūmi),* T30.994b22; and *I-chiao ching lun* ("Commentary to the *Bequeathed Teachings [of the Buddha] Scripture*"), T26.283b26–29; *Ta-chih-tu-lun,* T25.125a629. The doctrine resonates with the *Abhidharmakośabhāṣya*'s distinction between the interpretation of *pratītyasamutpāda* as "associated with the person" *(sattvākhya),* corresponding to our soteriological aspect *(jen),* and "not associated with the person" *(asattvākhya),* equivalent to our ontological aspect *(fa);* P. Pradhan, ed., *Abhidharmakośabhāṣyam,* p. 133.17. Note also the *Ratnagotravibhāga* distinction of the *adhigamadharma* ("the doctrine as realization") into "that which is realized" (i.e., the truth of extinction, corresponding to *fa*), and "that by which realized" (i.e., the truth of the path, corresponding to *jen*); see Takasaki, *A Study on the Ratnagotravibhāga,* p. 182.

19. *KAZ,* p. 334.
20. *KAZ,* p. 264.
21. *KAZ,* pp. 278–311.

22. *KAZ*, pp. 143–154.
23. *KAZ*, p. 300.
24. *KAZ*, p. 333.
25. *KAZ*, p. 147.
26. *KAZ*, p. 266 and passim.
27. *KAZ*, p. 148.
28. *KAZ*, p. 145.
29. *KAZ*, pp. 295, 304, 330.
30. *KAZ*, p. 300.
31. *KAZ*, p. 299, following Yen-shou.
32. *KAZ*, p. 143.
33. The theory of sudden awakening/sudden cultivation is covered in more detail in *KAZ*, Introduction, pp. 59–60.
34. For Tsung-mi's treatment of the realization-awakening, see *KAZ*, pp. 353, n. 113.
35. *Liu-tsu t'an ching* (*T*48.353b4–5) for the relevant passage.
36. *KAZ*, pp. 102–124; 150–155. For general discussion on this need to balance samādhi and prajñā, see also Guy Bugault, *La notion de "Prajñā" ou de sapience selons les perspectives du "Mahāyāna": Part de la connaissance et l'inconnaissance dans l'analogie Bouddhique, Publications de l'Institut de Civilisation Indienne,* vol. 32 (Paris: Editions E. de Boccard, 1968), pp. 89–93.
37. See, for example, the parallel discussion on the use of *samatha* (calmness) and *vipassanā* (insight) in E. Muller, ed., *Atthasālinī* (London: Pali Text Society, 1897), i.131: "And here they are given as forming a well-yoked pair *(yuganaddha)*" (Pe Maung Tin, trans., *The Expositor* [*Atthasālinī*] [London: Pali Text Society, 1958], vol. 1, p. 173).
38. See Pralhad Pradhan, ed., *Abhidharmasamuccaya of Asaṅga, Visva-Bharati Studies,* no. 12 (Santiniketan: Visva-Bharati, 1950), p. 75.
39. These teachers are being studied by Shotaro Iida. Fa-lang was a disciple of Seng-ch'üan (fl. ca. 512), who was himself one of the ten main disciples of the Koguryŏ monk Sŭngnang (fl. ca. 494), who played an important role in the development of the early San-lun School; see Pak Chonghong, *Han'guk sasang-sa,* pp. 38–41.
40. For the correlations between samādhi and dhyāna see *Visuddhimagga,* iii.5; Ñāṇamoli, trans., *Path of Purification* (Kandy, Sri Lanka: Buddhist Publication Society, 1979), pp. 85–90.
41. *Ch'an-yüan chu-ch'üan-chi tu-hsü, T*48.399a.
42. *KAZ*, pp. 104–105.
43. See, for example, excerpts in Hu Shih, ed., *Shen-hui ho-shang i-chi* (rev. ed., Taipei: Hu Shih chi-nien kuan, 1970), pp. 128–9; partially translated in Philip Yampolsky, *The Platform Sutra of the Sixth Patriarch* (New York, Columbia University Press, 1967), p. 33.
44. For the metaphor of prajñā as radiance, see *Chao-lun,* translated by Walter Liebenthal, *Chao Lun: The Treatises of Seng-chao* (1948; repr., Hong Kong: Chinese University of Hong Kong, 1968), pp. 64–80, 66 and n. 259, 79 and n. 333, 97 and n. 455. Paul Demiéville, "Le miroir spirituel," *Sinologica,* vol. 7 (1927) (noted in Liebenthal, *Chao lun,* p. 26, n. 105) says specifically, "Dans le Bouddhisme chinois, *tchao* désigne techniquement la fonction de la gnose, *prajñā.*" See also Alex Wayman, "The Mirror-like Knowledge in Mahāyāna Buddhist Literature," *Asiatische Studien,* vol. 25 (1971), pp. 353–363; idem., "The Mirror as a Pan-Buddhist Metaphor-Simile," *History of Religions,* vol. 13 (1974), pp. 264–265.

45. *KAZ*, p. 153.
46. *KAZ*, p. 151.
47. *KAZ*, p. 111.
48. The *Avataṃsaka Sūtra* was translated by Śikṣānanda in Lo-yang, under the auspices of empress Wu Chao (r. 684–704); translation was begun in 695, third month, fourteenth day (2 April 695), and completed in the second year of Sheng-li, tenth month, eighth day (5 November 699); *K'ai-yüan shih-chiao lu*, *T*55.565c15, cited in Lewis Lancaster and Sung-bae Park, *The Korean Buddhist Canon: A Descriptive Catalogue* (Berkeley: University of California Press, 1979), p. 44.
49. *Pojo pimyŏng*, p. 338.3–4. See also Chinul's own description of his experience in the preface to his *Hwaŏmnon chŏryo*, pp. 1–3; translated in *KAZ*, pp. 24–26.
50. For a valuable survey of Li T'ung-hsüan's influence in East Asian Buddhism, see Robert M. Gimello, "Li T'ung-hsüan and the Practical Dimensions of Hua-yen," in Robert M. Gimello and Peter N. Gregory, eds., *Studies in Ch'an and Hua-yen* (Honolulu: University of Hawaii Press, 1983), pp. 321–389.

    Despite Li T'ung-hsüan's importance in the history of post-T'ang Buddhism throughout East Asia, he has been surprisingly neglected by modern scholarship. For short exegeses of his life and thought, see Kim Ingsok, *Hwaŏm-hak kaeron* (Seoul: Pŏmnyunsa, 1974), pp. 131–146; Takamine Ryōshū, *Kegon ronshū* (Tokyo: Kokusho kankōkai, 1976), pp. 403–426; idem, *Kegon shisōshi* (Kyoto: Kōkyo shoin, 1942), pp. 200–208; idem, "Ri Tsūgen no shisō to Zen," *Ryūkoku daigaku ronshū*, no. 346 (1953), pp. 1–21 (reprinted in idem, *Kegon to Zen to no tsūro*, pp. 131–146), which is the best treatment of his significance for the later development of Ch'an thought; Chang Wŏn'gyu, "Hwaŏm kyohak wansŏnggi ŭi sasang yŏn'gu," *Pulgyo hakpo*, vol. 11 (1974), pp. 41–43; Yi Chong'ik, "Chinul ui Hwaŏm sasang," in Sungsan Pak Kilchin paksa hwagap kinyom saŏp hoe, eds., *Han'guk Pulgyo sasang sa: Sungsan Pak Kilchin paksa hwagap kinyŏm sa* (Iri, Korea: Wŏn Pulgyo sasang yŏn'gu wŏn, 1975), pp. 528–532, for his importance in Chinul's thought. I have discussed Li's interpretation of Hua-yen and his influence on Chinul in *KAZ*, Introduction, pp. 50–55, and 199–237 passim.
51. This is not to imply that patriarchal Hua-yen never used meditative techniques; rather, as Robert M. Gimello has pointed out (in his "Early Hua-yen, Meditation, and Early Ch'an: Some Preliminary Considerations," in Whalen W. Lai and Lewis R. Lancaster, eds., *Early Ch'an in China and Tibet* [Berkeley: Asian Humanities Press, 1983] p. 152), the problem instead involves in exactly what sense meditation was practiced in early Hua-yen. While there is some validity to Gimello's contention that early Hua-yen doctrine might be considered a type of "meditative concept" (p. 156), by Chinul's time the point is moot, and whatever meditation might have been practiced in previous times had for all intents and purposes vanished. Given this development, the view of later Ch'an polemicists that Hua-yen is divorced from practice is not overly exaggerated. For accounts of the development and practice of Hua-yen meditation, see Unno Taitetsu, "The Dimensions of Practice in Hua-yen Thought," in *Bukkyō shisōshi ronshū: Yūki kyōju shōju ki'nen* (Tokyo: Daizō shuppansha, 1964), pp. 51–78; and Kobayashi Jitsugen, "Kegonshū kangyō no tenkai ni tsuite," *IBK*, vol. 15 (1967), pp. 653–655.

52. Kim Ingsŏk, *Hwaŏm-hak kaeron*, p. 133.

53. See discussion in Yi Chong'ik, "Chinul ŭi Hwaŏm sasang," in *Pak Kilchin Festschrift*, pp. 518–519.

54. *Hsin Hua-yen ching lun*, T36.761b.13 ff.; *Hwaŏmnon chŏryo*, p. 210.

55. See *Hsin Hua-yen ching lun*, T36.809b; cited in *KAZ*, pp. 222, 280; cf. *KAZ*, p. 219, for Tsung-mi's parallel view.

56. For the theory of nature-origination, see especially Kamata Shigeo, "Shōki shisō no seiritsu," *IBK*, vol. 5 (1957), pp. 195–198; Sakamoto Yukio, "Shōki shisō to aku ni tsuite," *IBK*, vol. 5 (1957), pp. 469–477; Endō Kōjirō, "Kegon shōki ronkō," *IBK*, vol. 14 (1965), pp. 214–216 and vol. 15 (1966), pp. 523–528. For general discussions, see Kim Ingsok, *Hwaŏm-hak kaeron*, pp. 230–239 and Whalen Lai, "Chinese Buddhist Causation Theories: An Analysis of the Sinitic Mahāyāna Understanding of *Pratītya-samutpāda*," *Philosophy East and West*, vol. 27 (1977), pp. 249–259.

57. *KAZ*, p. 206.

58. *KAZ*, pp. 205–6.

59. *KAZ*, p. 233, n. 32, citing Li.

60. See *KAZ*, p. 203.

61. The "ordinary man of great aspiration" *(taesim pŏmbu)* is defined by Li (*Hsin Hua-yen ching lun*, T36.756c) as a person who "seeks only the inscrutable vehicle of the Tathāgatas" and is unsatisfied with only the provisional teachings of the three vehicles. This refers specifically to a person who has achieved the initial understanding-awakening and is engaged in the gradual practices that will eventually lead to the realization-awakening. See *KAZ*, pp. 117, 209, 212, 218–219. Note also Chinul's comment (*KAZ*, p. 299) that "the approach of sudden awakening/gradual cultivation . . . has been established specifically for ordinary men of great aspiration."

62. *KAZ*, pp. 203, 207.

63. *KAZ*, p. 102.

64. *Hsin Hua-yen ching lun*, T36.941b; quoted in *KAZ*, p. 204.

65. *KAZ*, p. 219.

66. *KAZ*, p. 219. Note the passage from the "Fan-hsing p'in" (Brahmacaryā chapter) of the *Avataṁsaka Sūtra* that "at the initial moment of the activation of the bodhicitta, full enlightenment is attained." See *Ta-fang-kuang fo hua-yen ching*, T9.449c14; *Ta-fang-kuang fo hua-yen ching*, T10.89a1–2.

67. *Hwaŏmnon chŏryo*, p. 451.

68. *KAZ*, p. 116-7.

69. For references to "tracing back the radiance," see *KAZ*, Index, s.v. For comparable uses of *panjo*, see Liebenthal, trans., *Treatises of Seng-chao*, p. 71 and n. 289; *Lin-chi lu*, T47.497c19, which Ruth Fuller Sasaki has translated as "turning your own light inward upon yourselves" (*The Recorded Sayings of Ch'an Master Lin-chi Hui-chao of Chen Prefecture* [Kyoto: The Institute for Zen Studies, 1975], p. 10); *Hsin-hsin ming*, T48.376c2; Po-chang Huai-hai (720–814), in *Chodang chip*, in Hyosŏng Cho Myŏnggi paksa hwagap kinyŏm kanhaeng wiwŏnhoe, eds., *Pulgyo sahak nonch'ong: Hyosŏng Cho Myŏnggi paksa hwagap kinyŏm* (Seoul: Hyosŏng Cho Myŏnggi paksa hwagap kinyŏm kanhaeng wiwŏnhoe, 1965), Appendix, fasc. 14, p. 92b; *Ch'an-yüan chu-ch'üan-chi tu-hsü*, T48.411c5, 17; *Ta-hui yü-lu*, T47.922c. The term ultimately can be traced to religious Taoist origins; cf. the use of the term *fan-kuang* which Schipper translates as "retourner la lumière (vers l'intérieur);" Kristofer Marinus Schipper, *L'Empereur Wou des Han dans la légende Taoiste: Han Wou-ti nei-tchouan*

(Paris: École française d'extrême-orient, 1965), p. 48, n. 1. Schipper notes that "les yeux étant considérés comme des sources de lumière, des luminaires, qui éclairent le monde et nous permettent ainsi de voir." Cf. also the usage in Bhāvaviveka, *Ta-sheng chang-chen lun* (*Karatalaratna;* "Jewel in Hand Treatise"), *T*30.277c20.

70. For this quotation see *CYKM,* fol. 27b9–10.
71. *Anguttara-nikāya,* 1.10 *("pabhassaraṃ idaṃ bhikkhave cittaṃ, tañca kho āgantukehi upakkilesehi upakkiliṭṭhaṃ");* see F. L. Woodward, trans., *The Book of the Gradual Sayings* (1932; London: Pali Text Society, 1979), vol. 1, p. 8; this passage is treated with considerable perspicacity by Ñāṇananda Bhikkhu, *Concept and Reality in Early Buddhist Thought: An Essay on "Papañca" and "Papañca-Saññā-Saṅkhā"* (Kandy, Sri Lanka: Buddhist Publication Society, 1971), p. 58; the implications of the mind's inherent luminosity in spiritual cultivation are brought out in a fascinating discussion by Ñāṇananda Bhikkhu, *The Magic of the Mind: An Exposition of the Kalākārāma Sutta* (Kandy, Sri Lanka: Buddhist Publication Society, 1974), p. 83 ff.
72. See *KAZ,* p. 341, n. 7, where I trace the term from *Shou-leng-yen ching (Śūraṅgama-sūtra)* (*T*19.103a29–b1) to Ch'eng-kuan, Tsung-mi, and finally into Ch'an materials.
73. *Lin-chi lu, T*47.497c19; translated in Sasaki, *Recorded Sayings of Rinzai,* p. 26.
74. Cf. Ñāṇananda, *Concept and Reality,* pp. 46–68, on the non-manifestative consciousness *(viññāṇaṃ anidassanaṃ)* of the enlightened person.
75. For valuable comparative discussion, see Ñāṇananda, *Concept and Reality,* pp. 2–22, and *Magic of the Mind,* pp. 57–67.
76. *KAZ,* p. 147.
77. *KAZ,* p. 332.
78. *KAZ,* p. 145.
79. Further discussion on the meaning of "awareness" is found in *KAZ,* p. 343, n. 20; see also Peter N. Gregory, "Tsung-mi and the Single Word 'Awareness' *(Chih)."*
80. *KAZ,* p. 312: "The mind of numinous awareness is exactly the self-nature of suchness; it is neither the discriminative consciousness which arises in relation to objects in the conditioned realm nor the wisdom produced by the realization-wisdom."
81. See discussion in *KAZ,* p. 343, n. 20.
82. *KAZ,* p. 334.
83. *KAZ,* p. 207.
84. *KAZ,* p. 218.
85. *KAZ,* p. 144.
86. *KAZ,* p. 334.
87. For the historical background of the development of *kung-an* practice in Ch'an Buddhism, see Isshū Miura and Ruth Fuller Sasaki, *The Zen Koan: Its History and Uses in Rinzai Zen* (New York: Harcourt Brace and Javanovich, 1965), pp. 3–16; reprinted in idem, *Zen Dust: The History of the Koan and Koan Study in Rinzai (Lin-chi) Zen,* pp. 3–16.
88. See *Shan-fang ye-hua* ("Evening Talks in a Mountain Room") by Chung-feng Ming-pen (1263–1323), in his *T'ien-mu Chung-feng ho-shang kwang-lu* ("The Expanded Records of Master Chung-feng of T'ien-mu Mountain") (repr. ed., Pulguk-sa, Korea: Pulguk-sa sŏnwŏn, 1977), fasc. 11a, fol. 54–55; this text has only been reprinted from the Shanghai *P'in-ch'ieh* edition

of the Tripiṭaka, published in 1911. See also Miura and Sasaki, *Zen Dust,* p. 6.

89. See, for example, *Lin-chi lu,* T47.506b8; *Ching-te ch'uan-teng lu,* T51.358c14; *Pi-yen lu,* case 2, T48.141c6, case 49, p. 184c14, and case 60, p. 192b5.

90. Its best-known occurrence is in *Wu-men kuan,* T48.292c.

91. *Leng-ch'ieh shih-tzu chi,* T85.1289b–1290a; the quotation appears at p. 1289c29. See the discussion in Ch'üan An, "Wu-tsu Hung-jen ch'an-shih," *Hsien-tai Fo-hsüeh,* no. 82 (1957), pp. 26–29. Cf. the chapter by Bernard Faure in this volume for a different interpretation of this phrase.

92. Yi Chong'ik (*Chogye chong,* p. 83) has speculated that Chinul probably contracted with Sung or Koryŏ traders to bring a copy of *Ta-hui yü-lu* from China during his stay at Ch'ŏngwŏn-sa, a temple located near the seaport of Naju in the southwest of the Korean peninsula (*KAZ,* p. 83, n. 110).

93. *Pojo pimyŏng,* p. 338.6–13.

94. The *Sŏnmun yŏmsong chip* was an anthology of 1125 *kongans* in thirty fascicles, compiled by Hyesim in 1226. Beginning with stories concerning Śākyamuni Buddha, the work includes sūtra extracts, cases involving the twenty-eight traditional Indian patriarchs and their six Chinese successors, and episodes from the lives of later Ch'an masters. To each case are appended interpretative verses by both Hyesim and other Ch'an and Sŏn teachers. The first edition of the text was burned by the Mongols, and the revised editions of 1244 and 1248 added 347 new cases, to make a total of 1472 *kongans.* For a brief description of the work and its different editions, see Tongguk taehakkyo pulgyo munhwa yŏn'guso, ed., *Han'guk pulgyo ch'ansul munhŏn ch'ongnok* (Seoul: Tongguk taehakkyo ch'ulp'anbu, 1976), pp. 123–124. For a discussion of "verses of critique (lit., 'fingering')" *(yŏmsong)* and other verse-explanations of Sŏn *kongans,* see Iriya Yoshitaka, Kajitani Sōnin, and Yanagida Seizan, trans., *Setchō jūko, Zen no goroku,* vol. 15 (Tokyo: Chikuma shobō, 1981), pp. 291–304.

There has as yet been no adequate treatment of Hyesim and his important role in the popularization of the *hwadu* technique in Koryŏ Buddhism. Perhaps the best study produced so far has appeared in Ko Hyŏnggon, *Haedong Chogye-chong ŭi yŏnwŏn mit kŭ choryu: Chinul kwa Hyesim ŭi sasang ŭi chungsim ŭro* (Seoul: Tongguk University, Tongguk yŏkkyŏng wŏn, 1970), pp. 60–84. For general studies of his life and thought, see Nukariya Kaiten, *Chosŏn Sŏn'gyo-sa,* Chŏng Ho'gyŏng, trans. (1930; trans., Seoul: Poryon'gak, 1978), pp. 292–305; Han Kidu, *Han'guk Pulgyo sasang* (Iri, Korea: Wŏn'gwang taehakkyo ch'ulp'an'guk, 1973), pp. 217–242. The *Chogye Chin'gak kuksa ŏrok* is published in Kim Talchin, trans., *Chinul, Hyesim, Kakhun, Han'guk ŭi sasang taejŏnjip,* vol. 2 (Seoul: Tonghwa ch'ulp'an kongsa, 1977), pp. 205–375; the Chinese text is included in pp. 461–499, but with many misprints. Hyesim's associations with Chinul are discussed, and some excerpts from his memorial stele are translated, in *KAZ,* pp. 30–32.

95. For T'aego Pou, Naong Hye'gŭn, and the latter-Koryŏ Sŏn tradition, see Nukariya Kaiten, *Chosŏn Sŏn'gyo-sa,* pp. 350–357, 360–384 (Naong); Takahashi Tōru, *Richō bukkyō* (1929; repr., Tokyo: Kokusho kankōkai, 1973), pp. 321–344; Han Kidu, "Koryŏ hogi ŭi Sŏn sasang," in *Pak Kilchin Festschrift,* pp. 598–613, 613–639; idem, *Han'guk Pulgyo sasang* (Iri, Korea: Wŏn'gwang taehakkyo ch'ulp'an'guk, 1973), pp. 243–272, 273–310; Yi Nŭnghwa, *Chosŏn Pulgyo t'ongsa,* vol. 3, pp. 500–514.

96. *KAZ*, p. 339.
97. See *KAZ*, pp. 238–239 for details.
98. *KAZ*, p. 246–247.
99. *KAZ*, p. 250.
100. *KAZ*, p. 296.
101. *KAZ*, p. 334; cf. p. 264.
102. *KAZ*, p. 338–340.
103. *Visuddhimagga*, xxiii.24, Ñāṇamoli, trans., *Path of Purification*, p. 826; and see discussion in Padmanabh S. Jaini, ed., *Abhidharmadīpa with Vibhāṣāprabhāvṛtti* (Patna, India: K. P. Jayaswal Research Institute, 1967), pp. 84.
104. *KAZ*, pp. 337–338. Ta-hui also comments: "Training on this path is not bothered by a lack of intelligence; it is bothered instead by excessive intelligence. It is not bothered by a lack of understanding; it is instead bothered by excessive understanding" (*Ta-hui yü-lu*, T47.935a23–24).
105. *KAZ*, pp. 244, 264.
106. *KAZ*, p. 334.
107. For these two types of investigation, see especially *KAZ*, pp. 249–253.
108. *KAZ*, p. 252.
109. *KAZ*, pp. 252–253. See also discussion in *KAZ*, pp. 260–261, nn. 54, 56.
110. See Chang, Chung-yüan, *The Original Teachings of Ch'an Buddhism* (New York: Pantheon, 1969), p. 271. The terms are also used by Ta-hui, from whom Chinul probably adopted them; see, for example, *Ta-hui yü-lu*, T47.870b and passim.
111. *KAZ*, p. 240.
112. *KAZ*, p. 264.
113. *KAZ*, p. 338; quoting *Ta-hui yü-lu*, T47.921c. See also the discussion in Hyujŏng (Sŏsan *taesa*), *Sŏn'ga ku'gam* ("Divining-Speculum on the Sŏn School"), *Chŏng'ŭm mun'go*, vol. 131, translated by Pŏpchŏng (Seoul: Chŏng'ŭmsa, 1976), p. 41; Yŏndam Yuil (1720–1799), *CYKM*, fol. 29a12–29b6.
114. *Chin'gak kuksa ŏrok*, p. 497 [Kor., p. 367]: " 'Why did Chao-chou reject the claim that all sentient beings had the Buddha-nature?' 'Because they all are subject to the activating-consciousness.' "
115. *Ta-sheng ch'i-hsin lun*, T32.577b; Yoshito S. Hakeda, trans., *The Awakening of Faith Attributed to Aśvaghosha* (New York: Columbia University Press, 1967), pp. 47–48.
116. See the comments by Yüan-wu K'o-ch'in (1063–1135), in *Pi-yen lu*, case 99, T48.222c18; translated by Thomas and J. C. Cleary, *The Blue Cliff Record*, vol. 3 (Boulder: Shambhala, 1977), pp. 628–635.
117. *P'abyong* is discussed at *KAZ*, p. 255, n. 12. For both of these types of expression, see *KAZ*, p. 241.
118. I have attempted to sort out some of the conflicting views of Tsung-mi and Chinul on these two types of awakening in *KAZ*, pp. 358–359, n. 143. See also *KAZ*, pp. 241–242: "Hence the first stage of abiding after the levels of faith are fulfilled is called the access to realization."
119. *KAZ*, p. 250.
120. *KAZ*, p. 336, quoting *Ta-hui yü-lu*, T47.891a.
121. *KAZ*, p. 336.
122. The term *p'a* is used at *KAZ*, p. 252.
123. Summarizing *KAZ*, p. 246.
124. *KAZ*, p. 252.

125. Sung-bae Park, *Buddhist Faith and Sudden Enlightenment* (Albany: State University of New York Press, 1983), p. 8; see also pp. 6–8, 73–77, 123–125.
126. *KAZ*, p. 253.
127. The "three mysterious gates" were methods of instruction first used by Lin-chi I-hsüan and subsequently adopted by Fa-yen Wen-i (885–958), Yün-men Wen-yen (?862–949), and Fen-yang Shan-chao (947–1024). See *Lin-chi lu*, *T*47.497a19–20; Sasaki, *Record of Rinzai*, p. 6; and Lin-chi's biographies in *Ching-te ch'uan-teng lu*, *T*51.291a14 and 300b24. For their use by Fen-yang Shan-chao, see *Ching-te ch'uan-teng lu*, *T*51.305a17, and *Hsü ch'uan-teng lu*, *T*51.469b20. For Fa-yen and Yün-men, see *KAZ*, p. 250.
128. See *KAZ*, p. 90, n. 182.
129. See Tsung-mi's accounts, translated in *KAZ*, pp. 90–91 nn. 183, 184, 185.
130. Summary of *KAZ*, pp. 214–215, 244–245.
131. *KAZ*, p. 246.
132. *KAZ*, p. 240, quoting Fen-yang Shan-chao, from *Fen-yang Wu-te ch'an-shih yü-lu*, *T*47.603b; see also *Jen-t'ien yen-mu*, *T*48.302b1–2.
133. *KAZ*, pp. 214, 240; the quote is from Li T'ung-hsüan (*Hsin Hua-yen ching lun*, *T*36.721a) but is often quoted by Ch'an masters.
134. *Ch'an-yüan chu-ch'üan-chi tu-hsü*, *T*48.400a; quoted in *KAZ*, pp. 251, 321–322.
135. *KAZ*, p. 251.
136. *KAZ*, p. 240.
137. *KAZ*, p. 338–339.
138. For this term, see *Pi-yen lu*, case 17, *T*48.157a16; translated by Thomas and J. C. Cleary, *The Blue Cliff Record*, vol. 1, p. 110.
139. See Ñāṇananda, *Concept and Reality*, passim; and for background on the Indian attitude toward conceptualization, see A. K. Warder, "The Concept of a Concept," *Journal of Indian Philosophy*, vol. 1 (1970/71), pp. 181–196.
140. The term "terse" *(saengnyak)* is used at *KAZ*, p. 251, and passim.
141. *KAZ*, p. 214.
142. See *KAZ*, pp. 214–215; pp. 244–245.
143. *KAZ*, p. 242; see also *Hsin Hua-yen ching lun*, *T*36.834b, quoted in *KAZ*, pp. 242, 250. The most accessible treatment of the Ch'an usage of the term appears in D. T. Suzuki, *The Zen Doctrine of No-mind* (London: George Allen and Unwin, 1958). For the distinct Indian background to the term, where no-thought *(acintya; acittaka)* almost always carries a negative connotation, see Edward Conze, *Buddhist Thought in India: Three Phases of Buddhist Philosophy* (1962; repr., Ann Arbor: University of Michigan Press, 1973), pp. 113–114. Virtually the only positive use of the term in Indian texts is when no-thought is taken to be an attribute of the attainment of the cessation of thought *(asaṃjñinirodhasamāpatti)*; see *Abhidharmako-śabhāṣya*, edited by P. Pradhan, p. 8; Buddhaghosa, *Visuddhimagga*, xxiii.18; Ñāṇamoli, trans., *Path of Purification*, p. 824.
144. See discussion in *KAZ*, pp. 241–250, where Chinul clarifies this for both the Sŏn and *kyo* schools.
145. *KAZ*, p. 250; cf. *KAZ*, p. 246: "At the moment of entering into realization, they slough off their former acquired understanding and, through absence of thought, come into conformity [with the Dharmadhātu]."
146. See discussion in *KAZ*, pp. 290–291.
147. *KAZ*, pp. 148–149, quoting *Ch'an-yüan chu-ch'üan chi tou-hsü*, p. 403a; and see *KAZ*, p. 266. This phrase is the hallmark of the Southern School of Ch'an and appears in the Tun-huang edition of the *Liu-tsu t'an ching*,

T48.338c15–16, translated in Yampolsky, *Platform Sutra,* p. 137; see pp. 137–138, n. 69, for references to secondary studies on no-thought.

148. This phrase is first used by Tung-shan Liang-chieh (807–869); see *Tung-shan yü-lu,* T47.525a24; noted by Yi Chong'ik, "Chosasŏn e issŏsŏ ŭi musim sasang," *Pulgyo hakpo,* vol. 10 (1973), p. 241; see also his discussion on pp. 241–243. For references to *musim* in secondary literature, see Yampolsky, *Platform Sutra,* pp. 137–138, n. 69. For the Ch'an usage of the term, cf. Suzuki, *The Zen Doctrine of No-mind.*
149. See *KAZ,* pp. 169–173. Numbers three through six are adopted directly from Lin-chi I-hsüan.
150. *KAZ,* p. 119; see full discussion at *KAZ,* pp. 116–124.
151. *KAZ,* p. 119; T10.911c.
152. *KAZ,* p. 119.
153. See *Vimalakīrtinirdeśa-sūtra:* "One who wants to purify the Buddha-land should purify his mind. To the extent one's mind is purified, the Buddha-land is purified" (*Wei-mo-chieh so-shuo ching,* T14.538c); *Liu-tsu t'an ching:* "If there are simply no impurities in the mind-ground, the Western Paradise will be near at hand" (T48.352a26 and b1); *KAZ,* p. 119.
154. *KAZ,* p. 120.
155. For problems surrounding the authorship of this text see Ono Gemmyō, *Bukkyō no bijutsu to rekishi* (Tokyo: Kanao bun'endō, 1943), pp. 1213 ff.; Minamoto Hiroyuki, "Kōrai jidai ni okeru Jōdokyō no kenkyū: Chitotsu no *Nembutu yōmon* ni tsuite," *Ryūkoku daigaku bukkyō bunka kenkyūjo kiyō,* vol. 9 (1970), pp. 90–94; and *KAZ,* p. 191.
156. For these schemes, see Mochizuki Shinkō, *Jōdokyō no kigen oyobi hattatsu* (Tokyo: Kyōritsusha, 1930), pp. 306–314.
157. *KAZ,* pp. 193–195, for these stages. The use of such terminology as "one true Dharmadhātu" to describe the state of realization recalls Chinul's earlier treatment of both Sŏn and Hwaŏm practices, described previously, and lends credence to the traditional attribution of this work to Chinul.
158. *KAZ,* pp. 103, 216.
159. *KAZ,* p. 218.
160. See, for example, *Sutta-nipāta,* vv. 796–803; cf. discussion in Ñāṇananda, *Concept and Reality,* pp. 16–18, 34–52.
161. *KAZ,* p. 212.
162. *KAZ,* pp. 216, 217.
163. See *KAZ,* pp. 338–339.
164. *KAZ,* p. 294.
165. *Hua-yen chin-kuan* is listed in Ŭich'ŏn's catalog, *Sinp'yŏn chejong kyojang ch'ongnok* ("New Compilation of a Comprehensive Catalogue of the Repository of the Teachings of All the Schools"), T55.1167b6, as *Hua-yen chin-kuan ch'ao,* in four (alt. two) fascicles. Yuil tells us (*CYKM,* fol. 15a.4) that this was an explanation (perhaps an outline?) of Ch'eng-kuan's massive *Hua-yen ching shu* (T#1735).
166. *Hwaŏmnon chŏryo,* p. 3.

Contributors

Carl Bielefeldt, assistant professor in the Department of Religious Studies at the Stanford University, received his Ph.D. in Buddhist Studies from the University of California, Berkeley. He has recently completed a monograph on Dōgen's meditation manuals and is coediting an anthology of Japanese scholarship on Dōgen. His current research is in the area of the earliest Zen schools in Japan.

Robert E. Buswell, Jr. completed his Ph.D. in Buddhist Studies at the University of California, Berkeley and is currently an assistant professor in the Department of Oriental Languages at the University of California, Los Angeles. His principal publication is *The Korean Approach to Zen: The Collected Works of Chinul,* which provides annotated translations of all the works of the founder of the Korean Sŏn tradition. He is editor of, and contributor to, *Buddhist Apocryphal Literature,* forthcoming as volume 10 in the Berkeley Buddhist Studies Series, and coeditor of the *Abhidharma Buddhist Philosophy* volume of the *Encyclopedia of Indian Philosophies.* His current research centers on East Asian Buddhist apocryphal scriptures that resonate with Ch'an, with special reference to the *Vajrasamādhi-sūtra.*

David W. Chappell teaches Chinese Buddhism and comparative religion at the University of Hawaii, where he is a professor in the Department of Religion. He did his doctoral work at Yale University on the Chinese Pure Land pioneer Tao-ch'o (562–645). His publications include *T'ien-ta'ai Buddhism: An Outline of the Fourfold Teachings,* a translation of the teachings of the fourth Ch'an patriarch Tao-hsin (580–651), and coeditorship of *Buddhist and Taoist Studies,* volumes I and II. He is also the founding editor of the journal *Buddhist-Christian Studies.*

Bernard Faure teaches Asian religions at Cornell University. After studying in Japan for several years under the guidance of Professor Yanagida Seizan, he obtained his doctorate from the University of Paris-VII in 1984 with a dissertation on the emergence of Ch'an orthodoxy in eighth-century China. He has recently finished a French translation of the so-called "Treatise of Bodhidharma" and is working on a book tentatively entitled "On the Margins of the Ch'an and Zen Traditions." He is also conducting research on the early development of Japanese Zen, focusing on the instrumental role of the "Japanese School of Bodhidharma" (Nihon Daruma-shū).

Peter N. Gregory is director of the Kuroda Institute for the Study of Buddhism and Human Values and assistant professor in the Program in Religious Studies and Center for East Asian and Pacific Studies at the University of Illinois, Urbana. He received his Ph.D. in East Asian Languages and Civilizations from Harvard University with a dissertation on Tsung-mi's *Yüan-jen lun.* He has coedited, with Robert Gimello, *Studies in Ch'an and Hua-yen* and "The Sudden/Gradual Polarity in Chinese Thought." In addition to a number of articles on Tsung-mi and Hua-yen thought, he is currently finishing a monograph on the *Yüan-jen lun* and is working on a book-length study of the life and thought of Tsung-mi.

Alan Sponberg is an assistant professor and the D. T. Suzuki Preceptor of East Asian Religions at Princeton University. He received a Ph.D. from the University of British Columbia with a dissertation on the Vijñaptimātratā philosophy of the seventh-century Chinese Buddhist monk K'uei-chi. His research has focused on the transmission of Buddhism from India to China, and he is especially interested in early Yogācāra. Recent work includes "The Thirty Verses: An Introduction to the Yogācāra Buddhism of Vasubandhu" and a symposium volume, *Maitreya, the Future Buddha,* coedited with Helen Hardacre.

Daniel Stevenson, assistant professor in the Department of Philosophy and Religion at Butler University, received his Ph.D. from the Department of Religion at Columbia University. His dissertation involves the investigation of the development of early T'ien-t'ai thought and practice with particular emphasis on the formulation of its meditative system.

Glossary

a-tzu kuan 阿字觀
an-hsin 安心
An-lo chi 安樂集
an-lo hsing 安樂行
An-lo hsing i 安樂行義
Bendō hō 辨道法
ch'amgu 參句
ch'amjŏng chŏlch'ŏl 斬釘截鐵
ch'amŭi 參意
ch'an 禪
"Ch'an chen" 禪箴
Chan-jan 湛然
ch'an-hui 懺悔
"Ch'an-men kuei-shih" 禪門規式
Chan-men shih-tzu ch'eng-hsi t'u 禪門
　師資承襲圖
Ch'an-men yao-lüeh 禪門要略
ch'an-na 禪那
ch'an-ting 禪定
chan-ting chieh-tieh 斬釘截鐵
Ch'an-yao 禪要
Ch'an-yüan ch'ing-kuei 禪苑清規
Ch'an-yüan chu-ch'uan-chi tu-hsü 禪源
　諸詮集都序
ch'ang chao 常照
Chang Chün 張均
ch'ang-hsing san-mei 常行三昧
Chang Lu 張魯
Ch'ang-lu 長蘆
Ch'ang-lu Tsung-tse 長蘆宗賾
Ch'ang-lu Ying fu 長蘆應夫

ch'ang-tso san-mei 常坐三昧
Chang Wan-fu 張萬福
Chang Yüeh 張說
Chao-chou Ts'ung-shen 趙州從諗
chao-liao 照了
ch'e 體
ch'ejung-hyŏn 體中玄
Ch'en Chen 陳鍼
chen-hsin 眞心
Ch'en Hsü 陳詡
chen-[ju] kuan 眞如觀
chen-ju san-mei 眞如三昧
Ch'en Shih 陳實
chen-li 眞理
Chen-ting 眞定
chen-tsung 眞宗
chen wu-nien 眞無念
Chen-yen 眞言
cheng 正
ch'eng-ch'ang fo-ming 稱唱佛名
cheng-hsiu 正修
ch'eng i fo ming tz'u 稱一佛名字
Ch'eng-kuan 澄觀
ch'eng ming 稱名
cheng-nien 正念
cheng-nien erh tso 正念而坐
Cheng-tao ko 證道歌
cheng-tsung 正宗
cheng-wu 證悟
Ch'eng-yüan 承遠
chi 知

chi-ch'i hsin 集起心
ch'i-fo pa-p'u-sa ch'an-fa 七佛八菩薩
　懺法
Chi-tsang 吉藏
Chia-ts'ai 迦才
chiao-wai pieh-ch'uan 教外別傳
chieh chia-fu tso 結跏趺坐
chieh-wu 解悟
chien 見
Chien-chung ching-kuo hsü teng lu 建中靖
　國續燈錄
ch'ien-hsiang cheng-hsing 遣相證性
chien-hsing 見性
ch'ien-hsü ts'un-shih 遣虛存實
chien-shih hsin 堅實心
chih 止
chih 知
chih 智
chih-chih hsin-hsing 直指心性
Ch'ih-chüeh 慈覺
chih-hsin ch'an 制心禪
Ch'ih-hsiu Po-chang ch'ing-kuei 勅修百丈
　清規
Chih-i 智顗
chih-jen-yün 直任運
Chih-kuan fu-hsing chuan hung-chüeh 止觀
　輔行傳弘決
Chih-p'an 志磐
chih seng shih 知僧事
Chih-shen 智詵
Chih-ta (Hui-ta) 智達(惠達)
Chih-wei 智威
Chih-yen 智儼
Chin'gak Hyesim 眞覺慧諶
Chin kuang-ming ch'an-fa 金光明懺法
ch'ing 情
Ching-chüeh 淨覺
Ching-hsien 景賢
ching-hsing 經行
ching-jen 淨人
Ching-kang san-mei ching 金剛三昧經
Ch'ing kuan-yin ch'an-fa 請觀音懺法
Ch'ing kuan-shih-yin hsiao-fu tu hai t'o-
　lo-ni ching 請觀世音消伏毒害陀羅
　尼經
Ch'ing kuan-yin hsing-fa 請觀音行法
Ching-ming ching 淨名經

Ching-te ch'uan-teng lu 景德傳燈錄
Ching-t'u fa-shen tsan 淨土法身讚
Ching-t'u lun 淨土論
Ching-ying Hui-yüan 淨影慧遠
Chinsim chiksŏl 眞心直説
Chinul 知訥
Chodang chip 祖堂集
Chogye 曹溪
Chogye Chin'gak kuksa ŏrok 曹溪眞覺
　國師語錄
cho'gyŏn chasim 照見自心
chŏnghye ssangsu 定慧雙修
Ch'ŏngwŏn-sa 清源寺
chŏnje 全提
Ch'ŏnt'ae 天台
ch'osinji 初信地
Ch'u-chi 處寂
Ch'u-chin 楚金
chü-yüan 具緣
Ch'uan-ao ta-shih 傳澳大師
chuan ch'eng fo-ming 專稱佛名
chüan ching 勸請
chuan hsin 專心
Ch'uan fa-pao chi 傳法寶紀
Chüan hsiao wen 勸孝文
"Chüan ts'an-ch'an jen chien hsiu
　ching-t'u" 勸參禪人兼修淨土
chüeh 覺
chüeh-i 覺意
chüeh-i san-mei 覺意三昧
Chüeh-i san-mei 覺意三昧
Chüeh-i san-mei hsing-fa 覺意三昧行法
Chung-feng Ming-pen 中峯明本
chŭngip 證入
chŭngo 證悟
Ch'ung-hsüan tsung 重玄宗
Chung-hua ch'uan-hsin-ti Ch'an-men
　shih-tzu ch'eng-hsi t'u 中華傳心地禪
　門師資承圖
Chung-tiao pu-chu Ch'an-yüan ch'ing-
　kuei 重雕補註禪苑清規
Daikaku zenji zazen ron 大覺禪師坐
　禪論
Denjutsu isshinkaimon 傳述一心戒文
Dōgen 道元
Eihei kōroku 永平廣錄
Eisai 榮西

Enni Ben'en 圓爾辯圓
Erh-shih-wu wang san-mei 二十五王
　三昧
Fa-chao 法照
fa-chieh ting-yin 法界定印
fa-chieh wu-ai yüan-ch'i 法界無礙緣起
Fa-chih 法持
Fa-chü ching 法句經
Fa-hsiang 法相
fa-hsing 法性
fa-hsing chi-jan 法性寂然
Fa-hua ch'an-fa 法華懺法
Fa-hua ching an-lo hsing i 法華經安樂
　行義
Fa-hua hsüan-i 法華玄義
fa-hua san-mei 法華三昧
Fa-hua san-mei ch'an-i 法華三昧懺儀
Fa-ju 法如
Fa-tsang 法藏
Fa-yen Wen-i 法眼文益
Fa-yüan 發願
Fa-yün Fa-hsiu 法雲法秀
"Fan-hsing p'in" 梵行品
fan-nao chang 煩惱障
fang-pien 方便
fang-pien sui-yüan ch'an 方便隨緣禪
Fang-teng ch'an-fa 方等懺法
Fang-teng san-mei hsing-fa 方等三昧
　行法
Fang-teng t'o-lo-ni ching 方等陀羅尼經
Fang-wang ching 梵網經
fei 非
Fei-hsi 飛錫
fei-hsing fei-tso 非行非坐
fei-hsing fei-tso san-mei 非行非坐三昧
fen-pieh 分別
Fen-yang Shan-chao 汾陽善昭
fo-hsing 佛性
Fo-kuo Wei-po 佛國惟白
Fo-tsu t'ung-chi 佛祖統紀
Fu ta-shih (Fu Hsi) 傅大士 (傅翕)
Fukan zazen gi 普勸坐禪儀
"Fukan zazen gi senjutsu yurai" 普勸
　坐禪撰述由來
Gijō 義讓
gozan 五山
Gyōhyō 行表

haeo 解悟
Ho-tse 荷澤
hoe'gwang panjo 廻光返照
Hōnen 法然
Hottō 法燈
Hottō kokushi hōgo 法燈國師法語
Hou-mo-chen Yen 候莫陳琰
hsi-ch'an 習禪
hsi erh-pien fen-pieh ch'an 息二邊分
　別禪
hsi-wang hsiu-hsin 息妄修心
hsiang 相
Hsiang-erh 想爾
hsiang hsin-chung k'an i-tzu 向心中看
　一字
Hsiang-mo tsang 降魔藏
hsiang-tai 相待
hsiang-t'ung 相同
Hsiang-yang 襄陽
Hsiao chih-kuan 小止觀
hsin 心
Hsin-hsin ming 信心銘
Hsin Hua-yen ching lun 新華嚴經論
hsin jo yu nien ch'i chi pien chüeh-
　chao 心若有念起即便覺照
hsin-shih liu-tung 心識流動
hsin-shu 心數
hsin-ti 心地
hsing 性
hsing-ch'i 性起
hsing-ch'i yüan-t'ung 性起圓通
Hsiu-hsi chih-kuan tso-ch'an fa yao
　修習止觀坐禪法要
Hsiu-hsin yao lun 修心要論
hsiu-k'ung 修空
Hsü ch'uan-teng lu 續傳燈錄
Hsü kao-seng chuan 續高僧傳
Hsü-k'ung-tsang pa-pai jih t'u-ts'e
　虛空藏八百日涂測
Hsüan-lang 玄朗
Hsüan-shih 宣什
Hsüan-tse 玄賾
Hsüan-tsang 玄奘
Hsüeh-feng Hui-jan 雪峯慧然
hua-t'ou 話頭
Hua-yen 華嚴
Hua-yen chin-kuan 華嚴錦冠

Hua-yen chin-kuan ch'ao 華嚴錦冠鈔
Hua-yen ching 華嚴經
Hua-yen ching hsing-yüan p'in shu-ch'ao 華嚴經行願品疏鈔
Hua-yen ching k'ung-mu chang 華嚴經孔目章
Hua-yen ching sui-shu yen-i ch'ao 華嚴經隨疏演義鈔
Hua-yen fa-chieh hsüan-ching 華嚴法界玄鏡
Hua-yen fa-chieh kuan-men 華嚴法界觀門
Huai-jang 懷讓
Huang-po 黃檗
hui 慧
Hui-an 慧安
Hui-chen 惠真
Hui-ch'i 慧持
Hui-chi ssu 會稽寺
Hui-hai 慧海
Hui-hung 慧洪
hui-hsiang 廻向
Hui-jen 慧忍
Hui-jih 慧日
Hui-k'o 慧可
Hui-li 慧立
Hui-neng 惠(慧)能
Hui-ssu 慧思
Hung-chi ch'an-yüan 洪濟禪院
Hung-ching 弘景
Hung-chou 洪州
Hung-jen 弘忍
hwabyŏng 話柄
hwach'ŭk 話則
hwadu 話頭
hwaje 話題
hwalgu 話句
Hwaŏm 華嚴
Hwaŏmnon chŏryo 華嚴論節要
hyŏnjung-hyŏn 玄中玄
i 意
i 頤
i chi 理智
i ch'i chi hsiu san-mei 意起即修三昧
I-fu 義福
i-hsiang 一相
i-hsiang san-mei 一相三昧
i-hsin chieh 一心戒

i-hsing 一行
i-hsing san-mei 一行三昧
ilchin pŏpkye 一眞法界
illyŏm hoe'gwang kyŏn chabonsŏng 一念廻光見自本性
i-nien san-ch'ien 一念三千
i-p'ien 一片
I Shih 頤師
i t'ang tso-ch'an 依堂坐禪
i-tsung 一宗
jen 人
Jen-t'ien yen-mu 人天眼目
Jion Daishi denki monjū 慈恩大師傳記文集
jo yu wang ch'i chi chüeh 若有妄起即覺
"Ju fa-chieh p'in" 入法界品
ju hsiang nien 如相念
Ju-ju chü-shih tso-ch'an i 如如居士坐禪儀
ju-lai ch'an 如來禪
"Ju-lai hsing-ch'i p'in" 如來性起品
Ju-lai hsing-hsien ching 如來興顯經
ju p'u-sa wei 如菩薩位
ju-t'uan hsin 肉團心
kaisetsu 解説
k'an-hsin 看心
k'an-hsin fa 看心法
k'an-hua 看話
k'an-hua ch'an 看話禪
Kanhwa kyŏrŭi ron 看話決疑論
kanhwa sŏn 看話禪
k'an wu-so ch'u 看無所處
Kanazawa bunko 金澤文庫
kanna 看話
Keizan 瑩山
kikutsu 鬼窟
Ko Hung 葛洪
ko i 古意
kōan 公案
kongan 公案
kongjŏk yŏngji 空寂靈智
Kōjō 光定
k'ou-chüeh 口決
kōzen gokokuron 興禪護國論
ku-jen 古人
k'u-mu ssu-hui 枯木死灰
kuan 觀

kuan fo 觀佛

kuan-hsin 觀心

Kuan-hsin lun 觀心論

Kuan-hsin lun shu 觀心論疏

kuan i wu 觀一物

kuan ju-lai 觀如來

Kuan p'u-hsien p'u-sa hsing-fa ching 觀普賢菩薩行法經

Kuan-ting 灌頂

Kuan wu-liang-shou ching 觀無量壽經

kubak pŏmbu 具縛凡夫

K'uei-chi 窺基

Kuei-feng Tsung-mi 圭峯宗密

Kuei-shan ching-ts'e 溈山警策

ku'gyŏng chi 究竟地

kujung-hyŏn 句中玄

k'ung 空

kung-an 公案

k'ung-chieh i-ch'ien 空劫以前

kuo 果

K'uo-an 廓庵

Kuo-ch'ing pai lu 國清百錄

kwanjo 觀照

kwanjo chasim 觀照自心

Kwŏnsu Chŏnghye kyŏlsa mun 觀修定慧結社文

kyo 教

kyosŭng 教乘

kyŏng chasim 鏡自心

kyŏngjŏl-mun 徑截門

Lan-ch'i Tao-lung 蘭溪道隆

Leng-ch'ieh pao-chi ching 楞伽寶積經

Leng-ch'ieh shih-tzu-chi 楞伽師資記

li 理

Li ch'an-hui 理懺悔

Li chih fa 立制法

li-hsin 理心

Li Hua 李華

li-ju 理入

li kuan 理觀

li-nien 離念

Li-tai fa-pao chi 歷代法寶記

Li T'ung-hsüan 李通玄

lien-hua sheng-hui 蓮華勝會

"Lien-hua sheng-hui lu wen" 蓮華勝會錄文

Lin-chi I-hsüan 臨濟義玄

Lin-chi lu 臨濟錄

Lin-chien lu 林間錄

ling-chih 靈知

liu-ken ch'an-hui 六根懺悔

Liu-tsu t'an-ching 六祖壇經

Lo-chou 洛州

Lo-pang i-kao 樂邦遺稿

Lo-pang wen-lei 樂邦文類

Lu-shan Hui-yüan 盧山慧遠

Lu-shan lien-tsung pao-chien 盧山蓮宗寶鑑

Lüeh chu-ching-lun nien-fo fa-men wang-sheng ching-t'u chi 略諸經論念佛法門往生淨土集

Lüeh-ming k'ai-meng ch'u-hsüeh tso-ch'an chih-kuan yao men 略明開曚初學坐禪止觀要門

lung shen-hun 弄神魂

Lung-shu ching-t'u wen 龍舒淨土文

Ma-tsu Tao-i 馬祖道一

Mang-lo chung-mo i-wen 芒洛聚墓遺文

manhaeng 萬行

meng-wang 夢王

mi 味

mi-yao 密要

men 門

mieh 滅

mo-chao 默照

Mo-ho chih-kuan 摩訶止觀

Mo-ho po-jo po-lo-mi ching chüeh-i san-mei 摩訶般若波羅密經覺意三昧

Mo-ho-yen 摩訶衍

mo-shih 魔事

Mochizuki Shinkō 望月信亨

mu 無

Muhon Kakushin 無本覺心

mukcho 默照

mumi 無味

munyŏm 無念

musain 無事人

Musang 無相

musi 無始

musim 無心

musim hapto mun 無心合道門

naejo 內照

Naishō buppō sojo kechimyakufu 內證佛法相承血脈譜

Nan-wu O-mi-t'o fo 南無阿彌陀佛

Nan-Yüan Hui-yung 南院慧顒

Nan-yüeh Hui-ssu 南嶽慧思
Naong Hye'gŭn 懶翁慧勤
nien 念
nien ch'i chi chüeh 念起即覺
nien-fo 念佛
Nien-fo ching 念佛經
"Nien-fo fang-t'ui fang-pien wen" 念佛
防退方便文
"Nien-fo hui-hsiang fa-yüan wen" 念佛
廻向發願文
nien-fo san-mei 念佛三昧
Nien-fo san-mei pao-wang lun 念佛三昧
寶王論
"Nien-fo ts'an-ch'an chiu tsung-chih
shuo" 念佛參禪求宗旨説
nien i 念巳
nien Tz'u-shih p'u-sa 念慈氏菩薩
ning-hsin ch'an 凝心禪
Niu-t'ou 牛頭
Ōjōraisan shiki 往生禮讚私記
Ono Gemmyō 小野玄妙
ŏpsik 業識
p'a 破
Pa-ch'iung shih chin-shih pu-cheng
八瓊室金石補正
p'abyŏng 破病
pan chia-fu tso 判跏趺坐
p'an-chiao 判教
pan-hsing pan-tso san-mei
半行半坐三昧
P'an Shih-chen 潘師正
pan'gwan chasim 返觀自心
panjo 返照
panjo chasim 返照自心
panjo chasŏng 返照自性
pao chang 報障
Pao-p'u-tzu 抱朴子
Pao-t'ang 保唐
"Pao-wang ju-lai hsing-ch'i p'in"
寶王如來性起品
pen-hsin 本心
pieh 別
pieh ch'ang ch'an-hui 別場懺悔
pieh hsing 別行
Pan-chou cheng-hsiang hsing-fa
般舟證相行法
pan-chou san-mei 航舟三昧
Pan-chou san-mei ching 般舟三昧經

pi-mi chih tsang 秘密之藏
Po-chang ch'ing-kuei 百丈清規
Po-chang Huai-hai 百丈懷海
"Po-chang kuei-sheng sung"
百丈規繩頌
po'gwangmyŏng chi 普光明智
Po-jo po-lo-mi-to hsin ching yu-tsan
般若波羅密多經幽贊
pŏp 法
*Pŏpchip pyŏrhaeng nok chŏryo pyŏngip
sagi* 法集別行錄節要並入私記
pŏpkye muae yŏn'gi 法界無礙緣起
pudong chi 不動智
P'u-hsien 普賢
P'u-hsien kuan ching 普賢觀經
"P'u-hsien p'u-sa chüan-fa p'in"
普賢菩薩勸發品
P'u-hui 普慧
P'u-sa chieh-fa 菩薩戒法
pu-ssu pu-kuan 不思不觀
P'u-chi 普寂
P'u-tu 普度
pulbyŏn 不變
pulsŏng 佛性
Rankei Dōryū 蘭溪道隆
Rinzai 臨濟
Ryōchu 良忠
sabutsu 作佛
saengnyak 省略
sagu 死句
Sagul-san 闍崛山
Saichō 最澄
samhyŏn-mun 三玄門
san chang 三障
san chih-kuan 三止觀
san-hsüan men 三玄門
san-hsüeh 三學
San-kuan i 三觀義
San-lun 三論
san-ti 三諦
Sankon zazen setsu 三根坐禪説
Satō Tetsuei 佐藤哲英
Seng-ch'ou (Hui-ch'ou) 僧稠(慧稠)
Seng-ts'an 僧璨
Shan-fang ye-hua 山房夜話
Shan-tao 善導
she-lan liu-ch'un 捨濫留純
she-mo kuei-pen 攝末歸本

Shen-hui 神會
Shen-hsiu 神秀
shen-k'eng 深坑
sheng-hsin 聖心
Shibu roku 四部錄
shih 事
shih ch'an-hui 事懺悔
Shih ch'an po-lo-mi tz'u-ti fa men
　釋禪波羅密次第法門
Shih chu pi-po-sha lun 十住毗波沙論
shih-hsiang nien-fo 實相念佛
shih-hsin 十信
shih-kuan 事觀
Shih kuan-ching 十觀境
Shih-niu t'u 十牛圖
shih sheng kuan-fa 十乘觀法
Shih-yüan tz'u-lin 釋苑詞林
shikan taza 只管打坐
Shōbō genzō 正法眼藏
Shōbō genzō zazen gi 正法眼藏坐禪儀
Shōichi kokushi hōgo 聖一國師法語
Shōsōin 正倉院
Shou-chih (Shou-chen) 守直(守真)
shou-hsin 守心
shou-i 守一
shou i pu i 守一不移
Shou-leng-yen ching 首楞嚴經
Shou-leng-yen san-mei ching
　首楞嚴三昧經
shuang-chao 雙照
shuang-chi 雙寂
simji 心地
sinhae 信解
Sinp'yŏn chejong kyojang ch'ongnok
　新編諸宗教藏總錄
sipchu 十住
sipsin 十信
[so]-yüan 所緣
Sŏn 禪
sŏng 性
sŏnggi 性起
sŏngjok tŭngji 星寂等持
Sŏnmun yŏmsong chip 禪門拈頌集
Sŏnwŏnjip tosŏ so 禪源集都序疏
Sŏsan Hyujŏng 西山休靜
Sōtō 曹洞
Ssu chiao i 四教義
ssu chü 四句

ssu chung san-mei 四種三昧
Ssu-ming Chih-li 四明知禮
Ssu-ming Pao-ying 四明寶英
ssu yün hsin hsiang 四運心相
ssu-wei 思惟
su-shih 俗事
sui-hsi 隨喜
sui-tzu-i 隨自意
sui-tzu-i san-mei 隨自意三昧
Sun 孫
Sung kao-seng chuan 宋高僧傳
sŭpki 習氣
Susim kyŏl 修心訣
suyŏn 隨緣
Ta-chih-tu-lun 大智度論
Ta-chu Hui-hai 大珠慧海
*Ta-fang-kuang fo ju-lai pu-ssu-i ching-
　chieh ching* 大方廣佛如來不思議境
　界經
Ta-hui Tsung-kao 大慧宗果
Ta-hui yü-lu 大慧語錄
Ta-pao-chi ching 大寶積經
Ta-p'in ching 大品經
Ta-sheng ch'i-hsin lun 大乘起信論
Ta-sheng fa-yüan i-lin chang 大乘法苑
　義林章
Ta-T'ang hsi-yü chi 大唐西域記
*Ta-T'ang Ta-tz'u-en-ssu Fa-shih-chi-
　kung pei* 大唐大慈恩寺法師基公碑
*Ta-T'ang ta-tz'u-en-ssu San-tsang-fa-
　shih chuan* 大唐大慈恩寺三藏法師傳
Ta-tsang i-lan 大藏一覽
taech'i 對治
T'aego Pou 太古普愚
taesa 大事
taesim pŏmbu 大心凡夫
T'ai-p'ing 太平
T'an-luan 曇鸞
tao-ch'ang 道場
Tao-ch'o 道綽
Tao-hsin 道信
Tao-hsüan 道宣
Tao-hsüan (Dōsen) 道璿
T'ao Hung-ching 陶弘景
T'an-yü 壇語
"T'ang Hung-chou Po-chang shan ku
　Huai-hai ch'an-shih t'a-ming" 唐洪
　州百丈山故懷海禪師塔銘

tang-nien 當念
Te-hui 德輝
Tendai 天台
t'i 體
t'i-chen ch'an 體真禪
t'i-chen chih 體真止
ti-i i 弟一義
t'iao-ho 調和
T'ien-i I-huai 天衣義懷
T'ien-mu Chung-feng ho-shang kuang-
lu 天目中峯和尚廣錄
T'ien-sheng kuang teng lu 天聖廣燈錄
t'ien-shih 天師
T'ien-t'ai 天台
T'ien-t'ai Chih-i 天台智顗
T'ien-t'ai chih-kuan 天台止觀
ting 定
ting-li 定力
Ting shih-fei lun 定是非論
Tōdaiji 東大寺
tono chŏmsu 頓悟漸修
tono tonsu 頓悟頓修
Tsan-ning 贊寧
tse 賾
tso-ch'an 坐禪
tso-ch'an chen 坐禪箴
Tso-ch'an chen 坐禪箴
Tso-ch'an i 坐禪儀
tso-ch'an ming 坐禪銘
tsu-shih ch'an 祖師禪
Tsu-t'ang chi 祖堂集
Ts'ui Kuan 崔寬
Tsui-shang-sheng lun 最上乘論
Tsung-ching lu 宗鏡錄
Tsung-mi 宗密
tu 都
Tu-Shun 杜順
tun-chiao 頓教
tun-wu 頓悟
tun-wu chien-hsiu 頓悟漸修
Tun-wu ju-tao yao men 頓悟入道要門
tun-wu tun-hsiu 頓悟頓修
Tun-wu yao-men 頓悟要門
t'ung 通
t'ung hsing 同行
t'ung-kuan 通觀
Tung-shan Liang-chieh 洞山良介
Tung-shan Shou-ch'u 洞山守初

Tzu-men ching-hsün 緇門警訓
Tz'u-min Hui-jih 慈愍慧日
Ŭich'ŏn 義天
ŭijŏng 疑情
ŭisim 疑心
wan-shan t'ung-kuei 萬善同歸
Wan-shan t'ung-kuei chi 萬善同歸集
wang-chü 妄俱
wang-hsin 忘心
wang-nien hsin 妄念心
Wang-sheng ching-t'u chi 往生淨土集
Wang-sheng li-tsan chi 往生禮讚偈
Wang-sheng-lun chu 往生論註
wang-yüan 忘緣
wei-hsin 唯心
wei-na 維那
wei-nien 未念
Wei-shih chang 唯識章
Wen-shu-shih-li so-shuo po-jo ching
     文殊師利所説般若經
Wen-shu shuo ching 文殊説經
Wen-shu-shih-li wen ching 文殊師利
     問經
Wo-lun 臥輪
Wŏndon sŏngbullon 圓頓成佛論
wŏndon sinhae mun 圓頓信解門
Wŏnhyo 元曉
wu 無
wu-chi hsin 無記心
Wu-chu 無住
wu-ch'ung wei-shih kuan 五重唯識觀
Wu fang-pien i 五方便義
Wu fang-pien nien-fo men 五方便念
     佛門
wu fu i yüan 無復異緣
wu-hsiang 無相
Wu-hsiang 無相
wu-hsiang chieh 無相戒
wu hsiang hsing 無相行
wu-hsin 無心
wu-hsing 無形
wu hui 五悔
wu-i 無意
Wu-men kuan 無門關
wu-nien 無念
Wu-shang-i ching 無上依經
wu-shang sheng 無上乘
wu-sheng 無生

Wu-sheng fang-pien men 無生方便門
wu-shih 五時
wu t'ing-hsin kuan 五停心觀
wu-tso 無作
wu-tso-i 無作意
wu-t'ung 五通
wu-wei 無爲
Yang-ch'i 楊岐
Yang Wei 陽畏
Yao-chüeh 要決
yeh chang 業障
Yen Ping 顏丙
yin 因
yin-lüeh hsien-sheng 隱劣顯勝
yŏmbul 念佛
Yŏmbul yomun 念佛要門
yŏmsong 拈頌
Yŏndam Yuil 蓮潭有一
yong 用
yŏngji 靈智
Yōsai 榮西
yu 有
yu hsiang hsing 有相行
yu-hsin 有心
yu-lou ting 有漏定
Yü-ch'üan ssu 玉泉寺
Yü Hsiang 虞翔
yü hsin-hsiang chung 於心想中

yü nien 欲念
yüan 圓
Yüan-chao 元照
yüan-ch'i chih shu 緣起之殊
Yüan-chüeh ching 圓覺經
Yüan-chüeh ching hsiu-cheng i 圓覺經
　修證儀
Yüan-chüeh ching ta shu ch'ao 圓覺經
　大疏鈔
Yüan-feng Ch'ing-man 元豐清滿
yüan-kuan 圓觀
Yüan-kuei 元珪
yüan-lü hsin 緣慮心
yüan-tun 圓頓
Yüan-t'ung ch'an-shih 圓通禪師
Yüan-wu K'o-ch'in 圓悟克勤
Yün-men Wen-yen 雲門文偃
yung 用
Yung-chung 永中
yunghoe 融會
Yung-ming Yen-shou 永明延壽
Yung-nien 永年
zazen 坐禪
Zazengi 坐禪儀
Zazen yōjin ki 坐禪用心記
zen 禪
Zemmon shishi shōshū zu 禪門師資承
　襲圖

Index